THE SIRENS OF THE HOTEL LOUVRE

A volume in the NIU Series in

Slavic, East European, and Eurasian Studies
Edited by Christine D. Worobec

For a list of books in the series, visit our website at cornellpress.cornell.edu.

THE SIRENS OF THE HOTEL LOUVRE

AN ACTRESS, A WRITER, AND THE CREATIVE LIFE IN THE SILVER AGE OF CHEKHOV

SERGE GREGORY

NORTHERN ILLINOIS UNIVERSITY PRESS
an imprint of

CORNELL UNIVERSITY PRESS
Ithaca and London

Copyright © 2025 by Cornell University

All rights reserved. Except for brief quotations in a review, this book, or parts thereof, must not be reproduced in any form without permission in writing from the publisher. For information, address Cornell University Press, Sage House, 512 East State Street, Ithaca, New York 14850. Visit our website at cornellpress.cornell.edu.

First published 2025 by Cornell University Press

Library of Congress Cataloging-in-Publication Data

Names: Gregory, Serge, 1948- author.
Title: The sirens of the Hotel Louvre : an actress, a writer, and the creative life in the silver age of Chekhov / Serge Gregory.
Description: Ithaca : Cornell University Press, 2025. | Series: NIU series in Slavic, East European, and Eurasian studies | Includes bibliographical references and index.
Identifiers: LCCN 2024029687 (print) | LCCN 2024029688 (ebook) | ISBN 9781501780417 (hardcover) | ISBN 9781501780424 (paperback) | ISBN 9781501780431 (epub) | ISBN 9781501780448 (pdf)
Subjects: LCSH: I︠A︡vorskai͡a, Lidii͡a Borisovna, 1871–1921. | Shchepkina-Kupernik, T. L. (Tat︠ʹ︡i͡ana Lʹvovna), 1874–1952. | Women in the theater—Russia—History—19th century. | Women in the theater—Russia—History—20th century.
Classification: LCC PN2723 .G74 2025 (print) | LCC PN2723 (ebook) | DDC 792.092/52 [B]—dc23/eng/20240913
LC record available at https://lccn.loc.gov/2024029687
LC ebook record available at https://lccn.loc.gov/2024029688

To Rachel and Hana

Contents

Acknowledgments ix

Notes on Transliteration, Dates, and Currency xi

Introduction	1
Prologue: Korsh's Private Theater	4
1. "Ma Petite Sappho"	20
2. "I Spent Two Weeks in Some Sort of a Daze"	37
3. "In Paris Things Don't Happen So Quickly"	54
4. "Don't Forget the One Who Loves Only You"	63
5. *The Dream Princess*	77
6. Princess Baryatinskaya	95
7. Reconciliation	113
8. *Sons of Israel*	131
9. The New Theater	151
10. Marriage	177
11. 1905 Revolution	188
12. The Wandering Star	202
13. English Debut	215
14. "I Don't Need a 'Happy Life,' I Need the Stage"	230

15. "A Princess in Real Life, but in the
    Theater a Queen" 238
16. *Anna Karenina* 249
17. Divorce and Revolution 258
18. "Out of the Bolsheviks' Clutches" 271

Notes 281
Bibliography 303
Index 309
Illustrations begin on page 167

Acknowledgments

Without access to the University of Washington Libraries' extensive Slavic collection, I would never have been able to start researching this book. What a pleasure it was to spend hours in the microfilm room, reading articles and reviews in late-nineteenth-century Moscow and St. Petersburg newspapers. They provided a vivid, contemporaneous account of the world of the theater during Russia's Silver Age.

I had planned to continue my research by working in Russian archives, but Vladimir Putin's war against Ukraine made that impossible. Fortunately, I was able to turn to Renee Stillings and the archive support services of US-based SRAS (School of Russian and Asian Studies) to get the primary source materials I needed to finish my book. I am particularly grateful to SRAS researcher Andrei Nesterov for photocopying hundreds of pages of Lidia Yavorskaya's letters, telegrams, and postcards to Tatiana Shchepkina-Kupernik. Back home in Seattle, Mariana Markova provided invaluable assistance in transcribing Yavorskaya's often illegible handwriting. Kelby Fletcher read the first three chapters and suggested some stylistic changes. In an email exchange, Marina Litavrina, Yavorskaya's Russian biographer and a professor of theater history at Moscow State University, kindly responded to my questions and offered words of encouragement.

Finally, I was buoyed by the enthusiasm of Amy Farranto, Northern Illinois University Press senior acquisitions editor, and Christine Worobec, editor of the NIU Series in Slavic, East European, and Eurasian Studies, after reading the first few chapters of my manuscript. During the sometimes challenging peer review process, they remained unruffled and supportive. Their suggested additions and revisions helped shape a better book. The meticulous copyediting of Katherine Pickett under the guidance of Mary Kate Murphy, production editor at Cornell University Press, saved me from numerous errors, infelicities, and inconsistencies. Kendra Millis applied her years of experience in creating an index that will serve as a valuable tool for readers.

Notes on Transliteration, Dates, and Currency

I have used a simplified Library of Congress transliteration of Russian names and places, for the most part, with the following modifications: ий and ый—"y," ю—"yu," я—"ya," ё—"yo." The soft sign (ь) has been omitted. I have preferred commonly accepted English spellings of Russian names over consistency (for example, *Lidia* rather than *Lidiia*, *Chaliapin* rather than *Shaliapin*). Although Lidia Yavorskaya spelled her name *Yavorska* when she was living in London, I continue to use *Yavorskaya* when writing about this period. Similarly, I use the American spelling of *theater* unless I'm naming a British venue (for example, the Ambassadors Theatre). I use city names as they were called at the time (for example, *Tiflis* rather than *Tbilisi*), and as they were commonly spelled at the time (for example, *Lvov* instead of *Lviv*).

The endnote text and bibliography revert to the standard Library of Congress system.

All translations from Russian are my own. In quoted material, a three-point ellipsis (". . .") indicates that suspension points appear in the original text—Russian writers of the time had a particular fondness for ellipses. I use a four-point ellipsis (". . . .") to indicate that I have omitted a few words from the original text.

Dates are primarily according to the Russian calendar, which in the nineteenth century was twelve days behind the Western calendar. In the twentieth century, the difference was thirteen days until February 1918, when the Soviet government adopted the Western calendar. I use Western dates when writing about Yavorskaya's time in Great Britain.

Because actors' earnings, the cost of tickets, and so forth, are mentioned in the book, it's helpful to have a basic understanding of the value of the ruble at the turn of the twentieth century. At the time, both Russia and the United States were on the gold standard, and exchange rates were relatively stable. Between 1899 and 1903 the ruble was worth 78 cents (one US dollar equaled 1.29 rubles). To get a sense of the buying power of the ruble, in 1902 a hotel room in St. Petersburg ranged between two and ten rubles a night; lunch at a restaurant cost two to three rubles; an orchestra seat at the Mariinsky Theater cost about six rubles. In 1892, when Anton Chekhov felt he had a sufficiently substantial income to buy his small estate at Melikhovo, he was making a thousand rubles a month.

Introduction

In 1887, Anton Chekhov, already established as a writer of short stories and humorous sketches, decided to try his hand at writing a four-act play. For several years, in his column Fragments of Moscow Life, he had enjoyed skewering Moscow theater productions, particularly the low-brow fare offered by the impresario Fyodor Korsh. But Chekhov now found himself attracted to the prospect of earning considerably more money by writing plays rather than stories, for which he was paid by the line in kopecks. He surprised his friends, and even himself, by signing a contract with Korsh to have his play *Ivanov* staged at Korsh's theater. Chekhov soon discovered, however, that in return for increasing his income, a theatrical production demanded its pound of flesh—the loss of artistic control.

Chekhov possibly would never have turned to writing plays had not Alexander III issued a decree five years earlier permitting the opening of commercial theaters in Moscow and St. Petersburg in direct competition with established government-supported theaters. Previously, laws going back to the time of Catherine the Great had established a state monopoly in those two cities, limiting the performance of Russian plays to just two theaters: the Alexandrinsky in St. Petersburg and the Maly in Moscow.

Twenty years after the end of the state monopoly, Moscow and St. Petersburg could boast of twenty-six commercial theaters.[1] They staged works by Russian playwrights, but also exposed audiences to both contemporary and classical Western European dramatic literature. Private theaters premiered productions directed by such innovators as Konstantin Stanislavsky, Vladimir Nemerovich-Danchenko, and Vsevolod Meyerhold of plays by Chekhov, Maxim Gorky, Leonid Andreev, and others. They also introduced Russian audiences to the modernist plays of Henrik Ibsen, August Strindberg, and Maurice Maeterlinck. The turn of the century saw productions of even more daring expressionist and symbolist works by Frank Wedekind, Knut Hamsun, and Gabriele D'Annunzio.

Although they were successful in their day, neither the actor Lidia Yavorskaya nor the dramatist Tatiana Shchepkina-Kupernik are now considered among the luminaries of Russia's Silver Age (roughly 1890–1920). Yavorskaya is remembered as a flamboyant but not gifted actor, a Sarah Bernhardt manqué, less beloved than her rival Vera Komissarzhevskaya, who died tragically from smallpox in 1910 at the age of forty-five. Shchepkina-Kupernik's fame rests on her memoirs of the period and her translations of Western European plays. Her own plays, stories, and verse, some of which were based on her familiarity with Yavorskaya's life and career, are little known. In fact, Donald Rayfield, the preeminent biographer of Chekhov, wrote a monograph on Shchepkina-Kupernik with the title "The Forgotten Poetess."[2]

Catherine Schuler, in *Women in Russian Theatre: The Actress in the Silver Age*,[3] self-described as a work of "feminist intervention," was the first Western scholar to recognize that Yavorskaya was more than a crass exhibitionist. In her chapter on Yavorskaya, subtitled "The Silver Age Actress as Unruly Woman," she pointed out that Yavorskaya, like Komissarzhevskaya, was an actor-entrepreneur who, like her male counterparts, played a significant role in exposing audiences to all that was new in Russian and European drama. In addition, Schuler wrote: "Her experience raises intriguing questions about women who publicly flaunt the boundaries of the bourgeoisie and about female transgression in general. Most importantly, her career, public persona, and the response to it reflect changes in Russian theatre and society that had tremendous resonance for women."[4] This book expands that theme, seeking through a biographical and cultural historical narrative to make clear to the reader the ways in which Yavorskaya and Shchepkina-Kupernik rebelled personally and creatively against the social dictates that confined them.

Yavorskaya's and Shchepkina-Kupernik's careers intersected with those of virtually all the period's major Moscow and St. Petersburg theatrical entrepreneurs, directors, actors, and writers. Yavorskaya was a popular leading lady at two of Russia's most prominent private theaters—Korsh's in Moscow and Alexei Suvorin's in St. Petersburg. She starred in productions of French plays translated by Shchepkina-Kupernik that cemented the actor's reputation as "the Russian Sarah Bernhardt." Yavorskaya went on to start her own company, the New Theater, with a repertoire that reflected a commitment to modernist drama that was serious and prolonged, if not always popularly received.

Shchepkina-Kupernik came from a distinguished Russian theatrical family long associated with Moscow's Maly Theater. She used her family connections to convince Korsh to hire her as an actor. But she soon discovered that she much preferred writing and translating for the stage to acting. In addition to collaborating with Yavorskaya, Shchepkina-Kupernik wrote stories, narrative poems, and plays that made life in the theater their central subject, focusing on the challenges faced by actresses in balancing their professional careers, personal relationships, and family responsibilities in a society that gave men the power to oppress women.

Chekhov declared himself infatuated when he first met Yavorskaya and Shchepkina-Kupernik, her close friend and collaborator. He wryly called them "the sirens of the Louvre," blaming them for distracting him from his writing and seducing him to spend countless hours in their company at Moscow's Hotel Louvre, a favorite residence of the city's more prominent actors.

When Nicholas II came to the throne in 1894, he continued the reactionary policies of his father, Alexander III, that severely limited opportunities for women to work outside the home. Women were not allowed to attend universities, as they had been briefly in the 1860s. Shchepkina-Kupernik noted that with higher education unavailable to them, many women friends of her generation turned to literature, art, and the theater to achieve creative satisfaction, as well as financial and social independence. The story of Yavorskaya and Shchepkina-Kupernik is the story of two women who, against the background of the flourishing of the dramatic arts during the Silver Age, successfully fashioned careers for themselves at a time when the theater was one of the few professional paths available to women who wished to escape the constraints of traditional family life.

Prologue
Korsh's Private Theater

In the early spring of 1880, the young actor Alexandra Glama-Meshcherskaya returned to St. Petersburg from Vilnius, where she had performed during the winter season. She was having considerable success playing in provincial theaters after being frustrated by the lack of opportunities in St. Petersburg and Moscow. If you were accepted into the company of one of the two imperial dramatic theaters, you would be assured of a salary, but there was no guarantee that you would get any roles. The popularity of acting as a career for women, who otherwise had limited professional options, had resulted in an oversupply of actresses.

In her brief time at the Alexandrinsky Theater, Glama-Meshcherskaya had to compete with more than a dozen other young actresses for available ingenue roles. These actresses, she recalled, "didn't have enough work, and most of them sat around on their hands, happy if any sort of role turned up, or if they were chosen to be the understudy for one of their more fortunate predecessors. Getting a good, new role was like winning two hundred thousand rubles in the lottery."[1]

Glama-Meshcherskaya was staying in the Grand Hotel in a two-room suite that looked out onto the golden cupola of St. Isaac's Cathedral. She performed in a few small clubs while weighing where to go next. One day her maid announced that a gentleman had arrived from Moscow and was waiting to see her in the vestibule. She came out to find a rather unattractive man in baggy clothes pacing about the room. He introduced himself as Vasily Burlak, representing a new private theater scheduled to open in Moscow. "I've come from there," he said, "with instructions from the administration, from Anna Brenko, to invite you to join us. The troupe will be a strong one: everyone in it is already a celebrity."[2]

In spite of the imperial monopoly on theaters, sporadic attempts had been made over the years to circumvent the law through amateur performances and readings. Starting in 1879, Anna Brenko, an enterprising actor from the Maly Theater who was unhappy with its repertoire, took it upon herself to test the limits of the law. She made repeated trips to St. Petersburg to obtain permission to perform public readings, first as literary-musical benefit performances sponsored by the Society of Christian Assistance, then more audaciously in silent partnership with a benefactor, Samuel Malkiel, who agreed to transform one of his mansions on Tverskaya Street into what came to be called the Pushkin Theater. Officially, Brenko received permission to perform scenes from plays, but in reality she and Malkiel spent lavishly to produce full-fledged productions using well-paid provincial actors.

Burlak offered Glama-Meshcherskaya an annual contract, including one so-called benefit performance, for which she would be able to select the play and keep most of the evening's proceeds. "It only remains for you to fill in what you want for a monthly salary and sign the contract," he said.[3] Glama-Meshcherskaya was overjoyed at the prospect of returning to Moscow and asked for a modest salary of four hundred rubles a month (the average for an established actress was six hundred).

As soon as she arrived in Moscow in early August 1880, Glama-Meshcherskaya decided to visit the new theater and introduce herself to its director. The Malkiel mansion was an imposing three-story structure. Four caryatids loomed above its entrance as Glama-Meshcherskaya went inside and up the stairway to the theater hall. There she found Brenko, who greeted her with what struck her as "typical Moscow heartiness." Still in her early thirties, Brenko gave the impression of being a well-educated "new" woman, having come of age in the liberalizing 1860s. As Brenko gave Glama-Meshcherskaya a tour of the hall, the stage, and the dressing rooms, she described the goals of the theater, the makeup of the acting company, and the planned repertoire. Even though the theater was barely lit, Glama-Meshcherskaya sensed the intimate elegance of the place, the tasteful decor. The severe white walls were set off by blue silk and velvet trimming. The stage curtain was blue as well, as were the seats and the drapes above the doorways leading to the loges. Glama-Meshcherskaya took it as a good sign that the actors' dressing rooms were clean and spacious. She felt blessed, as if she "had woken up in a new world."[4]

But in reality, Brenko was still battling the old world of the imperial monopoly. Fearing a denunciation from a single low-level civil servant could shut down her company, she made one more trip to St. Petersburg at the end of 1881 to legalize the performance of plays in their entirety, this time with the backing of Moscow's governor-general. Her persistence and politically powerful supporters prompted the new tsar, Alexander III, to form a theater commission to look into the matter. The tsar was open to the argument that private theaters could be a vehicle to help "renew patriotic nationalism."[5] On April 6, 1882, the commission agreed to end the state monopoly and no longer prevent the creation of private theaters.

However, by then Brenko was bankrupt and had lost ownership of her theater. Lawsuits unrelated to the Pushkin Theater had forced Malkiel to withdraw his financial support. Her small theater primarily attracted the city's educated elite, and a full house brought in no more than a thousand rubles. Ticket receipts were not covering expenses. Even worse, previously, in March 1881, the state had decreed that all theaters were required to close for six months of mourning following the assassination of Alexander II. Brenko later admitted that in her enthusiasm to create a "perfect" theater, she had taken on an excessive level of debt.[6] But above all, she blamed Fyodor Korsh for her ruin.

Korsh was a thirty-year-old trial attorney who had benefited financially from the judicial reforms instituted in 1864, which established an independent judiciary with public hearings and jury trials. With a passion for theater and a reputation for wily business dealings, he had rented the cloakroom at the Pushkin. Taking advantage of the Russian custom requiring all theatergoers to check their coats, he made a handsome profit by charging twenty kopecks for each coat, regardless of whether the patron had paid for a full-price ticket or had a complimentary pass.

From his vantage point, Korsh watched as Brenko expended all her energy on overcoming the imperial monopoly and all her money on sustaining the theater. Already a wealthy man, he could have come to her aid, but instead chose to wait and pounce once she was gravely wounded. Korsh sought to create a sense of panic among her creditors that put him in a position to take over. When the insolvent Pushkin

Theater shut down in February 1882, he offered the troupe a new location on Gazetny Lane, having signed a joint venture agreement with the building owners to remodel their space into a theater.

Brenko spent the rest of her life struggling to make a living, mostly by teaching acting classes. She was only occasionally remembered for her pioneering role in changing Russia's theatrical landscape.

Korsh's Russian Dramatic Theater opened on August 30, 1882, with a production of Nikolai Gogol's *The Inspector General*, a reliable warhorse. The premiere was preceded by a celebratory breakfast and dedication of the building, which was temporarily marred by the refusal of the invited priest to sprinkle holy water on the stage and dressing rooms. He explained that he was not empowered to bless the walls of the "pagan temple of Thalia and Melpomene."[7] Korsh sent out for another, more tractable priest.

Glama-Meshcherskaya, who had been performing again in the provinces after Brenko's collapse, returned to Moscow fully expecting that Korsh's endeavor, with the same acting company, would be a continuation of what Brenko had begun, only now in a larger theater. But for Glama-Meshcherskaya the joy of reuniting with her old acting company was soon diminished by the palpable absence of Brenko. Having gotten used to Brenko's calm, collegial leadership, the actors now had to adjust to Korsh's mercurial intrusiveness. Burlak and fellow actor Modest Pisarev, who had formed a creative troika with Brenko, soon found themselves pushed aside. Korsh had spent tens of thousands of rubles renting and restoring the new theater. He felt he had the right to do whatever was necessary to maximize a financial return. He abandoned Brenko's repertoire in favor of lighter fare, seeking to attract an audience of shop owners, merchants, low-ranking officials, servants, and their families who never frequented the more expensive Maly Theater. Korsh also expanded Brenko's practice of matinee performances at reduced prices. Seats in the upper gallery, where you could reach up and touch the ceiling, cost only ten kopecks. He premiered a new play every Friday, often after only one or two rehearsals. With so little time allowed for adequate preparations, the role of the prompter, hidden in the stage footlights, became crucial, even more important than that of the director, since some actors barely knew their lines.

Korsh admitted that in his first three years he was guilty of numerous "errors and omissions" while trying to put the theater on a sound financial footing. It was his lawyerly way of characterizing his heavy-handed, sometimes blundering management. A thin man with a neatly combed, fan-shaped beard that jutted out from his chin at an angle, he had the demeanor of a well-connected bureaucrat, exuding respectability, walking briskly, often carrying an overstuffed briefcase. His voice, a reedy falsetto, turned squeaky when agitated.

When he chose to be affable, Korsh became smarmy. It irritated Glama-Meshcherskaya that he would constantly call her "my dovie." He seduced playwrights and actors with flattery, but once they were under contract, he treated them like factory workers. In his first season, when the time came to issue paychecks on the eve of the theater's Lenten hiatus, Korsh decided to reduce the actors' wages for February because the month had three fewer days. For Pisarev, Burlak, and Glama-Meshcherskaya, this was more than they could bear. They quit, saying they intended to file a court complaint.

Young Anton Chekhov, recently hired by a St. Petersburg newspaper to write a twice-monthly column on Moscow cultural life, had already commented on the sad demise of Brenko's undertaking, and told his readers he was shocked to learn that the Pushkin Theater was about to be reopened as a café-cabaret by a group of St. Petersburg Frenchmen. He now turned his attention to press accounts of the dispute between Korsh and the actors who had previously been in Brenko's troupe. He thought Korsh's penuriousness soiled his entire undertaking, the way "a single dirty fly can smear up a whole wall."[8] As the cheeky flaneur of Fragments of Moscow Life, Chekhov regularly paraded his disdain for Korsh's vulgarity. He complained that the impresario had nothing fresh or original to offer, observing that the actors struck the same poses in the same tiresome French farces. The very act of going to Korsh's theater soured Chekhov's mood. He found himself enduring night after night of "vodka, stuffy smoking lounges, a crush in the cloakroom . . . You come out of the theater, and outside it's dirty and cold; the sky is bleak; the waiting coachmen are freezing."[9]

Korsh was losing money. He staged a lavish production of the historical play *Tsar Vasily Ivanovich Shuisky*, spending more than twenty thousand rubles on eleven performances that won favorable reviews but put him heavily into debt. Even after focusing primarily on comedies during the next season, Korsh was unable to sustain the level of subsidy required. He was forced to turn over his theater and all its sets and costumes to Savva Mamontov, the entrepreneur and arts patron who was eager to find a venue for his new private opera company.

Chekhov could barely contain his glee: "The reasons for such a precipitous death are not known, but they most likely sit with Korsh himself. You recall that at the first opportunity Mr. Korsh took on this endeavor with great passion. But marriages based on passionate love and great undertakings with passionate beginnings are both inherently unstable."[10] On February 3, 1885, Chekhov attended Korsh's farewell performance and closing ceremonies. From the audience, men in their tailcoats and women in their best gowns shouted out "Thank you!" Deeply touched, Korsh came out on stage surrounded by actors in tears. The actor Sophia Volgina stepped forward to recite a poem, in which, according to Chekhov, "syntax said farewell to rhyme, rhyme said farewell to meaning, and meaning said farewell to even a grocer's concept of verse."[11] This was followed by a speech given by a young man who said much "about banners being raised high, about unity, about mission, energy and so forth, but the passionate esthete said nothing about *The Inspector General* being put on after only one rehearsal, about a beating that took place in the gallery, about the [torn] tights that Mr. Kiselevsky wore in *Richelieu*."[12]

The pronouncements from the stage about unity and solidarity were a sham, given that the next day almost the entire troupe signed a complaint denying newspaper reports that they had anything to do with a gold pin with diamonds being given to Nikolai Volkov-Semyonov, the theater's director. Chekhov concluded: "This announcement was not collegial and is of no interest to the public. In general, it's time for actors to stop acting familiar with the public and thrusting themselves onto them with farewell kisses, bad poetry, and backstage nonsense. We're sick of it!"[13]

As was the case with some of his other pronouncements about Moscow artists and cultural figures, Chekhov was wrong about Korsh's demise. Korsh had many supporters in the public, in the press, and, most importantly, among Moscow's wealthy merchant families, who were beginning to actively participate in the city's cultural life. He put together a prospectus for a new theater that would respond to the public demand for "elegant, light comedy." He pointed out that the relative failure of large-scale productions had shown him that "the key to the success of the enterprise lies exclusively in the painstaking production of pure comedy performed by an impeccable ensemble."[14]

Alexei Bakhrushin, a wealthy leather merchant with a passion for theater, offered to lease land to Korsh that he owned on Bogoslovsky Lane at below market rates, and set aside fifty thousand rubles for construction of a new theater. Korsh again turned to the architect Mikhail Chichigov, who had remodeled both the Pushkin Theater and the one on Gazetny Lane. But this time he commissioned Chichigov to design a structure from the ground up in the fashionable Russian Revival style. Chichigov worked almost without sleeping to draw up detailed plans. The theater's exterior was exposed red brick with decorative niches and panels, reminiscent of a medieval Russian church. The elaborate roof featured turrets in the shape of *kokoshniki*, the traditional semicircular Russian peasant headdress. To this day the building remains a masterpiece of Moscow neo-Russian architecture.

Inside, the theater had 1,047 seats consisting of a ground level with side loges (the most expensive seats), two balcony levels, and an upper gallery. The entire theater—the stage, theater hall, foyer, corridors, and dressing rooms—was lit by electricity. Both the Bolshoi and Maly theaters still used gaslights. The construction team and interior designers worked at a breakneck pace. The first stone was placed on May 5 and on August 30—110 days later—the theater, its walls still smelling of damp plaster, held its opening performance.

Meanwhile, Korsh had lured his "dovie" Glama-Meshcherskaya back into the troupe by offering a contract of seven hundred rubles a month, one benefit performance, and a month's vacation to be taken at any time during the regular season (she had complained to him about being overworked). She was impressed with the electrical lighting—the dramatic effect of going from total darkness to light in an instant was remarkable. But the lighting was far from perfect; the bulbs gave off a yellow light and burned unreliably. Actors had to abandon their old ways of putting on their makeup. The electrical light was unforgiving, exposing wrinkles and any crude application of shading, pancake, and blush. It also undermined Korsh's economizing on stage sets, since the lights made the use of cheap scenery and furnishings obvious. However impressive the theater's exterior was, Glama-Meshcherskaya felt the architect failed to put any thought into providing comfortable facilities for the actors. Dressing rooms consisted of two parallel rows of stalls, each divided by wooden partitions, along a narrow corridor. In most stalls it was possible to extend your arms and touch both walls. The theater lacked a backstage actors' foyer, so there was always a loud crush of people standing in the corridor leading to the dressing room stalls.

Writing about Korsh's new theater, Chekhov remained unmoved: "The members of the troupe in quality and quantity are reminiscent of a Lenten mixed salad: everything's there except for the most important thing—meat."[15] Yet a year later Chekhov did a surprising thing—he confessed to fellow writer Maria Kiselyova: "I'm writing a play for Korsh (ahem!),"[16] as if to say, "I bet you never thought I would stoop so low." It was not such a great leap—he had published numerous humorous sketches in the form of dialogues that were not unlike one-act farces. A produced play paid well, better than the eight kopecks a line he was getting for writing Fragments. He had previously described most actors as "decent, but uneducated bar flies,"[17] but now he made some exceptions, notably Vladimir Davydov, who had recently left the Alexandrinsky Theater for Korsh's: "My goodness, what an actor the city of Peter has let slip through its fingers!"[18] With Davydov in mind, Chekhov turned one of his short sketches into a dramatic etude called "Swan Song."

In this, his first theater piece, Chekhov used a Shakespearean conceit—an actor alone on stage—as a metaphor for all lives. The curtain opens on the stage of a provincial theater. Piles of rubbish and a knocked-over stool lie on the floor. Several doors on the right lead to dressing rooms. Vasily Svetlovidov, an elderly comic actor, still dressed as Calchas, the Greek oracle-priest in Jacques Offenbach's *La Belle Hélène*, stumbles out of his dressing room, where he had fallen asleep drunk after a benefit performance. He sets the stool upright and sits down. It's the middle of the night and he thinks the theater is empty. He wallows in self-pity: "Whether you want to or not, it's time to start rehearsing for the role of corpse."[19] Svetlovidov is startled to discover that he's not alone—the old prompter Nikita comes out of another dressing room in his nightshirt. Homeless, he has nowhere else to sleep. Nikita tries to coax Svetlovidov to leave, but the actor refuses, saying he lives alone and no one's there to put an old drunk to bed. He laments that over the years he has allowed himself to be corrupted by vulgar comic roles: "This black pit chewed me up and swallowed me!" With Nikita's assistance, he conjures bits of monologue by Lear, Hamlet, and Othello, moments of theatrical greatness that only make more evident to him what has been lost, never to return. He says to Nikita: "What sort of talent do I have? I'm a squeezed-up lemon, a melting icicle, a rusty nail."[20]

With the self-deprecation that he often used as a defense against criticism, Chekhov claimed to have written his little play in an hour and five minutes. But the piece was a noteworthy beginning for the young playwright. In it Chekhov expressed an ambivalence about the theater that became a constant concern for him and led him toward a new approach to drama. Here was an art form that consisted of life itself—real people interacting with each other before your very eyes. Unfortunately, Chekhov had often witnessed life on stage being distorted by hackneyed acting that undermined verisimilitude.

When the play premiered at Korsh's theater on February 19, 1888, Davydov was so carried away with his role as Svetlovidov that he ad-libbed much of it, making numerous asides about famous Maly Theater actors of the past. Chekhov seemed not to mind, but by then he had already experienced the frustration of having little control over a Korsh production of his work.

"Swan Song" was published in January 1887, but a year passed before it appeared on stage. In the meantime, Korsh encouraged Chekhov to write a full-length play. In mid-September 1887, he sat down to write *Ivanov*, finishing the play in less than two weeks. He felt unsure about how good it was, given how quickly he wrote it. But Korsh liked it, commenting that the play avoided making any "theatrical mistakes." Chekhov was flattered by Korsh's reaction. It reassured him that he instinctively understood how a play worked. He explained to his brother Alexander: "The plot is complicated and not stupid. I finish every act like a short story: the entirety of the act is peaceful and quiet, and then in the end I punch the audience in the face." Chekhov was also pleased with his characterization of Ivanov, "a type who has a literary significance," and he could only see an actor like Davydov doing justice to the role.[21]

Chekhov initially seemed satisfied when Korsh presented him with a contract for 8 percent of gross receipts, which typically averaged 1,100 to 1,500 rubles a night. But once preparations were underway, acceptance turned to nervous apprehension. He felt ignored, unable to share his growing concerns about the quality of the production. Most actors in the troupe were "capricious, vain, half-educated." Only Davydov buoyed his spirits. The evening of the contract signing, he and Davydov stayed up until three in the morning going through the play. Listening to Davydov, Chekhov was convinced the actor was a "most colossal artist." Davydov, in turn, said *Ivanov* was better than all the rest of the plays written for the current season. The actor felt the problem was the rest of the troupe. Davydov told Chekhov that *Ivanov* had five superlative roles in it, but "for this very reason it will fall with a thud at Korsh's because there's absolutely no one to play them."[22]

Chekhov understood this was not something that concerned Korsh, a merchant who had "no need for an artist's or a play's success, but only a full house." He found fighting Korsh on the assignment of roles "upsetting and very unpleasant. If I had known, I wouldn't have agreed to have anything to do with it." Chekhov heard belatedly that the Maly Theater would have agreed to take on his play. He went to see Korsh about voiding his contract, but the suggestion made Korsh so livid that his arms and legs twitched as he spoke. Chekhov resigned himself to the fate of a "'beginning playwright' who willy-nilly had climbed into someone else's sled."[23] Korsh had promised ten rehearsals; there were only four.

When Glama-Meshcherskaya, who had the role of Ivanov's dying wife, Anna, arrived backstage at the first rehearsal, she noticed a solitary figure sitting on a stool by the stage entrance. He was taking windup toys out of his pocket and, to everyone's amusement, letting them go, one after the other, along the stage floor. One of them stopped at her feet, and Glama-Meshcherskaya asked an actor passing by, "Who's that strange fellow sitting there?" The actor peered across the stage into the darkness and said, "Oh, that's probably Anton Pavlovich. Yes, of course, that's him, Chekhov."[24] As a practicing physician, he had just come from treating some children who had stuffed his pockets with toys.

As the rehearsal proceeded, she noticed that Chekhov mostly sat quietly in the stalls; he neither interfered with the director's instructions nor made any comments to the actors. But privately he complained to his brother Alexander that only two of the rehearsals were productive, "since the other two turned into tournaments, in which the gentlemen artists practiced arguing about words and swearing."[25]

The journalist Vladimir Gilyarovsky dropped in on one of the rehearsals and found two of the actors arguing in the buffet. Nikolai Svetlov, for whom the premiere performance was a benefit, was "cursing the play up and down: 'What sort of play is this for a benefit? Just the title itself—*Ivanov*. Who's interested in some sort of Ivanov? Nobody will come.'" The comic actor Leonid Gradov-Sokolov objected: "No, brother, you're mistaken. First, the author is a talented writer, and secondly, the title is the best kind for a benefit: *Ivanóv* or *Ivánov*. Every Ivanóv and Ivánov will be interested in finding out what Chekhov wrote about him. And if only Ivanovs come—you'll have a guaranteed full house."[26]

Ivanov premiered on November 19, 1887. With a mixture of surprise, glee, and some exaggeration, Chekhov described to Alexander the tumult resulting "from such insignificant crap as my little play." Anton was seated to the side of the orchestra pit in the small director's loge, which felt to him like a prisoner's holding cell. His family sat "trembling" in lower-level loge seats. Backstage the actors "were on edge" and nervously crossed themselves. Yet Chekhov, much to his surprise, was calm. As the play began, it was clear to him that only Davydov and Glama-Meshcherskaya knew their lines. Everyone else either relied on the prompter or simply improvised. Ivan Kiselevsky, who played Shabelsky "didn't say a single phrase correctly. Literally: *not one.*" Notwithstanding the fact that Chekhov couldn't recognize the play being performed, "the first act was very successful. There were many curtain calls."[27]

Act 2 began with the same confusion: "A mass of people on stage. Guests. They don't know their roles, get mixed up, talk nonsense. Every word slices me like a knife along my spine." But at the end of the act, Chekhov was twice called out, followed by three ovations at the end of act 3. Each time the actors had to drag an unwilling Chekhov onto the stage. He seemed embarrassed, exchanging bows with Davydov, who heartily shook Chekhov's hand while Glama-Meshcherskaya pressed his other hand to her heart. There was a long intermission after scene 1 of act 4, which seemed to surprise the audience. Chekhov heard them grumble as they stood up and made their way to the buffet.

The conclusion of the play left Chekhov exhausted and disappointed. Kiselevsky's bumbling in particular disturbed him. He told his brother, "My Kiselevsky doesn't know his role, is as drunk as a shoemaker, and his short poetic dialogue turns out to be something slow and vile." It was obvious to him that Ivanov's fatal heart attack in the final scene confused the audience. When the curtain fell, "they made noise, a racket, clapped, hissed; they almost started fighting in the buffet, and in the balcony the students wanted to throw someone over, and the police hauled two of them out of the theater. . . . Our sister almost fell into a faint." The prompter told Chekhov that he had not seen such excitement both in the audience and backstage in over thirty years of working in the theater.[28]

But such excitement did little to allay his continuing ambivalence about writing for the stage, where he found himself and his craft exposed in ways he could not control. Several days later a scathing review of the play appeared in the *Moscow Leaflet* by Pyotr Kicheev, whom Chekhov considered a swindler from their early days working together for a Moscow weekly. Kicheev wrote that based on what he had already heard from others, he expected little from the play, but "we never suspected that a young man with a university degree would risk presenting to the public such a deeply immoral, such a nakedly cynical confusion of ideas, as has been presented by Chekhov in his *Ivanov.*"[29] Kicheev found it offensive that the playwright sought to justify the shameless behavior of Ivanov, who ignores his dying wife while falling in love with his neighbor's daughter. To him, Ivanov was a weak-willed man whose suffering was unworthy of our compassion. The finale, when Ivanov implausibly, out of shame, drops dead of a heart attack, was nothing more than a failed effort to win over the audience's sympathy.

A more positive review was published the following day in the *Moscow Gazette*. The writer found the play to be the work of a young, inexperienced, but unmistakably talented author, and the performances to be superior to the standard productions at Korsh's theater. Chekhov's talent was primarily reflected in the way he characterized the people who inhabit the provincial town of the play: "There is absolutely nothing tendentious. People are simply depicted as people."[30] Nevertheless, like others, the critic found Ivanov's motivations to be muddled and the finale to be stilted. A third review in *News of the Day* blamed Korsh rather than Chekhov for producing a play in such an "unfinished state."[31] Victor Alexandrov-Krylov, a popular playwright whose works were part of the Maly Theater's repertoire, approached Chekhov and offered to make some revisions and additions in exchange for being listed as the coauthor and dividing the royalties. Without revealing how deeply offended he was by the very notion of another writer fixing his work, Chekhov "delicately refused."[32]

After the third and final performance, Chekhov left for St. Petersburg, bringing *Ivanov* with him. He wanted the publisher Alexei Suvorin, his new literary benefactor, to read it. Suvorin had borrowed money to purchase the *New Times*, a failing St. Petersburg newspaper, which he turned into "the nation's most powerful newspaper."[33] He leveraged the success of the newspaper to create a major publishing company. His monopoly on train station bookstalls selling mass-produced, low-cost books made him very wealthy. Suvorin, who was now thinking about starting his own theater, found Chekhov's play to be very good, and considered it a mistake that Chekhov had given it to Korsh. He felt that neither Korsh's troupe nor the Moscow public or critics were capable of understanding *Ivanov*. Chekhov was encouraged by Suvorin's response; perhaps he need not make changes to the play. He wrote to Davydov in Moscow: "The end of the play doesn't sin against the truth, but nevertheless it amounts to a 'stage lie.' It's able to satisfy the viewer only on one condition: that it be played extremely well."[34] His St. Petersburg friends were telling him that the ending could remain as is only if an actor like Davydov played the role of Ivanov.

Chekhov vacillated between wanting to revise the play and simply setting it aside. He told his family: "When I think about how Korsh's shits sullied *Ivanov*, how they mangled and broke it, I want to throw up and start feeling sorry for the public, who left the theater empty-handed."³⁵ After Korsh's successful staging of "Swan Song" in February 1888, Chekhov saw the virtue in sticking with short humorous sketches—they lacked pretense and paid well.

Later that year, Suvorin told Chekhov he was interested in buying Korsh's theater and asked him to act as a go-between. Korsh's reaction was typically mercurial—at first he acted stunned and frightened, then overjoyed; he assured Chekhov that it would be "absolute bliss" for him to put the theater in such trustworthy hands. Korsh promised to show Chekhov all the books at intermission, but Chekhov protested that he didn't know the first thing about bookkeeping. "I spoiled the whole evening for him," Chekhov told Suvorin: "He wandered the corridors acting crazed, as if weighed down with grief. He went looking for me so that he could unburden his soul." He found Chekhov in the buffet and told him that he would take no less than one hundred thousand rubles. Chekhov was surprised that he wasn't asking for a million. "Well, my dovie," Korsh replied, "I'm just giving you an approximate random figure . . . I'll show you the books."³⁶

The next day Korsh sent Chekhov a letter to forward on to Suvorin in which he detailed the income and expenses of the theater and his conditions for selling. Chekhov better understood Korsh's willingness to sell "his shrine of glory" when he saw the financial records, which indicated that the theater's bottom line still depended on Korsh's personal subsidies and the support of outside investors.³⁷ Chekhov asked Suvorin to keep the matter secret, "or else my Korsh will shoot himself." Suvorin decided to pass on Korsh's offer. Chekhov promised to calm Korsh down the next time he saw him, and he reassured Suvorin that it was all for the best. Owning a theater was more oppressive than exciting: "You expend your energy working with actors, actresses, and authors; try to guess public tastes; constantly see in your theater the mugs of newspapermen, demanding free tickets and writing for who knows what publication."³⁸

By now Chekhov committed himself to making radical changes to *Ivanov* in the expectation that it would be staged at the Alexandrinsky Theater in St. Petersburg. Meanwhile, he had written *The Bear*, which he considered a "frivolous, Frenchy little vaudeville" well suited for Korsh's stage.³⁹ In the play, Elena Popova is a widowed landowner who has been mourning the death of her philandering husband for over a year with great display. She is visited by Grigory Smirnov, another landowner who has come to collect a debt owed by her husband. When she refuses to pay, a comic battle of the sexes ensues. Exasperated by her stubbornness, Smirnov challenges her to a duel, to which she readily agrees, fetching her husband's brace of pistols. Her audacity so excites Smirnov that he decides he's in love with her. In the final scene, he grabs her by the waist with Popova still yelling "I hate you! To the barrier!" before she willingly submits to a prolonged kiss.

The drama censor was offended by the "vulgarity and unpleasant tone" of the play,[40] but he was overruled by the head censor, who decided it could be staged if some of the crude language was removed. All plays were subject to prior censorship by police authorities working for the Ministry of the Interior. With no defined standards for what was permissible, "each censor had his own biases, interpretations, moods, and whims."[41]

The Bear premiered on October 28, 1888. Popova was played by Natalia Rybchinskaya, who was promised the role after expressing disappointment that Anna in *Ivanov* had been given to Glama-Meshcherskaya instead of her. Although Chekhov was delighted by the audience's applause and laughter, he felt the actors played their roles clumsily, failing to add any nuance to their "one-note" performances.[42] Nevertheless, reviews were favorable, and Korsh was certain it would consistently do well at the box office.

Unfortunately, after the first performance, as Chekhov put it: "A coffee pot killed my bear." Rybchinskaya was drinking coffee when the pot burst and the steam scalded her face. Glama-Meshcherskaya stepped in to play Popova in the second performance. She spent the whole night memorizing her role. But she was unwilling to do more than one performance—she had already given notice to Korsh that she was taking her midseason vacation as stipulated in her contract, and already had tickets for St. Petersburg. Korsh was furious, but she stood firm and got on the train. Chekhov was upset as well: "My fur-bearing animal unwillingly dropped dead, not having lived even three days."[43] He took a swipe at Glama-Meshcherskaya for falling out with Korsh: "Who now is going to play sick kitties in psychopathic plays?"[44]

As soon as Glama-Meshcherskaya arrived in St. Petersburg, Korsh started bombarding her with telegrams, sometimes two or three in a day. Then he switched to letters, which Glama-Meshcherskaya characterized as "plaintive, angry, full of lyrical digressions,"[45] sometimes so lyrical that she couldn't figure out what he was asking of her. For a while the letters stopped. Then Korsh changed his tactics. Having failed to get her to return early, he wrote Glama-Meshcherskaya a flattering letter, saying they should forget their differences. Once she was back in Moscow, he was anxious to make up for his losses by heavily rotating *The Bear* into his repertoire. Meanwhile, Chekhov turned his attention to getting his play on the stage of the Alexandrinsky Theater, where it opened on February 6, 1889, with Maria Savina, one of St. Petersburg's most renowned actresses, in the role of Popova.

Chekhov continued to have reservations about letting himself get too mired in the theater, which he referred to as "a snake who sucks up your blood."[46] He did, however, like the money, having earned a thousand rubles from *Ivanov* and *The Bear* in a little over a year. He wrote to a colleague: "Writing plays is advantageous, but being a playwright is upsetting and doesn't come naturally to me. I'm not made for ovations, backstage excitement, successes and failures, since my soul is lazy and can't bear a sharp rise and fall in temperature. The smooth and even profession of a belletrist strikes my soul as something much warmer and kinder. That's why it's unlikely that I'll ever turn out to be a decent playwright."[47] But, if anything, he was becoming even more embroiled in the messy business of writing for the stage. The truth was that he was being seduced by the world of the theater, and as is the case in any seduction, initial wariness was giving way to irresistible attraction.

Chekhov had been holding onto another farce, *The Proposal*, for almost a year, so as not to compete with the success of *The Bear*. But in September 1889 he decided to give *The Proposal* to a new private theater formed by Elizaveta Goreva. After all, a revised version of *Ivanov* was set to open at Korsh's theater at the same time. But after three performances of *The Proposal*, Chekhov asked Goreva to remove the play from her repertoire. He was unhappy with the quality of the provincial actors in her troupe, which he found to be "watery" and casually thrown together. *The Bear* was having much greater success at the Alexandrinsky Theater. The same month, Chekhov allowed another new private theater run by Maria Abramova, the wife of the writer Dmitri Mamin-Sibiryak, to start performing *The Bear*. The two stars of the original production, Nikolai Solovtsov and Rybchinskaya, left Korsh to continue their roles at Abramova's theater. Korsh, in his own words, was "thrown for a loop," since he felt he had exclusive rights to the play being performed in Moscow. Chekhov wrote to his friend, the playwright Ivan Shcheglov: "There's a whole revolution going on with my vaudevilles." He recounted that he had pulled *The Proposal* from Goreva, that Korsh was furious at Abramova for taking away *The Bear*, that Solovtsov felt *The Bear* was his "because he's already played it 1,817 times," and that the Maly Theater and its actor/manager Alexander Lensky were offended that the new *Ivanov* was playing at Korsh's.

Chekhov told Shcheglov: "You theater folks, you're a lot of trouble!"[48]

Chapter 1

"Ma Petite Sappho"

As the 1892–1893 theater season came to an end, the actor Alexandra Glama-Meshcherskaya felt a growing sense of oppression working for Fyodor Korsh's theater. She was tired of doing two performances a day; the company was without a permanent director; she considered the repertoire to be "drab and shallow" and refused to take part in his more vulgar farces: "More and more often I was filled with a complete revulsion for the work I had previously loved."[1] When Solovtsov, who had left Korsh in 1890, invited her to join a company he was forming in Kiev, she jumped at the opportunity. Glama-Meshcherskaya never performed for Korsh again.

With four actors having left his company before the fall 1893 season, Korsh sought out new talent from the provincial theaters to replenish his troupe. Among the actors he invited to meet with him was Lidia Yavorskaya. She was twenty-two years old and had just completed a stint as a member of Alexandrinsky actor Nadezhda Vasilieva's summer company performing in Revel, Estonia. From the moment she walked into his tiny backstage office, Korsh sensed she was different from the typical aspiring ingenue. She was not in the least intimidated by him. She had not come hoping to start out by being cast in small roles, but instead audaciously announced that she wanted to debut as Marguerite

Gautier in *The Lady of the Camellias*, a role made famous by Sarah Bernhardt and one she had already played in Revel.

Korsh looked at her through his pince-nez and smiled. She was an attractive woman with grayish-blue eyes, blond hair, and a thin but full-bosomed figure. There was nothing demure about her. Her eyes and smile were nervous and lively. Her voice was strangely hoarse and cracked. There was something high-strung, unsettling, and capricious about her that was unmistakably erotic.

Her bold manner intrigued Korsh, but he responded with his usual offer to a promising newcomer: "I'll gladly give you some small roles. Take advantage of them, my dear, and then we shall see . . ."

"Take a risk," she shot back in a way that momentarily took him aback.[2]

Aware that Yavorskaya had a successful run in Revel performing in *The Bear*, Korsh decided to cast her in two one-act comedies set to open within the next two weeks at his newly repainted and remodeled theater. From the outset, audiences took note of the young beauty's charismatic presence. Critics for Moscow's two leading newspapers, the conservative *Moscow Gazette* and the more liberal *Russian Gazette*, were less enthusiastic. Both newspapers complained about the sloppy preparation of the actors in Korsh's troupe and the theater's focus on low-brow comedies.

An overflowing matinee crowd packed Korsh's theater on September 9 to see Yavorskaya in her first dramatic performance in Alexander Ostrovksy and Nikolai Solovyov's *Light but No Heat*. Korsh quickly capitalized on her appeal, reviving Boleslav Markevich's *The Haze of Life* with Yavorskaya in the lead role of the social climber Olga Rantseva. Chekhov so loathed the play that when it first came out, he thought of writing a parody of it. He considered the author a "Moscow dandy and salon habitué" whose depiction of high society lacked originality. He said the play was "written with a horribly smelly toilet mop."[3]

It had been three years since Korsh last staged *The Haze of Life* with Glama-Meshcherskaya as Rantseva. When the play opened on September 24, *Artist*, a monthly journal popular with Moscow's theatergoing public, noted that the production was consistent with the theater's practice of reviving old dramas rather than presenting new works. The critic concluded, however, that these old plays were still preferable to being subjected to the tiresome farces that made up the rest of Korsh's repertoire.[4]

Yavorskaya's first lead role in a five-act drama gave audiences an opportunity to take stock of the new actor's talents. The critical response was mixed, sometimes contradictory. In general, newspaper reviews were unreliable, too often influenced by the critic's personal relationship with a given theater, acting company, or director, and by the publisher's political leanings. Everyone recognized the radiance Yavorskaya displayed on stage, especially when elegantly costumed. But one critic complained of the "excessive realism" in Yavorskaya's acting, in which she often resorted to shrieks and wringing of her hands to underscore Rantseva's fits of passion. Another critic, however, praised her ability to go through a range of emotions, from flighty to nervous to scornful to self-loathing. In two separate reviews in *Artist*, one critic wrote that Yavorskaya had "an audible voice with a pleasant timbre," while a different critic wished she "had more clarity of diction at the end of her phrases, more sonorousness in her speech, and less rushing through."[5] Not surprisingly, Yavorskaya's quick rise to fame despite mixed reviews grated on the other actors in Korsh's troupe. Her Gallic elegance and flamboyance, particularly the way she so obviously projected her sexuality on stage, reflected an approach that was startlingly different from that of her fellow actors and considered by many of them as unseemly for a Russian actress.

Lidia Yavorskaya was born Lidia Borisovna Hubbenet in Kiev in 1871 to a father who was a descendant of French Huguenots and a mother who came from a family of German Estonians. She grew up in luxury in a government-owned apartment thanks to her father's position as the Kiev police chief. The household was steeped in French language and culture. She later recalled that her first acting role was as an impulsive nine-year-old in a performance at her home of the children's play *Heureuse comme le reine* (*As Happy as a Queen*). She spoke the lines: "*Je veux nègre; je veux la lune*," boldly stating that she wanted the unattainable. "It foretold my future as an actress," she said, "much to the horror of my parents."[6]

They enrolled her in the Fundukleyev Girls Gymnasium hoping the rigors of the school would distract her from pursuing an acting career. Instead, the school, with its young teachers still under the sway of the student radicalism of the 1860s, only made Lidia rebel more fiercely against her parents. "In our circle," she recalled, "it was a time of rejecting 'art for art's sake,' a time of utilitarianism, Dobroliubov, Pisarev... Like many of my girlfriends, I cut my hair short and dreamed of 'serving mankind.'"[7] Lidia came to regard her father as a pawn of an oppressive ruling class. To show her defiance, at the age of fourteen she went up to a portrait of the tsar hanging in his study and gouged out the eyes.

She also continued to insist that her parents support her unwavering desire to be on stage. The actor Maria Krestovskaya, who like Lidia had performed as a teenager in amateur productions in Kiev, recalled once being told at the last minute that Lidia was taking her place in a role she had been promised. Lidia played the role even though the posters had Krestovskaya's name on them, and when some people in the audience hissed when she came on stage to take her final bows, Lidia spread the rumor that Krestovskaya had planted claques to cause the disturbance.[8]

In her last year of school, Lidia fell in love with her history teacher, L. Alexeev,[9] who thought of himself as a nihilist. Alexeev's political beliefs had such a strong influence on Lidia that even ten years later, at the height of her theatrical career, she spoke fondly of her education at the gymnasium, about how it made a deep impression on her soul and left her with "a head full of burning ideas and dreams."[10] As soon as she graduated, attempting a final break with her disapproving parents, Lidia married Alexeev. The naive seventeen-year-old quickly learned, however, what her husband's nihilism meant with respect to his marriage vows—no financial support, no fidelity, no belief in bourgeois values. He gambled away what little money he had; he spent many evenings getting drunk in nearby taverns; and when she tearfully objected to his womanizing, he reproached her for behaving like a typical philistine. One night she returned home earlier than usual from a rehearsal and found him in bed with the maid. She threw him out of the house. Under a cloud of shame and once again dependent on her parents, Lidia decided to go to St. Petersburg with the goal of joining the Alexandrinsky Theater. To further cut herself off from her past, she took on the stage name "Yavorskaya"; she liked that it sounded energetic and defiant.[11]

In the ten years since Glama-Meshcherskaya attended the Alexandrinsky drama school, the level of competition, especially among aspiring actresses, had increased significantly. Yavorskaya was ambitious, writing in her diary about her dreams of fame, but she understood that her limited experience in Kiev amateur productions would not get her far. She would have to first study with a recognized master before applying for admission to the school. Yavorskaya enrolled in classes given by Vladimir Davydov (the originator of the role of Chekhov's Ivanov), who had returned to St. Petersburg in 1888 after several seasons in Korsh's company.

Davydov was able to attract students because of his renown as an actor, but they soon learned he was an indifferent teacher who had no interest in advancing the careers of his students, particularly those who showed real talent and might become rivals for critical acclaim. He could not help but notice Yavorskaya's beauty and charisma, but was unsparing in criticizing her weak voice. She had already noticed in Kiev a tickling sensation in her throat and a dryness that affected her vocal cords and made her gasp for breath. Drinking water didn't help. She was suffering from chronic asthma, but her doctor told her it was only allergies.

In spite of her strained relationship with Davydov, Yavorskaya was accepted into the imperial school. After successfully completing her first year, she was allowed to wear the blue wool dress, the uniform of a full-fledged drama student. She had almost no friends among her classmates, most of whom came from much less educated and less Europeanized backgrounds. Undaunted, she plunged into her coursework, rehearsals, and long evenings spent memorizing roles. She particularly enjoyed attending premieres at the Mikhailovksy Theater, home to touring French companies presenting the latest plays from Paris. Davydov continued to give her advice as she prepared for student roles as Elizabeth in Freidrich Schiller's *Mary Stuart* and as Joan of Arc. "Learn to master your voice," he told her. "Pay attention to the lower and middle registers. Try to get out of the habit of speaking with a certain flatness in your voice and with a shrillness in your higher tones ... Don't raise your eyebrows when reciting—it makes you look naive and surprised. Your look should be completely confident ... stop rushing ... "[12]

Yavorskaya passed her examination performance but was not invited to join the theater company. She never spoke publicly about the rejection or its impact on her, but her friends later speculated that Davydov had a hand in convincing the theater's administration to dismiss her. The trajectory of Yavorskaya's career from here on can be seen as a concerted effort to prove how wrong Davydov and her detractors were to deny her entry into the imperial theater system.

Almost immediately she left St. Petersburg for Paris to study with Edmund Gôt, an elderly Comédie-Française actor who had been one of Sarah Bernhardt's mentors. We know nothing about Yavorskaya's first experience in Paris, but in retrospect it profoundly shaped her subsequent character, professional persona, and ambitions. She would return to Russia thoroughly Westernized, speaking French, dressed in Parisian fashions, and with an assertiveness completely at odds with the broadly accepted Russian notions of femininity.

When Yavorskaya arrived in Paris in late 1892, Bernhardt was almost fifty years old. Over the previous thirty years she had established herself as a stage celebrity of unparalleled worldwide fame. After quitting the Comédie-Française in 1880, Bernhardt took complete control of her own career, organizing highly profitable tours throughout Europe and even to the United States. While at home in Paris she leased the Théâtre de la Renaissance, serving as her own producer. Her flamboyant stage presence was as controversial as her love life, and both only served to heighten the public's fascination with her.

Muscovites flocked to the Bolshoi Theater when Bernhardt performed there for the first time in November 1881. Young Chekhov, writing for *The Spectator*, joined the throng, but he refused to be dazzled by Bernhardt, who "emerges from the upstage-center door, walks slowly and majestically forward to the footlights without looking anywhere, like a high priest advancing to perform a sacrifice." He was put off by her artifice and exaggeration: "Every sigh of Sarah Bernhardt, her tears, her convulsive death throes, the sum of her acting—is nothing more than a game, a clever and perfectly learned lesson. . . . Her every step is profoundly thought out, underlined a hundred times. Out of her heroines, she makes extraordinary women, just like herself."[13]

George Bernard Shaw had very much the same reaction: "She does not enter into the leading character, she substitutes herself for it."[14] Similar criticism would be leveled at Yavorskaya throughout her career.

After returning from her studies in Paris, Yavorskaya was invited to join Vasilieva's summer company in Revel. Vasilieva had been one of Yavorskaya's teachers at the imperial school and, unlike Davydov, was willing to help launch her student's career. Her debut in *The Bear* was favorably reviewed in the *Revel News*: "Miss Yavorskaya has rare theatrical abilities: a splendid appearance, a versatile and sonorous voice and an unusual agility. Even in a minor comedy, Miss Yavorskaya immediately drew the attention of the audience and was unanimously called out in the middle of the act. We hope to see Miss Yavorskaya in a major role in a comedy or drama."[15] In fact, over the course of the next three months, she played in comedies and dramas by Alexander Ostrovsky, Ivan Turgenev, and Nemirovich-Danchenko, as well as the lead in *The Lady of the Camellias*.

In the fall of 1893, after joining Korsh's troupe, Yavorskaya moved into the best suite in the Hotel Louvre, Glama-Meshcherskaya's former apartment. The corner suite was furnished in blue with a large semicircular living room looking out onto Tverskaya Square. The three-story building, only two blocks from Korsh's theater, contained two hotels—the lushly appointed Louvre and the smaller, more Spartan rooms of the Madrid. When touring theatrical companies stayed there, the director and lead actors typically had rooms in the Louvre, while the rest of the troupe stayed in the Madrid. The two hotels were joined by a dark, stuffy corridor that the editor Victor Goltsev christened "the Pyrenees." Wags joked that it was as difficult for a journeyman actor to move from the Madrid to the Louvre as it was to cross a mountain pass from Spain into France.

Tatiana Shchepkina-Kupernik, a former actor in Korsh's troupe, lived in room 8 of the Madrid. Barely five feet tall, she had been relegated to playing "pistachios," children's roles performed by adults. She came from an illustrious theatrical family with long-standing ties to Moscow's Maly Theater. Her Jewish father, the lawyer Lev Abramovich Kupernik, converted to Orthodoxy when he married her mother, Olga Petrovna Shchepkina, whose grandfather Mikhail Shchepkin dominated the Maly Theater's stage for the first half of the nineteenth century. Her aunt Alexandra Shchepkina-Chernevskaya joined the Maly in 1877 and was married to Sergei Chernevsky, one of the theater's leading directors. But Shchepkina-Kupernik herself could not hope to join the Maly, since as an imperial theater it only took on graduates of one of the state-run drama schools.

Shchepkina-Kupernik arrived in Moscow from Kiev in the spring of 1891 with a degree from the Fundukleyev Girls Gymnasium, from which Yavorskaya had graduated three years earlier. By the fall of 1892, Shchepkina-Kupernik decided to approach Korsh, asking him to let her play walk-on roles. Three days after talking to Korsh, she received a thick package from the theater—it was the script for the lead role in a one-act vaudeville, *The Heart Responded*. Terrified, she rushed to see Korsh, insisting she was incapable of taking on a speaking part. As Shchepkina-Kupernik recalled, Korsh replied: "Oh, it's nothing, nothing—in for an inch, in for a mile! Come to rehearsal tomorrow, and know your role by heart. (His tone was decisive.) My dovie, in our world it's unacceptable to refuse a role. Discipline!"[16]

Her aunt declined to help her prepare for the role, convinced that the eighteen-year-old was in over her head and concerned that she would bring shame to the Shchepkina name. The veteran Maly Theater actor Nadezhda Medvedeva was more supportive, as was the eccentric actor and librettist Konstantin Shilovsky, who doted on

Shchepkina-Kupernik. The production opened on September 21, 1892. The *Russian Gazette* wrote: "Miss Shchepkina, the great-granddaughter of the famous actor, debuted with great success in the role of the merry, frisky young Nina. The completely genuine joyfulness and lively acting of the young debutante made a very pleasant impression and earned the loud approval of the audience."[17] But neither Shchepkina-Kupernik nor her family placed much significance on her debut in one of the myriad Korsh vaudevilles that he trotted out week after week. The November issue of *Artist* noted that she was "charming" and "sweet" in "the role of the 'girl with berries,' consisting of only two or three words" in *From Crime to Crime*, but lamented: "Why or for whom was this old vaudeville dragged out of the dusty archives?!"[18]

Surrounded by a theatrical family deeply connected with the more prestigious Maly, Shchepkina-Kupernik quickly grew to disdain Korsh's repertoire. She wrote in her memoirs that although Korsh's theater was the most famous of Moscow's private theaters: "It was primarily a 'theater to aid digestion' for the merchant crowd that lived across the Moscow River and demanded only one thing: that theater shouldn't make you think and was allowed to make you laugh. Rosy, overfed merchant sons and daughters sat in the loges, sucked on candies during the performance, or ate apples and serenely watched scenes in which equally overfed, rosy actresses twittered naive and easily understood clichés."[19]

Theater critics continued to wish in vain for Korsh's demise. Several years earlier, Ivan Ivanov wrote in *Artist*: "Art doesn't forgive those who turn it into a vulgar amusement for the mob," predicting that the public, having grown sick of the constant mindless entertainment, would eventually abandon Korsh for healthier fare.[20] But it didn't happen. Of course, Korsh's theater offered more than just farces designed to generate a brisk trade at the buffet during intermission. He staged the first Russian production of Ibsen's *A Doll's House* in 1891, and followed it up the next year with the Moscow premiere of *Enemy of the People*. Over the next twenty years Scandinavian drama would prove very popular among Russian theatergoers, who felt an affinity for the literature and culture of their near neighbors beyond the Baltic Sea. The social dramas of Ibsen and Strindberg paved the way for audience interest in plays by Chekhov and Gorky. Works by Hamsun and Maeterlinck influenced the emergence of Russian symbolist theater in the early twentieth century with plays by Alexander Blok, Fyodor Sologub, and others.

Korsh was also proud of his bargain matinee performances of Russian and European classics, having distributed during the past decade over one hundred twenty thousand tickets to students so they could see the dramatic works they had been studying in class.[21] He still charged the students to check their coats, the income from which was sufficient to cover a performance's expenses. In part, Shchepkina-Kupernik's dissatisfaction with Korsh came from the realization that opportunities for her as an actor were limited. She told a friend: "I'm so small that I can only play.... little ingenues in vaudevilles. This is all fine while I'm young. And then come the 'fateful forties' and what will I do then?"[22]

During her stint with Korsh's company, Shchepkina-Kupernik began to write short stories and one-act plays. This time her aunt was more encouraging, asking her to flesh out a play that had been acted out one evening at a family gathering. She read the finished play to her "Uncle Seryozha" Chernevsky, who was impressed by the piece's sophisticated understanding of stagecraft. He agreed to submit the one-act play, *Summer Picture*, for consideration by the Maly Theater's literary-theatrical committee. It was accepted. She was summoned to the theater's office to sign a contract, which gave her the option of taking either a one-time payment of one hundred rubles or 2 percent of receipts each time it was performed. She took the one hundred rubles, which seemed like an enormous sum to her at the time, although subsequently, given the number of times it ran in Moscow, St. Petersburg, and the provinces, she realized she could have earned several thousand rubles from the play.

Shchepkina-Kupernik attended all the rehearsals, thrilled to have found a way to become part of the Maly Theater. Her aunt was cast as the heroine. Amused by Shchepkina-Kupernik's youth and diminutive size, the troupe dragged out the throne of Ivan the Terrible from the property storage and seated her in it to watch as they rehearsed. But unfortunately, she was prevented from attending the premiere. She had previously committed to play a male student in a vaudeville the same night at Korsh's, and the impresario refused to find a substitute. "Discipline! My dovie," Korsh said. After her performance she rushed to her aunt's apartment where the cast of *Summer Picture* was gathered around a festive table to celebrate the play's success. The reviewer in *Artist* wrote: "Miss Kupernik's *Summer Picture*.... makes a surprisingly fresh and bright impression. It is without banal vaudeville situations, without the usual vaudeville comedy—everything is suffused with a certain charming, poetic atmosphere of child-like joy."[23]

A few days later Shchepkina-Kupernik was finally able to see a performance. She recalled being "completely besotted by the feeling of creative joy."²⁴ She had found her calling as a writer. She decided to finish out the season at Korsh's, which ended in February 1893, and quit acting. Although comfortable on stage, she wrote in her memoirs: "I never experienced excitement and the feeling of forgetting myself on stage.... This wasn't the purpose and joy of my life."²⁵ She discovered she was much more nervous and excited reading her own works in public than performing the words of others on stage.

While no longer an actor, from the very beginning of her writing career Shchepkina-Kupernik chose to focus on the world of the theater as the setting for many of her stories. "Backstage," one of her first published works, appeared in the February 1893 issue of *Artist*. The story is remarkable in that it touches on a major theme that would define the course of her life: the power, if not the social status, that women could attain on stage that was otherwise denied to them in their traditional roles.

In "Backstage" Bronislava Lesnovskaya is a thirty-year-old leading actor with a company spending the summer in a provincial town. Already a widow, she has a lover, Arkady Rudnev, who has refused to consider marrying her because of a promise he made to his mother that he would never make an actor his wife. To add insult to injury, Rudnev announces to Lesnovskaya that he has become engaged to Natasha Krechetova, a naive seventeen-year-old provincial girl from a good family. Lesnovskaya decides to take revenge. Knowing that Natasha is in awe of the theater in general and of her in particular, Lesnovskaya invites her backstage during a performance intending to literally seduce her. Rudnev and Natasha enter her dressing room. Lesnovskaya reaches out with both arms to the blushing Natasha:

> "So this is your fiancée?" She looked at the thin girl with a lovely tender smile. "You should thank fate, Rudnev, that I'm not a man!"
>
> "What would happen?" Rudnev made up his mind to act uncomfortable.
>
> "I would steal this charmer from you!" Bronislava laughed and kissed the girl, who was looking at her with silent adoration. Emboldened by the tenderness of the "divine prima donna," she responded with a sincere, warm kiss.
>
> "Oh, oh ... how well we know how to kiss ... my child!" Lesnovskaya smiled slyly and sitting down on the couch, she pulled the girl down with her.²⁶

Over the next several weeks Natasha becomes Lesnovskaya's constant companion. One day while shopping, the two women are thoroughly drenched during a summer downpour and race back to Lesnovskaya's apartment:

> Laughing, they threw off onto the floor their wet dresses and wore only their short skirts. They looked at each other and burst out laughing again.
>
> "We're the spitting image of 'happy peasants returning from the field' in the *corps de ballet*, right, Nata?" Lesnovskaya laughed and, grabbing the girl by the waist, suddenly started to dance mischievously and dragged her into the bedroom. . . . It was clear to her that the feeling that Natasha had for her fiancé, whatever it was, it wasn't love, and that Natasha experienced a feeling for Bronislava that occurs among many very young girls for grown and experienced woman, a certain naive infatuation. She sincerely was carried away by Bronislava. It was pleasant for her to hold Lesnovskaya's finely chiseled hands in her own, to kiss her. Kissing the actress was incomparably more pleasant than kissing her fiancé, "whose beard became prickly after three days."[27]

Lesnovskaya succeeds in her plan to have Natasha join the company and wrest her away from Rudnev. She tells Natasha that she has convinced the theater director to let Natasha join the company. In a final melodramatic scene at the train station as the troupe prepares to leave town, Lesnovskaya confronts a furious Rudnev: "Did you really think that I wouldn't pay you back in kind? Only, as a good actress, I was able to hide my feelings, and my dear . . . sometimes in life you need to be a good actor!" Rather than an act of villainy, Lesnovskaya's revenge conveys a sense of triumph in which a woman has used her celebrity and her sexuality to assert her power over a thoroughly conventional man who made the mistake of treating her with aristocratic condescension.

Shchepkina-Kupernik reveled in her newfound independence after moving to Moscow. In Kiev at the age of fourteen, against her parents' wishes, she became engaged to the twenty-one-year-old Leonid Munshtein, a lawyer and aspiring poet. But their relationship became strained when she became infatuated with the forty-two-year-old actor Konstantin Shilovsky, a family friend who was best known for having collaborated with Tchaikovsky on the libretto for the opera *Eugene Onegin*. Shchepkina-Kupernik met Shilovsky while spending the summer at her aunt Alexandra's dacha outside Moscow. After dinner, at

Alexandra's request, Shilovsky took out his guitar and started to sing the aria *"Di quell'amor, quell'amor ch'è' palpito"* from *La Traviata*. The teenager swooned: "His voice, velvety, both strong and tender, poured into me like the magical potion of Tristan and Isolde. Every nerve of mine vibrated in unison with these sounds and responded to them. I grew quiet and, opening my mouth, stared in wonder at him."[28] She returned to Kiev the next day, and they began a correspondence. Shilovsky was married, yet took it upon himself to play the role of Shchepkina-Kupernik's romantic knight, writing her letters and verse in which he called her his hummingbird. He visited her when his theater company was on tour in Kiev. "I snuggled up to him like a child," she recalled. "I loved to sit in his lap, leaning my head against his coarse blue jacket, which smelled of 'Fresh Hay' cologne and cigars, and listening to his beating heart." For his part, Shilovsky managed to suppress the desire he felt for his little bird.

Shchepkina-Kupernik considered Shilovsky her first true love, and reacted with indifference to Munshtein's jealousy. She visited Shilovsky soon after her arrival in Moscow. But in time she realized it would be impossible to sustain this secret infatuation with a married man in the presence of both her family and his. They began to see each other less frequently. In the fall of 1891 Munshtein arrived in Moscow still hoping to marry Shchepkina-Kupernik. He was struck, and somewhat intimidated, by how quickly she found her way into Moscow literary and theatrical circles. Impatient with his timidity, she used her connections at the *News of the Day*, where a few of her stories had already appeared, to convince the newspaper to publish some of his verse. At the same time, she struggled to find a way to end their relationship. "I had already tasted sweet freedom," she wrote in her memoirs, "and only thought of how to painlessly break off with him. . . . There were tears and threats, including a revolver, but I had already found the stubbornness in me to insist, and after several painful scenes I felt myself finally to be free."[29] It was soon after ending their engagement that she took the bold step of approaching Korsh.

Well aware that the Shchepkina name opened doors for her, she actively sought to expand her contacts beyond those she had met through the Maly and Korsh theaters. She started to attend the soirees hosted by Sophia Kuvshinnikova, the wife of a police doctor who was openly carrying on an affair with the landscape painter Isaac Levitan. The Kuvshinnikovs lived in a four-room apartment eccentrically furnished *a la russe* below a police precinct watchtower near the Khitrovka slums. Kuvshinnikova, sometimes followed from room to room by a surly domesticated crane, presided over regular gatherings that attracted many of the city's most prominent writers, painters, actors, and singers. At the Kuvshinnikovs, Shchepkina-Kupernik met Lidia Mizinova (everyone called her "Lika"), a schoolteacher with dreams of becoming an actor or singer. She was struck by Mizinova's extraordinary beauty, describing her as a "Swan Queen" who seemed unaware of the effect that her charms had on others.[30] She had "downy ash-blond hair, dark sable brows, striking gray eyes, soft well-rounded features ... She was stately, shapely with a graceful walk and restrained gestures, shy, deep, secretive about much of herself."[31] In turn, Mizinova introduced Shchepkina-Kupernik to Maria Chekhova, Anton Chekhov's sister, who taught at the same girls' gymnasium as Mizinova. For the past several years Mizinova and Chekhov, who appreciated her charms but was wary of her attentions, had been engaged in a disjointed dance of a romance in which both often used humor to avoid expressing their honest feelings.

In April 1892 a scandal erupted within Kuvshinnikova's circle as a result of the publication of Chekhov's story "The Grasshopper," which many considered a thinly veiled caricature of the ménage à trois involving Kuvshinnikova, her husband, and Levitan. Chekhova blamed Shchepkina-Kupernik for goading Levitan, who had been a close friend of her brother's, to take greater offense at the story than he otherwise might have been inclined. In her memoirs, Chekhova recalled that Shchepkina-Kupernik arrived at Kuvshinnikova's apartment, "sat on the floor at the feet of the mistress of the house, took out her comb, let down her hair and said loudly: 'I don't understand how Chekhov ... It's all very strange ... He's been at your house, enjoyed your hospitality, was considered a friend, and suddenly he published this disgusting story ... How is this possible? It's totally incomprehensible.'"[32] At this point she had not even met Chekhov, who only infrequently attended Kuvshinnikova's soirees, offended by the way she openly humiliated her physician husband.

That fall Shchepkina-Kupernik had also been following with interest Yavorskaya's disruptive, meteoric rise within Korsh's company, although she herself was no longer a member. She noticed that Yavorskaya "suddenly arrived in this atmosphere of bourgeois well-being like a stone thrown into standing water—a disturbing female figure, neither roundish nor rosy ... Instead of chirping, one heard a nervous, harsh voice; instead of the bobbing up and down of a sweet little doll, there flashed a snake-like grace and a Parisian way of dressing that was striking to see."[33] By chance, Shchepkina-Kupernik during a brief visit to Kiev met Yavorskaya's mother, who strongly disapproved of her daughter's acting career. She asked Shchepkina-Kupernik about Yavorskaya's lifestyle in Moscow. "I told her what little I knew," she recalled, "but the kind old lady made the saddest conclusions from my words that her daughter was being extravagant, that she was surrounding herself with unseemly people and so on, and she wrote her a stern letter with references to me."[34]

Back in Moscow, the writer Vasily Mikheev, visiting Shchepkina-Kupernik in her room at the Madrid, told her Yavorskaya was complaining about her for saying "God-knows what" to her mother. Shchepkina-Kupernik claimed to be outraged by the accusation that she had gossiped about someone she had never met. She knew where Yavorskaya was living in the Louvre, and she quickly decided to cross the "Pyrenees" along the poorly lit corridor with the corpulent Mikheev puffing behind her, reaching the carpeted corridor of the Louvre. Shchepkina-Kupernik described the meeting in novelistic detail in her memoirs:

> I firmly knocked on the door and heard: "Come in!" from a very unusual, raspy, seemingly cracked voice. . . . There were a lot of flower baskets and a lot of people in the room. A very fine-figured, elegant woman in a white cloth house dress came up to meet me. What first struck my eyes was her golden hair tied behind her neck in a Greek knot, her look shining with a gray-blue light, and the nervous smile coming from her large but wonderfully formed mouth.[35]

Shchepkina-Kupernik rushed to explain what happened in Kiev:

> "Your mother asked about you. I literally said three phrases to her: that I know you're having great success in Moscow, that you are visited by many literary figures and actors, and that they say it's very interesting. And when she asked whether we lived in the same building, I said, not exactly, since the Louvre is much more elegant, and that in the Madrid the rooms are not so nice as here." "Does she have a good room?" "They say it's the best one in the Louvre. . . . That's all I said to her: I give you my word and ask you to believe me. And now forgive me that I broke in on you in such an unceremonious fashion and disturbed you."[36]

Yavorskaya grabbed both of Shchepkina-Kupernik's hands and graciously accepted her explanation. Shchepkina-Kupernik mingled with the other guests in the apartment, and by the time she left late at night, she was thoroughly in love with her newfound friend. She was struck by Yavorskaya's "brilliant ability to converse, her liveliness, a sort of snake-like grace, free, a slightly imperious attitude toward those around her manifested by their worship of her, and her unusual tenderness toward me."[37]

The next day Shchepkina-Kupernik found herself unable to shake a pervasive feeling of sadness. Toward the evening of a rainy fall day, she sat alone in her room thinking about her mother and her beloved Shilovsky, both of whom had recently died unexpectedly. She squeezed herself into the corner of her couch and wept. There was a knock on the door and she answered "Come in," expecting it to be the servant coming to light the lamps. Much to her surprise Yavorskaya entered the room.

"How good it is that I found you at home," she said, but quickly noticed Shchepkina-Kupernik's tears. Yavorskaya embraced her, saying: "My sweet girl, what's the matter? What happened?" This is how Shchepkina-Kupernik described her reaction:

> Not expecting such tenderness and not having experienced any kind of tenderness for a long time, I suddenly felt as if a living spring welled up in my starved heart: I pressed my head to this woman I didn't know and poured my tears onto her dark red manteau... And she caressed my hair, kissed my wet eyes, and called me tender and gentle names that no one had called me in a long time. She later said to me that when she saw me, so young and alone, her heart turned over and she was immediately attracted to me.
>
> From this day on, we were inseparable over the course of many years, and I am indebted to Lidia for many wonderful moments in my life. We were seized by an intense "friendship at first sight." They laughed at us, and made our friendship more difficult, convinced that we were actually in love with each other and couldn't live without each other—and in truth there is always a smack of romanticism and rapture with each other in these young friendships. With every hour we discovered something new about each other. In less than three weeks we shared everything: friends, how we spent our time, tastes, amusements, and even work. She asked me to go through her roles with her, select costumes. She gave me

ideas for stories. Her boundless energy overwhelmed my tendency to be lazy.[38]

Both women openly expressed their feelings of love to each other, although the depth of their intimacy is unknowable. Donald Rayfield has spoken of Shchepkina-Kupernik's "lesbian preferences."[39] In late-nineteenth-century Russia, lesbianism was, unlike male homosexuality, not "subjected to sanctions under the criminal code."[40] In 1895 Ippolit Tarkovsky, an assistant director at St. Petersburg's main maternity hospital, published a study on lesbianism in which he wrote that love between women could actually be "psychologically and neurologically healthy in every respect."[41] Legally and medically, lesbian sex was simply too rare and too benign to be of concern. Socially, however, it was considered deviant behavior. To the extent that love between women could be interpreted as a desire to be free of male dominance, it was also seen as a threat to the social order.

As an elderly woman, writing her memoirs in Stalinist Russia, Shchepkina-Kupernik understandably chose to be circumspect, to describe her feelings for Yavorskaya as "romanticism and rapture." But Yavorskaya's blizzard of notes sent to her in room 8 of the Madrid in the fall of 1893 were anything but circumspect, often ending with declarations such as "I firmly kiss you, how I love you" or "I embrace you with all my heart while fearing that I irritate you."[42] The notes were written mostly in French, which became their *langue d'intimité*.

Yavorskaya also came to rely on Shchepkina-Kupernik to keep her from becoming too distracted by the dissipations of her social life, to inspire her to take herself more seriously as a creative artist. "Yes, my poetry has forsaken me," she told Shchepkina-Kupernik. "Prose, prose, and prose! . . . And so it is from day to day. Every word, letter, poem, telegram from my dear Farfadette are bright rays of a golden sun, lighting up my faded, boring life."[40] Late one night, having returned to the Louvre from a tavern with "gypsies, oysters, declarations, triangles . . . . sleepless faces, spirits of the *fin du siecle*," she sent a note to Shchepkina-Kupernik about how tired she was of all this, how she couldn't bear doing this every night. She had to fend off a certain Garfield, a sulking "twenty-eight-year-old boy with a genius for doing nothing and drinking brandy. Oh, the same story as my husband. . . . . Oh, I've had enough. Work, healthy work, poetry."[43]

Many of the notes began with endearments that played on Shchepkina-Kupernik's short stature: "my dear beloved little girl," "*chere Farfadette*" (a sprite or imp), and "*ma petite Sappho*." The bits of poetry that Yavorskaya sent to her, whether heartfelt or the incoherent romantic effusions of someone enjoying play-acting, were unmistakable expressions of an ardent love that sometimes felt transgressive:

> Au nom de l'amour
> Nous serez punis par l'Eternel
> Pour avoir voler un coin du paradis
> Ensoleillé d'un rayon d'amour brulant.

> (In the name of love
> We will be punished by the Lord
> For stealing a piece of heaven
> Sunny with a burning ray of love.)[44]

Within their artistic circle, there were those who saw the relationship as a scandalous affair, which would soon make life difficult for both of them.

Chapter 2

"I Spent Two Weeks in Some Sort of a Daze"

By the middle of 1893, the romance between Mizinova and Chekhov had become increasingly dissonant. She sensed he was less interested in seeing her or even writing to her, and in a letter written in late August, she attributed this to his egotistical passivity:

> You only need people so that when the weather is lousy and the nights are long and there's nothing to do and it's too early to go to bed, there's someone around to drive away your boredom. And as soon as this passes, you no longer think about them. . . . You and I look at our relationship very differently. I just want to see you, and I'm always the first one to do something about it! You, on the other hand, want everything to be nice and calm, and to have people who have come to visit sitting beside you, but you yourself don't take a step to make it happen. I'm convinced that if, over the course of a year, for some reason I didn't come see you at all, you wouldn't budge to make the effort to see me.[1]

Chekhov replied that he was amazed by this attack "for no reason at all." He promised to see her "without fail" in September on his way to Petersburg, but he never made the trip. She wrote again on October 7: "I currently find myself in such a state. I so want to see you, so terribly want this, but I know that this will remain only a wish!" Her desperation was prompted by her decision to go abroad with her friend, the soprano Varvara Eberle, to take singing lessons in Paris: "I only have three or four months to see you, and after that, possibly, I'll never see you."[2] Chekhov tried to reassure her: "Why the melancholia, Lika? We'll see each other not for three or four months, as you write, but for forty-four years, because I will come for you, or put more simply, will never let you go. We will see each other until you throw me out."[3] He again promised to come to Moscow in the next few days, but when he failed to appear, Mizinova decided to accompany Maria Chekhova to Melikhovo, Chekhov's estate about forty miles south of Moscow. The visit did nothing to reassure Mizinova that Chekhov felt any deep affection for her.

On October 27, two days after Mizinova left Melikhovo, Chekhov arrived in Moscow, staying at the home of his brother Ivan. Within the first few days, Mizinova introduced Chekhov to Shchepkina-Kupernik. Almost immediately, he found himself embraced by a coterie of writers and actors who gathered most evenings at Yavorskaya's apartment at the Hotel Louvre. The journalist Pavel Sergeenko recalled that "at one party so many women were flirting with Chekhov that someone in jest compared him with Admiral Avelan," the head of the Russian fleet whose lavish reception during an official visit to France was the focus of lengthy daily reports in the *Moscow Gazette*. "Chekhov happily seized on the joke," Sergeenko added, "and with comic seriousness took on for a period of time the persona of the admiral."[4] In addition to Sergeenko, members of "Avelan's squadron" included the writer Ignaty Potapenko, the journalist Vladimir Gilyarovsky, Fyodor Kumanin (the founder and editor of *Artist*), Mikhail Sablin (editor of the *Russian Gazette*), Shchepkina-Kupernik, Yavorskaya, Eberle, and Mizinova.

A note has been preserved in Moscow's Russian State Literature archives in which several members of "Avelan's squadron" entice Shchepkina-Kupernik and Eberle to join them one evening at Yavorskaya's apartment. Chekhov wrote: "Avelan also awaits you. The hostess said that she's not writing you because she's illiterate." But, in fact, Yavorskaya signed the note "Fantasy" (some in the group had taken to calling Shchepkina-Kupernik and Yavorskaya "Poetry and Fantasy," respectively).[5] At other times the squadron met up at Kumanin's or Sablin's editorial offices, or dined together at the chic Yar or Strelna restaurants, both of which were famed for their gypsy entertainers.

Mizinova regretted introducing Chekhov to her lady friends. When they met alone on November 1, Chekhov irritated her by talking about how charmed he was by Yavorskaya and Shchepkina-Kupernik. She sent him a note the next day:

> Why did you start talking yesterday about the theater? So that I again could thoroughly torment myself all day! Here's what I want to ask you. You know very well how I feel about you, and so I'm not at all hesitant to write about this. I also know your feelings—or condescending pity—or complete indifference. My deepest wish is to be cured of this awful condition which I find myself in, but it's so hard. I beg you. Help me.[6]

By the time he left Moscow, Chekhov had managed to assuage Mizinova's hurt feelings. As soon as he was back in Melikhovo, he received a letter from her reverting to the playful tone (often with an intentional pinch of malice) that characterized much of their correspondence. She told him she had "once again spent an impossible evening" carousing with Eberle and "Madamoiselle Yavorskaya," going to bed at eight o'clock in the morning. Mizinova reported that Yavorskaya "said that Chekhov was fascinating and that she wanted to marry him without fail. She asked for my assistance, and I promised to do everything possible for your mutual happiness. . . . Will you soon come here to propose to Madamoiselle Yavorskaya? It would be good even if you came for that! Write three lines about whether you love Lidia Borisovna—of course to me, not her! . . . Come see me, you tormenter of my soul."[7] She had written the letter in Shchepkina-Kupernik's room at the Madrid, where she was spending the night. Shchepkina-Kupernik sat next to her, composing her own note to Chekhov in comic verse:

> Heartfelt greetings to Avelan!
> He's always in my head;
> And I never cease to be bored,
> While he's not in Moscow.
> My soul is struck
> By the incomparable Avelan—
> As no other romance
> Has entranced me in my life!
> All, all my dreams are of Avelan,
> All we talk about is only him,
> As he appears in secret
> As if in a rosy mist
> We await Avelan without fail

To come to us at the end of the week.
Would that he think of Tatiana
At least from time to time! . . .
And so on, all in this vein, to the end of time.[8]

Chekhov readily admitted that all this fawning attention had gone to his head. He wrote to Suvorin: "Three days ago I returned from Moscow, where I spent two weeks in some sort of a daze. This was because my life in Moscow consisted of a continuous series of feasts and new acquaintanceships. They kept teasing me, calling me 'Avelan.' I have never before felt so free, . . . and the girls, girls, girls . . . "[9] He wrote to Mizinova: "Do you often go to the Louvre? Greetings to the sirens of the Louvre, and tell them that even running away hasn't unsnarled me from their nets: I'm still under their spell."[10]

Although Shchepkina-Kupernik playfully posed as one of the girls dreaming of Avelan, in retrospect she refused to see herself or her friends as mere sirens intent on seducing the men of his "squadron," and distracting them from their creative work. She thought of her friends as a new generation of women who were the intellectual and artistic peers of the men in her circle. She recalled this period as one of "deaf and dumb reaction." Women weren't allowed to attend universities, so "the best of the girls . . . . threw themselves one way or the other into the arts. . . . We knew how to have fun, drink up champagne, sing gypsy romances, but we also knew how to talk about Nietzsche, about Dostoevsky, about searching for God. We knew how to read through a scientific abstract, correct proofs and so forth." They had to constantly struggle to have their talents taken seriously by their male counterparts: "They didn't see, and didn't want to understand that we were 'the first swallows,' . . . who, at the price of our young lives, our reputations, with a smile on our lips and with a steadfast effort, in the midst of condemnation, persecution, sexual advances, opened the way for future women, destroyed the thickets of centuries-old traditions, prejudices and slavery with our own weak hands and served a greater cause: women's liberation."[11]

Yavorskaya's quick rise to fame rested on a sexuality that she used to assert her power over men. As an actor she could be brazen in a way impermissible for most society women. Her liveliness and charm masked the technical flaws in her acting, but also overshadowed her intelligence and desire, even as a beginning actor, to use theater as a force for social progress. Her fellow actors, mostly with provincial backgrounds, mocked her for her fluency in French, for her Parisian elegance. "The cream of Moscow—professors, writers and so forth—were drawn to her," wrote Shchepkina-Kupernik. "But fatally they were more interested in the woman in her rather than the actress or person."[12]

Shchepkina-Kupernik was also attracted to Eberle, who had a more "infectiously cheerful," less mercurial personality than Yavorskaya. Tall, redheaded with green eyes, the twenty-three-year-old Eberle had just left the opera company at the Bolshoi Theater, where she had debuted the previous year in Tchaikovsky's *Eugene Onegin*. To everyone's amusement, Eberle enjoyed taking snuff and singing folk songs while accompanying herself on the balalaika, which she had learned to play as a child growing up on the steppes far from Moscow. Shchepkina-Kupernik painted an idyllic, eroticized picture of their affection for each other:

> I can recall a bright day in early spring, in blue and gold, in Moscow. Varya had just been to some sort of fortune-teller and had insisted that I accompany her. The fortune-teller had told her all sorts of nonsense, and leaving the place, we were as happy as a couple of kids. We got into a horse-cab. A lively crowd scurried all around us. The greenery on the boulevard sparkled as if newly washed. The cupolas of the churches glowed. We both started laughing, neither one of us knew why—and here outdoors we loudly smothered each other in kisses, again not knowing why—for the sunny day, for our freedom . . . and most of all, for our youth. Nothing happened, but it seemed to us that something precious had been given to us.[13]

Mizinova and Eberle had formed a close friendship as well; the two of them made plans to go to Paris together. Unlike Eberle, Mizinova was very much an amateur singer, still too insecure to perform in front of anyone but her friends and teachers.

Maria Chekhova joined Shchepkina-Kupernik's circle of friends as well. At first, Shchepkina-Kupernik had a hard time warming up to her. She was used to the more outgoing personalities of her theatrical friends, and Chekhova struck her as too serious and reserved. But she eventually came to enjoy her wry humor, so similar to that of her brother, even if she never seemed to lose her "womanly composure" when the rest of group became rowdy. Chekhova, by nature, was circumspect, not prone to flirting, and worried that the rumors about Shchepkina-Kupernik's relationship with Yavorskaya would somehow taint her own reputation.[14]

Chekhova and Mizinova once again visited Melikhovo in mid-November, followed by Chekhov's departure for Moscow a few days later. This time he stayed for almost a month, first at Ivan's apartment, then moving into a room at the Loskutnaya Hotel just outside the Kremlin walls. Ostensibly he was in Moscow to review additional proofs for *Sakhalin Island* with Victor Goltsev. He asked Mizinova to organize a piroshki lunch for him and Goltsev at her apartment, ending his note to her with "Until we meet, sweet matchmaker," jokingly referring to her caustic offer to act as a go-between for Yavorskaya. Chekhov was in fact again responding to the siren calls coming from the Louvre. He received a note from Shchepkina-Kupernik: "Perhaps you will honor us with your presence at the modest room No. 8. And I won't say how happy the hostess will be."[15] Yavorskaya herself pleaded: "I don't at all feel well. If you can, if you are able to find such goodness in your heart, write me the prescription that you cruelly tore up yesterday. I don't dare count on your magnanimously coming to visit the ailing Yavorskaya, but I'm hoping . . ."[16]

At this early stage in their relationship, Shchepkina-Kupernik seemed naively willing to encourage, even stage manage, the flirtation between Yavorskaya and Chekhov, but over time jealousy complicated her feelings toward both of them. In her memoirs, she wrote that Chekhov "had dual feelings toward Lidia. Sometimes he liked her, sometimes he didn't like her, but without a doubt she interested him as a woman."[17] She maintained that their relationship never went farther than a "light flirtation." While this initially might have been true, Chekhov would eventually succumb to the actor's charms. Yavorskaya herself seemed to enjoy spreading the rumor that she was having an affair with Chekhov. Ivan Shcheglov noted in his diary on December 7, after stopping by the Loskutnaya Hotel, that Chekhov said to him: "You fall in love with an actress, you live like a heavenly bird."[18]

One evening in early December, Yavorskaya and Shchepkina-Kupernik dropped in to see Chekhov at his hotel on their way to a performance of a touring Ukrainian troupe at the Paradise Theater. Finding him not at home, Shchepkina-Kupernik left a note asking him to make sure no one was staying at his sister's apartment because Yavorskaya would be spending the night there. Chekhova had invited Yavorskaya to use the apartment as a place to hide from the unwelcome attention of her former husband Alexeev, now a government official in the customs department. Several months later, Yavorskaya recounted these events in her characteristic overwrought style in a letter to Chekhov:

> You recall how last November I was fleeing from a man who was chasing after me and I fell back on your hospitality.... Maybe my fleeing seemed crazy to you and possibly exaggerated. You asked me more than once, when both revulsion and pity for this man was roiling inside me, "What was I after?" As an artist and a human being, you talked to me about the right of a person to take command of her own feelings, to love or not love, freely relying on her own inner feelings.[19]

The intimidating power that Alexeev had over Yavorskaya, who by now was surely experienced in fending off unwanted admirers, was due to the fact that they weren't legally divorced.

In the midst of this turmoil, Yavorskaya maintained a busy performance schedule of light comedies, including Nemirovich-Danchenko's *The Christmas Party*. But these trifles were dwarfed by Korsh's decision, in recognition of Yavorskaya's quick rise to fame, to let her take on the role she had audaciously asked to play when they first met five months previously—Marguerite Gautier in *The Lady of the Camellias*. It was set to premiere on December 27, 1893. Additionally, Korsh scheduled the benefit performance promised in her contract for February 18, 1894. Since it was customary to feature a new play at a benefit performance, Yavorskaya asked Chekhov to write a light one-act piece. He apparently agreed because a few days later, after he returned to Melikhovo, Mizinova wrote him that she heard he was "busy writing a drama for Yavorskaya's benefit performance."[20]

Three years of enduring Chekhov's ambivalent feelings toward her, now compounded by Yavorskaya's personal and professional pursuit of Chekhov, finally drove Mizinova into the writer Potapenko's arms. Chekhov had invited both Mizinova and Potapenko to spend New Year's at Melikhovo. When Mizinova returned to Moscow, she announced to Chekhov: "I have completely fallen in love . . . with Potapenko! Papa, what am I to do? You, of course, will always have the ability to get rid of me and dump me on someone else!"[21] It was a declaration of love expressed as an act of revenge. Falling in love with a married man with children was hardly something Chekhov would likely encourage Mizinova to do, even if it relieved him of the burden of her emotional demands.

In late December 1893, Shchepkina-Kupernik left Moscow to spend the holidays with her father in Kiev just as Yavorskaya was about to star in *The Lady of the Camellias*. Without Shchepkina-Kupernik for the first time since they had declared their love for each other, Yavorskaya felt abandoned: "Oh, my life as an artist, where is it after my poet has flown away? . . . Oh, my holidays won't be complete without you." Sitting alone in her backstage "cage," Yavorskaya wrote Shchepkina-Kupernik that her only consolation was the theater, her "empire of dreams," especially now that she had thrown herself into playing Marguerite Gautier in spite of the jealous scorn directed at her from some actors in the ensemble.[22]

Shchepkina-Kupernik wrote back from Kiev telling Yavorskaya that she had taken it upon herself to visit the Hubbenet family, and letting her know that her mother expressed an interest in coming to Moscow after the holidays. This prompted a distraught Yavorskaya to fire off a telegram to Shchepkina-Kupernik: "Terrible state of mind. Arrange it so that mother does not come."[23] Yavorskaya followed up the telegram with a lengthy letter explaining that she feared her mother's visit would be another attempt to force her to quit acting: "For God's sake, calm Mama down. They can't make me leave." She went on to say that her relationship with her family was completely spoiled, that they suspected her of living a tawdry life, and that she was determined to remain free of them: "The oppression of this sweet, artistic, intelligent, most of all artistic family so brightly stood before my eyes that I recalled all the difficulties that I have endured from its vulgar, stupid yoke. Oh no, no, not at any price! I've had enough!"[24]

Yavorskaya and Shchepkina-Kupernik's shared desire to assert their independence and challenge conventional behavior deepened their affection for each other. Shchepkina-Kupernik published a poem titled "Credo" in January 1894, expressing to the extent possible, given the censorship of the day, her social and sexual rebellion. The poem was written in a way that the object of her love could be either a man or a woman:

> I want to be as free as the winds of the steppe,
> As the enchanting song of a poet,
> To rip my soul from its deadening chains,
> From the shackles of a hypocritical world.
> I want to never have to ask,
> I want limitless freedom—

I want to caress without inhibition and to love
Amid the splendors of an eternally youthful Nature
. . . .
I want, oh my friend, to feast my eyes on you
And the stars, and the scarlet dawn;
I want to be your fettered slave—
I want to be your queen!²⁵

Sometime soon after Shchepkina-Kupernik's return to Moscow from Kiev, the two women began addressing each other using the intimate form of "you."

Yavorskaya's desire to play Marguerite Gautier, a role first performed in 1852, was primarily motivated by her progressive inclinations, even if the heroine's tragic fate stemmed from the hypocrisy of the French bourgeoisie. She saw it more as an opportunity to join the ranks of the French divas who had gained fame through their portrayal of the doomed courtesan. Eleonora Duse and Sarah Bernhardt had already performed the role in Moscow. The critic for *Artist* made it clear that Yavorskaya's performance, although there was much to praise in it, was not on par with that of "the brilliant Duse and the famous Sarah Bernhardt." Yavorskaya was very attractive ("A marvelous figure, unusually mobile features, expressive eyes") but with some shortcomings in her technique ("a certain abruptness and monotony in how she moves her arms, and excessive number of gestures"). He felt her edgy, passionate acting style at times was consistent with the demands of the role, although it undermined her portrayal of the dying Marguerite in the last act, where her strong voice and physicality failed to convincingly depict a person in the last stages of consumption. Nevertheless, as in previous reviews of Yavorskaya's major roles, the critic saw much promise in the young actor: "We make all these criticisms of the actress because we can be especially severe about her gifts; she has shown us what she is capable of, and we, in truth, hope that she fully takes advantage of her rich gifts."²⁶

Chekhov did not see *The Lady of the Camellias* on his return to Moscow. There was a performance on January 12, but it conflicted with his previous commitment to Potapenko to spend the evening at the apartment of the pedagogue Dmitri Tikhomirov with his "squadron" and the staff of *Russian Thought*. The festivities commemorated Tatiana Day, a church holiday traditionally celebrated as a drunken revelry by university students marking the end of the semester. Chekhov had written his brother Mikhail, who was 145 miles away in Uglich, urging him to come to the party, which promised to be a rare opportunity to have "one hell of a good time" in the company of "the most popular professors, performing artists, and representatives of the press."[27] Mikhail received the letter on January 11 and quickly got himself ready, first traveling seventy miles by sleigh in the fierce cold to the nearest train station, arriving in Moscow on the evening of the twelfth. When he entered Tikhomirov's apartment, he recalled: "It was loud, joyous, and bright, and I saw all the luminaries of the Moscow intelligentsia at the time sitting at an enormous table."[28] Mikhail had just found a place to sit down when Sablin and Goltsev approached him and begged him to go immediately to the Louvre to bring Shchepkina-Kupernik and Yavorskaya to the party as soon as possible. The revelers, already slightly drunk, felt the evening would not be complete without the presence of the two ladies.

Mikhail felt it was awkward to refuse them, and, despite being tired from his journey, went off to the Louvre. There he was told that Shchepkina-Kupernik was at Korsh's theater watching Yavorskaya's performance. He found Shchepkina-Kupernik sitting in the staff loge and told her about the invitation to the party. She went backstage at the end of the third act and returned to report that Yavorskaya asked them to wait, that "it remained for her 'just to die,' and then she would be ready." It was "with a heavy heart" that Mikhail sat out the last two acts in the loge watching Yavorskaya's performance: "I was never an admirer of her talent. I especially didn't like her voice, which was husky, cracked, as if she constantly had a sore throat. But she was an intelligent woman, progressive, ... and she had a clearly defined literary taste."[29]

To his further dismay, Mikhail discovered that Yavorskaya was so nervously agitated after her performance that she needed time "to calm herself down and restore herself." He continued to sit in the loge and wait. When Yavorskaya finally emerged, she announced that she had to go back to her apartment to take her makeup off and get changed. By the time they set off for the Louvre, it was already midnight. When they finally arrived at Tikhomirov's, everyone had left and the servants were clearing the table. The next morning, Mikhail dropped in on his brother at the Great Moscow Hotel. Chekhov looked at him and said "Oh, you!," shaking his head in disappointment that these two women had managed to ruin his brother's evening.

The next day Chekhov returned to Melikhovo with Mikhail, soon followed by his sister and Mizinova, who arrived to celebrate his birthday.

During their stay, Chekhov learned that he had managed to offend Shchepkina-Kupernik, most likely having said something about her relationship with Yavorskaya. He wrote to her on January 20, inviting her to visit him: "Sweet Tania, don't be angry with me. Come today or tomorrow to Melikhovo. We'll drink to peace and *basta*. Be a good girl." He signed the note "Resident of the Louvre (No. 54) A. Chekhov. I await you."[30]

But Shchepkina-Kupernik was too busy helping Yavorskaya prepare for her benefit performance to go to Melikhovo. On February 2, Yavorskaya wrote an insistent letter to Chekhov, reminding him of his promise to write a one-act play for the event and asking him to deliver it within six days to meet the publicity deadline. It was exactly the kind of letter that would cause Chekhov to balk at providing any further assistance. She appealed to his "magnanimity and goodness," confident that he understood "how important this is for a young, beginning actress" whose future depended on its success. Her tone was presumptuous:

> Dear Anton Pavlovich, don't refuse to adorn my benefit with your play. Putting aside the sparkle of poetry that you would give even to a one-act piece, your name alone would arouse the kind of interest that is unattainable to me as a novice before the Moscow public. Support me, a timid debutante. This will be infinitely precious to me, and I'll say a great thanks to you for this.
>
> If you have the least sympathy, not just to me personally, but for an actress, you will fulfill my request, more so because in comparison to the good you will have done for me and the pleasure you will give the public, it won't involve much effort on your part—two evenings and it will be ready.[31]

When they last met, Chekhov had described to Yavorskaya an idea he had in mind for the play. She found the plot to be "fascinating" and now suggested to him that the piece should be called "Reveries," based on "the concluding words of the countess: 'It's a dream!'" In support of Yavorskaya, Kumanin, the editor of *Artist*, wrote Chekhov the next day that the "young, talented actress L. B. Yavorskaya . . . . sleeps and dreams" that he would fulfill her request.[32] But Chekhov did not respond. In place of Chekhov's play, Shchepkina-Kupernik offered her one-act farce "At the Station."

With less than three weeks left until the event, Yavorskaya finally decided on the main play for her benefit. "They brought to me," she recalled, "several melodramas to choose from with champagne, gypsies, shootings, poisons, and other such noisy effects."³³ But instead, she selected Sophia Kovalevskaya's *The Struggle for Happiness*. It was an unusual, provocative choice, but one consistent with Yavorskaya's progressive inclinations. Kovalevskaya was one of the most remarkable "women of the sixties"—a mathematician of genius who, despite the professional constraints placed on women, managed to earn a doctorate at the University of Gottingen and went on to hold the departmental chair at the University of Stockholm. At the age of thirteen, Kovalevskaya showed an aptitude for algebra, which so alarmed her father that for several years he forbade her to be tutored on the subject. She and her older sister Anyuta felt "incarcerated" by life on the estate and frustrated by their father's refusal to support their aspirations. Anyuta secretly began to submit stories to the Petersburg journal *The Epoch*, which led to her being briefly courted by its publisher, Fyodor Dostoevsky, until she realized that he demanded a level of submissiveness in a wife that she found unacceptable.

Kovalevskaya decided that she wanted to go to a Swiss or German university. However, in the 1860s Russian women were allowed to travel abroad only while accompanied by a parent or husband. This led some of the more radical youths to arrange fictitious marriages as a means of emancipating women. She found a willing coconspirator in Vladimir Kovalevsky, a Petersburg Darwinist with an interest in geology and paleontology. He went through the motions of a courtship and gained her father's consent. After their marriage, they spent five years in Europe, at the end of which Kovalevskaya received her doctorate based on the three published dissertations she submitted in lieu of formal coursework. During their stay in Europe, the Kovalevskys spent time in London, where Vladimir met with Charles Darwin and Thomas Huxley, and Sophia attended the Sunday soirees of George Eliot. They also went to France in April 1871 at the height of the Paris Commune to assist Anyuta in her hospital work during the insurrection.³⁴

Back in St. Petersburg, both Kovalevskys, despite their advanced degrees, were unable to find suitable academic positions. By now, the marriage was no longer fictitious (a daughter was born in 1878), but it became increasingly strained. Vladimir failed miserably as a businessman trying to take advantage of Russia's rapid industrialization. Sophia spent long periods in Europe trying to find a teaching post. In 1883 Vladimir committed suicide by inhaling a bottle of chloroform. Toward the end of the year, Sophia was offered a provisional teaching post in Stockholm, which controversially led to a permanent position as professor of mathematics. August Strindberg, in a newspaper article, wrote that "a female professor of mathematics is a pernicious and unpleasant phenomenon—even, one might say, a monstrosity."[35]

Achieving a lifetime appointment in Stockholm unleashed a flood of creative energy in Kovalevskaya. She turned to writing in addition to her mathematical research, starting with a memoir of her meetings with George Eliot. Kovalevskaya had become friends with Anna-Carlotta Leffler, a Swedish feminist novelist. They decided to collaborate on a play called *The Struggle for Happiness*. Kovalevskaya provided the concept, characters, and plot line, while Leffler did the writing in Swedish. The idea for the play was original but highly impractical in theatrical terms. It was, in fact, two plays subtitled *How It Was* and *How It Might Have Been*. Both had the same characters and began with the same prologue, but from there the plots diverged. The intention was to have the plays performed by the same actors two nights in a row. In *How It Was*, the heroine, the baroness Alisa, turns her back on Karl, the man she loves, to marry her cousin in order to retain ownership of the family factory. In the final lines of the play Karl says to Alisa: "One thought is unbearable. The thought of how all this might have been."[36] In the second play, Alisa eventually marries Karl, and they turn the factory into a cooperative venture in partnership with the workers. Although the setting was Scandinavian, Yavorskaya felt that Alisa "was our Russian girl, related to us in mind and spirit." The actress recognized that the play had technical defects, yet "something strong, bright, ideological emanated from it."[37] It expressed the liberal aspirations she first felt as a gymnasium student.

The play was translated into Russian in 1892 and published in Kiev, which was how it came to the attention of Yavorskaya and Shchepkina-Kupernik. When Yavorskaya proposed the play to Korsh, he resisted, convinced that it was a deadly bore and would lose money. But she was insistent, since a benefit performance provided an opportunity to choose a work and a role that best represented her personal beliefs. She was convinced that making a compromise now at the beginning of her career would set a bad precedent. Yavorskaya performed only the second part, *How It Might Have Been*, both for practical reasons and because it focused on workers' rights. Shchepkina-Kupernik scrambled to polish the play with little time to spare. As it was, only a week would be set aside for a read-through and rehearsals. The work had been translated by Maria Luchitskaya, a Ukrainian whom Shchepkina-Kupernik felt had an incomplete mastery of Russian. On February 4, Yavorskaya appeared in a revival of Alexei Pisemsky's *Men above the Law*. During the last act, the woman she played was banished to a cellar below stage, from which she emerged at the very end. Shchepkina-Kupernik waited for her below as Yavorskaya lowered herself into the trap: "It was there by the light of candle ends, perched amidst dusty set decorations that both of us worked on the play, taking advantage of every minute. I can recall the Rembrandt-like illumination in the underground darkness, the candle ends lighting up Lidia Borisovna dressed in a white peignoir with her cascading curls."[38] They sat there working through the script until Yavorskaya heard her cue, suddenly started wailing loudly, and threw herself "into the gaping maw of the trap" back up onto the stage. Not surprisingly, she gave a distracted performance.

Beyond revising the script, Shchepkina-Kupernik also took charge of the celebratory aspects of Yavorskaya's first benefit. She wrote to Chekhov asking him to participate in the gift of a silver engraved blotting pad signed by Yavorskaya's closest friends. All he needed to do was to provide the engraver with two or three samples of his signature and a brief salutation. She gave as an example Levitan's message "Believe in yourself," obviously goading Chekhov, since the two men were not speaking to each other. Chekhov replied that "Lidia Borisovna is an outstanding person, and I'm ready to jump into flames to ensure that her return home from the theater after the benefit is joyous, but I beg you on my knees to allow me not to participate in giving the gift."[39] He feared offending the other actors who previously appeared in his plays at Korsh's theater and to whom he had not offered a comparable tribute.

Chekhov left for Moscow on February 18, staying this time at the Louvre. He attended neither Yavorskaya's benefit that evening nor her after-party. The premiere attracted significant press coverage. Uncharacteristically, in advance of the opening, the *Russian Gazette* published a long background article on *The Struggle for Happiness* and on Kovalevskaya's life. The performance sold out. When Yavorskaya appeared on stage for the first time, she was presented with two laurel wreaths, a lyre made out of flowers, a luxurious bouquet, several boxes of flowers, and the engraved blotting pad. Shchepkina-Kupernik recalled that the theater that night was packed with university students who had heard that factory workers figured in the cast. She claimed that when Alisa says, "There's only one way to better the situation of the workers—that's to encourage them to close ranks and form a union," those sitting up in the cheap gallery seats drowned out her words with applause, causing the police in the hall to start looking around nervously. Alexandra Kollontai, who would later become Shchepkina-Kupernik's close friend and a prominent communist revolutionary, subsequently told her how much the play, naive as it was, excited her young compatriots, who were attracted to the work of a Russian woman who had achieved such widespread fame in the West.[40] *Artist*, often supportive of Yavorskaya given that its publisher Kumanin was a member of the "squadron," considered the production to be sufficiently significant to warrant a lengthy feature article: "Despite the obvious lack of stage-worthiness and its excessive length, the play makes an illuminating impression. Having seen it one night, you come out of the theater better than when you entered it."[41]

While Chekhov failed to attend Yavorskaya's benefit performance, he still spent time with his "sirens" during his brief stay in Moscow. Kumanin sent him, together with Yavorskaya, Shchepkina-Kupernik, Mizinova, and Eberle, to a studio to be photographed individually and in groups for *By the Way*, a collection of poetry and prose that he was publishing. The last sitting involved Shchepkina-Kupernik, Yavorskaya, and Chekhov. When the photographer said "Look into the camera," Chekhov turned and made a stone face, which caused the women to lean forward and burst out laughing.[42] In the resulting photograph, Chekhov faces the camera with an inscrutable look while the two women, seemingly infatuated, gaze intently at him. When Chekhov saw the photograph, he called it "The Temptation of St. Anthony."

In *By the Way*, "Avelan's squadron" collaborated on an anthology on the theme of amorousness, sometimes playfully, sometimes in earnest. Chekhov contributed his story "The Beauties," an etude on how seeing an attractive woman can give rise to feelings in a man of sadness and melancholia. Mikheev contributed "Beneath the Mask," a story of love lost and found, dedicated to Yavorskaya. The first story in the collection was Shchepkina-Kupernik's "Sappho," presented as "pages from the diary" of a frivolous divorcee who admits that "all sorts of nonsense seems terribly important and interesting to me," and who decides to take revenge on a suitor for preferring the perfume Karylopsis ("Barbarian," she screeches) over her favorite called Sappho. Silly as it is, this comic sketch has elements in it that unmistakably reflect Shchepkina-Kupernik's feminist slant on love and desire. The diarist displays considerably more affection for her friend Lily—they greet each other with profuse kisses—than for Yuri Andreevich, her suitor, whom she would rather taunt than embrace. Lily is the one who introduces her to the perfume Sappho, telling her that "for your friends you have always been Sappho," calling her (as Yavorskaya called Shchepkina-Kupernik) "*ma petite Sappho.*" It is Lily who comes up with a way to take revenge on Andreevich for preferring Karylopsis. They buy cases of the "suffocatingly sweet perfume," spray it all over Lily's clothing, furniture, and drapery, and even pour drops of it into his coffee instead of liquor: "I allowed him to kiss my hands only so that he would more strongly smell the perfume." Finally, his head aching, Andreevich falls on his knees and begs her to change her perfume.

For the story's narrator, Sappho represents more than just the name of her favorite perfume: "In general, I love Sappho. Her image from the mists of time shines like a faraway star." Bored by her first husband, wary of getting married a second time, the narrator has come to appreciate Sapphic lyrical yearning: "No, there is something higher in unsatisfied passion. With satisfaction comes the end of striving. But eternal striving . . . eternal desiring . . . What beauty! What poetry!" She mentions reading a book by a German scholar who pointed out "that Sappho was not at all that unattractive, masculine woman that many considered her to be," a reference to Friedrich Gottlieb Welcker, who wrote "Sappho Liberated from a Prevalent Prejudice." "On the contrary," the narrator continues, "she was a short, elegant woman with a fine figure, an extraordinary Sappho with splendid hair, as the madly in love Alcaeus [the Greek lyric poet] says of her. Oh yes, yes! Only a woman in all the significance of this word could write such hymns to Cypris [Aphrodite]."[43]

Accompanying Chekhov's story in *By the Way* was a photograph of all four "sirens" in an intimate vignette, billows of gauze draped over their shoulders, their heads affectionately touching each other. On the back of Chekhov's copy of the photograph, Shchepkina-Kupernik inscribed a Sapphic poem in which each woman is compared to a flower—she is a tea rose, Mizinova is a poppy, Yavorskaya is a camellia, and Eberle is a tobacco flower:

> In this picture are four blossoms. Their smiles are clear, their look is calm. I bow before you, Aphrodite. No mortal is worthy of such a garland. Living flowers! How beautiful is the enchanting dream of splendid summer. It breathes love, and life is filled with the fragrance of a tea-rose as fresh as youth, as hot as a sultry day. Here is the poppy, bright crimson, happy and bold. Here proudly and purely shines the bright corona of a white camellia. And this

is a fragrant tobacco flower. Let night fall—its aroma flatters us. I greet you, Aphrodite. No mortal will ever attain such a garland.⁴⁴

The taking of this photograph marked the end of an idyll. With the beginning of Lent on February 28 and the closing of Moscow's winter theater season, "Avelan's squadron" dispersed, and the four "sirens" left for Europe. On March 2 Shchepkina-Kupernik and Yavorskaya went to the Kursk station with a bouquet of tulips and hyacinths to see Chekhov off for Crimea, where he hoped the warm air would improve his health. The next day Yavorskaya left Moscow with plans to join Korsh in Italy and then travel on to Paris, this time not as a failed Petersburg drama student but as a Moscow leading lady looking for new French plays to perform. Potapenko left for Paris on March 4 to join his wife and children. Mizinova and Eberle followed a week later to take up singing lessons offered through the Grand Opera. Feeling abandoned, Shchepkina-Kupernik talked "grandfather" Sablin, as editor of the *Russian Gazette*, into funding her so that she could join Yavorskaya in Italy in exchange for writing a series of feuilletons for his newspaper. For her this first trip to Europe would prove to be a whirlwind of excitement, a chance to experience the Roman and renaissance culture she had only imagined in *Eternity in a Moment*, and to share it in the company of her beloved Yavorskaya. For Mizinova, the journey was filled with melancholy and a sense of foreboding—she felt that Chekhov had abandoned her and that her hopeless love for Potapenko would only bring her sorrow. When she found out she was pregnant, she was convinced she was going to die.

CHAPTER 3

"In Paris Things Don't Happen So Quickly"

As Mizinova made her way by train to Paris, she imagined Chekhov spending the spring sitting in sunny Crimea enjoying a steady stream of telegrams and letters from Shchepkina-Kupernik and Yavorskaya. On April 11, 1894, Shchepkina-Kupernik sent him a flirtatious poem from Naples in which she told the wind to convey to him "all the wondrous sounds that sing in our hearts, all the kisses that burn on our lips."[1] In truth, Chekhov was bored, not because he missed the company of his lady admirers, but because he felt oppressed by the burden of having to spend most of each day writing, his only amusement being attending the rehearsals of a local amateur production of *Faust*. On March 23, Yavorskaya sent him a long, desperate letter from Rome in which she revealed that her relationship with Shchepkina-Kupernik had brought on a family crisis. Her former husband Alexeev, whom she had spurned the previous November, had taken his revenge by sending a letter to her father in which he wrote:

> Yesterday I received the news from Moscow that your daughter left for Italy with Miss S-K, and with this departure, I'm of course obliged to burn my bridges and will not attribute to your daughter a single word of reproach . . . The matter has nothing to do with me, but your daughter is flying off a horrible precipice. Her

relationship with S-K has become a filthy tale in Moscow, and it's not surprising—this lady is a well-known *M-lle Giraud, ma femme*, and contact with her is not without consequences. I know that I am distressing you, but just the same I consider it my duty to explain this situation to you . . .[2]

Yavorskaya's father had forwarded the letter to her. She had no idea who M-lle Giraud was, but correctly guessed it was meant as an insult. *Mademoiselle Giraud, Ma Femme* was a salacious 1870 novel by Aldolphe Belot, in which a husband discovers that his wife and the wife of a friend are lovers. Yavorskaya was distraught that the letter had revived the strained relationship with her parents, who had only recently started coming to terms with her acting career. It had also thoroughly shattered her Italian idyll: "I was feeling so good: the Forum, Capitoline Hill, muses, emperors, vestal virgins . . . and suddenly from these heights into this mess, into this unexpected awful mud."[3] Above all, Yavorskaya was livid because the letter had maligned Shchepkina-Kupernik, whom she defended as totally innocent of any offense. She explained to Chekhov:

> I *sincerely* fell in love with Tatiana Lvovna. It's so painful, and I don't have the strength to explain to you what they have blathered about her because of me. I so treasure that feeling of family, of pure affection, of female caresses that Tanechka introduced to me that to throw her out of my house, to not treat her as a sister would be terribly difficult for me. She knows nothing, but, of course, if because of me she will be exposed to shame—my duty will be, without saying a word to her, to estrange myself from her.[4]

The previous November, Chekhov said he was willing to talk to Alexeev about his harassment of Yavorskaya, but she had turned down his offer. Now, at the end of her rambling, agitated letter, she asked Chekhov "to write a few lines to Petersburg," either to Alexeev or to someone with connections at the customs office where he now worked, "so that he will stop making a nuisance of himself." Chekhov apparently ignored her request. Nor did Yavorskaya take any steps to distance herself from Shchepkina-Kupernik.

Shchepkina-Kupernik too had experienced the distress of being harassed by a former lover. Still smarting over her decision to break off their engagement, Munshtein became even more upset when he found out about her relationship with Yavorskaya. In his 1931 memoir in verse, *Moscow Faraway*, the stanza describing their breakup is immediately followed by a stanza on Yavorskaya's meteoric rise at Korsh's theater: "The press rushed to dethrone others, it started to praise and glorify her. She wasn't very talented, but there was intelligence and splendor and stylishness, and zest, an attractive figure, self-assurance, culture . . . She knew how to choose friends and acquaintances. A host of men and women buzzed about her, attracted by her . . . She knew how to make a noise, become the 'news of the day,' and make a 'boom.'"[5] In his humorous pieces for *News of the Day*, Munshtein gossiped about Shchepkina-Kupernik and her friends. As a rising celebrity, Yavorskaya was particularly vulnerable to attacks in the press. "It was especially easy for him to do this with regard to Lidia," Shchepkina-Kupernik recalled, "which depressed me terribly because I understood that he was pursuing her for the sole purpose of doing me harm."[6] Eventually he fell in love with and married another actor in Korsh's company, and stopped tormenting Shchepkina-Kupernik. But years later, after Shchepkina-Kupernik published her memoirs, in which she wrote that there had never been any serious feelings between them, that it was all "taken from plays and novels," Munshtein lamented in *Moscow Faraway* that she had cruelly mocked the love they had once shared.

Yavorskaya spent a month in Italy with her benefactor Korsh while Shchepkina-Kupernik returned to Russia, staying with her father in Odessa. Concerned that Shchepkina-Kupernik might jump to the wrong conclusions, Yavorskaya wrote to her that Korsh was being the perfect gentleman. As he left for Paris in advance of Yavorskaya, she "warmly thanked Korsh for the wonderful month in Italy, since he had made the most of it as much as he could, in word and in deed. I hasten to let you know that Korsh is very nice. He's a person we were mistaken about. You and I have a staunch defender in him. His relationship with me is delicate and without reproach. He doesn't display anything towards me but the warmest, most sincere feelings."[7]

Korsh met Yavorskaya at the train station on the morning of her arrival in Paris. He delivered her to her hotel room, after which, as she wrote to Shchepkina-Kupernik, "we celebrated at breakfast with sparkling wine and drank to your health." Yavorskaya also mentioned that Korsh's room was one floor above hers, for which "I'm indebted to him for his delicacy." In the evening they went to the Palais Royal to see Georges Faydeau's "horrible" farce *Un fil à la patte* (*Tied by the Leg*). Having gotten up at four in the morning to meet Yavorskaya's train, Korsh fell asleep at the theater—he "was so tired that he almost fainted

(It's already obvious that my fate is to make my friends pass out from exhaustion; it's no accident that you've said that I'm hardy enough for two)!" They left before the end of the third act.[8]

While in Paris, Yavorskaya promised Shchepkina-Kupernik to find a publisher for her book of verse, *Fleurs de Russie*. The work, a celebration of the feminine, expanded the metaphor she had previously developed of poetically representing Russian women as different types of flowers. Yavorskaya had shown some of the poems to a Monsieur Lenoir, a literary friend of Korsh's, who had found them delightful, and talked of having the book printed in an elegant edition. But then Lenoir kept putting off meeting with Yavorskaya, and when they did meet, he found some of Shchepkina-Kupernik's language infelicitous and in need of revision. "In Paris things don't happen so quickly," Yavorskaya wrote. "Everyone rushes, hurries, promises, and having deceived you twice, they then do it a third time, don't I know it. We need a month at least, perhaps more to fulfill the projected plan."[9] The poems were apparently never published.

Meanwhile, Yavorskaya spent most of her time with Mizinova and Eberle, often going to the theater thanks to Korsh, who "only needs to send his calling card to the administrator" for them to get seats even at sold-out performances. Sarah Bernhardt's Théâtre de la Renaissance, according to Yavorskaya, was "the most current, most elegant. To not see Sarah in something is a sign of bad form." At a private viewing at a dress salon on the Champs-Elysées, she caught a glimpse of Bernhardt, who made an appearance in the hall as if she were a "crowned figure." Uncharacteristically, Yavorskaya confessed: "I hid myself as much as I could so as not to embarrass the Russians!"[10]

Yavorskaya's letters to Shchepkina-Kupernik at times became despondent, recalling happier times when they were together in Italy: "How pitiful is mercantile, bourgeois Paris compared to Florence, Rome!" When she caught a cold, she complained there was "no one to take care of me, to be concerned about me, my dear, good, blessed little one! . . . There's nowhere in Paris where you don't feel yourself to be foreign, never has there been such need for a quiet home, your own home, which would be a shrine to that which is dear, unchanging, without noise, tawdriness, traveling salesmen! Oh, my child, get married to a good, simple person! After all, I'm now starting to get old, lonely, gloomy."[11] Yavorskaya was twenty-three.

But as Shchepkina-Kupernik's long-awaited arrival in Paris became imminent, Yavorskaya's melancholy dissipated: "I now have lots of energy, a return of strength, a thirst to work." She attended the salon of Madame Juliette Adam, a feminist author and founding editor of *Nouvelle Revue*. "What a crude old lady," she told Shchepkina-Kupernik, "vulgar like a Parisian usherette," but fascinating and smart. She was certain that Shchepkina-Kupernik would charm the Parisians: "You can create a sensation in Paris, but you need a décolleté bodice. Joking aside, it's the chief requirement to be successful at receptions such as those of Madame Adam." Yavorskaya also reminded her to bring copies of her published work and theater reviews: "You will need to work a lot here, my little one."[12]

As Yavorskaya predicted, once in Paris, the irrepressible Shchepkina-Kupernik had no trouble forming her own social circle. The Russian-born soprano Felia Litvinne, whom she had previously met in Moscow, welcomed her to her elegant apartment and introduced her to the small Parisian community of expatriate Russian artists, including the portraitist Yuri Leman, who asked Yavorskaya to sit for him. Shchepkina-Kupernik's main guide to Paris was the Parnassian poet Catulle Mendès. She did not much care for his verse, which she found to be a strange mix of mysticism and eroticism, "often bordering on the pornographic." But he was a wonderful companion who opened her eyes to the splendors of the city. He took her to the newspaper office where he worked, which struck her as the opposite of the quiet of Sablin's *Russian Gazette*. Here the atmosphere was frenzied. Telephones were ringing constantly; reporters and stenographers rushed about from floor to floor. They visited the "colossal" department stores—the Louvre, Bon Marché, and Printemps—"their massive maws swallowing every minute hundreds, thousands of women, dazed, having lost all feeling of time and space," she wrote. Russia had no such palaces of consumerism. She walked through the Grand Market with its displays of "mountains of meat, wildfowl, fish, vegetables, and fruits that Paris consumed in a day." At Versailles, they wandered along the lanes of the old park while bicycle riders raced by, some on tandems, some pulling carriages "from which dangled the little legs of a small child." On the banks of the Seine, they ate fried fish in small taverns entwined in clematis and stopped at fair stalls while Mendès recited his verse to her.[13]

Mizinova, too, had quickly embraced the cultural life that Paris had to offer, although her letters to Chekhov and his sister complained of loneliness and abandonment. Potapenko could visit her only occasionally, briefly, and in secret. She was sure his wife was faking her hysterical claims of illness. She pleaded in vain for Chekhov to come to Paris.

Meanwhile, she was having some success with her singing lessons. One of her teachers said her voice had a wonderful timbre that was well suited for a dramatic soprano. But she sarcastically described to Chekhov the morning lessons in her pension, where she and Eberle practiced with a group of German, French, and English women singers with only one skinny German male to accompany them. She saw Charles Gounod's *Faust* and Giuseppe Verdi's *Othello* at the Grand Opera. She herself performed at student concerts. She attended the annual salon exhibitions at the Elysian Fields and Field of Mars, but was not sure she liked what she saw and wondered what her friend Levitan would say about the paintings. She found Parisian street life fascinating as she looked down on it from the top of an omnibus, and hoped to write down her impressions in articles for *Artist*, but nothing came of it.

Now reunited, Yavorskaya and Shchepkina-Kupernik focused their efforts on gaining entry to the world of Parisian theater. Shchepkina-Kupernik was embarrassed by what she saw at the Comédie-Française. The declamatory acting style struck her as false and old-fashioned. She much preferred the lively repertoire of the boulevard theaters. Her favorite actor was Gabrille Réjane, whose style of performance she found simple and realistic. "She was not beautiful," she recalled, "but in her lack of beauty, there was something captivating. A snub little nose, a large but pretty mouth, cat-like eyes and a cat-like grace. A soft femininity and a mischievous child-like animation . . . "[14] By comparison, Shchepkina-Kupernik was thoroughly disappointed when she finally saw Bernhardt perform:

> Her "golden" voice, as the Parisians expressed it, was indeed very beautiful. . . . Its every note, every word was clearly separated, masterfully pronounced, sometimes almost sung out in the typical French manner. But it didn't stir your soul; it was hard to believe her sufferings, and you had the feeling that as soon as the curtain came down, she would wrap herself in her elegant manteau, get in a carriage, and go have dinner with her admirers.[15]

Through Litvinne, Yavorskaya and Shchepkina-Kupernik were invited to an intimate dinner at the home of Edmond Rostand, the young playwright whose first significant work *The Romantics* premiered during their stay in Paris. Rostand came from a wealthy and cultured family, and Shchepkina-Kupernik felt out of place arriving in her simple, black dress. The other ladies, she recalled, "looked more like some work of art than ordinary women. They were made up and coiffed so that not one hair was out of place."[16] They dressed, as was the custom, with a very low décolletage. The men wore frock coats with flowers in their boutonnieres. Melon was served as an appetizer, followed by fatted fowl, puff pastries, and an iced punch served in the middle of the meal. After dinner, the small gathering moved to a spacious hall to have coffee. The conversation turned to theater gossip, particularly about Bernhardt. Litvinne went up on a small stage to sing while the guests sat on couches strewn with many-colored pillows. Rostand was asked to recite some of his own verse. He nervously passed his hand over his dark, smoothly combed hair. Shchepkina-Kupernik found his voice to be surprisingly pleasant.

Although Shchepkina-Kupernik was to gain fame for herself and for Yavorskaya over the next several years as a translator of Rostand's plays, she came to have mixed feelings about his talents. His versification was elegant and masterful, but given her more egalitarian sympathies, she felt his plays lacked depth and pandered to the audience's desire to be comforted rather than challenged. She wrote: "Everything was so clear, so noble, so accessible to everyone that an audience member in the theater felt himself to be in a fragrant winter garden far from the storms and severe frost of real life. The *beautiful* was largely beyond him; it was replaced by the *pretty*."[17] Yavorskaya, by contrast, was much more receptive to the romantic excesses in his work and perhaps also to his sexual advances. Shchepkina-Kupernik disparaged Rostand's propensity to "change women like handkerchiefs."[18]

At another gathering at Rostand's, Shchepkina-Kupernik met Bernhardt in passing as the diva sat warming herself by a fireplace on a rainy, cold day. She was strikingly dressed in an outfit of muslin, embroidery, lace, and fur. Shchepkina-Kupernik found her face terrifying, not because it lacked beauty ("there wasn't an inch of her skin that was without any cosmetics"), but because she read into it "a desperate vanity, a thirst for power and success . . . It seemed to me that for her own glory, she was capable of trampling on the corpse of her competitor."[19]

In late spring, Shchepkina-Kupernik went off on her own to the Isle of Jersey, to finish working on her first novella, *Happiness*, based on an idea Yavorskaya gave her. While she was gone, Korsh conspired with Yavorskaya to secretly copy a production of Victorien Sardou's wildly popular play, *Madame Sans-Gêne*, being performed by Réjane at the Théâtre du Vaudeville. Sardou fiercely protected the text of his play, keeping the only complete manuscript to himself. Actors were given only their own parts and cues; the play was performed without the presence of a prompter. Without Sardou's knowledge, Korsh hired several stenographers to attend performances and jot down the actors' words. He asked Yavorskaya to memorize every gesture and the phrasing used by Réjane. Korsh took notes on the mise-en-scène, itemizing the props used.

When Shchepkina-Kupernik returned to Paris, Yavorskaya organized a lavish celebratory evening. Potapenko reported to Maria Chekhova that "Louvre-skaya is enraptured by the arrival of her girlfriend."[20] Mizinova too commented to Chekhova on Shchepkina-Kupernik's ongoing romance with Yavorskaya: "Recently Tania has been preaching *her own fin de siècle*. She was saying that there was nothing more vulgar than a man, and on the contrary—two women in beautiful underwear—this was simply poetry, etc." Mizinova also mentioned that Shchepkina-Kupernik hoped Chekhova would "fall in love, get married or, at least, lose your virginity, which according to Tania (and she's a smart woman) is worth having only until you're twenty years old."[21]

The two women returned to Italy, visiting Florence, Venice, and the mountain resort of San Martino di Castrozza, where Shchepkina-Kupernik sent off a poem to Chekhov, hoping he could get it published in *New Times*: "If not, keep it for yourself as a teaching and in memory of the Woman in Violet [Shchepkina-Kupernik]. The Woman in Green [Yavorskaya] kisses you (as do I, God knows) and sends her ardent greetings." The poem is an exalted ode to the enchanted Italian landscape. It ends:

> I do not want to dream or suffer
> In this wonderful land of beauty:
> There are magical sounds in my heart
> Talking to me of happiness . . .
> My tender friend! In this period of separation,
> Remember this day, this moment![22]

Once back in Paris, Shchepkina-Kupernik and Yavorskaya began preparing for their return to Moscow prior to the opening of Korsh's fall season on August 15. Before leaving they made a pilgrimage to Montmartre cemetery to visit the grave of Alphonsine Duplessis, who had served as the prototype for Alexandre Dumas's *Lady of the Camellias*. During her stay Yavorskaya had visited the elderly Dumas at his home in the village of Marly-le-Roy on the outskirts of Paris. The two hours of conversation with him made an indelible impression. She thanked Dumas for giving her the most successful role of her career and was eager to impress on him that she fully understood the character of Marguerite Gautier as a woman of "patrician dignity," who by misfortune "fell into the filthy and vulgar milieu" of a courtesan. Dumas said he wanted to show Yavorskaya a portrait he had of Duplessis. "We went into a completely dark, unused room," she told Shchepkina-Kupernik. "He pulled aside a curtain, slightly raised the portier, turned on the light, and I saw a marvelous portrait of Marguerite Gautier just as I had imagined her. Elegant, standing gracefully in a black dress, wearing white gloves as was the style then, a headband covering her hair."[23] At Montmartre, the two women found Duplessis's grave among the dark cypresses of the cemetery. Yavorskaya placed a branch of live camellias on the grave beside a bouquet of artificial camellias that Dumas had been bringing for the past forty years. Shchepkina-Kupernik wrote in her memoirs that as they stood by the railing: "We both then thought about death. . . . We thought of it as the young do: with both dread and disbelief that it existed."[24]

CHAPTER 4

"Don't Forget the One Who Loves Only You"

Following his time spent with Yavorskaya in Italy and France, Korsh fully committed himself to featuring her as his leading actress in her second year with the company. They had not become lovers, which may have disappointed Korsh, since Chekhov noticed his jealousy toward the men (including himself) whom she did favor with her attentions.[1] Korsh's fall repertoire reflected a desire to put more emphasis on new comedies and dramas from Western Europe. If the intent was to peel audiences away from the Maly Theater, the decision made sense, since the Maly was continuing to focus on classical and some new Russian works. But as the season unfolded, critics pointed out that there were inherent flaws in Korsh's troupe and in his management that made it very difficult for the theater to present serious artistic work successfully. The acting company consisted of players who had spent countless nights performing in lightweight farces in which, as the *Artist* described, "there were no roles, in essence, only humorous words, witticisms, and amusing body gestures."[2] Many of the actors had lost the ability to develop a character and build a performance. The weekly turnover of productions, with a new play every Friday, only exacerbated the problem. Most plays had fewer than five days of rehearsal, not enough time to even memorize a role much less flesh out a fully formed character. The first few nights of performance, in effect, became a continuation of rehearsals, with actors dependent on the prompter. It was not unusual for critics to notice that actors only "found their roles" after the second or third performance.

The fall 1894 season opened with a proven crowd-pleaser, Ostrovsky and Solovyov's *The Marriage of Belugin*, with Yavorskaya in the role of the ingenue Elena. The next play, Tolstoy's *The Fruits of Enlightenment*, proved to be more of a challenge. The role of Betsy would appear to be a perfect fit for Yavorskaya. Tolstoy described her as "a society girl around twenty years old with a relaxed manner, affecting masculinity. She wears pince-nez, is coquettish, and is given to guffawing. She speaks quickly and very precisely, pressing her lips together like a foreigner."[3] The comedy satirizes the upper class's fascination with spiritualism and séances. Wary of Tolstoy's popularity and his criticism of the nobility, the censors initially permitted the play to be performed only in "amateur theaters." In February 1891 the Moscow Society of Art and Literature, started by Konstantin Stanislavsky and incorporating an acting company that stretched the definition of "amateur," organized a closed premiere performance of the play with Vera Komissarzhevskaya as Betsy. At the time she was still an acting student of Davydov's, who no more encouraged her professional career than he did Yavorskaya's. By fall the censors allowed *The Fruits of Enlightenment* to be performed in the imperial theaters, but it wasn't until the spring of 1894 that permission was granted for private theaters to put on the play. As usual, Korsh's sloppy preparation led to unfavorable comparisons of his production of *The Fruits of Enlightenment* with those by Stanislavsky and the imperial theaters.

Yavorskaya and Shchepkina-Kupernik had moved back into the Hotel Louvre, but Chekhov was spending very little time in Moscow. In early August he went off to the Volga with Potapenko, much to the distress of his sister, who could not forgive Potapenko for seducing Mizinova and abandoning her in Europe. Chekhov briefly returned to Melikhovo, then set off late in the month for the south, meeting up with Suvorin, with whom he set off for Europe without telling his family. From Vienna he wrote to Mizinova asking her "where exactly are you in Switzerland so I can look for you."[4] She was overjoyed, but warned him: "Don't be surprised by anything! Come if you're not afraid of becoming disenchanted with the former Lika! There's not a trace of her left."[5] She was afraid of his disapproval once he saw that she was pregnant: "It seems to me that you've always been indifferent to people and to their inadequacies and weaknesses!" While Potapenko may have said nothing to Chekhov about Mizinova's condition during their travels together, her letters to him now made it obvious. Chekhov wrote his sister that Potapenko was "a Yid and a swine." However sympathetic he was to her plight, Chekhov was reluctant to embroil himself in the tumult of Mizinova's life. He backed away from his promise to visit her, telling her it would be "awkward to drag Suvorin along." Feeling abandoned, Mizinova returned alone to Paris to have her baby. Potapenko was present in November when Mizinova gave birth to a daughter, Christina, but left soon afterward, never to see Mizinova again.

While he was in Europe, Chekhov missed the premiere of Yavorskaya's triumph of the season, *Madame Sans-Gêne*, which opened on September 16. The title role of Catherine Hubscher, the "madam without inhibitions," was loosely based on a historical figure, Marie-Thérèse Figueur, who served as a soldier in the French revolutionary wars, during which she first encountered Napoleon as a young officer and unceremoniously criticized his behavior and his looks. Figueur and Napoleon later crossed paths when he was emperor and she was a dragoon in Paris famed for her bravery in battle. Recalling their first meeting with gracious humor and impressed by her accomplishments, Napoleon welcomed her into high society and court life at Saint Cloud.

In the first act of Sardou's play, which takes place in revolutionary Paris in 1792, Catherine is a plain-speaking washerwoman who hides Count Neipperg, a wounded Austrian officer, in her bedroom during a skirmish with the French militia. She manages to convince her fiancé Lefebvre, who is a sergeant in the revolutionary army, not to betray the enemy officer to his comrades and help him escape. The remaining three acts of the play take place in Napoleon's court in 1811. Although her husband, Lefebvre, is now the Duke of Danzig, Catherine remains true to her nickname and continues to speak bluntly, scandalizing court society. Napoleon tells Lefebvre that he must divorce his wife, but after meeting with Catherine and learning of her military exploits, he is charmed by her. Meanwhile, Napoleon clashes with the Austrian consul, who is none other than Count Neipperg. He suspects Neipperg, who has become friends with Lefebvre, of having an affair with his wife and orders him to be shot, demanding that Lefebvre be the one to carry out the execution. At the last moment, Napoleon finds a letter from the empress that absolves Neipperg. The cloud is lifted from the Duke and Duchess of Danzig, and Napoleon drops the demand that they divorce.

Korsh's production featured lavish sets and costumes. Its "glitter and novelty" proved popular with audiences. But *Artist* continued to complain about the troupe's lack of range and Yavorskaya's overacting. Critics had no idea that Yavorskaya was basing her performance on how she had seen Réjane play the role in Paris. So successful was Yavorskaya's mimicry that Vladimir Nelidov, the manager of the Maly Theater, recalled that when Réjane later performed the role in Moscow, people commented to him: "She's copying Yavorskaya; they're doing everything like Korsh did."[6]

It was during preliminary discussions about bringing a French production of *Madame Sans-Gêne* to Russia that Sardou learned of Korsh's unauthorized Moscow premiere. Sardou had written to the director of the Mikhailovsky Theater about bringing Réjane on tour. The director informed him that Korsh was already preparing a translation of the play. Sardou, unaware of Korsh's clandestine copying of the original Paris production, assumed that Korsh was basing his production on a translation of a German text, having yielded production rights to the playwright and theater director Oscar Blumenthal. After hearing that Korsh and Blumenthal already had some sort of professional relationship, Sardou wrote Blumenthal a stern letter accusing him of giving the text to Korsh. Blumenthal protested that he was innocent and suggested that Korsh had obtained a printed copy of the play. Sardou knew this was impossible, since the play had not been printed anywhere. Sardou expressed his frustration to a Russian reporter: "What can I say? I've been robbed." There were no copyright agreements between France and Russia, so published plays could be developed for stage production without the author's permission or the payment of royalties. "*Madame Sans-Gêne* was not offered for sale anywhere," Sardou complained, "neither in French nor any other language. In order to obtain the text of the play, it was necessary to resort to actions that I have no doubt qualify as illegal: here there is either bribery, or deception, appropriation, misuse of trust, borrowing, or all of these together."[7] Korsh apparently had been telling people he had received permission from Sardou and had even paid him a royalty, but Sardou responded that this was a lie, that he had never been in contact with Korsh. "What can Mr. Korsh say in reply to this completely categorical declaration?"[8] asked the *Moscow Gazette*, hoping to provoke a response. Confident in his legal standing, Korsh chose silence. The play went on to have thirty-eight sold-out performances before the season ended. It was so popular that, as one theater historian noted, Yavorskaya's Catherine inspired an array of *Madame Sans-Gêne* products: bathroom soap, perfume, caramel candies, cigarettes, and two-colored women's blouses.⁹ Also contributing to the play's popularity was the fact that over half the scenes called for Yavorskaya to be either taking off her shoes or getting undressed.¹⁰

Munshtein, Shchepkina-Kupernik's former fiancé, jumped at the opportunity to satirize any scandal involving Yavorskaya. He recalled how Korsh had deflected reporters' questions about Sardou and royalties by gathering the press at intermission and going on about how he had spared no expense on this lavish production—fifteen thousand rubles paid to Fontainebleau for Bonaparte's snuff box, a hundred rubles for a single silver sconce. However, it was only after Munshtein overheard some departing theatergoers mentioning that they saw Shchepkina-Kupernik among the throng throwing flowers at Yavorskaya's feet, rekindling in him his feelings of betrayal, that he rushed home and decided to write "a 'pamphlet-parody' of the actors' milieu." In the parody, every time Korsh tries to say "Yavorskaya," he's only able to utter a "Yavor . . ." when suddenly the shadow of Sardou appears, "snarls, laughs, and cuts off the conversation." Although the piece in no way affected the popularity of the production, Korsh told Munshtein that he was offended he had been called a thief: "I love parodies and puns, but this is beyond the pale."

One evening, a short while later, Munshtein was shown to a table at the Hermitage restaurant when he noticed Yavorskaya sitting at the next table with a group of her friends. He sensed that this was a deliberate setup by his journalist colleagues accompanying him. His impulse was to flee, but one of his friends dragged him over to Yavorskaya, whispering to her: "Don't hold back, give it to the impertinent poet!" She pressed his hand with a smile and said, "I'm not angry . . . Sit with us." Charmed by her attentions and coming to a realization of "how wrong everything is in the world," Munshtein ended the evening sitting in Yavorskaya's suite at the Louvre writing verse in her guest book.¹¹

Unlike *Madame Sans-Gêne*, Korsh's next production, *Vasantasena*, based on a German translation of an ancient Sanskrit play, proved to be a disaster. Once again, Yavorskaya was cast in the title role. Once again, she portrayed a heroic, independent woman, this time a wealthy courtesan who declares her love for a married, impoverished Brahmin because she is drawn to his ideals and nobility of soul. Once again, Korsh spent lavishly on exotic sets and dressed Yavorskaya in provocative costumes. But the opening-night audience quickly realized that there was something terribly wrongheaded about the production. Before the curtain lifted, they were told that Yavorskaya was feeling ill but would nevertheless perform. She was forced to use exaggerated gestures to compensate for her weak, hoarse voice. If the troupe had a hard time transporting audiences to Napoleon's Paris in *Madame Sans-Gêne*, they failed even more miserably to create the illusion of Indian court life. People started laughing during scenes that should have been emotionally charged. One member of the audience was heard to say afterward that the actors had "performed an Indian drama in Chinese."[12] A week later, Alexander III died suddenly, and all theaters were ordered to go dark for a month of mourning.

Chekhov arrived back in Moscow on October 14, the day of the disastrous premiere. Unable to go on to Melikhovo because of a snowstorm, he spent several days in the city reading proofs for his short-story collection *Motley Tales*. He sent a note to Shchepkina-Kupernik and Yavorskaya at the Louvre announcing with a poetic flourish that he was eager to see them: "At last the waves have tossed the madman on the shore / And he has raised his arms to two white seagulls."[13] Yavorskaya responded that "a hot samovar, a shot of vodka, mushrooms, everything you want . . . . and, most of all, I will be awaiting you." She reminded him he held a special place in her heart: "When I am with you, I can relax from everything and everyone. . . . When I am with you, the sun peeks into my soul."[14] Shchepkina-Kupernik recalled that when Chekhov walked into the suite, Yavorskaya vampishly threw herself in front of him in the guise of Vasantasena: "She struck the pose of the Hindu heroine, dropped to her knees on the rug, stretching her thin arm out to Chekhov, exclaiming: 'The unique . . . the inscrutable . . . the charming . . .'"[15]

Chekhov started to take a more serious interest in Shchepkina-Kupernik's literary undertakings. She was busy putting the finishing touches on her translation of Rostand's play *The Romantics*, which Korsh had committed to producing in December. Chekhov invited her to come visit him in Melikhovo, where he would spend most of the next two months. In late November she wrote him she was finally ready to take him up on his offer. He was delighted but warned her that the road was still in horrible shape: "I fear that your tasty cartilage and bones may get crunched. . . . The last time I came from the station, my heart was jolted loose by the trip, so that I'm now incapable of falling in love." He also congratulated her on hearing that *Happiness* had been accepted for publication in *Books of the Week*, which he considered to be a "solid, attractive journal."[16]

Happiness is a feminist bildungsroman inspired by Yavorskaya's disastrous first marriage. Shchepkina-Kupernik sent an early draft to Yavorskaya around the time of the scandal resulting from Alexeev's letter to her father. The work deeply affected Yavorskaya, reminding her of how much suffering her husband had caused her. In a letter to Shchepkina-Kupernik, she wrote: "You have surrounded me with such tenderness, such solicitousness, which has helped me endure a most difficult time of shame and insult at every step."[17]

In *Happiness* Maria (Marusya) Nezvantseva, like Yavorskaya, falls in love with her gymnasium teacher and at age seventeen marries him. But she soon discovers that as a married woman, she has no meaningful role in life. Her husband, Alexander Torsky, prefers to spend his evenings at his club, drinking with his friends and gambling, eventually falling deeply into debt. Maria shares her feelings of disappointment in marriage with a new friend, Lyudmilla Pavlovna, an independent young widow, highly educated and widely traveled, who tells Maria that life is too full of possibilities to give up on her happiness at such a young age: "You don't need to be loved, you need *to be able to love*, dear girl, to be happy."[18]

Maria decides to leave her husband, and go with Lyudmilla to Italy and then on to St. Petersburg, where Maria studies music and becomes an accomplished pianist. However, she soon falls under the influence of a Petersburg high-society couple that introduces her to the world of modernist pessimism. In the midst of this descent into decadence, Torsky reappears, declaring that he has come to reclaim her as his wife, much as Yavorskaya's husband had done. One evening, after visibly flirting with his wife in front of others, he takes her home and forces himself on her: "She gave herself to her husband like a toy, a lifeless doll."

Maria visits Lyudmilla at her estate, telling her of the sordid life she has lived: "It's as if I have been swimming in mud, and have gotten used to this attractive mud." Lyudmilla tells her to forget her past. They return to Petersburg. Maria begins studying music again; she writes to Torsky telling him that she's moving ahead with the divorce. One day Lyudmilla visits Maria, who is now radiating happiness. She tells Lyudumilla the reason—she is pregnant.

Not surprisingly, some reviewers criticized *Happiness* for being a feminist attack on men and marriage. The story reflected not only the marital conflicts that Yavorskaya and Shchepkina-Kuperni had experienced in their young lives, but also their conviction that devotion to art allowed women to free themselves from stultifying subservience to men, that a woman even had the right to raise a child on her own outside of marriage, without shame. When Yavorskaya read the draft of the novel, she told Shchepkina-Kupernik with characteristic effusiveness that her life as an actor was "just as stormy, just as passionate as first love is for the soul of a 17-year-old girl." But now she felt that she had redirected that passion toward "a deep belief in our work—our *art*, as if it were a religion. Our life is a battle, a difficult battle to raise high its banner, our happiness is to be intoxicated with its glory—yes, these moments are our happiness."[19]

On December 3 Shchepkina-Kupernik, accompanied by Maria Chekhova, once again visited Melikhovo. As she stepped out from the stifling train carriage at Lopasnya, she was struck by the "blessed silence" of the countryside now before her. The winter air smelled of pine trees that lined the rough road to Melikhovo, "as if something fragrant was hiding beneath the snow."[20] Chekhov invited her to accompany him to Vaskino, the neighboring estate, to serve as godparents at the christening of Prince Shakhovskoy's daughter. Chekhov insisted that he had arranged this on purpose to prevent Shchepkina-Kupernik from forcing him to marry her (marriages between godparents were illegal): "Under no circumstances should we get married. You're a writer and I'm a writer, and we undoubtedly would get on each other's nerves."[21]

The friends returned to Moscow to attend the premiere of *The Romantics* on December 20. Chekhov told his sister that the play, Rostand's comic retelling of *Romeo and Juliet*, was very good and that Shchepkina-Kupernik's verse translation was "elegant."[22] Yavorskaya was well suited for the role of the ingenue Sylvette. *Artist* damned her with faint praise: "The external attributes of the artist and the character of her gifts are more appropriate for a refined, but not especially deep French comedy, not demanding much temperament and power from the artist."[23] Over the course of several nights her bombast softened; she gave smoother, more restrained performances where her sweetness better captured the light tone of Shchepkina-Kupernik's verse translation.

A few days later Chekhov spent the morning reading Shchepkina-Kupernik's story "Loneliness" in a cold classroom at the school where his brother Ivan taught. He wrote her a note praising the story in his typically backhanded fashion: "I forgave you for all your crimes. The story is quite good and without a doubt you are intelligent and thoroughly sly. I was especially struck by the artistry of the story. By the way, you don't understand anything."[24]

"Loneliness," like *Happiness*, reflects elements found in Yavorskaya's and Shchepkina-Kupernik's young adult lives. In the story, Zoya becomes engaged at seventeen hoping that she has found a soul mate. Instead she finds herself unable to understand the passion she has aroused in her fiancé, since she herself feels none. She discovers he is jealous not only of other men but also of her women friends. He is likewise jealous of her success as a painter, which is beginning to make her financially independent. When she tells him that she wants to break off the engagement, he brandishes a revolver vaguely threatening to shoot either her or himself, a scene reminiscent of the incident that ended Shchepkina-Kupernik's own engagement.

Zoya is drawn into the circle of Inna Pavlovna, "a young lady with a convenient husband, an independent character and a wonderful apartment, where on Thursdays the finest society gathered."[25] It is at one of Inna's soirees that Zoya—already beginning to suspect that her still life paintings, while selling well, were ultimately trivial—begins to feel a deep sense of loneliness and depression. Her doctor recommends that she admit herself to a hospital. Upon doing so, she is struck by the basic decency of her fellow patients, all from the lower classes, and their instinctive sense of compassion for each other. Zoya begins to realize the falsity of the high society she lived in and of her own selfishness. Returning to her studio, she decides that now, rather than painting flowers, she will paint subjects from schools, factories, and the small houses on the outskirts of the city. Zoya has learned from the hospital patients that in order to be happy, one mustn't demand happiness but give happiness to others. This Dickensian sentimentality toward her heroine, a hallmark of many of Shchepkina-Kupernik's stories, is what Chekhov found off-putting. He repeatedly advised her in her writing to refrain from telling the reader what to think. "In general," he said to her, "love your heroes but never say this out loud."[26]

For the next month, most of which he spent in Moscow, Chekhov allowed himself to once again be lured onto the rocks by the sirens of the Louvre. But this time, rather than just being enticed by their flattery and flirtations, he was drawn into an uncomfortable ménage à trois charged with an undercurrent of sexual jealousy. When he broke away briefly from them to go to Melikhovo to celebrate the New Year with his family, he received a mock official document from Yavorskaya imploring him to not stay away for long:

Official Document

By imperial command, issued in the city of Moscow on the first of January 1895, Anton Pavlovich, the son of Chekhov, the literary general and knight of the orders of the Great and Holy Martyrs Tatiana and Lidia the First, and private of our personal convoy, is free to go on leave until the third of February of this year to all cities of the Empire and abroad with the condition that he provide two replacements and appears at the designated time to carry out double his responsibilities of service.

Inscribed in her very own hand by Her Majesty, Lidia the First
Place inscribed
1 January 1895
In Moscow
Room 16—the private office of Her Majesty[27]

Chekhov responded to the summons by returning to Moscow on January 4, staying in room 5 of the Great Moscow Hotel for seventeen days. Two days before his arrival, Shchepkina-Kupernik visited Melikhovo, impulsively inviting the painter Levitan to accompany her. Having played a big part in stirring up the animosity between the two men, she now brought them together for the first time in almost three years. Chekhov and Levitan were reconciled, although their friendship would never be as close as it had been before the publication of "The Grasshopper." In Paris, Mizinova had gotten wind of Chekhov's renewed entanglement with her sister sirens. She wrote to him: "Well, has Tania settled in Melikhovo and taken my place on the sofa? Is your wedding to Yavorskaya soon? Invite me so that I can stop by and create a scene in the church."[28]

Judging from the flurry of notes Yavorskaya sent to Chekhov's room, their flirtation turned into a love affair within several days of his arrival. Her tone is no longer playful. It is heartfelt and amorous; she switches to the intimate form of "you." She tells him that even when her suite is filled with guests and admirers, she is bored without him. She misses him terribly and sends over a gift: "My darling, it's terribly difficult to part from you, as if the best part of my heart is being torn off. It's terribly cold today, allow me to take care of you: wrap yourself in this plaid cover, it will warm you like my hot kisses do. . . . Don't forget the one who loves only you, Your Vasantasena."[29] On January 8, addressing Chekhov as "Karudatta, worthy of envy! Darling, heavenly bliss on earth," she implores him to come to Korsh's theater to see her perform in *Madame Sans-Gêne*. He attends, writing to Suvorin the next day that "the play was lavishly produced and not badly performed. Yavorskaya plays the main role—she is a very sweet woman."[30]

For her benefit performance in early February, Yavorskaya decided to do Giuseppe Giacosa's *The Lady of Challand*, which he had written specifically for Sarah Bernhardt. Despite a full house and the usual accompaniment of valuable gifts, flowers, and laurel crowns bestowed on the evening's beneficiary, critics savaged the performance. The monarchist *Moscow Gazette*, consistently unsympathetic to Yavorskaya's "foreign" style of acting, wrote: "She wailed and rushed about, her voice was hoarse, and she made the most despairing gestures, but the efforts remained fruitless, and Miss Yavorskaya remained as before, a mediocre Russian amateur of the dramatic arts who for some reason imagines herself to be an artist."[31]

Chekhov, while availing himself of Yavorskaya's ardor, was not spellbound. She was "sweet," something he often called Mizinova, even as he held her at arm's length. In the midst of his affair with Yavorskaya, he described her to Suvorin: "This is a very good woman and actress, who could possibly make something of herself if she hadn't been spoiled by her training. There's something vulgar about her, but that doesn't matter."[32] Chekhov understood that Yavorskaya's acting career would have been better served had she not fallen under the baneful influence of her Parisian drama teacher and the extravagant example of Sarah Bernhardt.

The consummation of their affair upset Shchepkina-Kupernik. She felt possessive both of Yavorskaya's affections and of the role she was playing in advancing her professional career. At the same time, Shchepkina-Kupernik was buoyed by the interest Chekhov showed in her writing, and hoped it would bring them closer together. But now as a result of the affair, Chekhov was interfering with her relationship with Yavorskaya. For more than a year, the two women had acted as a pair (offering themselves as "poetry and fantasy," "the tea rose and the camellia," "the woman in violet and the woman in green") playfully fawning at the feet of Chekhov. Yavorskaya, however, was the one to go beyond flirtation to actual seduction. During his Moscow stay, Chekhov and Shchepkina-Kupernik quarreled. Possibly she gossiped to others about the affair. In response, he scolded her for her lesbianism in a way that deeply offended her. As soon as he returned to Melikhovo, Chekhov sent a note to Shchepkina-Kupernik asking her not to remain angry at him. He invited her to come visit him: "We'll make a toast to peace—and *basta*. Be a good girl." He signed the note: "Resident of the Louvre (Room 54)."[33]

Wary of what Chekhov honestly thought of her, Shchepkina-Kupernik responded to Chekhov's invitation cautiously: "I'm very glad, Anton Pavlovich, that your unusually strange mood has left you." She was, however, still stunned that he had judged her so priggishly. She refused to believe that he could act like other "dimwitted people." It had caused "a minor revolution in my entire view of things."[34] She immediately regretted sending him the letter. She wrote to him again to "apologize for the stupid, childish feeling that compelled me to write you such an answer in my last note." Since their relationship had shifted so rapidly from his encouragement of her to his disapproval, she agonized over how this had happened:

> Tell me directly, simply. What alienated you from me? What were you dissatisfied about? What? Do you really think that just *words* alone were all that I said to you, in sweet, dear Melikhovo . . . I will always, always do everything to make amends for my poor manners, if that's what they are, and again be in your good graces. Allow me to look right into your good, honest eyes: they cannot be mistaken—they will see that I was never against you either in word or thought, and I never will be, that I love you, and if I see in you a coldness or enmity—that will be very, very hard on me.[35]

But Chekhov did remain cool toward her. When Suvorin expressed an interest in meeting Shchepkina-Kupernik, Chekhov encouraged him to visit, but "don't come to kiss Kupernik's feet. She is a talented little girl, but I doubt that you will find her likable. I feel sorry for and annoyed at myself: three days a week I find her loathsome. She's a sly devil, but her motives are so petty that it turns out she's not a devil, but a rat."[36] Shchepkina-Kupernik's frequent visits to Melikhovo abruptly stopped. She was right to be wary of his distaste for her sexuality. Later in the year, awaiting a visit from Suvorin at a time when Yavorskaya and Shchepkina-Kupernik were both in St. Petersburg preparing for a stage production, Chekhov wrote him: "The weather in Moscow is good, there's no cholera, there's also no lesbian love . . . Brrr!! The recollection of those individuals about whom you write makes me nauseous, as if I'd eaten a rotten sardine. They're not in Moscow—and that's wonderful."³⁷

The winter theatrical season had come to an end. For the Lenten break, Korsh decided to import a series of French opera productions (including sets and costumes) that had originated in Paris. The endeavor turned out to be a fiasco. The Kapellmeister he hired knew nothing about French opera and, without the full scores at his disposal, he tried to lead the rehearsals using only a piano transcription. The French opera managers panicked and pulled out. The performances were canceled and subscribers got their money back. The *Moscow Gazette* crowed: "Woe to the shoemaker who starts to bake pirogi.... Woe it is if a person takes up something not knowing or understanding how it's done."³⁸

Yavorskaya went on tour with Korsh's troupe, performing for several weeks in Nizhni Novgorod. She stayed in the Great Nizhigorod Hotel, "Room 9, alas not Room 5," she wrote to Chekhov, referring to his room in the Great Moscow Hotel where they enjoyed their brief affair. Her letter was mostly in verse, in which she again took on the persona of the Indian courtesan:

> You don't know how your Vasantasena
> Your southern flower, your "little sun,"
> Is suffering here in this lighted puppet theater,
> Which charges her four rubles a day
> For a hotel room, completely unlike,
> Alas, that room in the Moscow hotel,
> In which she and you
> tasted true bliss!

Seemingly delirious with the flu, lying in her hot bed, she begs Chekhov to send Shchepkina-Kupernik to visit her, but fears she has been distracted by his "seductive company, for which, I agree, I would forget everything, not only friends, but the whole world." She rambles on about Korsh's thirty-thousand-ruble loss from the French opera, about how "a conversation about Tania is an anachronism," about her "mad love" for Chekhov, "my holy, unattainable, extraordinary one!"³⁹

As had happened with Mizinova, Chekhov now felt the need to pull away from Yavorskaya and her cloying passion. He was attracted to lively and intelligent women, but remained wary of the power of these "sirens" to ensnare, distract, and confuse a man, a theme he explored in "Ariadne," a story he wrote that spring. When he visited Levitan in his studio, he was struck by how much his old friend had aged, convinced that his numerous love affairs had worn him out as a person and as an artist. "Pfew! Pfew!" he wrote to Suvorin. "Women take away your youth, but not for me. In my life I've been just a sales clerk, not the boss, and fate has rarely toyed with me. I've only had a few romances, and I'm no more like Catherine the Great than a walnut shell is like a battleship."[40] He refused to be further seduced by the sirens calling to him. Instead, he withdrew into his writing, devoting himself in his fiction to reshaping the women around him and giving them new lives.

Chapter 5

The Dream Princess

Korsh's troupe returned briefly to Moscow from Nizhni Novgorod before traveling on to St. Petersburg for a month of performances at the Maly Theater starting in early April 1895. From room 6 of the Great Moscow Hotel (next door to the site of their January tryst), Yavorskaya wrote to Chekhov, reminding him "that I sincerely love you and miss you very much." She considered visiting him in Melikhovo but had been told the road from the train station was impassable. The main reason for her letter, however, was to ask Chekhov to put in a word for her to Suvorin, whose newspaper, *Novoe vremia* (*New Times*), was sure to review Korsh's performances at the Maly. "Since St. Petersburg is not Nizhni," she wrote, "and I positively cannot expect from it the same kind of ovations and tributes I had there, I hope you will carry out your sweet promise to help me a little regarding St. Petersburg." She also encouraged Chekhov to come to St. Petersburg to provide her with "moral support."[1]

Yavorskaya's return to St. Petersburg was extraordinarily significant for her and the source of considerable anxiety. It was obvious to Shchepkina-Kupernik, who spent time with Yavorskaya during her stay in the capital, that "she wanted to show those who had turned her down at the Alexandrinsky Theater that she was worth something, that she, a rejected student, after a little over two years was returning to

St. Petersburg as the leading lady in one of Moscow's major theaters."[2] Her popularity with audiences as an ingenue, who, as the preeminent theater critic Alexander Kugel put it, had an unmistakably erotic *"odor di femina,"*[3] was widely recognized. But she also craved an approval of her acting abilities that was largely being denied her in Moscow.

On March 30, Chekhov wrote to Suvorin, encouraging him to see Yavorskaya perform at the Maly. The letter, with its quasi-clinical description of her attributes, reflects both fascination and condescension:

> Go attend *Madame Sans-Gêne* and watch Yavorskaya. If you want to, introduce yourself to her. She's intelligent and dresses well, and is occasionally witty. She's the daughter of Hubbenet, the Kiev police chief, so that her arteries flow with an actor's blood, while her veins with police blood. I've already had the pleasure of expressing to you my psychiatric opinion about the continuity of these two bloods. All winter the Moscow papers have been hunting her down like a rabbit, but she hasn't deserved this. If not for her shrieking and a certain mannerism (also an affectation), she would be a genuine actress. In any case, she's a curious type. Pay attention to her. If you're interested in the plays, take a look at the first act of Korsh's *The Romantics*.[4]

As soon as she arrived in St. Petersburg, Yavorskaya wrote to Chekhov again, unaware that he had already contacted Suvorin and even more deeply fearful of what the critics would say about her. As before, she took on the persona of the Indian courtesan writing in verse to her lover:

> Oh tender, beloved Karudatta,
> Condescend to a poor, forgotten one,
> Put in a word in defense of your unfortunate
> Beautiful Vasantesena,
> Otherwise Suvorin and the critics
> Will destroy your Lotus with a savage fury,
> Will tear Vasantesena into pieces
> And calmly toss her wondrous body
> To be devoured by hungry Moscow critics . . .
> Oh, save me, Karudatta!!

As part of her effort to generate positive press coverage, Yavorskaya twice met with Viktor Burenin, the *New Times* lead writer, before opening night. He was kind to her and urged her to invite Suvorin to come to the theater, but she sensed that Burenin was "a venomous man beneath a mask of amiability," an opinion that Chekhov agreed with. The two men shared a long-standing enmity. Burenin teased Yavorskaya about Chekhov, asking her whether she was in love with him. "You see, darling," she wrote Chekhov, "it's clear to everyone, yes, yes, yes!" Still, she was afraid of approaching Suvorin without Chekhov's intercession. "I'm terribly nervous about the upcoming performances," she confessed.[5]

Korsh's stay at the Maly began on April 5 with a production of *The Flirt*, a comedy in which Yavorskaya had one of her first roles soon after joining the troupe. Built in 1876–1878, the Maly Theater was an impressive structure facing the Fontanka Canal. It seated fourteen hundred people divided into stalls, three tiers of loges and an upper gallery. In its splendor, comfort, and acoustics, it was considered comparable to St. Petersburg's Mikhailovsky Theater.[6] Most recently, the theater had been primarily leased for French and Russian operettas as well as visiting companies like the Comédie-Française (Duse and Bernhardt had performed there).

On April 7 the *New Times* published an overview of the visit by Korsh's company written by "F" (most likely Mikhail Fyodorov, a writer who at times served as the paper's nominal publisher). Fyodorov noted the popularity of Korsh's light repertoire among St. Petersburg audiences, who appreciated the liveliness of the troupe's performances. He singled out Yavorskaya as a new actress in the company making her professional St. Petersburg debut. Mentioning that she had been a student in Vladimir Davydov's class at the St. Petersburg Theatrical School, Fyodorov recalled seeing her perform in scenes from Schiller's *Mary Stuart* as part of her final examinations: "Since then Miss Yavorskaya has apparently worked hard and significantly improved herself."[7] He noted that opinions about her acting in Moscow fell into two extreme categories—exaggerated praise or excessive criticism—both of which, he felt, were wrong. He was unable to make any firm judgments by watching her perform in *The Flirt*, a clichéd comedy in which she had an "accessory role," playing a coquette "who slips but does not fall." Her performance as Catherine Hubscher in *Madame Sans-Gêne*, a major role in a serious play, would more properly display her talents.

Suvorin attended the second performance of *Madame Sans-Gêne*. On April 8 he wrote a signed review in the *New Times*, perhaps as a favor to Chekhov. With his tendency to focus on the trivial, Suvorin left much to be desired as a theater critic. He told his readers he had been in

Paris to see Réjane perform at the play's premiere. Korsh's production struck him as very similar, even down to the insufferable length of the intermissions, which resulted in the play ending at one in the morning. One major difference, however, was that the Russian actors, reflecting Russian customs and manners, interacted with each other on stage in ways that were completely foreign to French social norms. It bothered Suvorin that in the salon of the Duchess of Danzig, a man sits down while the woman with whom he's speaking stands or walks around, or that a count would walk into a living room and sit down without waiting for the hostess to invite him to be seated: "I never saw this in Paris."

More to the point, in comparing Yavorskaya with Réjane, Suvorin found her to be less gifted and less experienced. It was obvious to him that Yavorskaya was mostly imitating Réjane, except for a "deliberate vulgarity and shouting in the third act that was totally unnecessary" and unlike anything Réjane would do. In contrast to Réjane's "wonderful voice," Yavorskaya's was dry and "incapable of modulation, intonation, and expressiveness." While Fyodorov hoped this play would reveal Yavorskaya's abilities, Suvorin came to the conclusion that in this role he was only able to judge "her ability to imitate, not to create."[8] The *St. Petersburg Gazette*, the city's oldest newspaper, expressed similar reservations, finding that Yavorskaya's interpretation of the role had a naiveté that might have been avoided under the guidance of a better director.[9] As was often the case with Yavorskaya's plays, in spite of the lukewarm reviews, the production was a popular success, enjoying six sold-out performances.

When Suvorin asked Chekhov whether he had treated Yavorskaya too harshly, Chekhov reassured him that the article did not strike him that way.[10] In any event, both men were more interested in another play that competed with Yavorskaya's performances for the attention of theatergoers, a production that resulted in a series of decisions that would shape her future career. On April 11, Gerhart Hauptmann's symbolist "dream poem in two acts" *Hannele* opened at the Panaev Theater, which had been leased by Suvorin's newly formed Literary-Artistic Circle. As first conceived, the Circle was an unusual organization—part entrepreneurial undertaking, part exclusive club for writers, actors, and capitalists whose members included Chekhov. Now over sixty years old and the owner of a vast publishing empire, Suvorin had never given up his dream of running a private theater company, one that would attract not only the city's intelligentsia but also high-society audiences that primarily attended the imperial Alexandrinsky Theater.

Now, under the auspices of the Circle, Suvorin decided to organize an "amateur" production of *Hannele* using well-known actors and setting high ticket prices intended to attract wealthy patrons. He had already championed Hauptmann as an innovative playwright whose work deserved to be read and seen in Russia. He mass-published *Hannele* as part of his Inexpensive Library series the year before, an example of how he could use his publishing arm to generate interest in a theatrical production. At the end of the same *New Times* article in which he had reviewed Yavorskaya's performance, Suvorin promoted his own upcoming production of *Hannele*, noting that the play had enjoyed wide success in Germany and France, and that it was part of the Literary-Artistic Circle's goal "of gradually producing all the leading works of foreign literature that are new in content and concept."

On the day of the premiere, the *New Times* pointedly compared *Hannele* to *Madame Sans-Gêne*, writing that while Sardou's play was pleasingly superficial, Hauptmann's was original "in plot and environment" and "leaves in the soul of the audience an impression that you rarely take away from the theater." Further building up self-serving anticipation, the newspaper reported that a large number of people from the literary and artistic world had attended the final dress rehearsal, which "made an affecting and sublime impression on everyone."[11]

Over the course of a dozen performances, Hauptmann's drama similarly excited general audiences. The critic for *The Week* noted that viewers felt they were seeing something similar to a medieval mystery play rather than a conventional drama. They experienced the deathbed delirium of a fourteen-year-old waif as if engaged in a religious ritual. In act 1, Hannele Mattern is pulled from a pond where she has tried to kill herself. She is brought to a poorhouse where residents attempt to revive her. Hannele's mother has died recently and she lives in fear of her abusive, alcoholic stepfather. In act 2, as Hannele lies dying in the poorhouse, she awakens filled with rapture. Her family, townspeople, and the beggars around her are transformed into apparitions. Her stepfather becomes the black angel of death; her mother is dressed as a deaconess. The local teacher appears as a Jesus-like stranger who speaks in verse of a heavenly kingdom, while the townspeople dress Hannele in the finery of a princess bride. An angelic choir of boys carries her off in a crystal coffin. In the last scene, Hannele lies again unadorned in her poorhouse bed, her heavenly death only a final dream.

The play's musical score, consisting of a backstage chorus with instrumental accompaniment by a double quartet, piano, harmonium, and harp, lent a serene majesty to the production. But what impressed critics the most was the naturalistic acting of Lyudmilla Ozerova, who was making her stage debut in the play. Just out of drama school, Ozerova, according to Shchepkina-Kupernik, was "a not especially attractive girl, very scrawny, inclined to hysteria, with a sickly face, large dreamy eyes and a weak, strained voice."[12] But it turned out that her attributes were perfect for playing the role of a dying, starving half-child. The Italian tragedian Ernesto Rossi, on tour in St. Petersburg, visited her backstage, praised her performance, and encouraged her to take on the role of Ophelia. The *New Times* shamelessly continued to proclaim the brilliance of Suvorin's new star. It gloated over a published report of the dashed hopes of the administration of the imperial theaters that Ozerova would make her debut at the Alexandrinsky Theater. She had told them that for now she belonged to the Literary-Artistic Circle.

Shchepkina-Kupernik dismissed the fuss over Ozerova and the play as nothing more than a jaded amusement for the "over-stuffed, happy-go-lucky audiences of Suvorin's theater. All these upper-crust old men, ladies dripping with diamonds, and golden youths from the guards regiments seemingly gushed over this depiction of poverty, sickness, and the touching death of the beaten-down Hannele."[13] Suvorin wrote to Chekhov about Ozerova's quick rise to fame, and apparently her neurotic temperament as well. Chekhov was intrigued: "Where is Ozerova going to spend the summer? I'd like to take a look at her and get to know her. You could invite me to treat her."[14]

Yavorskaya's St. Petersburg engagement included two additional signature roles: Alisa in *The Struggle for Happiness* and Marguerite Gautier in *The Lady of the Camellias*. Suvorin's newspaper favorably reviewed both performances. Its critic (possibly Burenin) thought Alisa was played "with an animation and agitation characteristic of this talented artist," although he found the play itself to be "clumsy, naïve, and very long-winded."[15] In a similar vein, the *St. Petersburg Gazette* concluded that Korsh's troupe performed "all this Swedish nonsense not too badly," with Yavorskaya's role a notable success. Shchepkina-Kupernik too was singled out for praise by the press during Korsh's St. Petersburg tour. Her translation of Rostand's *The Romantics* was performed in the capital for the first time, and the *St. Petersburg Gazette* noted its "sparkling language" and her ability to convey the humor found in Rostand's verse.

Korsh's St. Petersburg tour marked the end of the winter season. Yavorskaya now faced a decision whether to renew her contract for the next season, which would begin in the fall, or to seek other opportunities.

The runaway success of *Hannele* had convinced Suvorin to finally establish a permanent theater under the banner of the Literary-Artistic Circle. Even Chekhov was now supportive, sarcastically pointing out that well-attended plays and concerts would bring in more money for the Circle than relying on earnings from the card games it hosted for its members. Burenin, with Suvorin's approval, invited Yavorskaya to join the Circle.[16] As part of Suvorin's company, she would no longer have to play roles in the low-brow comedies and vaudevilles that were the staples of Korsh's repertoire. As the success of *Hannele* confirmed, Suvorin preferred importing serious European dramas. Yavorskaya had also grown tired of the negative press in Moscow. The St. Petersburg critics seemed less harsh, and, as Shchepkina-Kupernik discovered, were more easily corruptible, something Yavorskaya would use to her advantage. She could rely on Suvorin's newspaper, oblivious to any conflict of interest, to promote his own productions and his company of actors. Additionally, Ozerova proved to have a very narrow dramatic range, and Suvorin needed another ingenue to take her place.

Around this time, Chekhov began writing "Ariadne," a story in which the heroine's personality was similar to Yavorskaya's, but with a plot that echoed the circumstances of Mizinova's affair with Potapenko. Chekhov had joked to the writer Elena Shavrova that he had the urge to break away from the "genteel" stories demanded by his publishers and write "about terrifying, volcanic women."[17] "Ariadne" was based on his observation of the effect that both Yavorskaya and Mizinova had on him and other men against the background of the ongoing public debate on the "women's question," particularly the controversy prompted by the "Kreutzer Sonata," in which Tolstoy argued that the seductive powers of women were an impediment to human progress.

In Chekhov's story, Ivan Shamokhin falls in love with Ariadne, the "shapely, extraordinarily graceful" twenty-two-year-old sister of his neighbor. However, he quickly senses that for her, passion is only a performance: "Unlike me, she was unable to genuinely fall in love, because she was cold and already rather corrupted."[18] Ariadne's coldness is reminiscent of one of Shchepkina-Kupernik's less flattering descriptions of Yavorskaya, in which she notes that others compared her to the water sprite of Slavic mythology who, much like the Greek sirens, enjoyed enticing men to their doom: "She [Yavorskaya] had very strange eyes: in them you felt a kind of emptiness, as if they neither reflected nor absorbed the external world. Sometimes wandering off, sometimes looking without blinking, wide open—not for nothing did her admirers call them 'Rusalka' eyes. These were eyes that had no bottom, didn't transmit any feeling, not living the life of her face with its very agitated and mobile features."[19]

Shamokhin delays asking Ariadne to marry him when "fate saw fit to add a twist to our romance"—Mikhail Lubkov, a married friend of Ariadne's brother, comes to stay with them, seduces Ariadne, and takes her off to Italy. Blaming his bitter feelings of jealousy on Ariadne's sensuality, Shamokhin, like Pozdnyshev in the "Kreutzer Sonata," unleashes a misogynistic diatribe: "Must I, a cultured person, gifted with a complex spiritual organism, really ascribe my strong attraction to a woman only to the fact that the form of her body is different from mine?"[20] A month later, Ariadne writes to him from Italy, saying she misses him and accusing him of having deserted her. Her accusations are like those that Mizinova made to Chekhov from France and Switzerland. Mizinova herself recognized the similarities. A year after the story came out, she ended a letter to Chekhov with "Goodbye. Twice spurned by you Ar, i.e. L. Mizinova."[21]

Eventually, Ariadne spurns Lubkov and agrees to marry Shamokhin. He is ecstatic about finally being able to physically possess her, but understands that their love was not genuine. What he notices most is her slyness: "She used her cunning constantly, every minute, apparently without any motive, seemingly instinctively, the same way that a sparrow chirps or a cockroach twitches its feelers. . . . And all this just in order to be attractive, to be successful, to be adored! She got up every morning with only one thought: 'To be attractive.'"[22]

The dual narrative of "Ariadne," a highly unusual structure for a Chekhov story, distances the author from his character's anti-feminist screed. Shamokhin tells his story in the first person to a narrator who identifies himself as a well-known writer inseparable from Chekhov himself. The two men strike up a conversation on the deck of a steamer going from Odessa to Sevastopol. After Shamokhin finishes his story, the narrator asks him: "Why generalize and judge all women based just on Ariadne? The very striving for women's education and equality of the sexes, which I understand as a striving for justice, in itself precludes any suggestion that we move backwards. But Shamokhin was hardly listening to me and smiled suspiciously. He already was a passionately convinced woman-hater, and it was impossible to change his mind."[23]

Just as he was able to rework aspects of the lives and personalities of Mizinova and Yavorskaya in "Ariadne," he also reworked attitudes and opinions he had previously expressed regarding women into

Shamokhin's rather more extreme misogyny. While Chekhov thought Tolstoy's ideas about chastity were peculiar, he did talk in several letters to Suvorin about women as distractions who used their sexual allure to wear men out. Chekhov castigated Mizinova for failing to follow through on her professional ambitions, whether as a writer, singer, actor, or millinery shop owner. These opinions are consistent with ideas he expressed as a young man just finishing medical school, when he wrote to his brother Alexander, admittedly while drunk, suggesting that they collaborate on a dissertation called a *History of Sexual Dominance*. His thesis was that as creatures evolved into mammals, the sexes became more equal, but among mammals, males still remained dominant. "Women," he wrote his brother, "are everywhere passive. They give birth to cannon fodder. Nowhere and never are they superior to men with respect to politics or sociology. . . . A superior organism creates, but a woman has never created anything. George Sand is neither a Newton nor a Shakespeare. She is not a thinker."[24] These may be the rash thoughts of a tipsy twenty-three-year-old, but they reflect Chekhov's long-standing propensity to be individually supportive but generally dismissive of women as artistic equals of men.

In the summer of 1895 Chekhov arranged a meeting between Shchepkina-Kupernik and Suvorin, who had requested it back in January. She arrived at Melikhovo on July 21. The next day Chekhov went to Moscow to fetch Suvorin, who insisted that the only reason he was agreeing to come to Melikhovo was to talk to Shchepkina-Kupernik about the launch of his theater in the fall. On the evening of July 24, Shchepkina-Kupernik and Suvorin went for a long walk in the woods under a full moon. She found Suvorin to be "a tall, imposing old man with the piercing eyes and the gray beard of a patriarch . . . He combined in himself the features of a Russian petty tyrant and a European journalist."[25] As they walked, she presumably told him that she was planning to translate Edmond Rostand's *La Princesse Lointaine* (known as *The Far-Away Princess* in English), which Yavorskaya hoped to do for her first benefit performance at Suvorin's theater. In early May, Sarah Bernhardt had originated the role of the heroine Mélissinde at the Théâtre de la Renaissance in Paris. The next day Shchepkina-Kupernik and Suvorin went back to Moscow together.

As fall approached, Shchepkina-Kupernik found herself spending most of her time in St. Petersburg with Yavorskaya, who had already moved there and was preparing for the opening of Suvorin's new theater. The impresario had leased the Maly Theater for a year and completely refurbished it. He widened the spaces between the seats and installed new stage lighting and ventilation. Painted on the new stage curtain was a landscape depicting the ruins of an ancient temple and the scattered fragments of a statue. The rays of a rising sun lit up the scene and the figure "1895" shown through the morning mist, implying that the theater represented a new era in art.[26] The management promised more reasonably priced tickets than had been offered in the spring. The cost of a subscription to twelve performances ranged from 168 rubles for a loge to 12 rubles for back-row seats. In late August the *New Times* listed the members of the troupe, and in early September the newspaper announced the proposed repertoire for the first season, which consisted of Russian classics (beginning with Ostrovsky's *The Storm* on September 17), European dramas, and new works, including plays promised by Potapenko and Chekhov. In promoting the new theater, the newspaper sought to temper what it described as unrealistic expectations, stating that the modest goal of the administration was "to have a home for 'literary' plays and plays by young playwrights, and to set young actors and actresses in motion."[27]

The decision to begin the season with a play that was more than thirty years old and already well known to St. Petersburg audiences resulted in a disappointing opening night with many empty seats. The cast consisted almost entirely of actors who were performing in St. Petersburg for the first time. Their hesitancy dragged out the pace of the drama, leading the *St. Petersburg Gazette* to describe the evening as a "depressing, long drawn-out proceeding."[28] Zinaida Kholmskaya, a provincial actor (and future wife of the critic Kugel) making her Petersburg debut, was savaged for her poor performance in the lead role of Katherine. She was ridiculed for her habit of hovering at the front of the stage near the prompter's box: "It never enters her mind that there is a whole stage at her disposal.... and that it's not pretty to give a very long monologue standing up at the footlights right in front of the audience."[29]

The next night the other half of the troupe performed Ibsen's *A Doll's House* (known as *Nora* in Russia) with Yavorskaya in the title role. The *St. Petersburg Gazette* was again withering in its review, calling the production "worse than mediocre" and remarking again on the small size of the audience. The *New Times*, not surprisingly, came to Yavorskaya's defense, saying that the "talented Miss Yavorskaya played the role of Nora superbly." The critic admitted that the play itself felt more didactic than dramatic, that Ibsen was dressing up ideas in theatrical costumes. Nevertheless, Yavorskaya was able to overcome the inadequacies of the play by performing a difficult role "with great originality, deliberation, beauty, and nervous energy."[30]

In preparing for the upcoming production of *La Princesse Lointaine*, Shchepkina-Kupernik was spending a great deal of time at Suvorin's theater, getting a sense of the atmosphere of the place. Whereas Moscow's state-funded Maly Theater, which she considered her theatrical home, cultivated the impression of a group of artists working together as a unified family, she quickly saw that Suvorin's theater was a monarchy with an all-powerful manager surrounded by a "court clique" of shareholders with their own agendas, with their own favorites (including, for some, their actor-wives). It was a "theatrical swamp," swarming with intrigue. Whenever the irascible Suvorin attended rehearsals, they would take much longer. The playwright Sophia Sazonova described him pacing around the theater like Ivan the Terrible with his fur cap and walking stick, interrupting the actors by bringing up trivial details or seizing on a word that bothered him, prompting a lengthy, pointless discussion.[31] Glama-Meshcherskaya, who had been recruited to join the company after performing for two years in Kiev, was cast to play the role of the queen in Schiller's *The Maid of Orleans*. At the first rehearsal, she recalled "old man Suvorin, sitting in the first row, pounding his stick on the floor, openly expressing his opinion and loudly abusing the actors and actresses he didn't like. It was something out of an aristocrat's serf theater."[32] Her fragile health couldn't take it. After being replaced at the last minute in Turgenev's *A Month in the Country*, she left the company.

Shchepkina-Kupernik characterized Yavorskaya's relationship with Suvorin as "armed neutrality." By default, he related to actors with disdain. But recognizing her ability to attract audiences, Suvorin's newspaper continued to devote considerable ink to promoting her performances. Gradually, however, the reviews became more mixed. Writing about her as the free-spirited Magda in Hermann Sudermann's *Homeland*, the *New Times* concluded that Yavorskaya was the kind of actor who is unable to get lost in a role, an observation often made about Bernhardt. In Paul Harvieu's *In a Vice* (*Les Tenailles*) she was again called on to play a woman wronged by a marital code that subjugates the wife, this time with somewhat more success. However, in general, the string of realistic, socially conscious plays that Suvorin imported from Norway, Germany, and France were not well suited to Yavorskaya's flamboyant approach to acting, even though she was deeply interested in their themes.

After *In a Vice* closed, Yavorskaya headed to Moscow for the Christmas holidays, settling into her favorite suite at the Louvre, where she and Shchepkina-Kupernik frantically prepared for the January 4, 1896, premiere of *La Princesse Lointaine*. Shchepkina-Kupernik had decided to change the title to *The Dream Princess* (Принцесса Грёза in Russian), more literally translated as the "reverie princess." This title reflected her intent to have the play seen as a symbolist fable, one of the first works in Russia to use the Silver Age trope of "the Poet and the Beautiful Lady" as a metaphor for the relationship between the artist and his or her muse. When Yavorskaya had first told Suvorin that she had selected *The Dream Princess* for her contractually promised benefit performance, he became enraged. He thought it was a terrible idea. Suvorin assigned the production to Evtikhy Karpov, best known for directing the Russian classical works of Ostrovsky. Karpov refused to devote much effort to staging a medieval romance in verse based on a Provençal legend about the love of a troubadour prince for the princess of Tripoli. Yavorskaya and Shchepkina-Kupernik were forced to become the de facto directors.

In the midst of all this, Yavorskaya agreed to host a large group of people in her blue living room at the Louvre to hear Chekhov read his play *The Seagull* for the first time. Shchepkina-Kupernik recalled that Yavorskaya did not like *The Seagull* at all, although she feigned delight. Korsh commented that it was bad theater to have a man shoot himself offstage and not even let him give a speech before he died. Shchepkina-Kupernik felt unable to respond to the play objectively because it was obvious to her that Nina Zarechnaya was based on Mizinova, "a girl I was close to and who was also close to Anton Pavlovich, and who at this time had gone through a difficult and sad affair with a writer. And I was most of all bothered by the thought: would her fate turn out to be just as sad as that of the poor Seagull?"[33] Chekhov responded to the noise and arguments following his reading with an expression on his face that was both embarrassed and stern. He told Suvorin that his play had failed without even being performed.

Toward the end of December, Yavorskaya and Shchepkina-Kupernik were back in St. Petersburg to rehearse *The Dream Princess*. During one rehearsal Suvorin, sitting in his front loge seat, interrupted the actors, pounded his staff on the floor, and shouted out in frustration at what he was witnessing: "Some idiot is going to his lady idiot on some sort of idiotic boat, and these little girls [meaning Yavorskaya and Shchepkina-Kupernik] imagine that St. Petersburg will go out of its mind in ecstasy from this!"[34] Given that the work was not the sort of Western play that

Suvorin sought out for his new theater, it was understandable that the management refused to budget new set decorations and costumes for the production. *The Dream Princess* is set in the twelfth century. Joffrey Rudel, the prince of Blaye and troubadour of Aquitane, has heard accounts from pilgrims of the beauty and virtue of Melissinde, the countess of Tripoli. He writes a series of poems and songs dedicated to her, and decides to make a treacherous journey by sea galley to see his "dream princess." By the time the galley enters the harbor in Tripoli, he is gravely ill. His friend and fellow troubadour Bertrand is sent to Melissinde's castle to bring her to Rudel. As Bertrand recites the romantic verse Rudel had composed in her honor, Melissinde, at first mistaking him for the prince, finds herself falling in love with Bertrand. He too is attracted to her but eventually decides to sacrifice his feelings in loyalty to his prince. The princess goes to the galley to give solace to the dying Rudel. From his deathbed Rudel speaks eloquently to her of the nature of his divine love for her. She is overwhelmed by his sacrifice, ceremoniously putting her ring on his finger and her amulet about his neck. She cuts off the hair that he grasps as he sinks back down with his dying breath. She tears off her jewels and gives them to Rudel's sailors. Urging the men surrounding her to "go fight for the Cross" under Bertrand's leadership, she decides to cloister herself on Mount Carmel. On a literal level, the story is trite. Its ability to move audiences completely depended on the power of its verse to convey a deeper symbolic meaning for the love expressed by Rudel and Melissinde.

In spite of the lack of management support, Shchepkina-Kupernik was buoyed by the actors and crew who, sensing the emotional power of her translation, seemed excited to do the play. The property masters gathered set decorations from previous productions. They took various items from Yavorskaya's apartment—pillows, vases, statues, brocade; it didn't matter that they weren't appropriate for the period as long as they created what they felt was the right atmosphere for Melissinde's castle. For her title role, Yavorskaya had already ordered a costume and tiara from the same Paris studio that produced costumes for Bernhardt. Friends promised to bring red roses and white lilies for the opening-night performance.

But Shchepkina-Kupernik also sensed the schadenfreude of the actors not involved in the production, who laughed and shook their heads as they watched the last-minute preparations. In fact, Shchepkina-Kupernik herself was still not satisfied with Rudel's profession of love in the first act. She had translated it literally, and felt it to be too prosaic to successfully introduce the desired leitmotif of the play. After repeatedly struggling to find a solution, she awoke in the middle of the night with new, less literal, more melodious stanzas singing in her head, beginning with the song-like "Love is an intoxicating dream, / The light of life, / a bracing spring." She rushed off to the printers to replace the previous text. When he was shown the new stanzas, Nikolai Krasov, who was playing Rudel, complained to her about having to learn new lines at the last minute.

Chekhov let Suvorin know that he planned to be in St. Petersburg on January 4 for the premiere, where he was sure he would "once again see how they'll shower the diva with bouquets and pieces of paper from the lettered loge seats and present her with something 'from the student youth.'" He added sarcastically that Shchepkina-Kupernik was "as good a specialist in arranging benefits as an undertaker is at funeral processions. She organizes the benefits in such a 'Jewy' way that by the end of the second act the theater audience starts to feel ashamed, and the actors come to hate Yavorskaya for the rest of their lives."[35]

Shchepkina-Kupernik arrived at the theater with a feeling of trepidation. She took her seat in Pyotr Gnedich's box located in the right front of the theater. Gnedich, the first president of the Circle before Suvorin took over, had drawn the sketches for the play's scenery. The first act begins on the deck of the galley, which is being battered by a storm as it sails toward Tripoli. When the sailors see land, the dying Rudel is carried out on deck. His arms and blond locks are draped over a blue bedspread onto which Shchepkina-Kupernik and the crew had sewn silver French lilies just the night before. At this point, Shchepkina-Kupernik turned around in her seat to look at the audience, fearing it would react to the play with hostility. Some of those in attendance were from court society. The men were dressed in top hats and frock coats, the women in sumptuous dresses, the guards officers in their glossy uniforms. Grand Prince Vladimir Alexandrovich, the uncle of Nicholas II, sat in the royal box. She caught sight of Dmitri Merezhkovsky, the renowned writer and literary critic, who was looking out from his loge threateningly, "disdainful of such mere mortals as ourselves."[36] But she also saw the familiar faces of her Moscow friends Sablin, Goltsev, and Chekhov. University students and women auditors filled the upper balcony seats.

To the sound of a lyre, Krasov began to speak the lines that Shchepkina-Kupernik had just revised for him:

> I love—and don't await an answer.
> I love—and don't expect a kiss. . . .

I love my wonderful Dream,
My bright-eyed Princess,
I dream of a dear, indistinct,
Far-away!³⁷

As the *New Times* described it, Krasov "recited the verse of the dying poet-troubadour so touchingly and with such deep feeling with the accompaniment of a lyre that it prompted the spontaneous applause of the entire theater hall."³⁸ Shchepkina-Kupernik looked over at Gnedich with relief.

During the first intermission, the conversation was joyful, animated. Acquaintances congratulated Shchepkina-Kupernik, although one of them reported overhearing Merezhkovsky saying that her translation was "verse for an organ-grinder." She went backstage to calm and reassure Yavorskaya, who was yet to make her appearance, that the first act had been very well received. She made her entrance in the second act wearing a crown of lilies, her golden hair flowing almost to the floor. The jewels sewn into her clothing glittered, and when Yavorskaya stood in front of the stage lights, it was obvious she was wearing nothing under her dress.³⁹

By the time the final curtain went down, the audience had become thoroughly enchanted by what they had seen. Yavorskaya's Russian biographer paints a vivid picture of the excitement in the theater as everyone jumped to their feet. High-society ladies dropped their binoculars and reticules, cupped their hands, and shouted "Bravo!" Their husbands, their faces flushed and eyes moist with tears, clapped with all their might, calling for "the splendid blond princess in her semitransparent tunic and the tiny Thumbelina-translator."⁴⁰ When the two women came out, the grand prince joined the others in standing and applauding, to which Yavorskaya responded with a deep bow. Backstage, Shchepkina-Kupernik and Yavorskaya hugged each other and wept. When Shchepkina-Kupernik saw Suvorin, she couldn't resist telling him, "So you see, Alexei Sergeevich, they liked the idiotic ship!" He laughed and said, "I didn't expect this, I really didn't expect this, I admit it. What can be done? An old man sometimes blunders." Suvorin shrugged his shoulders, and Yavorskaya reveled in her victory over him.⁴¹

Shchepkina-Kupernik marveled that "overfed Petersburg became just as enamored of the romantic story of pure love in a medieval legend as before they had been enamored at the depiction of poverty, despair, and death of the starving Hannele."⁴² Inevitably, just as there was following the success of *Madame Sans-Gêne*, merchants responded with a range of products inspired by the play. There was a *Dream Princess* waltz, *Dream Princess* perfume, *Dream Princess* chocolate, and sheets of letter paper printed with quotes from the play. Yavorskaya's celebrity was at its height. She played the role twenty times. After each performance, theatergoers waited for her to emerge from the stage door to autograph programs. They sent her inspired doggerel: "Your aroma is that of the mystery of suffering, / Your splendor is that of the rapture of a living soul . . ."[43]

Many theater critics reflected the public's enthusiasm. The *St. Petersburg Gazette*, Suvorin's journalistic rival, had mostly ignored his fall theatrical productions. But now it printed a lengthy review by V. V. Volodin (the pseudonym used by Prince Vladimir Baryatinsky), who wrote, "From this poetic, elegant play wafts something youthful, good, and pure that makes you forget the prose of life and the burden of everyday dramas." Like other critics, Baryatinsky especially noted the quality of Shchepkina-Kupernik's verse, which he found "so musical, tender, and graceful that without exaggeration it's possible to say that the translation of *La Princesse Lointaine*, if not better than the original, is at any rate in no way inferior to it."[44] The critic for the *Illustrated Theatrical Journal* responded in a similar fashion, noting how difficult it was to preserve the warmth and beauty of the original French while making it sound harmonious and fresh in contemporary Russian.[45]

Yavorskaya, for once, basked in the glow of positive reviews. "Even critics of Miss Yavorskaya admitted the quality of her performance this time," wrote the *New Times*.[46] Baryatinsky in the *St. Petersburg Gazette* noted the absence of Yavorskaya's usual faults: "Her pauses were completely normal (the actress knew her role very well), and her voice sounded cleaner and more melodious than usual." Her portrayal of Melissinde was above reproach: "The actress's excellent diction, beautiful gestures, elegant figure, wonderful appearance and striking costumes created for the viewer the complete illusion of the legendary 'Dream Princess.'" Baryatinsky ended his review by reporting that it was the unanimous opinion of those who had seen *La Princesse Lointaine* in Paris that the St. Petersburg version was better produced and better performed.

Chekhov was not among those enthralled by the play. The night after the premiere he was at Suvorin's, telling Sazonova that as far as he was concerned Yavorskaya in her role as princess was just a "washerwoman who had covered herself in floral garlands." Not surprisingly for someone in the midst of a struggle to get the censors to approve *The Seagull*, an unconventional and very contemporary work, he was not much interested in a medieval story all about "romanticism, stained glass, and the Crusades." In response to everyone's praise of Shchepkina-Kupernik's translation, Chekhov, ever the master of the backhanded compliment, said, "She has only twenty-five words. Ecstasy, prayer, quiver, murmur, tears, reveries. But using these words, she writes enchanting verse."[47]

There was, however, an artist sitting in the opening-night audience who found inspiration in the sound of Tatiana's words and the mise-en-scène unfolding before his eyes. Thirty-nine-year-old Mikhail Vrubel had only recently started making a name for himself as a controversial symbolist painter who used saturated, iridescent colors to depict romantic and mythical subjects, not only on canvas but also in ceramics, glass, and stage sets. He had been summoned to St. Petersburg by his patron, Savva Mamontov, the railroad baron and founder of the Moscow artists' colony at Abramtsevo, to take over the design of the sets for a Mamontov opera being staged at the Panaev Theater. Mamontov had also just commissioned Vrubel to paint two murals for the upcoming All-Russian Industry and Art Exhibition set to open in Nizhni Novgorod in the summer. For one of the murals, Vrubel decided to paint a scene from *The Dream Princess*, a painting that became embroiled in a scandal but would eventually achieve enduring fame long after Rostand's play faded into obscurity.

The enormous canvas depicts the dying Rudel lying on the deck of his galley strumming his lyre. A gauzy Melissinde, an apparition in a white tunic and crown of white lilies, hovers above him. Rudel's friend Bertrand stands on deck, holding the rigging. When Albert Benois, the landscape painter who was in charge of the art pavilion for the Nizhni Novgorod exhibition, saw Vrubel's painting, he considered its color palette "monstrous" and commanded it be removed. Furious, Mamontov rented some land outside the exhibition grounds and built his own pavilion to exhibit *The Dream Princess* and eight other Vrubel paintings. Needless to say, people flocked to see the notorious painting, even if the modernist fresco offended their tastes. Maxim Gorky found Tatiana's translation to be "full of pure and powerful idealism," but considered Vrubel's interpretation to be strange and laughable: "a deliberate attempt to appear eccentric in order to obtain fame."[48]

Mamontov, however, was unwavering in his support of Vrubel. In 1901, when he took on rebuilding the art nouveau Metropol Hotel, Mamontov decided the arched upper facade facing Theater Square should be decorated with a majolica panel reproduction of *The Dream Princess*. Today, if you turn around as you walk across the square toward the Bolshoi Theater, you cannot help but notice Vrubel's mosaic gracing the top of the newly restored Metropol Hotel. As for the canvas, after the Nizhni Novgorod exhibition, it was stored with Mamontov's opera props, which eventually became the property of the Bolshoi Theater. In 1956 when clearing out an old storage area, the theater's staff stumbled across the huge, rolled-up canvas. Creased, filthy, and torn, it was turned over to the Tretyakov Gallery for restoration, which was completed in the 1990s. The museum decided to devote a special room to the painting. In June 2007, on the 150th anniversary of the artist's birth, the newly reconstructed Mikhail Vrubel Room opened at the Tretyakov. The room's framed centerpiece, *The Dream Princess*, forty-five feet wide and twenty-five feet high, fills an entire wall.

CHAPTER 6

Princess Baryatinskaya

Within a week of the premiere of *The Dream Princess*, Yavorskaya started rehearsing another play, *The Anthill*, set to open on January 12, 1896. At a rehearsal two days before the premiere, she apologized to *The Anthill*'s author, Sophia Sazonova, for not knowing her role, but reassured the distressed author that she would master it by that evening. The next evening, however, Yavorskaya failed to show up at the dress rehearsal, sending a note saying that if the play couldn't be put off, they should give her role to someone else. Karpov, the play's director, was furious and sent for Suvorin, who soon arrived accompanied by Chekhov. Suvorin was so enraged by what Karpov told him that he was ready to expel Yavorskaya from the troupe, an unlikely prospect given that she was at the beginning of an extraordinarily successful run of *The Dream Princess*.

Suvorin sat down and struggled to compose a letter to be delivered to Yavorskaya. He wrote and discarded multiple drafts. Chekhov joked that it had never taken him as long to write a feuilleton as it was taking Suvorin to write his note to Yavorskaya. Chekhov offered to go see her but the group rejected the idea. Karpov suggested that Zinaida Kholmskaya take over the role, but when they sent for her, it turned out she was ill. Sazonova complained that the letter that Suvorin and Chekhov finally crafted was too obliging. Instead, she dictated her own note, which said: "The play must go on tomorrow. I ask you to learn the role and come to rehearsal tomorrow at 11 a.m.," the day of the first performance. The letter was delivered by a messenger who was asked to wait for a reply. He soon returned with her answer: "I will fulfill your command; I will play the role tomorrow."[1] The incident further strained Yavorskaya's relationship with her fellow actors and with Suvorin, who suspected that she was leveraging her popularity with audiences to assert more control over her career and the theater's decisions.

Without mentioning the backstage tumult preceding the premiere, Suvorin's newspaper declared *The Anthill* a success. The play was a contemporary satire on St. Petersburg high society's obsession with gossip and slander. The trite plot centers on an influential civil servant who is about to give his daughter away in marriage, while he himself has fallen in love with a notorious widow. Complications ensue when the mother of his daughter's fiancé announces that if he marries the widow, whom gossips have labeled a coquette, she will not let her son marry his daughter. The *New Times* critic found the play to be "prolix" (Sazonova subsequently made cuts), but praised its ensemble of actresses, including Yavorskaya.[2]

The *St. Petersburg Gazette*, on the other hand, in a brief, unsigned review, disparaged the play. Sazonova's comedy, it wrote, "turned out to be not a poorly conceived, but a poorly written play, with a pretense of knowing the habits, morals, and conversations of high society. It's shameful that a 'literary' theater puts on such plays, alongside the works of Schiller, Hugo, Rostand, and Hervieu."[3]

These comments offended Suvorin, who knew its author was the paper's Theater and Music columnist, Vladimir Baryatinsky. The twenty-two-year-old prince was raised in a family with close ties to the tsar's household. After graduating from the St. Petersburg Naval College in 1893, he was assigned to a naval guards company. But he had already made it clear to his father that he wasn't interested in a military career. He preferred translating French verse, and wrote and acted in plays that were performed at the naval college and private theaters.

Suvorin wrote a letter to Baryatinsky in which he insisted there was nothing "shameful" about putting on a play by Sazonova, whose talent had long ago been recognized by writers such as Mikhail Saltykov-Shchedrin and Nikolai Nekrasov and whose play he considered to be talented and witty, in contrast to Baryatinsky's "poor, adolescent dramas," which Suvorin had refused to stage.[4] Suvorin decided not to mail the letter. His spiteful tone may have been prompted by the suspicion that

Baryatinsky had encouraged Yavorskaya's failed last-minute attempt to pull out of the play. The two had met at a literary soirée sometime early in the run of *The Dream Princess*.[5]

Yavorskaya's schedule for the rest of the winter season was less demanding, consisting of alternating performances of *The Dream Princess* and *The Anthill* without having to take on anything new. Despite its popularity, Suvorin still hated *The Dream Princess*. On April 8, he dropped in to watch the second act but soon left: "What nonsense," he wrote in his diary. "How awful it is to listen to such romantic rubbish, and from the mouth of Yavorskaya." Neither did Suvorin think much of Burenin's *Diana Fornari*, a revision of Alfred de Musset's *Chestnuts out of the Fire* (*Les Marrons du feu*), which his colleague, acceding to Yavorskaya's suggestions, had stuffed with theatrical effects from various plays: "He's a gifted critic, an incomparable pamphleteer, and a surprisingly talentless playwright."[6]

The two men quarreled over Yavorskaya. Suvorin suspected that Burenin was under her spell, and wanted to turn the Maly into "Yavorskaya's theater" simply because she had the ability to fill seats. Burenin argued that it was up to the public which actors would rise to the top. Suvorin disagreed: "Our theater doesn't have to be that way. It should give space to other actors and actresses." He was repelled by Yavorskaya's all too obvious desire to eliminate "not only actual rivals, but even potential rivals." Suvorin was more interested in the artistic mission and prestige of his theater than its profitability. With the theater's first year coming to an end, he penciled out a budget for the fall. Over a five-month season, theater rental would cost him twenty-three thousand rubles; salaries for the troupe would come to sixty thousand rubles. Assuming an average income of less than a thousand rubles per performance, he concluded that a loss was inevitable. He knew the prudent thing to do would be to step away from the theater, but he couldn't talk himself into doing it.[7]

The Maly Theater's season ended on May 3. Yavorskaya's star was now sufficiently bright that she had the power to enter into a partnership with Mamont Dalsky, a leading actor with the Alexandrinsky Theater, to organize a troupe to go on tour to Moscow. The repertoire consisted of her plays from the past season at the Maly plus Dalsky performing scenes from classical works such as Pushkin's *The Covetous Knight* and Shakespeare's *Hamlet*. While in Moscow, Yavorskaya asked Konstantin Stanislavsky, the thirty-three-year-old cofounder of Moscow's Society of Art and Literature, to direct *The Dream Princess*, but he refused. He wrote his wife, "I have, by the way, no regrets about this, since only junk would come of it."[8] Stanislavsky's naturalistic style of acting and staging was diametrically opposed to Yavorskaya's approach.

But this refusal led to a dispute over sets. Stanislavsky had bought back from Yavorskaya some scenery from his production of *Othello* that he desperately needed for an upcoming play. But when he went to the property shed, it was nowhere to be found. Knowing that Shchepkina-Kupernik handled Yavorskaya's business affairs, he sent a note asking her to help him locate the scenery. Even though it was almost midnight, she begged him to come over immediately. Shchepkina-Kupernik was distraught, saying she had allowed herself to get embroiled in the business side of Yavorskaya's affairs, and now it was tearing her to pieces. With tears in her eyes, she asked Stanislavsky to do her a favor by agreeing to come to at least one of Yavorskaya's rehearsals. In other words, Yavorskaya had instructed Shchepkina-Kupernik to hold the scenery hostage until Stanislavsky came to see her. He recalled the advice of his wife, the actress Maria Lilina, that in theatrical matters he should never get involved with ladies who in the eyes of the public are prone to scandal. "Among such women," he wrote to Lilina, "Yavorskaya, of course, takes first place." He managed to extricate himself from this attempt at blackmail: "But it all came out very awkwardly and, of course, I have acquired a new enemy in the theater."[9]

Stanislavsky did attend the first Moscow performance of *The Dream Princess* on May 5. He told Lilina: "I've seen much in this world, but I've never had the experience of seeing such an abomination." He complained that Yavorskaya's "hangers-on" kept trying to entice him to her dressing room between acts "apparently for her own advertising purposes." After the performance, as he was coming down the stairs, Stanislavsky bumped into Suvorin, who had come to Moscow to attend the coronation of Nicholas II. They decided to go to the buffet, where they talked about theater matters long after the doors were locked and the lights were turned off. Someone told Yavorskaya in her dressing room that Suvorin was still in the theater. Holding candles, she and her entourage ran through the foyer to the buffet, where they tried to cajole the two men to come with them to her apartment, which was in the theater building. "And here I stood my ground," Stanislavsky told his wife. "With a coldness that was unlike me, I refused, and they dragged off the old man [Suvorin]. You should praise me for my success!"[10]

By the end of May, Yavorskaya and Shchepkina-Kupernik were back in St. Petersburg. That summer the high-society gossips, who had been the objects of Sazonova's satire, had much to whisper about. When Nicholas II had married Alexandra in 1894, he stopped seeing his mistress, the ballerina Mathilde Ksheskinskaya, and asked Grand Duke Sergei Mikhailovich to become her protector. It was now well known that the grand duke was lavishly supporting her as his mistress. In July rumors of a new affair involving the imperial court were making the rounds—Prince Vladimir Baryatinsky, the boyhood friend of the tsar, had fallen in love with the actor Lidia Yavorskaya. She was characterized as a perfidious, previously married, "much older" woman (at twenty-five she was three years older than the prince) who encouraged his literary endeavors and talked of marriage as a means of rebelling against the corrupt and arrogant milieu in which he was raised.[11] When Shchepkina-Kupernik was introduced to Baryatinsky, he struck her as a very young, very handsome "light blond, feminine, with elegant facial features and dark eyebrows." She called him "the porcelain prince."[12] Unlike the previous generation of Baryatinsky men, fierce officers who had put down the Chechens and served bravely in the Caucuses, the current brothers Baryatinsky—Anatoly, Alexander, and Vladimir—were characterized as effete, neo-romantics, more drawn to the world of culture than military service.

Prince Vladimir, still an active naval officer, was assigned to the Dowager Empress Maria Fyodorovna's private yacht, the *Polar Star*. His father, Vladimir Anatolievich, was also attached to the yacht, which allowed him to keep an eye on his willful son. In early August, the *Polar Star* set sail for Copenhagen, where the Danish-born empress usually spent her summer months. The yacht had already left the harbor when Vladimir Anatolievich went to look for his son. Much to his surprise, he was told that Prince Vladimir had reported himself ill and wasn't on board. Vladimir Anatolievich had seen his son the day before, and he looked to be in perfect health. He immediately telegraphed Dr. Gustav Hirsch, the tsar's personal physician, to check on the prince. Dr. Hirsch rushed to the Baryatinsky palace, where the doorman told him that Prince Vladimir was well and had left instructions that all his belongings be forwarded to a new apartment. The doorman informed the doctor that the prince had married Madame Yavorskaya at a church in Novgorod the previous day. Three days before the wedding, the couple had taken the necessary steps to finalize Yavorskaya's divorce from Alexeev.[13]

Dr. Hirsch went to Prince Anatoly's house, pulling him away from a dinner party to tell him what his brother had done. The doctor was worried about how the news would affect the parents, especially their mother, who had a heart condition and was recuperating at their dacha in Tsarskoe Selo. Prince Anatoly also realized that by leaving his ship without permission, his brother could be charged with desertion. He decided to go see the tsar and ask him to intervene. Anatoly told Nicholas that since, as far as he knew, Yavorskaya was not yet divorced from her husband, the marriage couldn't possibly be legal. Nicholas said he would send for the chief procurator of the Holy Synod, Konstantin Pobedonostsev, to discuss the matter. In the meantime, he suggested that Prince Anatoly call on Grand Duke Alexei, the admiral of the fleet.

The grand duke had already received official word of the marriage and confirmed that since Prince Vladimir was under age and had married without the permission of his commanding officer, he could be arrested for desertion. But the grand duke, in deference to the Baryatinsky family, promised to hush the matter up as long as Prince Vladimir resigned from the navy. After consulting with Pobedonostsev, the tsar notified Prince Anatoly several days later that the Orthodox Church had declared the marriage legal. Alexei Kolomnin, Suvorin's business lawyer, told Prince Anatoly that being under age and marrying without permission had no legal significance. The responsibility fell totally on the priest, and these days even when minors married, they could not be compelled to get divorced.[14] Nothing could be done, the matter was fait accompli. Prince Vladimir's parents quickly took steps to cut off his funds.[15]

Suvorin was visiting the All-Russian Exhibition in Nizhni Novgorod when he received a telegram with news of the marriage. "She's older than he is and doesn't love him," he wrote in his diary. "If she doesn't bear him a child, she won't stay with him for long, or he won't stay with her."[16] Two days later he was back in St. Petersburg. Shchepkina-Kupernik came to see him. With tears in her eyes, she told him about an argument she had just had with Yavorskaya over breakfast at the Baryatinsky apartment, where Shchepkina-Kupernik had spent the night. They had been joined at breakfast by Zoya Yakovleva, an elderly writer, and the conversation turned to Yavorskaya's and Shchepkina-Kupernik's Moscow past and the rumors about their relationship. "Well, where there's smoke, there's fire," Shchepkina-Kupernik offered puckishly. Yavorskaya became livid that Shchepkina-Kupernik had said this in the presence of her new husband. "What?" she exclaimed. "Do you think what they said about you and me is true?" Shchepkina-Kupernik corrected herself and said that she was talking only about herself, that she was the one who had conducted herself in a way that resulted in their being stigmatized. After breakfast Yavorskaya, switching to French in the presence of her maid who was clearing up, continued to scold Shchepkina-Kupernik for gossiping and dropping hints about their past.

"My husband is hysterical," Yavorskaya said.

"If you want," Shchepkina-Kupernik replied, "I'll go to him and explain that I wasn't talking about you at all."

"He doesn't want to see you anymore. You must leave right now."

"But I'm in my smock. Allow me to at least get changed."

"You can get changed," said Yavorskaya, and Shchepkina-Kupernik left the apartment without saying goodbye.[17]

Soon afterward Yavorskaya wrote to Shchepkina-Kupernik asking her to sell the bed they had shared and send her the money, which she and her husband needed to furnish their apartment.[18]

Suvorin could see that Shchepkina-Kupernik was very distressed. She told him the prince was always criticizing Burenin but Yavorskaya insisted on keeping him close, thinking he could help both of them with their artistic endeavors. Shchepkina-Kupernik borrowed five hundred rubles from Suvorin, telling him she planned to go abroad in the fall to attend university lectures.

Two weeks later Yavorskaya came to see Suvorin. Her visiting card read "Princess Lidia Borisovna Baryatinskaya (formerly Hubbenet)," with no indication of her stage name. She was in a pleasant mood, but when her falling out with Shchepkina-Kupernik came up, she blushed and Suvorin felt she started talking nonsense about how Shchepkina-Kupernik had gotten angry because Yavorskaya had dissuaded her from going back to Moscow, her beloved "maternal soil" to which she felt some sort of mystical connection. Yavorskaya spoke of her husband enthusiastically. She told Suvorin they planned to visit her parents in Kiev for two months and then possibly go abroad from there.

"Does that mean you won't be here in the winter?" Suvorin asked, concerned that meant she would leave his theater.

"We'll possibly return to St. Petersburg," she replied. "I'm trying to get my husband to settle in St. Petersburg. . . . My husband wants to leave, having listened to the advice of those who are telling him that he needs to leave for a year until everything is forgotten. But I think we need to stay here. Evil acts aren't forgotten."

Yavorskaya's words struck Suvorin as smart and sensible. She mentioned that her divorce had been finalized, and she was now legally married. But the whole affair had taken a toll on her sensitive husband. "His nerves are shot," she told Suvorin. "You must agree that to do what he has done, you need to have nerve and be very decisive. And now his nerves are completely frayed."[19]

In her memoirs, Shchepkina-Kupernik understandably said nothing about how Yavorskaya's marriage had driven a wedge between them. Instead, she wrote indignantly about how the marriage scandal exposed Petersburg aristocratic prejudice against actors:

> It struck us as monstrous that there could be such a law that an actress is considered a pariah, rejected by society. Had we not already progressed from the 17th century when actors couldn't be buried in a Christian cemetery, but were buried at the side of the road like a suicide? This caste hatred was incomprehensible and insulting, especially to me, descended from an actor's family and accustomed to Moscow's worship of Shchepkin, Ermolova . . . In Moscow, it was an honor to be introduced to Ermolova, but here they treated an actress like a creature from the lower classes. This attitude of "high society" upsets me to the depths of my soul.[20]

Baryatinsky said of his early days with his wife: "It was as if I were in a dream." As far as he was concerned, his love for her overwhelmed any disagreements they had: "Petty squabbles can't shake that exalted, all-encompassing feeling of adoration I have, more than ever, for my Lidochka. We argue about some sort of nonsense, but after a minute we approach each other with outstretched arms. Together we have experienced too much happiness, sadness, joy, and agitation to have our feelings for each other waver."[21] But Baryatinsky's Russian biographer blamed Yavorskaya for being more cunning than loving. The prince had "plunged with sincerity into the whirlpool of his first youthful reveries and into the tragedy of the sexually obsessed Lidochka Yavorskaya, who used the title of 'princess' solely for self-promotion, and she betrayed his more sincere feelings and his love at every convenient opportunity."[22]

In September the newlyweds traveled to France but were back in St. Petersburg by early October. Yavorskaya had no intention of missing the rest of the fall theater season, which had been in progress for almost a month. Together with her husband, she met with Suvorin and the theater's other administrators on October 12 to discuss rejoining the troupe. She asked for fifteen hundred rubles a month without any proceeds from a benefit performance, which the prince felt she should not take on. Kolomnin and Burenin thought she was asking for too much and offered eight hundred rubles a month plus the option of one benefit at the standard rate. Speaking openly to the prince, Suvorin said his presence was making the negotiations more awkward, since it introduced delicate political considerations. Suvorin was certain that everything having to do with the prince would come to the attention of the tsar, and the Literary-Artistic Circle could be accused of offering a contract that took advantage of the prince's financial vulnerability. Baryatinsky dismissed this concern, saying it was solely up to him to decide what to accept.

"And if it pleases the tsar to let it be known to you that he finds this unacceptable?" Suvorin asked.

"The tsar can only laugh about it," said Yavorskaya. She let the men negotiate as if they were in charge, knowing that the final decision rested with her.

"If the tsar says this to me," the prince responded, "I'll say to him: Give me 20,000 rubles and then I won't do it."

"Meaning that you wouldn't allow her to perform if you had the money?"

"Yes, but then in my salons I would be able to do much more for her as an artist than she could earn on stage."

In their negotiations, Suvorin and his partners had to consider not only the budgetary and political implications of renewing her contract, but also the morale of the other actors in the troupe, who had started the season without the added tension of Yavorskaya's presence. Suvorin worried that if he created the impression that the theater might perish without her star power, it would demoralize his other first-tier actors. Anna Paskhalova, a jealous rival, had already been promised two roles that would have to be given to Yavorskaya if she rejoined the company. Yavorskaya made it known she hated Grigori Ge, a provincial actor in his first season. She demanded that if she was asked to perform in *The Dream Princess*, he could not play the role of Prince Rudel. On top of this, the actors complained to Suvorin that they were unhappy with the allocation of dressing rooms. "In my old age the devil has dragged me into this theatrical abyss," he lamented. "It's costing me a mass of money and giving me very little pleasure." The next day Suvorin visited Yavorskaya and the prince with a firm offer of eight hundred rubles a month without a benefit, with the later possibility of six hundred rubles plus the proceeds from a benefit. They accepted.[23]

What Suvorin may not have fully realized at that moment was that he was not only extending his contractual relationship with a difficult lead actress, but was also enmeshing himself in the financial troubles of her husband, the disinherited "porcelain prince." Suvorin continued to marvel at her disarming and deceitful ways. "Yavorskaya has her husband wrapped around her finger," he wrote in his diary. At the meeting the prince had insisted on no benefit performance, but two days later she was already talking to Kolomnin about modifying the agreement to include a benefit. She had also told Suvorin that she wanted to change her stage name to Orskaya. She thanked him for the delicacy with which he conveyed this to the troupe. On October 22 the *New Times* announced that the following week the Literary-Artistic Circle, which had moved into the Panaev Theater, would put on *The Dream Princess* and a new comedy, *The Weary Soul*: "An actress, who is well known to Moscow and Petersburg audiences, will be performing in both plays. She is performing under the pseudonym Orskaya."[24] That same day Suvorin received a letter from Baryatinsky giving permission for his wife to appear on stage under the name Yavorskaya. Suvorin was embarrassed and furious about being caught up in what obviously had been a quarrel between the prince and his wife: "What a lying creature! She's totally made up of pretense, envy, debauchery, and lies. And her husband knows nothing of her soul. If he only knew what one one-hundredth part of her life was like." Marriage did nothing to inhibit Yavorskaya's flirtations. The diplomat Sergei Tatishchev told Suvorin about a party he had attended in which she "gave what-for to everyone around and mocked Baryatinsky. She takes you by the hand, leads you into the next room and locks the door. We sit and talk for an hour. We come out and everyone imagines we've been doing God knows what."[25]

On October 18, a week after the contract signing, Baryatinsky dropped by to invite Suvorin to dinner. He declined, feeling compelled instead to stay home to write a long review article about the premiere of Chekhov's *The Seagull* at the Alexandrinsky Theater, which he had attended the night before. Much has been written about the play's disastrous opening night. Chekhov biographer Donald Rayfield succinctly described the reasons for its failure: "The play had been put on in the wrong city, in the wrong month, at the wrong theater, with the wrong cast, and above all the wrong audience."[26] From the response to the reading he gave in Yavorskaya's Moscow suite the previous December, Chekhov knew the play was bound to confound audiences. It had its origins in the personal dramas consuming his close friends Potapenko, Mizinova, Yavorskaya, and Levitan. The play reshaped their lives and personalities, creating a tableau of insecure artists struggling to find their place in the world. Irina Arkadina is Yavorskaya aged twenty years, a self-deluding grande dame, an epigone demanding everyone's full confidence in her talents. Her son Treplev says of her: "You mustn't praise anyone but her, you must acclaim her and go into raptures over her wonderful acting in *The Lady of the Camellias* or *The Fumes of Life*." There is much in her self-intoxication and her origins in Kiev that is reminiscent of Yavorskaya. Like Yavorskaya posing as the courtesan Vasantesena and dropping to her knees when Chekhov entered her suite at the Louvre, Arkadina melodramatically kneels before the writer Trigorin, calling him "wonderful, charming, amazing, unique." The resulting hybrid comedy-drama defied theatrical conventions. While finishing the first draft, Chekhov wrote to Suvorin: "I'm writing it not without pleasure, although I'm violating terribly the rules of stagecraft. It's a comedy, three female roles, six male roles, four acts, a landscape (a view out onto a lake); lots of conversation about literature, little action, and 180 pounds of love."[27]

Potapenko had taken on responsibility for getting the play past the censors and through the Imperial Theater Committee. Once approved by the censors, the committee assigned the play to the Alexandrinsky Theater in St. Petersburg, rather than the Maly Theater in Moscow, the more respected dramatic theater. The Alexandrinsky was best known for staging French farces, and *The Seagull* was selected to be performed at a benefit night for Elizaveta Levkeeva, a comic actress who was celebrating her twenty-fifth anniversary on stage. Levkeeva, however, did not have a role in *The Seagull*. Instead, following Chekhov's play, she would perform selections from Ostrovsky and Solovyov's 1877 farce *Happy Day: Scenes from Life in a Provincial Backwater*. The benefit performance, especially because *The Seagull* was billed as a comedy, attracted an audience looking forward to an evening of lighthearted laughter.

Chekhov arrived in St. Petersburg on October 9 already sensing that the play was likely to fail. He skipped the first rehearsal. Three days later the forty-two-year-old Maria Savina, the Alexandrinsky's reigning actress who had been cast to play Nina Zarechnaya, quit, in large part because the other actors couldn't help laughing at her attempt to play an eighteen-year-old. She told the director she was willing to take on the smaller role of Masha, but Maria Chitau, who had already been cast as Masha, took offense and refused to step aside. Vera Komissarzhevskaya, who would go on to be one of the most celebrated actresses of the Silver Age, was chosen to play Nina. Chekhov attended the rehearsal on October 14 and was encouraged by Komissarzhevskaya's performance, but he failed to attend the dress rehearsal the next night. Sazonova was there, since her husband, Nikolai, was playing Trigorin. She was unhappy with Nikolai's makeup (gray hair with a red beard), and with the absence of Chekhov and of Modest Pisarev, who was playing Dorn (he had fallen ill and would perform on opening night with a noticeably bad cold). The sets, borrowed from some wholly inappropriate farce, had yet to be delivered. As she sat in the empty theater, Sazonova gathered that the ending had still not been worked out. When Karpov, who had directed Sazonova's comedy *The Anthill*, sat down next to her, Sazonova told him the piece felt poorly rehearsed. He left and didn't return.[28]

On the morning of the premiere, Chekhov met his sister Maria, who had come from Moscow, at the train station. Walking along the platform, he told her, "The actors don't know their parts. They understand nothing. Their acting is horrible. Only Komissarzhevskaya is good. The play will flop. You shouldn't have come."[29] On top of the stress of the impending performance, Chekhov had to ensure that Mizinova and Potapenko, who were both there to see the play, were kept separated. Mizinova was given a seat in Suvorin's box on opening night; Chekhov convinced Potapenko and his wife to attend the second performance.

Sazonova's diary entry for October 17 best captures the sense of outrage that writers and actors felt regarding what happened to Chekhov at the Alexandrinsky Theater that night. Sazonova, though not a close friend of Chekhov, felt he had been treated savagely by a boorish audience:

> *The Seagull* is an unprecedented flop. They hissed the play. The author was not once called out on stage.... They hissed at Chekhov, one of our best writers, as if he were a person completely without any talent. The audience was malicious. They said, "What the hell was this?" A bore, decadence, that it wasn't worth watching for free, and here they were charging you money. Someone in the stalls announced: *"C'est de Maeterlinck."* They laughed at the dramatic sections. The rest of the time they coughed to the point of rudeness. The audience didn't see the intelligence, the talent in this play. A watercolor isn't good enough for them. Give them a house painter, then they'll understand. The public didn't understand its gloomy, hopeless colors, but instead shouted: "Boring! Incomprehensible!" The very fuss over this flop on a stage where all sorts of crap is successful speaks in favor of the author. He is too talented and original compared with those who lack talent.

Chekhov hid the whole time backstage in Levkeeva's dressing room and disappeared when it ended. Suvorin searched for him in vain to calm down his sister, who was sitting in the loges. . . .

The celebration for Levkeeva for twenty-five years went on as usual with speeches, presentations, kisses from her colleagues, and tears from the beneficiary. Having hissed at our best writer after Tolstoy, the audience tempestuously applauded this so-so actress.[30]

The next day Chekhov took the noon train back to Moscow and home to Melikhovo.

Swayed by the audience's reaction, the *St. Petersburg Gazette* declared *The Seagull* to be a "complete failure."[31] Its critic felt the play was infected with "a mournful imprint of sickliness and . . . . decadence." He hoped this experience would convince Chekhov to turn away from modernist experimentation. In a startling display of wrongheaded critical judgment, he added, "We will hope that the public will forget *The Seagull*, that *The Seagull* will become lost among the rows of Mr. Chekhov's future works."

In response, Suvorin took it upon himself to write a full-throated defense of the play in his newspaper. As far as he was concerned, the almost celebratory abusive response by critics was just so much noise. These critics would soon be forgotten, and Chekhov would remain one of Russian literature's brightest talents. Suvorin recognized there were problems with the production. As was all too common, the play had been hurriedly put on stage so that the opening night felt more like a dress rehearsal. The actors had not learned their lines well, and some were hopelessly miscast. Suvorin was astute in attributing the failure to the preparation and the venue, not the work itself. The imperial Alexandrinsky was not the place to premiere a modernist play, and Chekhov had written a work that audaciously broke with accepted theatrical conventions: "All is done so simply in this comedy, as in our lives, without effects, without monologues that are shouted out, without a particular battle, but somehow *just like that* . . . " But the Alexandrinsky's audiences expected theatricality and bombast. "On the stage, they love everything that doesn't exist in life," Suvorin complained, and they are comforted by the use of familiar devices and familiar categories of stage characters "starting with the ingenue and ending with benevolent fathers." Suvorin blamed Chekhov for running away from his responsibility to communicate to the actors and the director the innovative approach that would be required to make the play a success. The real problem was that no theatrical company yet existed that would be receptive to this approach and capable of doing justice to Chekhov's play. Nevertheless, Suvorin was convinced that what he described as the "odd and accidental" opening-night audience was an anomaly: "I haven't lost hope that future performances will give the public a different *Seagull*, a *Seagull* with its unmistakable literary qualities, with its honesty, with its lifelike characters and bitter poetry."[32]

Potapenko attended the second and third of the four performances of *The Seagull*. The audiences struck him as more typical of the Alexandrinsky. They watched and listened to the actors attentively. If the applause was infrequent, it was only because the play lacked the type of dramatic flourishes that cause theatergoers to leap to their feet. He sensed that the actors were beginning to work well together and bit by bit creating something that was a unified whole. But still, the audience's restraint affirmed Potapenko's sense that it simply didn't know how to respond to the untheatrical tone of the play. He wrote a review for the *New Times* in which he argued it was a mistake for Chekhov to make a major character, Trigorin, a writer because audiences don't really care about the inner lives of writers (he must have guessed that Trigorin was, in part, based on him). To him it felt like the audience reacted to Trigorin's awareness of his own mediocrity with "condescending curiosity."[33]

While *The Seagull* was playing at the Alexandrinsky, Yavorskaya returned to the stage in a revival of *The Dream Princess* at the Panaev under her own name. Suvorin was pleased with its success—it brought in over twelve hundred rubles in each of its first two nights. But he still disliked the play and her performance: "Her diction is not so much foolish as casual. It's good, then it's completely awful, then it's good again. And so it goes, but with everything in an elevated tone and with expansive gestures that are sometimes good."[34]

The day after the premiere, Yavorskaya came to see Suvorin to ask him for a loan of three thousand rubles. She told him her husband's creditors were demanding that amount or else they would seize their apartment. In return for the payment, the creditors agreed to let Baryatinsky sign a promissory note for an additional fifteen thousand rubles. Suvorin loaned her the money. A few days later Pyotr Ivanov, the manager of the prince's estate, visited Suvorin for reasons that weren't immediately apparent. Ivanov showed Suvorin promissory notes signed by the prince's two brothers, Alexander and Anatoly; one was for sixteen thousand rubles (due within a month) and the other was for twenty-four thousand rubles. Ivanov said the two brothers should make peace with Prince Vladimir so that the three of them could approach their parents and grandmother as a united front to settle their debts. Their grandmother on their mother's side, Countess Nadezhda Stenbock-Fermor, was fabulously wealthy, in her eighties, and in poor health. Ivanov told Suvorin the countess had already made plans to leave each of her grandchildren a million rubles, and the money was already sitting in a bank. On his way out, Ivanov stammered that if Yavorskaya could get the money now from somewhere to purchase the prince's fifteen-thousand-ruble promissory note, it would simplify matters in the short term, and she would easily be able to repay the debt when her husband got his million. It dawned on Suvorin that Yavorskaya was behind this odd visit from Ivanov and his veiled request, to which he decided not to respond. He wished Ivanov well and decided not to further involve himself in the prince's finances beyond the money he had already loaned to Yavorskaya.[35]

With the money she had borrowed from Suvorin, Shchepkina-Kupernik left Russia and set out for Lausanne University, enrolling in the department of belles lettres. Like many Western European universities, Lausanne admitted women, a privilege not granted to women in Russia. It presented Shchepkina-Kupernik with the opportunity to grow intellectually beyond the limitations of a gymnasium education. In her novella *Happiness*, Tatiana pointed out that for boys, the gymnasium was only an intermediate step, something to endure on their way to a university education. "For the majority of girls," she wrote, "the gymnasium is both the beginning and the end of their educational journey." At graduation they were expected to be fully formed women ready at the age of eighteen to take on the challenges of adult life.[36]

The new university at Lausanne (chartered in 1890) sat on a hilltop in the old city looking out over Lake Geneva. On class days Shchepkina-Kupernik clambered up the steep stone steps to the main auditorium, where she attended courses in medieval and modern French literature, "northern literature" (Russian, German, and English), and philosophy. Many of the women at the university, however, were attracted to the medical courses offered. Shchepkina-Kupernik noticed that while some of the female medical students were of the "old type," with unkempt hair and a suspicious attitude toward everything, they were outnumbered by more "contemporary" young women, who dressed well, embraced their femininity, and understood "that it's not enough to turn yourself into a parody of a man to pass for an educated woman."[37]

Shchepkina-Kupernik, in this instance, seemed to identify more with the assertive femininity of Yavorskaya, who used her "charms" to wield her power over men, than with the political radicalism of the descendants of the women of the 1860s.

The popularity of Professor Renard's French literature class among Lausanne's gentry ladies (including his young wife, who sat by the window when he lectured) prompted the professor to be cautious about the writers and works he cited, lest he offend propriety. He made references to classical and romantic writers such as Jacques-Bénigne Bossuet, Alphonse de Lamartine, and Victor Hugo, but said not a word about contemporary decadents such as Joris-Karl Huysmans and Paul Verlaine. In the course of spending an academic year living among cheerful, bourgeois, hardworking Swiss students, Shchepkina-Kupernik was struck by how different their upbringings and attitudes were when compared to their young Russian counterparts.

Starting in the winter of 1896, she wrote "Lausanne," a series of feuilletons published in the *New Times*, in which she contrasted the orderly, constrained, yet happy lives of the Swiss with the chaotic way in which Russian women were educated. In these essays, we find her searching for what constitutes the right balance between rebellion and discipline that will enable women to achieve their full potential in society. Without access to universities, Russian girls received their formal teaching through "institutes, gymnasiums, music teachers, drawing instructors, and French governesses."[38] Parents had little time to guide the child's moral upbringing or focus on their intellectual growth. In Russian gymnasiums (unlike Swiss schools), girls from differing classes and backgrounds mixed and formed strong friendships that sometimes influenced their worldview more strongly than their parents did. She wrote:

> With the power of opposites attracting, the daughter of an important bureaucrat becomes close with the daughter of a popular actress; the daughter of a poor teacher becomes friends with the daughter of a wealthy big-shot. Each teaches the other; unfamiliar worlds open up before their eyes.
>
> And a girl learns about life from the stories and theories of an old, not infrequently corrupted girlfriend, from the babbling of an empty-headed governess, from newspaper feuilletons lying around the living room, from books left on the bookshelf that are vaguely "not allowed" to be read or, adhering to the principle of freedom to read anything, are given out indiscriminately.[39]

This unfocused upbringing turned young women away from the desire to take on the socially acceptable roles of wife, mother, mistress of the household:

> An average, ordinary girl with a weak character, easily falling under every influence in nature . . . . is now willy-nilly set free, carrying her weak luggage of knowledge and fantastic theories about life; she is let out into the wide world of literature that is equally capable of being a boundless sea or a filthy swamp; she sees everything that is shown in the theater without discrimination; and her weak head begins to spin involuntarily.[40]

These young women, Shchepkina-Kupernik concludes, wish to live daring, unusual lives, but they are too weak and insufficiently gifted

> to separate themselves from the crowd and become "somebody." And this is why there is a mass of broken creatures, divorced women unable to endure *"terre-à-terre"* [down-to-earth] family life, bad actresses, unsuccessful writers, music teachers, pathetic and hungry, dreaming about the career of Sophie Menter [a virtuoso pianist and composer], girls living in furnished rooms, poor creations, their eccentricity leading them toward the reality that they will be courted by many men, but none will marry them.[41]

Shchepkina-Kupernik considered herself and her close friends to be iconoclasts who were pushing the boundaries of acceptable roles and careers for Russian women in late nineteenth-century society. In comparing the messy freedoms allowed Russian women in their upbringing with the strict boundaries proscribed for Swiss women, she wasn't advocating that those freedoms should be denied or even curtailed, only that Russian women should be formally educated about how best to take advantage of the freedoms given to them. The gradual breakdown of patriarchal authority in postemancipation Russia (we need only look back to Yavorskaya's and Shchepkina-Kupernik's rebellions against their parents to see examples), in some instances, resulted in young women feeling aimless and undirected as they grew into adulthood. In contrast, Shchepkina-Kupernik marveled at the orderliness of a Swiss upbringing. Parents devoted much of their time to raising their children. There was striking uniformity in how each day was structured: "Lectures, activities, and work all start at seven or eight o'clock; at noon everyone goes home; all of Lausanne has lunch at 12:30, dines at seven, and is fast asleep at ten. And everything here is so peaceful and calm."[42]

Girls were under the firm control of their parents; they read only what was given to them, they went to the theater only when their parents took them. Even at the university, the young women seemed childlike to Shchepkina-Kupernik; between classes they played schoolyard games like leapfrog. The youths were happy and uninfected with pessimism:

> Possibly their life is meaningless, empty in the generally accepted sense of the word. But they don't experience the other side of the coin: the constant feverish pressure on the brain, the constantly heightened nerves; they don't know what the novels of Zola are, have never been to an operetta, don't carry on a desperate flirtation; they are not destroyed, crushed by the noxious breath of a merciless life, but rather they smile calmly, traveling along their life's journey.[43]

For Shchepkina-Kupernik, this explained why the Swiss lacked any great poets, painters, or sculptors. She found their literature to be undeveloped. "Yes," she concludes, "Dostoevsky could not have been born in Switzerland."[44] It was as if a certain Dostoevskian self-laceration was essential to the kind of creative genius found in Russia.

Shchepkina-Kupernik continued her studies, enduring winter storms blowing off the lake that shook the classroom walls. The wind beat against the windows, blowing in through cracks and causing the gas lamps to sputter. On Sundays in the spring, she joined the townspeople on their obligatory walks up into the hills and through meadows of pale golden snowdrops interlaced with rivulets of newly melted snow cascading down from the surrounding mountains. In the summer of 1897, she received a string of postcards from Yavorskaya in Paris imploring her to come visit. She hesitated, but then Yavorskaya sent her a hundred francs, and she made up her mind to go. She was ready to repair the relationship. She took a train that raced through countless tunnels opening up to marvelous Swiss mountain vistas, crossed the French border at Pontarlier at midnight, traveled on into the dazzling daylight of the Côte d'Or and up the Rhone valley until she noticed graying skies and sooty factory smokestacks out her window, and heard the rising commotion in her carriage as passengers stood up and started to pull down their suitcases and valises. They were approaching the outskirts of Paris.

CHAPTER 7

Reconciliation

While Shchepkina-Kupernik was studying in Lausanne, attaining a fluency in European literature and languages that would serve her well in her career as a translator, Yavorskaya, in her second season with Suvorin's theater, solidified her reputation as one of St. Petersburg's leading actresses. She was frequently cast in exotic costume spectacles in which she played women who turned away from earthly pleasures to devote themselves to a spiritual life (or death).

In *A New World*, Marcus Superbus, a Roman patrician, rejects the attentions of Nero's wife, Poppea, and falls in love with the beautiful Christian, Mercia (Yavorskaya). Unable to save Mercia from being sacrificed to the lions, Marcus converts to Christianity and together they go to their deaths. The play was a translation (by Suvorin and his son Boris) of Wilson Barrett's *The Sign of the Cross*, which had been a great success on stage in the United States and England. It was subsequently twice adapted into film versions, most notably by Cecil B. DeMille in his 1932 precode spectacle starring Frederic March, Claudette Colbert, and Charles Laughton.

St. Petersburg audiences were drawn to the play's lavish costumes and painstakingly made sets that re-created the atmosphere of ancient Rome. Particularly effective were the catacombs beneath the Coliseum with its damp walls, faded columns, and moonlight shining through a window.¹ Suvorin noted with pleasure that the sold-out performances were reducing his losses for the season.

Much less successful was Burenin's *Aphrodite's Necklace*, set in Alexandria under the Greeks. Yavorskaya played Hero, a Jewish concubine who has grown weary of Alexandrine decadence and dreams of finding a more spiritual love. Suvorin's lack of confidence in Burenin's playwriting abilities was reflected in the *St. Petersburg Gazette* critic's comment that "the attitude of the Literary-Artistic Circle to Mr. Burenin's work was much less attentive than one would expect."² Additionally, given his caustic and reactionary journalistic writings, Burenin was despised by many of the university students who often filled the upper balcony seats whenever Yavorskaya was performing. On the first night of *Aphrodite's Necklace*, they expressed their disapproval by hissing, guffawing, and shouting during some of the more emotional scenes. The play was pulled from the repertoire after two performances.

For her contracted benefit performance, Yavorskaya selected *Izeÿl*, written by Armand Silvestre and Eugene Morand specifically for Sarah Bernhardt. The play had enjoyed a successful run in 1894 on the stage of Bernhardt's Théâtre de la Renaissance. It was the second time that season that Yavorskaya had convinced Suvorin to produce a play translated by her husband, a sign of the couple's growing creative influence on the theater. In December the prince had translated *Griselda*, a medieval legend in verse, also written by Silvestre and Morand. At the final curtain call of the premiere, Baryatinsky came out on stage, first together with all the actors, then again alone with Yavorskaya, who performed the title role. In the absence of Shchepkina-Kupernik, he was assuming the role of his wife's literary partner.

Similar in plot and atmosphere to *Vasantesana*, *Izeÿl* tells the story of an Indian courtesan who attempts to seduce Prince Siddhartha, who has renounced his worldly privileges. Instead, she becomes captivated by the prince, who has become Buddha, and decides to follow his teachings. Prince Sindiya, who has replaced Siddhartha on the throne and is passionately in love with Izeÿl, threatens to have Siddhartha killed if she doesn't reciprocate his feelings. She murders Sindiya, is sentenced to be tortured and executed, and dies in the arms of Siddhartha.

Unlike *Vasantesana*, *Izeÿl* enjoyed critical acclaim. Even the *St. Petersburg Gazette* praised the "costume-laden" production and the "wonderful and thoughtful acting" of the lead actors: "Miss Yavorskaya artistically presented the role of the beauty Izeÿl, first appearing in the splendor of limitless self-deception, in celebration of sin and excess, and then refusing all earthly pleasure for the sake of spiritual pleasures."³ Not surprisingly, the praise by the *New Times* critic was effusive as well: "Miss Yavorskaya's acting stood out with its nervous agitation spontaneously transferred to the electrified viewers. The role of Izeÿl showed us once again that Miss Yavorskaya continues to move forward, that her talent is being perfected, and that she relates to her craft with a true artistic approach and study."⁴ Following the premiere performance, when Yavorskaya emerged from the theater onto the street, she was met by a crowd of students applauding loudly as she made her way to her carriage.

Suvorin continued to fret over the theater's finances. He had trouble making up his mind whether to renew his lease. "Everyone is pinching me," he wrote in his diary. "In order for Yavorskaya to get 2,000 rubles from her benefit, I've squandered 1,200 rubles on the set decorations and gave her 800 rubles to obtain the play *Izeÿl* from Armand Silvestre, totaling 2,000 rubles. I've done more for this actress than for anyone else."⁵ During the last weeks of February, prior to the enforced closing of all theaters during Lent, he put both *A New World* and *Izeÿl* into heavy rotation, grossing a total of 14,638 rubles for the month. But it wasn't enough to stem his losses. He decided there would be no spring season. Running a theater was seductive, but it was a bad business proposition that, in the end, wounded his pride:

> I have already made peace that there will be no theater and that it's for the better. To lose money, and a significant amount at that—30,000 rubles over the past two years, to endure the most carping criticism in the newspapers, to be blamed for being unfair, for having favorites, to not see gratitude from the artists but rather to be blamed beyond all reason, to have to be cunning, to try to make peace, to have to justify this or that action in order to spare hurt feelings, to be continually under stress, to be prepared for explanations, to be on call and other things—all this is hard and thankless. What will be will be.⁶

Suvorin's sour mood extended to the government's hypocritical policy of shutting down Russian theatrical productions during Lent. Russian actors were banned from performing, but Russian audiences were allowed to attend productions by European dramatic and opera companies that took up residence in St. Petersburg's and Moscow's main theaters. Back in 1884 Chekhov wryly noted in one of his feuilletons the three "Lenten enjoyments" Muscovites indulged in when they were forbidden to attend dramatic plays: "amazingly expensive" Italian operas, French can-can performances with "girls in décolleté outfits singing ditties," and so-called private "vocal-instrumental-literary evenings" that could be "put on by anyone, wherever, and however."[7] In his newspaper column, Suvorin complained about how unfair it was that actors in the imperial theaters continued to draw a salary during Lent while those in the private theaters, both in the capital and in the provinces, lost the right to work. To get around the policy, provincial governors allowed local theaters to promote "readings" from a play during Lent. "But in fact," Suvorin pointed out, "the play is performed as it regularly would be, in costume, and the audience knows very well that this is a Lenten comedy skirting the law and eagerly attends these fake 'readings.'"[8] Meanwhile in St. Petersburg, Suvorin pointed out (echoing Chekhov's comments about Moscow), all sorts of café and cabaret performances by gypsies, operetta stars and French chanteuses, lacking any sort of "religious-moral character," were allowed. He proposed that during Lent, Russian ensembles should be allowed to perform plays that have been deemed to have "a moral, instructive tenor."

With the closing of Suvorin's theater after Easter, Yavorskaya was free to pursue other engagements. In March she went to Warsaw, where she was offered a theatrical run during Lent for the following year. In April 1897, she made her debut at the Alexandrinsky Theater in the secondary role of Lady Milford in Schiller's *Love and Intrigue*. Suvorin, who continued to champion Yavorskaya publicly, wrote a very sympathetic review of the premiere and of her performance, noting that "the debutante was greeted with lengthy and warm applause"[9] when she first appeared on stage. Even the *St. Petersburg Gazette* felt compelled to mention that Yavorskaya was called out on stage almost as often as Komissarzhevskaya, who had the lead role as the ingenue Luise.

Like other critics and impresarios, Suvorin had been following Komissarzhevskaya's career with great interest. Since joining the Alexandrinsky troupe the previous year, her fame had begun to eclipse that of Maria Savina, who had been the theater's leading actress since the late 1870s. The *St. Petersburg Gazette* found her performance as Luise to be "masterful and touching.... In a single season this gifted artist has completely captured the sympathy of the public."[10] Suvorin too found her to be wonderful in her heartfelt scenes, but "powerful moments, apparently, are not part of Miss Komissarzhevskaya's talent." Komissarzhevskaya's appeal lay in her ability to sustain and expand on the kind of vulnerability on stage that Ozerova had unfortunately only been able to capture in her debut as Hannele. Kugel wrote that Komissarzhevskaya's fame was based on her ability to convey the sense that she was "a fragile, suffering child of our times."[11] She would always be known for being the actress who first created the role of Nina Zarechnaya in *The Seagull*. Yavorskaya, however, even when portraying a courtesan who turns toward the spiritual, still projected a sensuality that audiences ascribed to the West in general, and the French theater of Bernhardt in particular.[12] The two actresses were seen as rivals. But in the end, the Russian temperament preferred feminine fragility and self-laceration, and over time Komissarzhevskaya's fame eclipsed Yavorskaya's.

In early May, Yavorskaya went on tour with a troupe of imperial actors to Astrakhan. The city's newspaper enthusiastically reviewed her performance in *Izeÿl*, saying that as an artist she possessed "the spark of God."[13] Meanwhile, Suvorin, changing his mind again, was mulling over whether to bring his theater back to life in the fall. In June, he signed a lease with Count Apraksin, the owner of the Petersburg Maly Theater. His company would start from scratch and return to the venue where they held their first season. "We don't have any plays, nor actors, nor a director," Suvorin bemoaned. "Nothing except for backdrops, which however we'll have to redraw because the stage of the Maly Theater is lower than at the Panaev Theater."[14] But the Maly also had several advantages—it was larger and located closer to the center of the city.

That summer Yavorskaya and her husband went to Paris, this time to renew her friendship with the luminaries of the French stage and to meet up with Shchepkina-Kupernik. In her memoirs Shchepkina-Kupernik mentioned neither her breakup with Yavorskaya following her marriage nor their reconciliation. But at the end of her 1897 "Lausanne" feuilleton, she described her stay in Paris and an evening at Rostand's luxurious home during which the playwright insisted that Yavorskaya recite some verse from Shchepkina-Kupernik's translation of *The Dream Princess*. When Yavorskaya finished, the guests had a lively conversation comparing her "gestures and mimicry with the Parisian 'Princess,'" in other words, Bernhardt. Shchepkina-Kupernik noted with pleasure that "everyone finds the Russian verse to be harmonious and directly pleasing to the ear. They try to repeat the Russian rhythm," although they haven't understood a word of it.[15]

Suvorin followed Yavorskaya's progress in Paris from afar, reading with amusement an interview she had given in *La Justice*: "She praised herself to the sky. Sardou promised her a wonderful play with a good role and wonderful costumes. Dumas-fils was her friend; the cream of society gathers around her; she was the first to perform *Dame aux Camélias* in Russian. Burenin's *Aphrodite* 'was in the repertoire for a long time.' It was only put on twice." She showed the interviewer publicity photos of her in various roles. "One stands out," the reporter commented. "Madame Yavorskaya half reclines on elegant skins with bare arms on which she is wearing bracelets that look like gold serpents, and wearing a diadem on her elegant golden hair, underscored by an unwavering smile on her lips and sensuous eyes."

"That's me in *Aphrodite*. . . . ," she told the reporter. "I disdain many of our prejudices, and I have incurred hatred for the fact that I have undermined the absurd foundations of the established Russian theater and its infantile conventions."

Suvorin was dumbstruck: "Wonderful. What can I say? Here's more: 'In St. Petersburg there is a literary theater, which thanks to its unwavering stormy success over the course of several years is slowly undermining the prestige of the imperial theater, which is weak and senile, cranking out the same old musty repertoire.'"[16]

Over the course of her career, particularly when performing abroad, Yavorskaya developed a masterful ability to take advantage of gullible reporters who dutifully reported her extravagant pronouncements on her place in Russian theater. Here, however, Suvorin could not help but agree with the sentiments expressed by his wayward comet of a star.[17] He informed her that he was restarting his theater company. She was to receive eight hundred rubles a month. The theater's repertoire for the fall 1897 season consisted of a mix of revivals of proven crowd-pleasers from the previous season (*Izeÿl, A New World, Hannele*), classical fare (*Faust, Julius Caesar, Hamlet*), and a variety of new works from Russia and Western Europe.

On October 3, Countess Stenbock-Fermor, Baryatinsky's grandmother, died. Baryatinsky asked Suvorin to put off performances of Grigory Gradovsky's *In the Name of Love*, in which Yavorskaya was playing the main role. Suvorin agreed, since it would be awkward for her to perform on the day of the funeral, "even though she didn't know the deceased, who in addition could not forgive her grandson for this marriage."[18] He decided to delay the next performance until the following Friday. But after the Monday funeral, she told him she was ready to perform on Wednesday, irritating Suvorin, who had to again juggle the performance schedule. Countess Stenbock-Fermor, who owned more than two dozen factories throughout Russia, left her heirs more than twenty million rubles. Vladimir Baryatinsky's portion of the inheritance gave him the capital to independently fund any future theatrical or journalistic endeavors that he and his wife chose to pursue.

The success of *Hannele* with St. Petersburg audiences prompted Suvorin to ask Burenin to translate Hauptmann's most recent symbolist fairy-tale drama, *The Sunken Bell*, for an upcoming production. The play takes place in the world of gnomes, wood demons, and water sprites. Yavorskaya was selected to play Rautendelein, an elfin forest-daughter who casts a spell on Heinrich, a foundry artist whose ambition is to make a perfect, clear-toned bell. In *The Sunken Bell* Hauptmann used a folkloric setting to dramatize an artist's sense of failure as he is pulled in different directions by the quest for an unattainable ideal, by the seductive powers of Rautendelein, and by the everyday demands of marriage, family, and bourgeois society. The *New Times* declared Yavorskaya's role her best of the season: "Her light tread, the grace of a wild goat, sometimes with the mischievousness of a child, sometimes with the demonic laughter of a witch, the enchanting characteristic costumes—all this created the complete image of a fairy."[19] At the end of January, Stanislavsky's Society of Art and Literature in Moscow performed *The Sunken Bell* using Burenin's translation. Stanislavsky reprised his role as Heinrich in October 1898, this time as one of the first productions of his newly formed Moscow Art Theater.

Yavorskaya's popularity, particularly among young audiences, continued to make her impervious to the criticism she received in the St. Petersburg press, which by now was often as negative as the reviews she had previously received in Moscow. Her reputation for supporting liberal causes was enhanced by her frequent participation in readings and private benefits. She directed a group of amateur actors in a performance that raised funds for needy Turkestan students. On another evening, she raced from the Maly Theater to make an appearance at the very end of a concert in support of students at the forestry institute. She was mobbed by "a throng of youths who surrounded the artist and literally didn't let her leave until she read at least ten numbers."[20] Following the concert, she promenaded on the arm of the minister of agriculture as they walked around an arcade of rooms outside the hall to view various exhibits accompanied by shouts of "brava" from bystanders. To support the House of Industry at Alexandro-Nevsky Monastery, which provided work, food, and shelter to the poor, she organized an amateur performance at Konovksy Hall of Suvorin's *Tatiana Repina*, in which she played the title role. Baryatinsky also participated in these charity events, most often reciting French verse. At a literary-musical evening at the apartment of the Romantic poet Yakov Polonsky, the prince performed his translations into French of the Russian poets Alexander Pushkin, Afanasy Fet, Mikhail Lermontov, and Polonsky as well, managing in his verse to preserve the meter of the Russian original. Yavorskaya complemented the classical themes of the evening by reciting Polonsky's "Vestal Virgin" and Gavriil Derzhavin's "Aspasia."

Yavorskaya's growing star power continued to feed bitter resentment among the actors in Suvorin's company, which from its very beginning lacked a sense of cohesion and artistic collaboration. Alexander Chekhov's description to his brother of his disastrous first experience at having a play staged by Suvorin underscored the pervasive atmosphere of backbiting and intrigue at the theater, and the sense that Yavorskaya's influence was invidious. Alexander had a long, if sporadic, history as a contributor to the *New Times*. He had come to depend on Suvorin to prop up his floundering attempts to make money as a writer. In December 1897 Suvorin agreed to put on Alexander's one-act *Platon Andreevich*, a comic farce about a retired military officer. The play was set for three performances, but after the first night it was taken off the schedule and replaced by two other vaudevilles.

Alexander was deeply offended. He felt the first night had been a success. "The audience laughed uproariously," he told his brother. They called for the author, but Alexander didn't come forward, staying in his loge seats with his wife and children. When he went to see Suvorin for an explanation for the cancellation, the impresario said that while he set the repertoire, he didn't get involved in schedule changes and encouraged him to talk to the director. Suvorin also advised him to write another play with a strong female lead. Only later, after talking to others, did Alexander understand what Suvorin was hinting at. Burenin, Pleshcheev, and others told him that Suvorin's absolute control was a fiction, that Nikolai Kholeva, the company's lawyer and secretary-treasurer, ran the stage from day to day and was responsible for changing the schedule, and that Kholeva himself was "run by his concubine," the actor Maria Domasheva. Kholeva had replaced Alexander's play, which had no female lead, with two vaudevilles in which Domasheva had prominent roles. "In a word," Alexander wrote Anton, "our theater, headed by Yavorskaya is a pretty nasty cesspool, which it's best not to have anything to do with." His play's future had become "shamefully dependent on Miss Domasheva's vagina and Kholeva's penis."[21]

Word got to Kholeva that Alexander and others were spreading the rumor that he was responsible for pulling *Platon Andreevich* from the schedule. Kholeva sent Alexander a registered letter in which he insisted that these rumors were false, placing the blame on the play's director or Suvorin himself. Suvorin advised Alexander to defuse the situation by writing back that it was best to ignore such baseless gossip. Unable to let go of his resentment over the fate of his "misguided little vaudeville," Alexander now came up with the theory that he had "fallen, like a chicken into the soup, between two warring factions—Yavorskaya and Domasheva." He was exaggerating when he told Anton that his play had stirred up "an entire stinking cesspool." More likely, such dustups were commonplace. To make matters worse, his first experience with writing for the theater had cost Alexander money—Suvorin paid him four rubles, forty-one kopecks (2 percent of proceeds) for the single performance, but his wife had paid fifteen rubles for loge seats for the three performances that were initially scheduled. Making his humiliation worse, during all this Alexander was acting as Anton's agent. While Anton was in the south of France for the winter, Alexander collected royalties for his brother that totaled close to a thousand rubles a month.

Suvorin felt the need to close out his season with a new work that could be counted on to keep the theater solvent, particularly because he was still committed to a benefit performance for Yavorskaya, which would do little to enhance his bottom line. Fortunately, he had successfully lobbied the Ministry of the Interior to allow his theater to stage plays on a limited basis during Lent. He selected Mikhail Bukharin's *Izmail*, a historical drama based on a Russian siege in 1790 led by the renowned General Alexander Suvorov of a strongly defended Turkish fortress. In it, Yavorskaya played Olga Verstovskaya, a relation of Major General Sergei Lvov, who took part in the storming of the fortress. The play, with its strong patriotic overtones (and a villainous Jewish spy), was a huge success with St. Petersburg audiences, just the kind of uplifting production that Suvorin insisted was appropriate for Lent. It had an extended run and, as a result, for the first time his theater ended its season free of debt.

For her benefit, Yavorskaya decided she wanted to play Roxane in Rostand's *Cyrano de Bergerac*, which had premiered less than two months earlier at the Théâtre de la Porte Saint-Martin in Paris, where it continued to enjoy sold-out performances. Hoping to replicate the success of *The Dream Princess*, Yavorskaya asked Shchepkina-Kupernik to translate the play. Her preternatural exuberance notwithstanding, Shchepkina-Kupernik found the task daunting: "I received the text of the play at the end of January and the benefit was set for February 10.

I had ten days to translate it, and it had five acts of rhymed verse!"[22] She started working on it at Yavorskaya's apartment, where she was staying, but soon found the working conditions to be impossible. The constant flow of people, telephone calls, and telegrams interrupted her concentration. She tried moving to a hotel, but people soon found out where she was hiding. Shchepkina-Kupernik decided it was better to leave town and go to Moscow. She had not found it necessary to rent an apartment there since her return from Lausanne, choosing instead to stay with a woman friend. But that place too would be noisy and full of people.

Shchepkina-Kupernik asked a friend, Lev Rodionov, known affectionately as "Uncle Lyova," if she could temporarily move into his small apartment on Tverskaya Street. She had grown close to Rodionov both because of his intelligence and because he made no demands on her. Most men in her circle fell into two categories: "Some saw me as a female writer for whom I was a competitor, for whom I was material for exploitation. Some saw me as a young and absolutely lonely woman who could be courted and would be offended if I didn't respond to this courting." The forty-year-old Rodionov was neither. "I trusted in him completely, more than any girlfriend, and I wasn't afraid to talk to him about my weaknesses and uncertainties, knowing that he would understand everything and forgive everything."

Shchepkina-Kupernik settled into a routine:

> At around ten in the morning I would appear in his modest office where everything was prepared for me: on the writing table was paper, clean pens (I didn't yet know how to type then), a little vase with fresh lilies, my favorite candies . . . And total silence reigned. . . . At one o'clock the door would open: Lev Mikhailovich's sister-in-law would silently enter and bring my lunch on a tray. I hastily gulped it down and wrote some more. At six o'clock she just as silently brought me my dinner. Toward evening I would get so tired that I would lie on the couch and, translating on the fly, would dictate to Uncle Lyova. At eleven o'clock I would give him everything I had written. He would get into a "quick cab" . . . . and race to the station for the express train leaving at midnight. There he had the conductor deliver the manuscript directly to Suvorin's theater. At the theater they instantaneously made copies of it, handed the copies to the actors, and they rehearsed the scenes.[23]

In this way she was able to translate the first three acts in less than a week. But by the fourth act, she suffered a temporary breakdown. Scenes involving the siege of Arras included technical military terms and up until then she had been working without a dictionary. The thought of having to slow down and pore through a dictionary suddenly felt overwhelming. She burst into tears, frightening Rodionov. He sent for a woman friend, who took one look at her and exclaimed, "This is disgraceful! For the sake of Yavorskaya's laurels, she's making herself sick!" The woman bathed Shchepkina-Kupernik, made her drink a bromide, and put her to bed. By the next morning she had recovered, finishing the play in another two days, having worked on it for a total of eight days.

Two days before the premiere of the play, Baryatinsky wrote a preview article about *Cyrano de Bergerac* in the *New Times*, using his pseudonym "Baron Ondit." The prince sought to generate interest in the production by explaining to readers that its swashbuckling hero was in fact a real person: "Savinien-Hercule de Cyrano de Bergerac was one of the most significant poet-satirists of the first half of the 17th century, and also an extremely original personality, someone who falls between a Moliere and a d'Artagnan." Cyrano was known in French literature for wielding a "dangerous and merciless" pen that inspired the works of other, more well-known writers such as Fontenelle, Swift, Voltaire, and Moliere.[24]

The opening night sold out, with loge seats that normally sold for twenty rubles going for one hundred, guaranteeing Yavorskaya an income of at least two thousand rubles. In return for its generosity, the audience was subjected to a six-hour event that went on past two in the morning. With typical Russian tolerance for long novels, plays, and operas that are beyond the endurance of many Westerners, most stayed until the end. The evening was drawn out by the ceremonies honoring the beneficiary, most likely orchestrated by Shchepkina-Kupernik. Yavorskaya didn't appear until the second act. After the act ended, she was called out on stage and showered with "flowers, flowers, flowers, silver, and other sorts of gifts. There were so many flowers that the beneficiary was completely hidden behind them. Among these flowers, there was some sort of sacrificial altar in which an electric light was hidden that lit up the bouquet," something "Orest," the *New Times* critic, had never seen before. Fortunately, all the gifts were bestowed during this one intermission rather than spread out after each act. Otherwise,

Orest noted, "the play might have ended at four o'clock, which hardly anyone would have been able to endure, except for the dear youths, who were ready to sit in the theater until morning."[25]

Shchepkina-Kupernik's translation received higher praise than the performance, although it was noted that the efforts of the ensemble, which had only six days to rehearse the play, were as herculean as those of the translator. Not surprisingly, both Yakov Tinsky (as Cyrano) and Yavorskaya did not appear to be in command of their lines. Shchepkina-Kupernik was shocked to hear Yavorskaya doing "something insufferable with the verse!" She thought to herself: "Was it worth it for me to try so hard just so she could shamelessly garble it?" Shchepkina-Kupernik found Tinsky's performance to be cold and "lacking any internal fire."[26] Orest called Shchepkina-Kupernik a "poetic phenomenon." He was aware that she had translated the play in eight days, and marveled that she had nevertheless been able to preserve the "rhymed verse of all five very long acts, not leaving out a single line, not stopped by a single witticism, competing in virtuosity with the author."[27]

Over the course of her long life, Shchepkina-Kupernik witnessed many other productions of her translation of *Cyrano* far superior to its premiere, and some that were worse. Later that year, Korsh signed a contract to do the play in Moscow. Shchepkina-Kupernik, having just returned from abroad, decided to attend a rehearsal unannounced, sitting far back in the darkened theater to listen to how her translation sounded. To her amazement, she recognized nothing. It was "some sort of nonsense, with almost no rhythm, without any indication of poetic measure . . . I wasn't understanding anything." After the rehearsal, she approached the prompter and asked to see the script. "I could see that the entire printed book had been pasted over with handwritten sheets of paper. The entire role of Cyrano and all the cues of his partners—and indeed the play was nothing but a monologue by Cyrano—all had been crossed out and rewritten." She went to the offices of the Society of Drama Writers and Composers, which enforced copyright protection, and forbade the play to be put on. Korsh was informed, and he raced to see Shchepkina-Kupernik, claiming he had not been to any of the rehearsals and that the actor "K" (she refrained from naming him in her memoirs) had on his own initiative decided to rewrite the script for his benefit performance. It turned out that "K," whom Shchepkina-Kupernik described as "quite handsome but a bit dim," had a rich father who was a major donor to the theater. As a result, Korsh pampered him. Shchepkina-Kupernik agreed to let the performance go on but only if her name was taken off the posters and program as the translator, and "K's" name was substituted. But Korsh responded that this was impossible, since they would have to get permission from the censors to substitute a different translation. The performance was canceled. A year later Korsh put on *Cyrano* using Shchepkina-Kupernik's translation with a better actor taking on the lead role.[28]

In late spring Yavorskaya was invited to return to Paris to represent Russia in a charity performance. Among the other participating actors were Bernhardt and Duse. Suvorin too was in Paris. He was invited to a soiree at Bernhardt's, where he was introduced to Rostand. The playwright was interested in what theatergoers thought of Yavorskaya in Russia. "Is she talented?" he asked. "Yes," Suvorin replied diplomatically. "It seems she loves to imitate?" Rostand said. "Yes," Suvorin again replied, both men understanding that it wouldn't be prudent to elaborate in the presence of Bernhardt and others. It was clear to Suvorin that Rostand wasn't "favorably inclined toward Yavorskaya," even though she had told him that Rostand was in love with her. Suvorin recalled that the previous night, when Yavorskaya had come to have dinner with him, she mentioned that her admirers were constantly threatening to shoot themselves when she didn't respond to their professions of love. Suvorin laughed, replying, "You should say to them: 'Go ahead and shoot yourself.' There won't be any volunteers."[29]

Concurrent with her collaborations with Yavorskaya in St. Petersburg, Shchepkina-Kupernik continued to maintain her family and personal connections with the Maly Theater in Moscow. By 1898 the Maly's popularity with audiences was beginning to fade as Ermolova, its leading actress since the 1880s, took on fewer significant roles. In the fall of 1898, hoping to reinvigorate the imperial troupe, Alexander Lensky, the Maly's lead actor, opened the New Theater, which was formed to provide younger actors, singers, and dancers with more opportunities to perform than were available to them at the Bolshoi and Maly Theaters It was for the New Theater and her close friend, the actress Evdokia Turchaninova, that several years later Shchepkina-Kupernik translated Friedrich Halm's *Wild Winds* (*Wildfeuer*), which she had seen in Vienna. She was intrigued by the gender-bending premise of the play: a medieval princess is raised as a boy for political reasons and doesn't even know she is female until she falls in love. Turchaninova, who from the age of twenty was often, to her dismay, cast by the Maly to play old ladies, told Shchepkina-Kupernik that at first she was terrified to appear on stage as a young boy. But the audacity of the transformation grew on her. With her tall, slim figure, she was a natural, at least at the beginning of her career, to play the role of a girl disguised as a page boy or young swain.

At the same time as the opening of Lensky's New Theater, Stanislavsky launched his Moscow Art Theater, taking up residence at the Hermitage Theater on Carriage Row. He had long dreamed of turning his Society of Art and Literature, essentially an informal theater group, into a professional company housed in a permanent theater. On June 22, 1897, Stanislavsky met with Vladimir Nemirovich-Danchenko, a playwright he knew only by reputation, at two o'clock for lunch in the dining room of the Slavyansky Bazaar Hotel. The meeting famously continued until eight o'clock the next morning, ending with breakfast at Stanislavsky's Moscow home. Nemirovich-Danchenko, whose plays were primarily produced for the moribund Maly, had grown frustrated dealing with the imperial theater's bureaucracy and decided to contact Stanislavsky. Over the course of their eighteen-hour meeting, the two men agreed to form a theater that would set reasonable ticket prices, decided which actors to invite to form a troupe, and divided their responsibilities—Nemirovich-Danchenko was in charge of the repertoire, Stanislavsky was in charge of staging. They also agreed it would take a year to properly set up the theater.[30]

The Art Theater's fall repertoire began with Alexei Tolstoy's historical drama *Tsar Fyodor Ivanovich* and ended on December 17 with Chekhov's *The Seagull*. Shchepkina-Kupernik attended every premiere and noticed the changes that Stanislavsky had made to the practices that were common in Korsh's and Suvorin's theaters. People were no longer allowed to enter the theater after the curtain went up. At the Hermitage Theater, Stanislavsky got rid of the large scratched-up mirror in the foyer and the large buffet. Instead, Shchepkina-Kupernik recalled, "there now reigned a stern, soft lighting, a quite tone . . . . a sort of concentrated silence." At first people complained that it was like a monastery, and didn't like not being allowed in if they arrived late. But eventually other theaters started imitating the Art Theater and "ended the disgusting practice of people wandering around at the back of the theater where it was considered chic to come in during the play and make as much noise as possible." Stanislavsky's actors, Shchepkina-Kupernik noted, were for the most part not from the ranks of established professionals. Many of the men had university educations, a rarity among professional actors, and the women were students or teachers. "They all were paid very little, went around in flimsy, worn-out coats, and were able to spend the whole night arguing about art or quarreling with each other endlessly about a mistaken interpretation of a role."[31]

After the disastrous premiere of *The Seagull* in St. Petersburg, Chekhov was understandably reluctant to repeat the humiliation in Moscow. Nemirovich-Danchenko had been a close friend of Chekhov for ten years, ever since the premiere of *Ivanov*. He wrote to Chekhov asking permission to mount a production, saying that he alone understood how to stage the play properly. Chekhov refused several times before relenting.

Given their working arrangement, it was Stanislavsky, rather than Nemirovich-Danchenko, who took charge of preparing the play. As had recently become his practice, he developed a "score" for the play, in which he broke down every act, every scene with detailed notes on each actor's mannerisms, expressions, and blocking, and also indicated the sound effects to be added to underscore the desired mood.[32] Together, Stanislavsky and Nemirovich-Danchenko rehearsed the play twenty-four times, including three dress rehearsals—a level of preparation unheard of in a Russian theater company. They meticulously checked the sets, the props, the sound effects. Stanislavsky still felt the play wasn't ready and wanted to postpone the opening for a week, but somehow Nemirovich-Danchenko talked him out of it.[33]

During the summer of 1898 Shchepkina-Kupernik renewed her friendship with the Chekhov family, first with Maria in Moscow, then visiting Anton at Melikhovo for a couple of days in July and again in August. She found everything here just as it had been before—the people, the flowers, the animals. Chekhov once again adopted a playful tone in his conversations and correspondence with Shchepkina-Kupernik, a tactic he often used to keep his women admirers at bay. He started calling her "Tatiana Yezhova," after threatening to marry her off to Nikolai Yezhov, a minor writer whom Chekhov found to be particularly annoying. She played along, sending a note in doggerel the next month in advance of their meeting in Moscow:

> Then come to me around six
> Or seven: I will await you
> And take you in my embrace!
> From here we can
> Go out again upon the waves

With the amiable-hearted Avelan
(Do you agree with my plan?)
More modestly than before . . . but just the same
As of old, to booze it up until first light!
We'll sit in a loge at Korsh's
Then have a bite to eat at my place.[34]

She signed the poem "Tatiana Yezhova."

The purpose of Chekhov's trip to Moscow was to watch preliminary rehearsals of *The Seagull*. During this visit, he found himself smitten by the troupe's lead actor, Olga Knipper. A few days later, he left for Yalta, banished again by his doctors after another incident of spitting up blood.

Aside from the joking, Shchepkina-Kupernik continued to seek Chekhov's approval for the success she was having as a writer and translator. On September 26 she sent him a breezy letter, in which she told him about her recent literary accomplishments: three stories published in *The Russian Gazette*, *New Times*, and *Family*, and a translation in verse, "a trifle that will run at an imperial theater."[35] Two of the stories were part of a series she was calling The Nobodies of This World, portraits of the downtrodden painted with Dickensian pathos. In her fiction, Shchepkina-Kupernik was beginning to focus on stories about the growing chasm between the urban rich and the poor.

Included in the letter was a clipping from the September 23 issue of *New Times*. It was a caricature by the painter Alexandra Khotyaintseva of Chekhov standing in a line in a room of the Tretyakov Gallery to get a peek at his portrait painted by Osip Braz. Chekhov had confided to Khotyaintseva that he didn't much like the portrait, claiming it made him look like he had just inhaled a lot of horseradish. Shchepkina-Kupernik wrote Chekhov that Khotyaintseva and Maria Chekhova had "started painting my portrait, which possibly will look more like me than yours, but alas will never end up in the Tretyakov Gallery."

Shchepkina-Kupernik confessed that she missed the emotional intensity of those who used to gather at the Louvre. She and Maria Chekhova, whom she affectionately called "Musya," had recently gone to a club to listen to gypsies until 5 a.m. It reminded her of the old days, but the evening "was more sad than happy. One recalled how many people have broken away from our former group of friends." Like Mizinova, Shchepkina-Kupernik invented phony suitors to tease Chekhov into jealousy, telling him that she planned to visit him in Yalta "if I don't end up in Paris, where I am being summoned by a 70-year-old bishop from the Spanish court who is in love with me. Am I making good conquests? Instead of him, I would prefer a good officer, but alas, they disapprove of 'old ladies with plays,'" as Chekhov had jokingly called her and her peers.

Writing back, Chekhov complained he was "as bored as a sturgeon" and thinking of putting on an amateur production at the Yalta Women's Gymnasium. He asked her to send him her play *Eternity in a Moment*: "You see how I concern myself with your fame. No sooner do they mention an amateur production, I immediately bring up your work." But three days later in a follow-up letter, he turned his request into a joke: "I want to give a lecture here 'on the decline of dramatic art through degeneracy'—and I need to read selections from your plays and show the audience some photographs—of you and the actor Garin." In the same vein, he again brought up the rise of "ladies with plays," saying the only way "to combat this calamity" was to summon them all to the Muir & Mirrielees, the Scottish department store next to the Maly Theater, and set the place on fire. The humor of Chekhov's correspondence with Shchepkina-Kupernik reflected an easing of their previous strained relationship. He signed one of his letters "Your benefactor and godfather Povsekaky" ("Shit-on-everything").[36] Encouraged, Shchepkina-Kupernik made a concerted effort to stay in his good graces.

On December 17, Shchepkina-Kupernik attended the Moscow premiere of *The Seagull*, sensing, as the play began, a heightened tension among both the audience and the actors. There were empty seats in the house. Cast members had calmed themselves by taking Valerian drops. The audience remained hushed during the first act. Stanislavsky was so worried about Nina's monologue, which begins Treplyov's "decadent" play ("People, lions, eagles and partridges . . . "), that he sat in the dark with his back to the audience grabbing a foot that was starting to twitch. But unlike what had happened in St. Petersburg, there were no catcalls. At the end of act 1, Dorn gently comforts Masha, who has just confessed her hopeless love for Treplyov and kneels sobbing at the doctor's knees. Stanislavsky's stage directions called for a fifteen-second pause during which the sound of a waltz grows louder, a church bell tolls, frogs croak, and the night watchman pounds his staff. Then Dorn says, "What can I do, my dear child? What? What?" The curtain comes down. Shchepkina-Kupernik recalled that at first there was a prolonged silence, which the actors interpreted as failure. But then came wild applause, "a hurricane of enthusiasm." The actors took six curtain calls and by the end of act 3 they "were weeping with excitement and embracing one another."³⁷ Suvorin had been right in his defense of the play after the fiasco in St. Petersburg. All it had needed was the right production (at a private theater), one that understood the author's sensibilities, to be seen as the masterpiece that it was.

Shchepkina-Kupernik came out of the theater feeling intoxicated and at 12:20 a.m. sent Chekhov a telegram: "I warmly congratulate you on the colossal success of *The Seagull*. I am happy for you." Forty minutes later she sat down to write him a more detailed letter "with still fresh impressions having just returned from the theater." She described the curtain call after the third act, when the audience began to call for the actor and "Nemirovich, smiling like a cat who'd been scratched behind the ears, announced that the author wasn't in the theater. Shouts rang out: 'Send a telegram.' The noise was terrifying. He responded: 'Should I send a telegram?' The answer was a hundred voices saying, 'Yes, we want you to, we want you to! . . . It was a surprisingly emotional moment."³⁸

Her description continued in an ecstatic, lyrical tone: "I can say that something striking took place on stage: it wasn't a play, life itself was being created. The details of the production were masterpieces of directorial art." She praised Lilina, Stanislavsky's wife, as Masha: "I saw for the first time a real woman on stage." Meyerhold was "remarkable" as Treplyov, "nervous, young, touching." Knipper was "very good" as Arkadina. The only actor she criticized was Roskanova as Nina: "She was positively bad. There wasn't sufficient poetry: a common provincial girl with a southern Russian accent."

Chekhov was grateful for Shchepkina-Kupernik's missives: "I received your telegram and was touched to the depths of my heart. Your letter arrived first and you were, so to speak, the first swallow, bearing me news about *The Seagull*, my sweet unforgettable godmother."³⁹ He reminded her that he had requested a book of her verse and mentioned that he had read her poem "At the Cemetery," which had appeared in the *New Times*. In the poem, the poet, attending a funeral at which a cluster of "dark nuns stood motionless, indifferent to the tears of grief," notices two very young nuns who "suddenly lifted their eyes—and burned us with their glance," a glance of agonizing envy for those who suffer and cry but are free. Chekhov told her that the poem was "simply a charm, completely magnificent." He seemed to appreciate that like him, she understood that what makes us feel most alive is the recognition of our shared suffering in the absence of any expectation of a heavenly reward.

CHAPTER 8

Sons of Israel

In the spring of 1899, Shchepkina-Kupernik, Yavorskaya, and Baryatinsky were invited to take part in celebrations commemorating the centennial of Pushkin's birth. Accompanied by Yury Yuriev from the Alexandrinsky Theater, they traveled south to Pushkin's grave at Holy Assumption Monastery of St. Sviatogorsky. There, at a wooden theater specially constructed for the occasion, Shchepkina-Kupernik recited her poem "In Memory of Pushkin," recently published in the January 31 edition of the *New Times*. Yavorskaya read Lermontov's "On the Death of a Poet" and "Monument." Baryatinsky recited his French translations of an excerpt from *Eugene Onegin* and six other Pushkin poems. The evening was concluded with Yavorskaya and Yuriev performing scenes from Pushkin's *The Stone Guest* and *Boris Godunov*.[1]

The actors repeated their performance in nearby Pskov. Afterward they were invited by city officials to a farewell dinner aboard a steamer bathed in electric light docked at a wharf on the banks of the Velikaya River. At the dinner Baryatinsky was asked once again to recite from his translation of *Onegin*. When he finished, Yuriev recalled, someone in the audience expressed regret that Pushkin's birth wasn't being celebrated abroad.

Knowing that Yavorskaya and her husband often acted on impulse, Yuriev wasn't surprised when soon after their return to St. Petersburg, they invited him to join them in the summer for yet another celebratory evening of Pushkin that they had booked at a small theater on the Boulevard des Capucines in Paris. The twenty-seven-year-old Yuriev was thrilled by the experience of going abroad for the first time, traveling to Paris first-class on the deluxe Nord-Express and staying at Baryatinsky's two-story apartment on a lane off Avenue Victor Hugo, all at the prince's expense. Peeking through the curtain before their performance, Yuriev noticed a few Russian expatriates in the audience, but was most impressed to see Jean Mounet-Sully and his brother Paul, two stars of the Comédie-Française, also in attendance. Yavorskaya took advantage of their stay in Paris to once again visit Rostand, who diplomatically expressed gratitude for her championing of his plays in Russia.

Yavorskaya and Baryatinsky returned from Paris to their newly furnished "palazzo" at 65 Ligovsky Prospect not far from the Nikolaevsky train station. With the sizable inheritance Baryatinsky received upon the death of his maternal grandmother, which his father had no legal right to block,[2] they were now able to afford a splendid residence—its twelve rooms encompassed more than two thousand three hundred square feet on two floors. Shchepkina-Kupernik often stayed at "Ligovka 65" when she was in St. Petersburg. Yavorskaya turned the apartment into a stage set suitable for the high drama of her daily life. She remodeled the main staircase into a copy of the Paris Grand Opera. The entryway, with its Egyptian columns decorated with ibises and lotuses, led to a staircase winding up to the Ludwig XV salon on the second floor, a white and gold rococo living room suitable for hosting grand soirees. Yuriev recalled that at Yavorskaya's, "you could meet everyone there! Journalists, writers, artists, musicians, every possible sort of theater person, interviewers, photographers. They all crowded the house day and night after every performance almost until morning."[3] Shchepkina-Kupernik, whose own living quarters were purposefully modest, found the decor—the flower arrangements scattered everywhere, the Chinese porcelain vases, the heavy drapes—to be clumsy, a "veritable mishmash, amusing, motley, but appropriately framing the motley, fussy life that went on in the house."[4]

During one of her stays at Ligovka, Shchepkina-Kupernik was working at a desk when a servant came in to ask whether she should let in an artist who claimed that the princess had given him permission in her absence to draw the grand staircase as background for a portrait.

Shchepkina-Kupernik glanced out into the vestibule and saw a short man dressed in a shabby jacket and wearing a carelessly knotted tie. "He wasn't good looking," she noted. "He had long hair, a slovenly, stringy little beard. He had small, deep-set eyes, but they were penetratingly attentive—this, if you will, more than anything else in his appearance made him look like an artist." She told the servant to let him in but to be sure to keep an eye on their fur coats. Soon Yavorskaya returned and introduced Shchepkina-Kupernik to the painter—it was Ilya Repin. She was floored: "He was to me as great a painter as Titian."[5]

The two women came to know Repin quite well. He introduced them to his new wife, Natalia Nordman, who, Shchepkina-Kupernik soon discovered, had quite eccentric progressive views. Nordman on occasion insisted on seating her cook and doorman at the dinner table, which only managed to make both the servants and the guests uncomfortable. She also was a passionate vegetarian, converting a dutiful Repin to a diet of herbal soups, vegetable stew, rice and cabbage piroshki, custards, compotes, fruits, and nuts.

Repin's first attempt at a portrait of Yavorskaya went no further than an incomplete sketch, but in 1910 she sat for him at his studio, where he completed an oil painting now in a private collection in England. The year before, Repin had sketched Baryatinsky, and four years later he painted a strongly colored oil portrait of a cheerfully plump Shchepkina-Kupernik.

None of these paintings, however, achieved the masterfulness of Repin's remarkable portrait (1899) of Yavorskaya's and Shchepkina-Kupernik's mutual friend, Baroness Varvara Iskul von Hildebrandt, which now hangs in the Tretyakov Gallery. Shchepkina-Kupernik recognized the brilliance of the work: "In the portrait you see a shapely, tall woman in a bright red silk blouse, wearing a strange hat and with a remarkably drawn veil over her face. . . . It seems that you could lift the veil, so lightly does it fall over the face, covering but not hiding the delicate features of the beautiful face, dark eyes, gazing piercingly and boldly, and the strong chin."[6] The baroness lived in an elegant house filled with Roman paintings and sculptures—her husband was the Russian ambassador to Italy. Yavorskaya had consciously decorated her home in imitation of the baroness's, but Shchepkina-Kupernik felt that where the baroness furnished her rooms over the course of twenty years with a "quiet luxury," everything in the Baryatinsky house "felt like temporary decorations."[7] Iskul von Hildebrandt was the president of several societies that funded medical institutes, hospitals, and clinics.

According to Shchepkina-Kupernik, her charitable interests caused those in the highest society to look askance at her, branding her as a "red," but that didn't stop ministers, generals, and academics, as well as prominent artists, from attending her salons.

By 1899 Suvorin's stubbornly antisemitic views on the Dreyfus affair were causing friends and colleagues to disassociate themselves from him and his newspaper. He continued to doubt that the Jewish officer was innocent of spying for Austro-Hungary even after the French government acquitted Dreyfus. Suvorin had long accused liberals of pandering to Jews, whom he felt were competing with and displacing Russians, thereby weakening the nation. He had written two plays, the drama *Tatiana Repina* (1888) and the comedy *Stockmarket Fever* (1896), that featured villainous Jewish bankers. By the late 1890s Jews in Russia experienced harsher restrictions on their freedom than anywhere else in Europe. Most were confined to the Pale of Settlement, a section of western Russia established by Catherine the Great. In 1897 Moscow's governor-general ordered a massive expulsion of Jews illegally residing in the city.

That year, in his regular column, Suvorin complained about being forced to explain his use of the word "Yid" [zhid] when he wasn't responsible for creating its "offensive meaning," which was the "collective verdict of the Russian people . . . . the sum, so to speak, of the moral filth, which comprises the majority of Jewry [evreistvo]."[8] Such sentiments caused Chekhov to begin distancing himself from Suvorin, who had been the closest thing to a mentor for the past ten years.

Baryatinsky joined those who had decided to no longer write for the *New Times*. Now that the prince had come into his inheritance, he planned to spend it on a long-held dream: starting his own newspaper. However, more than just funding was required to launch a newspaper. The increasingly conservative government had stopped approving requests to publish newspapers that were not subject to prior censorship. Baryatinsky's only recourse was to find a publisher who already had been granted rights to put out a daily paper. After a long search, his colleague and business partner Konstantin Arabazhin located such an owner, paying him five thousand rubles for the *Severnyi Kur'er* (*Northern Courier*).[9] The first issue came out on November 1, 1899.

Judging by its contributors, the publication leaned decidedly to the left. Political and economic issues were covered by the moderate Marxist Peter Struve. Maxim Gorky wrote articles for the literature section.

Shchepkina-Kupernik had recently met Gorky at a literary evening in Moscow. She couldn't help but notice him—he wore a worker's blouse and high boots in a room full of elegantly dressed women and men in black frock coats. At first, she thought he was a plumber or mechanic who had come to fix something. "He had a face that wasn't handsome," she recalled, "but spontaneously attracted attention: a vigorous forehead, relatively long hair, a lock which fell across his forehead, bright eyes beneath stern brows, and a gaze that was bold, free, and piercing, the look of a man of significance. I continued to look him over, not sure who he was and what he was doing here."[10]

When she was introduced to Gorky, he blurted out, "Well, I'll be damned!" and proceeded to lavishly praise her translation of *Cyrano*, saying it was possibly better than the French original. She joined Gorky in writing for the *Northern Courier*. The newspaper struck her as having "the most curious mix of contributors from all parties and directions. . . . Here there were both Marxists and those who thought of themselves as Marxists, members of the People's Will, and Social Democrats, and terrorists. Here, of course, there were also provocateurs."[11] But it was clear they all had a common desire to battle with the current regime. She wrote a poem dedicated to the *Northern Courier* in which the newspaper was compared to a sower of seeds on a parched landscape who was filled with the hope that a future generation "will gather abundantly the rich harvest" of his efforts.[12]

From the start, the *Northern Courier* took on what it considered to be the *New Times*' "judo-phobia." On the "Jewish question," Baryatinsky wrote that it was a social question, not a national one: "There is no Jewish nationality, they have no common language, they have no national territory; they are, more or less, rightful and assimilated citizens of various countries."[13] For him Russia's Jewish population was sharply divided into two groups—a wealthy business class and a poor class of craftsmen and laborers. These two distinct classes shared a common interest only when they were both victims of exclusion. Otherwise, the differences among Jews were just as strong as those within other groups of people.

Suvorin saw Baryatinsky's publication as a personal betrayal and a competitive threat. It didn't help that when Suvorin wrote to Chekhov in Yalta in early January 1900, sharing the latest circulation numbers in St. Petersburg and asking why the *Northern Courier* was enjoying so much success, Chekhov responded, "Because our society is exhausted. It is rotting from hatefulness and souring like grass in a swamp, and it wants something fresh, free, light. It wants it desperately!" Chekhov confessed that he had previously misjudged Baryatinsky: "They will, of course, close down his newspaper, but his reputation as a good journalist will long remain after him."[14]

For Suvorin, Baryatinsky's success only intensified the rancor he felt toward him and, most especially, his wife. On March 5 at a rehearsal for Lermontov's *Masquerade*, he argued with Yavorskaya about her request to put *The Dream Princess* back into the repertoire. As far as he was concerned, it was a play designed only to appeal to those with vulgar tastes. The argument left him depressed: "I'm sick of the theater with its artists, requests, and debuts. Most importantly, I'm terribly sick of myself."[15] That night at his theater, he watched Yavorskaya perform her death scene in *Masquerade*. He was astonished: "She was on her hands and knees facing the audience, and while she crawled forward, her breasts spilled out of her corset. Very realistic! These Baryatinskys love advertising. The prince loves it just as much as his wife."[16]

However, for the past year, the notoriety of Prince Vladimir's marriage to Yavorskaya within Petersburg high society had been eclipsed by the scandal of his older brother Prince Alexander's affair with the astonishingly beautiful Italian café chanteuse, Lina Cavalieri. Alexander had met her in the fall of 1897 during one of her St. Petersburg engagements and followed her to Paris, where she was starring in the *Folies Bergère*. He spent lavishly on her and encouraged her to abandon the variety stage by paying for her opera lessons. By 1899 there were rumors in the Petersburg popular press that they had gotten married. Although Cavalieri, in her unreliable memoirs, claimed that she and Prince Alexander had gotten married, there's no legal record of it.[17] Given the Baryatinsky family's failure to prevent Prince Vladimir's marriage to an actress, it is very likely that they (and the tsar) this time took the necessary measures to prevent or invalidate a marriage to a low-born woman whom they saw as a femme fatale out to snag the Baryatinsky title and fortune. They found a suitable bride for Prince Alexander—Princess Ekaterina Yurevskaya, the daughter of Alexander II's mistress. Cavalieri went on to a long career in opera and silent films. In 1955 Gina Lollabrigida appeared in a fictionalized film about Cavalieri called *La Donna Più Bella del Mondo* (*The Most Beautiful Woman in the World*) with Vittorio Gassmann as Prince Sergei, who was modeled after Alexander Baryatinsky.[18]

In the spring of 1900 Vladimir Baryatinsky was again in the public spotlight, for less salacious reasons, as he continued to pursue a vigorous battle against the conservative press, which was attracting the attention of government censors. When Esper Ukhtomsky, the publisher of the *St. Petersburg Gazette* and a close confidant of the tsar, accused Baryatinsky of being a womanizer who was living off his wife's earnings, which were procured by "unknown services" for Suvorin and his organization, the prince decided to file a complaint before a civil "court of honor."[19] At the hearing, which took place on May 3, Ukhtomsky remained defiant. He spoke for ninety minutes, insisting that Baryatinsky had no moral right to accuse high society of being debauched, when he himself led a debauched life while his wife frequented "a thousand dressing rooms."[20] Yavorskaya had encouraged her husband to stand his ground, but the "porcelain prince" had a delicate nature not well suited to countering such bare-knuckled accusations. In his testimony he called Okhtomsky a "bald-faced liar," but then asked to have it stricken from the record. A delegation of students and workers attended the hearing to support Baryatinsky, but in the end the panel of jurists ruled against the prince's claim.

Yavorskaya dropped by Suvorin's apartment at midnight to tell him what had happened. She said Baryatinsky had defended himself poorly, that he had "become a bit flustered." Suvorin took no pleasure in the prince's humiliation, given that Ukhtomsky had used the incident to attack him as well as Baryatinsky. "You couldn't find a viler creature than this Prince Ukhtomsky," he wrote in his diary, furious that Ukhtomsky had publicly accused him of being a Machiavellian who supported both the *New Times* and the *Northern Courier*, two newspapers with opposite political views, for the sole purpose of destroying the *St. Petersburg Gazette*.[21]

Unhappy with the outcome, Baryatinsky decided to challenge Ukhtomsky to a duel, precisely the type of "satisfaction" that military and civilian courts of honor had been set up to quash. Yavorskaya and others unsuccessfully tried to talk him out of it. The encounter ended with Baryatinsky getting lightly wounded in the arm.[22] Afterward, he began to feel more pessimistic about his ability to continue his journalistic struggle. Lev Tolstoy had told him: "It's futile to fight against the conditions surrounding you while continuing to live within them. It makes more sense to create your own unique personal life."[23] But the prince's personal and professional life was inextricably linked with his wife's, who owed her livelihood to his journalistic and political rival. The arrangement was unsustainable, particularly because Suvorin felt increasingly fed up with Yavorskaya as an actor. When she performed

The Lady of the Camellias at the Oranienbaum palace theater outside of St. Petersburg that summer, Suvorin reacted with hostility to the *St. Petersburg Gazette*'s glowing review: "What scum these reviewers are, vulgar and ignorant, using nothing but clumps of clichés. . . . Yavorskaya plays Marguerite Gautier as a libertine, as a spent courtesan with her guttural voice lacking in intonation, lacking in expressiveness."[24]

In early November 1900, Suvorin announced to his actors that they were to begin rehearsing *Sons of Israel*. They were familiar with the play because in 1898 its authors, Savely Litvin and Victor Krylov, had approached them about putting on a production. After a few rehearsals, the troupe refused to take it on. Litvin, whose real name was Efron, was a Jew who had converted to Russian Orthodoxy and made a name for himself publishing antisemitic stories that were popular in reactionary circles. With the help of Krylov, an established playwright who in 1887 made Chekhov the unwanted offer to fix *Ivanov*, Litvin adapted one of his stories into the play *Sons of Israel*. At first the authors had hoped to have the play produced at the Alexandrinsky Theater, since Krylov had connections there as the head of its repertory department. The theater's chief administrator approved a production, but its managing director, Vladimir Telyakovsky, found it to be "a tendentious attack on the Jews, besides being written not seriously but shallowly."[25] Concerned that the play would "stir up a mob," he managed to delay scheduling the production until the theater appointed a new chief administrator, who, as it turned out, had no interest in having the play appear on the imperial stage.

Sons of Israel concerns a Jewish community living in the Pale of Settlement on Russia's western border, some of whom are involved in smuggling goods to avoid Russian-imposed tariffs. In the first act, on a melodramatic stormy night, two families gather at an inn and prepare to light the Shabbat candles as they await the return of one of the smugglers, Mikhel Reddikh. Sarah Goldenweiser, the daughter of the rich businessman Moshe, accuses her father of hypocritically condoning smuggling activities during Shabbat, when according to tradition all labor should cease. The theme of Jewish hypocrisy is further underscored when the local court magistrate appears at the door, his carriage having broken down nearby. The magistrate is attracted to Sarah, and he doubts her when she says that her arranged engagement to the repulsive rabbi Sender reflects her own wishes. "Wiliness—that's the greatest talent of your people," he tells her.[26] After the magistrate leaves, Mikhel finally returns to the inn. He has killed a border guard. Two guards come to the inn bearing the body. In the final scene of the first act, the guards witness the two families seated at a long table covered with food and lighted candles, Mikhel hidden among them. Sarah's cries of anguish are drowned out by the rising voices praying: "Bless me with peace, angels of peace!" The scene is designed to compel the audience to feel outraged by Jewish criminality disguised as religious devotion.

The magistrate, investigating the murder scene, finds Mikhel's revolver. Moshe and Sender decide to pin the murder on Yushke, an apostate Jew, by telling the magistrate the gun is his. They also concoct a scheme to compromise the magistrate, assuming he will be unable to resist making advances toward Sarah if they send her alone to him with the community's offer to donate money to the widow of the border guard. The magistrate arrests Yushke, who when interrogated admits to smuggling but implicates Mikhel as the murderer. When Sarah visits the magistrate, he asks her whether she thinks Mikhel took part in the murder. She understands that the magistrate is asking her to betray her community: "Do I really dare to prefer you over my own people? Place you, a stranger, a Christian, above my own? But this is a terrible sin! . . . But what can I do when my mind doesn't let me think otherwise? I see that you are good and honest, not they. I would like to hate you like they do, but I can't."[27] She cries on his breast. He embraces her, trying to calm her down. Her fiancé Sender bursts in, telling the magistrate he has come to take her home, just as Sarah had requested. Sensing that he has been set up, the magistrate heaps abuse on Sarah: "A Jewess, a Jewess to the very last drop of your blood! You are worse than they are . . . They deceive, steal, murder, but they are completely vile creatures to be wary of. But you came here in the guise of an angel . . ."[28]

In the last act, Sarah writes a note to her father saying she has decided to escape her forced marriage by going to live in St. Petersburg. When she goes to the magistrate's office to reconcile with him before leaving, he offers to marry her. She refuses, saying she would never convert to Christianity and, if necessary, is willing to follow her father into exile. Moshe enters and begs her to return to the community. She refuses and embraces him to say farewell. He turns off the lamp, then leads Sarah out the door into the garden where Sender and another accomplice grab her. Moshe then kills her. When Moshe confesses his crime, the magistrate screams out: "Religious fanatics!"

Suvorin assigned Karpov, who was responsible for the disastrous premiere of *The Seagull*, to direct *Sons of Israel*. Tinsky, a Jew, was cast as

Moshe. Karpov asked Yavorskaya to play Sarah. She had taken part in the preliminary rehearsals in 1898 and had even asked Krylov to help her establish the right tone in her portrayal of Sarah.[29] But this time, she refused to play the role. On November 12, she wrote to Karpov: "Having attentively reread the play *Sons of Israel*, I have come to the conclusion that on principle I cannot act in it. I consider this play an incitement to ethnic hatred and consequently a provocation of the worst instincts of the mob. I am sincerely sorry to have to turn down a role cast by you, but I think that in your heart of hearts you cannot but sympathize with me."[30] To save face, Karpov told Suvorin that Yavorskaya had been the choice of the play's authors, while he had always much preferred Maria Domasheva, the actress whom Chekhov's brother Alexander had called the "concubine" of the theater's lawyer Nikolai Kholeva. When Savina, Komissarzhevskaya's rival at the Alexandrinsky Theater, heard about the refusal, she wrote her husband that Yavorskaya was a scoundrel: "That hussy should be thrown out of the place."[31]

The next day Baryatinsky made Yavorskaya's protest public by printing in his newspaper that she had refused to take part in the play "in view of its tendentiousness, which has nothing in common with artistic literature or the tasks of art."[32] Hoping to deflect criticism of the play as an attack on Jews, Karpov retitled it *The Smugglers* and looked for ways to soften the script during rehearsals. On November 16, Suvorin speciously offered a correction to what had been written in the *Northern Courier*, publishing a note in the *New Times* that the Literary-Artistic Circle was not putting on *Sons of Israel*, but rather *The Smugglers*, which "depicted the morals of the Russian Jews living on the western border and engaged in smuggling. The Literary-Artistic Circle theater accepted this play precisely with this title, which accurately conveys the contents of the play."[33]

Suvorin's riposte only heightened the polemical battle between the two newspapers. In addition, two days before the premiere, Yavorskaya and Baryatinsky invited Tinsky to their apartment and tried to browbeat him into dropping out of the production. Everyone was having a late breakfast in the blue living room. The gathering included Baryatinsky's partner Arabazhin and the newspaper's head typesetter. The prince urged Tinsky to avoid being part of the inevitable scandal of the premiere. He made it clear that his newspaper was preparing an article that would blow up in the faces of every participant in the "foul production." Baryatinsky assured Tinsky that he and his wife wouldn't attend "in order not to be present at the torture that is being prepared for you."³⁴ Tinsky protested that it would be un-collegial to quit at this late date, but Yavorskaya said she doubted that an actor of his caliber would be fired for it. At the dress rehearsal that evening Tinsky declared he was quitting, but contrary to Yavorskaya's assurances he was told that this would result in his being expelled from the company.³⁵ Forced to continue, Tinsky became furious at Yavorskaya and her husband for engineering his humiliation in the presence of his fellow actors.

On November 22 and 23, the *Northern Courier* published two articles on *The Smugglers*. The first summarized the plot of the play based on Suvorin's published version. The second article, published on the day of the premiere, was a full-throated condemnation of the production:

> It is a slander against the entire Jewish people, shameless, not based on anything; a disturbing, indiscriminate accusation against an entire nation for the lowliest crimes, for immorality and a blind fanaticism . . . And this is the kind of play that they want to put on stage, albeit with some softening of the script, albeit under the modest title *The Smugglers*.
>
> Up until now antisemitism has been the lot of a few newspapers, acting on the confused thinking of its readers. Now in a live image, it wants to influence the feelings and fantasies of the viewer. This is a broadening of the sphere of nationalist intolerance and maliciousness, which threatens to result in the most grievous of consequences. Arousing the passions and ugly instincts of the crowd, antisemitism on the stage can lead to new pogroms.³⁶

The "Petersburger" columnist for the *New Times* replied: "Various 'singers of Judaism' are trying to convince the public, which isn't familiar with the play, that the authors 'slander' the Jews. Really? What are the authors and the management of the Literary-Artistic Circle guilty of if Jews really engage in smuggling, if in our western border provinces more than ninety percent of the smugglers are Jews?" The author asserted that data from the Customs Tariff Department backed these figures.³⁷ Baryatinsky countered:

> The defenders of Mr. Efron's play refer to the fact that the percentage of Jews among criminal smugglers is very high. This question, in reality, is of little interest to us . . . Jews live packed together in the Pale of Settlement. They are denied the opportunity to pursue many professions. Is it necessary to be surprised that living on the border, they comprise a huge percentage of smugglers? The entire

border population without exception smuggles . . . Enough with us hypocritically piling onto one unhappy tribe, driven out for a thousand years, such sins and inadequacies, which are completely evenly distributed among all peoples and various social classes.[38]

The *Northern Courier*'s attacks on *The Smugglers* and Yavorskaya's refusal to perform in it had drawn the attention of St. Petersburg University students, who had long been among her most devoted fans. Leading up to the premiere, students held meetings at the university and several technical colleges called for the closing of the production. This, in turn, resulted in the formation of coordinating committees that began to develop strategies "to prevent the performance of the play by any means necessary." The theater's box-office manager noticed that students were buying blocks of twenty to thirty seats in the gallery, not caring "whether they could see or not."[39] Fourteen student leaders met the night before the premiere to make final preparations for their protest. They distributed free tickets, called on everyone "to take care to bring noisemakers and whistles, but only such things that may be thrown on stage without harm to the well-being of the actors." Section leaders were assigned to signal when to start the disturbance. They agreed "not to leave the auditorium until the performance is conclusively ruined."[40]

Suvorin was aware that students were planning to create a demonstration at the premiere, and on November 18 he went to Moscow to see Chekhov, who was making preparations to leave for the south of France for the winter. In his diary Suvorin wrote that he had every intention of returning to St. Petersburg for the dress rehearsal on November 22, but that Chekhov had talked him out of it, saying that if he stayed, there was a chance they could visit Tolstoy. That left Suvorin's son-in-law Alexei Kolomnin in charge of the final rehearsal, and he is likely the one who had to deal with Tinsky's last-minute attempt to drop out of the production.

A mix of fashionable men and women and more shabbily dressed students streamed into the theater on the evening of November 23.[41] A notice indicating that the performance was sold out was posted at the box office. Nevertheless, a group of students who had been unable to get tickets had gathered outside the theater. Standing in front of them was a large group of police officers who had been summoned by the stage manager to maintain order. Inside the theater the audience took their seats and waited in tense silence for the curtain to go up. Suddenly there was an uproar in the gallery—a group of ticketless students had broken through the police lines and rushed into the theater. The police followed in pursuit and started evicting anyone without a ticket. After a few minutes, order was restored.

The audience started rhythmically clapping, signaling for the curtain to be raised. As soon as it went up, students in the gallery and balcony sections leaned over the rails and started yelling, "Bring it down!" People in the boxes and stalls yelled back, "Shut up, you bastards!" As the actors began speaking their lines, they were drowned out by the stomping of feet and the shriek of a chorus of boatswain's whistles coming from the balcony. The actors had to dodge volleys of cucumbers, onions, garlic, and potatoes being thrown at them as they moved about the stage. Tinsky noticed with fury that Baryatinsky, Yavorskaya, and Arabazhin, despite their promise to stay away, were in fact present. "From the stage," he later wrote, "I saw how Ms. Yavorskaya from her loge was enjoying the turmoil created by her genius."[42] Someone in the stalls yelled at her: "Tramp, numbskull, throw her out of the theater!" She stood up to say something, but was shouted down by hecklers. With people shaking their fists at her, she and the prince quickly left their loge seats. Yavorskaya decided to go to the home of her friend the Baroness Iskul von Hildebrandt to wait there until things quieted down. The prince went briefly to his newspaper office before returning home. Meanwhile, the police started pulling some students from their seats and escorting them out of the theater.

When the curtain went down on the first act, the audience applauded and the hall grew quiet, although there was still some shouting and commotion coming from the corridors and foyer. Karpov came out in front of the curtain and signaled that he wanted to say something. But before he could open his mouth, the stomping, whistles, and catcalls resounded again. He tried to shout over the din, but then someone hurled a galosh, which was followed by a barrage of pickles, potatoes, and onions. He retreated backstage. He was met by the writer Daniil Mordovtsev, who had been sitting in Yavorskaya's box. Mordovtsev begged Karpov to stop the performance, saying it had devolved into a political demonstration that would result in mass student arrests. An incensed Karpov shouted back at him: "Go ahead and let them!" Kolomnin, feeling sick, paced nervously backstage, his hands and lips trembling. He was upset that Suvorin had stubbornly insisted on staging the play, and then had left him to face the repercussions while his father-in-law sat having a nice dinner with

Chekhov at the Slavyansky Bazaar restaurant in Moscow. Kolomnin decided to call off the play but was told by a police official that the city provost's office had telephoned and ordered that the play must continue, no matter what.

The actors were told of the decision to continue. This time when the curtain went up, police officers ringed the stage, giving the demonstrators the opportunity to start throwing vegetables at them rather than the actors. A direct hit was met with laughter and applause, creating a carnival atmosphere. More seriously, a policeman who was removing a young woman from the gallery was tripped and the two of them tumbled to the floor. When he got up and started dragging her out by the hair screaming, a group of students rushed to help her, and they were joined by more police, resulting in a melee. Pandemonium followed. More protesters were dragged from their seats, beaten, and pushed down the stairs. Some ran to the box office demanding their money back. The final curtain was lowered and the actors, still wearing their makeup, escaped out the back door with the police escorting them. As people streamed out of the exits, a contingent of firefighters with torches and a platoon of mounted gendarmes held back the crowd that had started to gather on the embankment. During the riot in the theater, seventy-two people were arrested, forty-three of them students. Over the next few days, almost a hundred more were briefly taken into custody and released.[43] Two thousand students staged a walkout at the university, resulting in thirty-two expulsions.

Late in the evening Yavorskaya returned home, but she was awakened at 3 a.m. by a police officer bearing a summons. She screamed at him that she wasn't some sort of criminal to be seized in the middle of the night on false pretenses, and declared that she would immediately lodge a complaint with the minister of internal affairs, which she did later in the morning. The ministry backed off.[44] The police, however, continued their informal surveillance of Yavorskaya, having started a dossier on her earlier in the year that listed performances and gatherings that could be considered political agitation. One entry noted a reading she gave in February at a workers' hall on the outskirts of the city, where she recited the banned verse of Vladimir Bogoraz-Tan, a writer who had been arrested and exiled for his association with the revolutionary wing of the radical group the People's Will. Another entry described an evening soiree in March at the Baryatinskys' apartment attended by fifty students. "Yavorskaya's house," wrote one police officer, "is a breeding ground for harmful inclinations among the youth."[45]

Suvorin arrived by express train from Moscow at noon on November 24. When he got home, the servants told him about the riot at the theater. He went upstairs hoping to get more details from Kolomnin but was told that his son-in-law had gone to the Senate to defend a case. Suvorin decided to go to his office and write one of his "Little Letters" to be published in his newspaper. In it he made light of what had happened, insisting that the play was nothing more than "cheerful nonsense, a vaudeville," whose significance the public had exaggerated. After all, he pointed out, all sorts of negative types are depicted in Russian literature and on stage, not excluding "Jews, Armenians, Greeks, and Tatars." As soon as he finished the piece, his wife and son came into his office with the shocking news that Kolomnin, having gone to the Suvorin bookstore after his Senate appearance, had suddenly collapsed and died of a heart attack. Suvorin was dumbstruck. "This death," he wrote in his diary, "painted the scandal in different colors. That which I heard later from Yavorskaya, Arabazhin, and Prince Baryatinsky, who fomented the scandal, was beyond impudent." He was certain that for Kolomnin the stress of being backstage during the riot had "cut short his life."[46] Suvorin pulled his "letter" and substituted another in which he said that due to Kolomnin's death, "my readers will understand that right now I cannot participate in any way in current publishing activities."[47]

Nevertheless, the *New Times* did manage to publish several antisemitic letters to the editor regarding the performance before the Central Press Directorate decided to issue official instructions forbidding newspapers to print anything about *The Smugglers* or the scandal at the theater. One reader noted that "the whistling came exclusively from the upper seats, jam-packed with young students of the splendid Jewish kind." The desire to protest the performance, according to this reader, was the result of "a new 'Exodus' of Jews to the theater, turning it with their endeavors into a cow barn with its noise and filth." He quoted a Hungarian government official who was reputed to have said, "You only have to step on one Yid's toes to raise a shout and hubbub throughout all of Europe." Another reader said he had overheard one of the students racing to the box office say: "Let's get our money back and use it to get a ticket for the next production!" A third reader protested that the general censor had allowed the play to be produced, "but for Jews one censor for the Russian theater isn't enough. They want to have their own personal censor for everything that has to do with Judaism."[48]

Suvorin, a consistent foe of press censorship, wrote a sharp letter to the head of the Press Directorate opposing the instructions. Together he and the head of the directorate went to see Ivan Durnovo, president of the Council of Ministers, who refused to wave the decree. Durnovo blamed Suvorin for putting on the play in the first place, and for allowing the sale of block tickets to students. The minister feared that continued press reports about the riot would only serve to exacerbate tensions over the "Jewish question." Suvorin argued without success that muzzling the press would only make martyrs out of Baryatinsky and Yavorskaya.

On November 25, thirty-seven actors signed a petition demanding that Yavorskaya be thrown out of the troupe. Two days later, Burenin visited Yavorskaya and her husband. He reported to Suvorin that they felt embarrassed by what had transpired. Burenin accused the prince of being in the hands of Jews. "He protested," Burenin told Suvorin, "when I said that I know that he borrowed 50,000 rubles from Levi." The next evening at the producers' meeting, Suvorin told the managers it was pointless for the actors to declare they didn't want to work with Yavorskaya: "When soldiers go into battle, they don't say: 'Among us is one person with whom we don't want to go. First get rid of him.'"[49] When this comment was passed on to the troupe, one of the actors, Mikhail Mikhailov, came up to Suvorin and said:

> We don't really know what role Yavorskaya had in organizing the scandal and whether she took part. Let's assume that she had no part in it. But when they threw eggs, galoshes, and binoculars at us, she should have come to us and said: "You, my comrades, are being innocently blamed, and I want to be together with you." Instead of this, she sat in her loge and accepted applause from the very people who were blaming us. That's what prompted us to sign the protest. We decided on this not in the heat of the moment, but calmly two days afterwards, and we think what we did was right.[50]

Suvorin sympathized with Mikhailov but wasn't ready to acquiesce to the actors' demands. The decision would have to be made by the management of the Literary-Artistic Circle.

In a conversation with Suvorin, Burenin said Yavorskaya had confirmed to him that she had organized the demonstration and wanted to arrange a meeting to explain herself to Suvorin. Suvorin was wary. "I know how sly and cunning she is," he said. "But to give the troupe the right to expel artists—that's a last resort. Yavorskaya needs to say that she has her own newspaper, that in this newspaper I have been defamed, that Prince Baryatinsky told Plyushchevsky-Plyushchuk [the stage manager] that the *Sons of Israel* is only the prologue to the agitation against the *New Times*."[51]

Suvorin and Yavorskaya met for three hours on December 1. They both spoke calmly and Suvorin concluded that "she's not guilty of anything. It's just a difference of convictions. It was all organized by Yids, banker-Yids, and 500 Yids who came to Petersburg that day." She assured him she had been in the theater for only twenty minutes before leaving for Baroness Iskul's apartment. She accused him of wanting to have the *Northern Courier* shut down. Suvorin responded that it would be "the height of stupidity for the government to ban the play and the *Northern Courier*." He proposed to Yavorskaya that she submit a request to the theater's management to sort out the conflict between her and the troupe. He himself felt it could be settled either in a court of arbitration or a court of honor with the assistance of the Russian Theatrical Society.

Later that evening, Suvorin vented in his diary. He called Baryatinsky "an aristocratic degenerate, a pea-brain, seeking popularity through any sort of humiliation, who lifts his head and forcefully slanders." Yavorskaya had tried to convince Suvorin that the student demonstration was motivated in part by comments Suvorin had made in his newspaper arguing that too many Jews had been admitted to Kharkov University. This led Suvorin to fall back on one of the points he most frequently made about the "Jewish question": if Jews were allowed to freely assimilate, despite their small numbers they would soon dominate Russian society. The admissions policy at Kharkov University meant, he wrote in his diary, "that soon at the expense of the Russian peasant, all Jews will be educated," that Russian peasants were unable to compete with the Jews. "The Jews are pushing aside the Russians; the Jews are banning the play."[52]

The next day the troupe officially presented a statement to the theater's management that there was proof that Yavorskaya was complicit in inciting the demonstration, which resulted in their humiliation before the public. The actors asked for her to be dismissed immediately. Yavorskaya in a series of letters continued to plead her case to Suvorin, who became exasperated and once again blamed himself for willingly getting embroiled in running a theater. "What a tormenting lady," he wrote in his diary. "Nothing's ever her fault! Her enemies, who persecute her, are to blame, not her.... She doesn't want to understand anything. I should leave the theater. It's impossible to run it with the help of several masters. When there's a profit, the shareholders take the money. When there's a deficit, I bear the costs."[53] Recognizing that there was no unanimity among the actors and management on how to resolve the dispute, he feared it would drag on endlessly.

Suvorin began rehearsals for another performance of *The Smugglers*, encouraged by the minister of internal affairs, Dmitri Sipyagin, who told Suvorin that if Russians were allowed to "put on *The Inspector General*, then let the Jews watch *The Smugglers*." Suvorin asked Sipyagin to keep the police away and not interfere with the performance: "The master here is the audience, not the police."[54] Suvorin recognized that aspects of the play were vulgar, so he ordered changes, including eliminating the use of Yiddish accents. On the evening of December 23, two hundred people watched a full rehearsal.

The next morning, when employees of the *Northern Courier* approached the editorial office, they saw a group of porters under police supervision taking down the newspaper's sign. They found out that an order, authorized by the Ministries of Internal Affairs, Justice, and Public Education and by the procurator of the Holy Synod, had been issued to close down the publication for "its intentionally harmful direction."[55] Although Chekhov and others had predicted the government would inevitably ban the newspaper, it still came as a shock to the staff. After the *Smugglers* incident, its circulation had increased dramatically, and the office manager had felt elated by all the money orders for subscriptions that were coming in from the provinces.

Yavorskaya was incredulous: "They shut down a *newspaper* because of something that happened in a *theater*."[56] But, of course, the authorities had long been looking for an excuse to close the newspaper, primarily because of its leftist sympathies. One detective wrote in Yavorskaya's dossier: "It seems to me that it's a sin not to take advantage of the opportunity to thrash the Baryatinskys and exile Yavorskaya." The police noted that Yavorskaya had been taking an active part in the newspaper's affairs and that she had rather theatrically declared that she didn't fear being sent into exile together with the *Northern Courier*'s Marxists contributors. They quoted her as saying, "We'll go together with them in the same train carriage—it will be fun." It appears the police didn't take Yavorskaya's provocations very seriously. One officer considered it to be "some sort of crazy ravings" when, "as an excited Lady Macbeth in makeup, she tragically exclaimed: 'They are pursuing us Marxists, but we will not put down our weapons. Let them shut down this newspaper, we will start up another. The government is afraid that we have an entire army of Marxists supporting us.'"⁵⁷

People assumed that Suvorin would be pleased by the demise of a bitter rival and that perhaps he even had a hand in it. But he too was shocked: "The closing of the *Northern Courier* torments me. What government stupidity! They say that three ministers and the procurator of the Synod decided this during breakfast. Calmly and pleasantly! What sort of Christmas present is this for many poor writers, typesetters, workers, etc.? This is penal servitude for a journal. In the evening Burenin said Yavorskaya is crying, refuses to do the benefit, and wants to act.... I feel sorry for her."⁵⁸

Shchepkina-Kupernik had been in Moscow and missed the premiere of *The Smugglers*. But when she returned to St. Petersburg, she attended a gathering of theater people who were discussing Yavorskaya's behavior, and she witnessed the growing animosity toward her friend. A critic whose wife worked for the Maly Theater pounded his chest expansively and shouted out: "An idea, gentlemen, that's one thing, gentlemen, but actions, gentlemen, that's something else entirely, gentlemen!"⁵⁹

She noticed how deeply affected Yavorskaya was by the closing of the *Northern Courier*, in spite of her pose of defiance. The actor began to overeat and gain weight. She briefly attempted to find funding to start another newspaper, but soon gave up. Shchepkina-Kupernik could see "she was no longer the former burning Lidia Borisovna—she had somehow completely burned out."⁶⁰ With her characteristic flair for self-dramatization, Yavorskaya told her:

> I'm worn out. Everything has become so narrow.... When I lived as part of the general pulse of social interests, it seemed to me that I was taking part, albeit as a small nut or screw, in the larger mechanism of intellectual life in Russia—and suddenly to lose it all, and live a narrow egotistical life, seasoned with a bit of literary-artistic flavor... I sigh... Will I never any more feel myself in the ranks of those fighting for freedom, for the happiness of the majority, for righteousness? I have died... it seems to me that I will no longer live now that they have killed my child [the *Northern Courier*].⁶¹

Yavorskaya also confessed that Baryatinsky's despair was putting a strain on their marriage. He would disappear from the house for long stretches and not return for dinner. And, according to Shchepkina-Kupernik, "their intimate life became sporadic." On February 1, 1901,

Baryatinsky shot himself in the chest. He left a suicide note in which he said he felt as much despair over the hounding directed at his wife as over the demise of his newspaper:

> No one is to be blamed for my death. There has been too much slander, foulness, and lawlessness against which it is impossible to battle. Decent people are much too powerless. There is nowhere to turn for help, even my parents. It's time to kill myself. There is only one thing that weighs on me—I am leaving my sweet Lida alone, my guardian angel, with whom I have shared my joys and sadness. But I am consoled by the fact that possibly my death will silence those who hate her. Forgive me, my friends.[62]

He was seriously wounded, but the bullet missed his heart and lungs.

On February 25, the General Assembly of Suvorin's theater met to resolve the charges against Yavorskaya. The management recommended that she be dismissed from the troupe for breach of contract. In fact, no such contract existed; her agreement with Suvorin had been verbal. Nevertheless, thirty-two voted for the recommendation; twenty-nine voted against. She was expelled. Suvorin noted in his diary that the matter was finally settled, but once again wrote: "I feel sorry for her."[63]

In a letter to Shchepkina-Kupernik from Biarritz, where she and her husband went to escape the shame they had endured in St. Petersburg, Yavorskaya considered turning her back on the theater: "I don't want to be a *cabotine* [a ham actress]. I don't want to live with actors and their empty heads."[64] Robbed of the independence that a professional career as an actor had given her, she recoiled in the face of her husband's reassertion of his dominance over her: "My husband, with his humiliating despotism makes me look ridiculous, discredits me, *insisting* that I fall back on the friendship of people, whom I hardly know, whom he prefers to me as an influence. . . . I, a free spirit, am reduced to a slave, to a wet hen, an old lady! . . . I'm in pitiful dependence, squeezed by a cruel ring around my neck from soft aristocratic hands."[65]

She tried to revive her former intimacy with Shchepkina-Kupernik: "You, my dear little girl, were a ray of light in my dungeon. More than once, you were a gust of freeing wind when I was suffocating . . . Now you have flown away. . . . I sit here rotting alive, surrounded on one side by a misogynist husband, and on the other by the intrigues of old friends. What is to be done?"[66] Yavorskaya asked her to come live with her and Baryatinsky for a while. But accepting such an invitation would be awkward. Shchepkina-Kupernik had fallen in love with someone else—the feminist writer Maria Krestovskaya.

CHAPTER 9

The New Theater

Maria Krestovskaya was the daughter of the writer Vsevolod Krestovsky, whose most famous novel, *The Slums of St. Petersburg* (1864), was a Dickensian tale of the squalid underworld of the capital.[1] Raised in St. Petersburg by her grandmother after her parents divorced, Krestovskaya dreamed of becoming an actor, and in 1879 at the age of seventeen she moved to Moscow to become part of Korsh's company. At the age of twenty-one, Krestovskaya adapted for the stage Émile Zola's *Nana*, the portrait of a prostitute turned actor, but it was banned by the censors. Around the same time, she fell in love with Nikolai Dobrovolsky, a landscape painter who was a member of the Itinerant movement, already married, and twenty-five years older than she was. In 1883 she gave birth to a son, Vsevolod. Three years later, Dobrovolsky set off for Siberia to paint landscapes in Irkutsk and Lake Baikal. Krestovskaya eventually joined him there with their child. But when they were reunited, Dobrovolsky shunned both her and Vsevolod. She returned to St. Petersburg and decided to pursue a career as a writer. Victor Klyushnikov, the editor of *The Russian Messenger*, recognized her talents, took her under his wing, and published her stories in his thick journal.

Krestovskaya quickly established herself as a writer of popular stories about female love. As a fellow woman writer who was just starting out, Shchepkina-Kupernik read Krestovskaya's stories with great interest, but with some ambivalence. Critics called Krestovskaya the "Russian George Sand," but Shchepkina-Kupernik felt she was unworthy of the comparison: "She wasn't able to turn her lyrical openness into a comprehensive and finished worldview, and more than many female writers, she was guilty of the sin they were usually blamed for: she wrote only about her own romances."[2]

Toward the end of the 1880s, Krestovskaya met Evgeny Kartavtsev, a wealthy banker and the treasurer of the Literary Fund, who fell deeply in love with her. However, he was reluctant to marry her, concerned that within his social milieu he would be ostracized for having as his wife a Bohemian writer with an illegitimate son. After a long period of hesitation, he relented and married her in 1891, agreeing to adopt Vsevolod as his own son. Krestovskaya embraced the role of a high-society woman, and her literary output slowed dramatically. Her husband encouraged her to take charge of building a villa that she called "Marioki" on land near the Gulf of Finland that he had purchased as a surprise for her. She worked closely with a young architect who turned her clumsily drawn plans into blueprints for what Shchepkina-Kupernik called "one of the most enchanting summer houses that I have ever seen—well-built, full of light and air."[3]

Shchepkina-Kupernik met Krestovskaya around 1900. In her memoirs, she wrote that "we quickly became close to each other, and soon she held no secrets back from me."[4] Krestovskaya confided to her that she could never forgive Kartavtsev for wavering so long before he finally decided to marry her, which caused a strain in their relationship. The intimacy between the two women is reflected in an entry in Shchepkina-Kupernik's notebook in which she jotted down an aphorism uttered by Krestovskaya in a dream: "Condescension kisses you on the forehead, friendship kisses you on the cheek, tenderness kisses you on the eyes, respect kisses you on the hand, love kisses you on the lips, and passion kisses you there and everywhere else."[5]

Shchepkina-Kupernik, like Krestovskaya, wrote about female love, but from a less traditional perspective and only sometimes in lyrical terms. In her feuilleton "From the Diary of a Superfluous Woman," published in a 1903 collection, she created the persona of a woman who feels she is slowly being drained of all desire, "a degenerative disease no different than TB."[6] She had tried falling in love with men, but it turned out to be a mirage: "The most passionate kiss aroused in me only a feeling of cold. Not even revulsion but a light confusion: 'Why am I doing this?' And I became unable to continue this game."[7] Rejecting heterosexual love, she tried turning friendship with men "into a cult." But here too she was unsuccessful. From her perspective, all men fell into two categories: those who are free (single and available) and those who are not (married or already in love). "For those who are not free, friendship is impossible, for them only one woman exists in the world: she with whom at the given moment they are in love. For those who are free . . . they feel somewhat offended, why *friendship*, when it could be something else?"[8]

But neither were relationships between women necessarily based on equality: "Female friendship has a place to the extent that one side needs a confidante, and the other side is willing to be one. A woman must either submit or dominate: equality is not in her nature."[9] Here Shchepkina-Kupernik describes a dynamic (and some biographical similarities) that makes it sound like she is describing her relationship with Yavorskaya:

> I have no desire to dominate anyone. I didn't need anything. I didn't have intimate, sweet secrets that I, inflamed and shaking, could share with a girlfriend: my life is so free and independent that for one of my female friends I had to concoct a secret as if it were a mise-en-scène. She was such a romantic that being an orphan and completely independent, she could not agree to marry her fiancé unless it was an elopement.[10]

Unwilling to dominate, the "superfluous woman" allows herself to play the role of passive confidante until one day she begins to question whether her friend really has any sincere feelings for her. She begins to think she exists only to "smile at the right time, sympathize at the right time, harmonize at the right time" in support of whatever "crazy idea" was currently gripping her friend. Meanwhile, she was denying herself the ability to be driven by her own "crazy idea," to be driven by a desire that would cause her to take action in her own life and give it meaning and happiness. She was convinced that such an idea "supplies the oil in a lamp, and it makes a woman burn, makes her live." The example she gives of a woman under the spell of such an idea is unmistakably based on Yavorskaya's passionate involvement with the *Northern Courier*:

> I recall my acquaintance, a young woman, beautiful, loved by her husband. She could have lived in bourgeois satisfaction, carefree and idle, i.e., happy in the opinion of the crowd. But her dream

was to publish a journal, and so she convinces her husband to do this—and her life becomes filled. She sits for nights at the press, she herself looks over the articles, becomes agitated over polemics, quivers from joy over every new subscriber—not because of the money—she is unable to think about money: when there are temporary cash-flow problems, without thinking, she gives away her family pearls "for the business." She cries hot tears of emotion over a thank-you letter from a student; she blazes with indignation at a sally from a hostile newspaper. She lives for this. She responds with her whole being to the typesetters—her friends—to every minor event in the life of the journal, to the typographers, to the workers. And when the journal is closed because of conditions "not related to the publication," she tries to poison herself.

This is a life full of agitation, unpleasantness, unrest—but it is *life* . . . and I don't have something like this.[11]

This discussion of active and passive roles in a relationship explains why Shchepkina-Kupernik was beginning to personally and professionally distance herself from Yavorskaya. She was no longer devoting as much time to translating French plays in support of Yavorskaya's stage career. By now she had published several collections of verse. In 1902 she was nominated as a candidate for the Academy, a distinct honor, although in the balloting she received only one vote.[12] Her relationship with Krestovskaya was different from the submissive role she had been playing in her relationship with Yavorskaya. Her fame was increasing as Krestovskaya's career stalled while she devoted herself to family life and the management of Marioki.

In February 1901, Shchepkina-Kupernik was in St. Petersburg, staying at Krestovskaya's apartment at 12 Kirochnaya Street, when Yavorskaya was fired from Suvorin's theater. She was depressed and unable to decide what to do next. The *Sons of Israel* scandal and her rejection by both the theater's actors and management meant that neither the Alexandrinsky nor any private St. Petersburg theater was interested in having her join their company. One possibility was returning to Moscow. As it turned out, Stanislavsky's Moscow Art Theater had just arrived in St. Petersburg for a monthlong tour. Yavorskaya, with a characteristic lack of restraint, set out to win over Stanislavsky, Nemirovich-Danchenko, and in particular the theater's leading actress, Olga Knipper.

While staying in St. Petersburg, Knipper met and was charmed by Krestovskaya, sensing they shared "a mutual sympathy for each other."

She wrote to Chekhov in Yalta about her first dinner at Krestovskaya's. She found the host to be "elegant, soft, feminine, smart, and she doesn't write like an old lady. She herself came for me today in a carriage with two chestnut horses, took me along the embankment, and brought me to dinner. I had a splendid time at her place." Knipper was less charitable toward Shchepkina-Kupernik and her father, who were also at the dinner: "Papa Kupernik ate a lot, gobbled up masses of candies—and kept purring something to himself. Although he's intelligent, he's very repulsive. Tanka lay near him on the floor, on his lap, and caressed him—it was somehow repulsive."[13] Thus began a whirlwind of visits, teas, and dinners with both Krestovskaya and Shchepkina-Kupernik. Knipper also wrote to Chekhov's sister in Moscow about her newfound friend. Maria Chekhova responded, "I too like Krestovskaya very much. You must send her my greetings." But she chided Knipper for her malicious comments about others: "I will not allow you to speak badly of my friends, about Yavorskaya and Tanechka. Apparently with your impudence, you've become a 'Protopopov,'" referring to a disagreeable offstage character in *The Three Sisters*.[14]

Knipper had ample reason to dislike Yavorskaya, not only because she knew about her brief affair with Chekhov, whom Knipper would marry in May. She was repulsed by stories she had heard about Yavorskaya's onstage antics, in which she would fuss with her costume, the better to show off her body.[15] Knipper told Chekhov that after the first act of the February 21 performance of *Uncle Vanya*, "Yavorskaya wormed her way into my dressing room to get acquainted. For what reason? Her flattery was vulgar, disgusting. After the fourth act, she took a red carnation from between her breasts and tossed it from the parterre to Stanislavsky—how touching! Her prince was also there—pale, stooped."[16] On top of this, Knipper was deeply upset over the scathing reviews she was receiving in the press. Although the theater sold out every night, St. Petersburg newspapers were generally dissatisfied with the actors' performances, focusing particularly on Knipper.[17] Chekhov reassured her that what they were writing was nonsense, that he expected nothing but "muck" from the *New Times*, and that Kugel, writing for the *St. Petersburg Gazette*, was attacking Knipper only because he could never forgive her for taking the role of Yelena Andreevna in *Uncle Vanya* away from his mistress, the "absolutely talentless actress" Kholmskaya.[18]

Several days later Knipper complained again about Yavorskaya coming to her dressing room: "She crawls, she flatters, she invites everyone to stay with her. The brazen woman."[19] Yavorskaya invited Knipper to a banquet she was arranging for the entire company, but Knipper had no intention of going: "I can't bear the sight of that coarse woman and have given orders for her not to be allowed in my dressing room during intermissions."[20] Chekhov gently chided Knipper for overreacting to Yavorskaya's overtures, which he found to be comical rather than threatening: "So, she's been coming to you at the theater in the spirit of Sarah Bernhardt, with none other than the sincere desire to make the entire troupe overjoyed by her attention. And you almost get into a fight with her!"[21]

Stanislavsky, unlike Knipper, did attend Yavorskaya's banquet, but their conversation would hardly have resulted in him asking her to join his company, given how much he disliked her acting. While Yavorskaya's attempt to attach herself to the Moscow Art Theater was a failure, surrounding herself with the company and its actors at a time when all doors seemed closed gave her an idea—perhaps the way forward was to start a theater company of her own.

In the spring of 1901, Yavorskaya rented the Nemetti Theater on Officer's Street to stage a production of Rostand's *The Eaglet* (*L'Aiglon*) in a verse translation by Shchepkina-Kupernik. Rostand had written the play for Bernhardt, who debuted in the title role of the Duc de Reichstadt, the exiled son of Napoléon, at her own Théâtre Sarah-Bernhardt in March 1900. The patriotic verse drama was a phenomenal success, notwithstanding the fact that the fifty-six-year-old actor had cast herself as a twenty-year-old man. The theater enjoyed eight months of sold-out performances, after which the production went on tour to the United States.[22] Originally *The Eaglet* had been promised to Suvorin prior to Yavorskaya's dismissal. Shchepkina-Kupernik, reflecting the change in their relationship, said she had "translated it for her in memory of old times."[23] She uncharacteristically wrote very little in her memoirs about her translation of the play or its staging. She did again defend Yavorskaya from accusations by St. Petersburg critics that her performance was modeled after Bernhardt's, since she knew that Yavorskaya had not yet seen Bernhardt in the role.

Yavorskaya found the burden of assuming responsibility for the production of *The Eaglet* extremely stressful. "I'm in despair," she wrote to Shchepkina-Kupernik. "I don't know what to do. I'm worn out. Until 7 p.m. I *directed* and rehearsed *The Eaglet*.... It's going terribly.... Tomorrow I'm scheduled to rehearse at 10 a.m. It's very hard for me to get up early. I'm so exhausted."[24] After fifteen performances at the Nemetti, Yavorskaya took her production on tour to Kiev. The Kiev correspondent for the illustrated weekly magazine *Teatr i Iskusstvo* (*Theater and Art*) attended the premiere and remarked that Yavorskaya was completely unable to recite Shchepkina-Kupernik's verse, choosing to just shout out her lines regardless of whether she was expressing joy, despair, hope, irony, or anger: "The audience, which wasn't very large, started to leave the theater after the second act."[25]

Over the past four years, *Theater and Art*, edited by Kugel and Kholmskaya, had established itself as the preeminent and most comprehensive journal covering the Russian theater. Kugel, writing his reviews and essays under the pseudonym "Homus Novus," became the country's most prominent theater critic. He frequently attacked the growing tendency of directors to present themselves as auteurs of a production, which he felt constrained actors and their performances. Stanislavsky and Chekhov hated his antimodernist views but grudgingly respected his formidable intellect.

Although by now the marriage between Yavorskaya and her prince was beginning to show strains, the idea of forming their own theater company suited both their interests. For Baryatinsky it could serve as a forum for presenting his own plays and his translations of classic and contemporary European works. His inherited wealth would provide the capital to launch the endeavor. There was no expectation, however, that the theater would be profitable. For Yavorskaya the theater would allow her to cast herself in roles as she saw fit, a power that she had never previously possessed and one that understandably would become a source of friction with the other actors in the troupe.

They decided to call their company the "New Theater," a public declaration of their intent to align themselves with the progressive elements in St. Petersburg culture and society. The theater was housed in Kononovsky Hall, located along the Moika canal embankment . It was a less than ideal venue, since to enter the theater, patrons had to climb a gently sloping staircase with multiple landings up to the fourth floor. The theater was comparatively small—the orchestra level had six hundred seats with a balcony and gallery; the loges provided another two hundred seats. The stage was cozy with low, hip-high footlights reminiscent of the Théâtre de la Renaissance in Paris. Backstage it was dusty, dark, and cramped. Most of the dressing rooms were below stage level; the actors had to climb a set of stairs to make an entrance.[26]

The beginning of the fall theater season was preceded by a calamity: on the night of August 19, 1901, Suvorin's Maly Theater caught fire for unknown reasons. The main hall, the stage, and all its props and sets burned to the ground. Suvorin noted in his diary that he had heard rumors that the cause of the fire was arson and the police had received letters blaming Yavorskaya. But he assigned the blame to "our short-sightedness and negligence."[27] The building manager had "stupidly economized," failing to continue to employ the firefighters who normally lived in the theater during the season. Suvorin was forced to return to the Panaev Theater. But because it had already been rented out, he had to buy out the lease and cover the expenses of the other company moving to a new theater. He estimated that this would cost him around one hundred thousand rubles for five months. As encouragement (and to preserve their own jobs), Suvorin's actors offered to reduce their salaries by 25 percent, but he graciously thanked them and rejected the offer. He was willing to take a loss to keep his theater intact.

The refurbished New Theater opened on September 15, 1901. The *New Times* critic noted that "Kononovsky Hall now looks like an elegant living room instead of the previous gray and boring barracks. In everything one sees the fine taste of the proprietress, who has put much effort into decorating her salon properly."[28] Everyone described the theater as Yavorskaya's, not Baryatinsky's, despite his significant financial and creative contributions.

The evening began with a one-act poetic "conversation" written by Shchepkina-Kupernik that included four people: a writer, a theatergoer, a journalist, and a young actress, played by Yavorskaya. Over the course of the conversation each participant is asked the same question: Do you believe in theater? The writer is frustrated by how difficult it is for a young playwright to get the attention of producers. To the theatergoer "the stage is almost the only free arena, from which it is possible for us to toss out to a crowd of people life-giving grains that sow good feelings."[29] He is drawn to the shared catharsis of a spectacle that "excites all hearts." The journalist, by implication a theater critic, is more jaundiced: "The theater is only a fiction, an empty entertainment."[30]

The actress is the last to appear on stage. She tells the audience what to expect from the New Theater—Tolstoy, Ibsen, Henryk Sienkiewicz (a dramatization of *Quo Vadis*), and starting that night, Shakespeare's *The Tempest*, which had rarely been staged in Russia, in a translation by Baryatinsky and with Yavorskaya in the role of Ariel. Over the next six seasons the company would mix new works with European classics. In her conversation in verse Shchepkina-Kupernik gives Yavorskaya the opportunity to get back at her critics. The actress tells the journalist:

"You often vent your bile on us. You are unfair, sometimes malicious... And we are helpless to defend ourselves from the attacks."[31]

But for her it is all worth it for the chance to attain moments of ecstatic unity with the audience. She gets the last word. Standing before a full house in her small theater, she says to them:

> It has been my singular dream for many years to fight against vulgarity and narrow mindedness; and to find happiness in my livelihood. Yes, this is my happiness: and I won't hide that when at times it happens that I arrive at the theater feeling the heavy burden of my own deep despair—only the realization that everyone who is close to you, that everyone who is possibly like you, is seeking to forget themselves, and you give it to them completely, if only for a moment. Suddenly inspiration flies down from the heavens, and you feel in that moment with all your heart that you are alive, that you are living for others, forgetting yourself.... Such happiness... there is nothing like it, and for me in this is all of life's meaning and light.[32]

Shchepkina-Kupernik wrote these words knowing that what Yavorskaya sought most as an actor was this deeply Romantic feeling of self-oblivion on stage. But in truth, audiences were more drawn to her as a charismatic celebrity than as an artist able to disappear into her roles. She, in turn, felt particularly energized by public adulation, especially by university students, who sensed she shared their liberal values. The opening-night audience heard her extol "that living, ebullient spirit, fiery and free-thinking, that the young carry within them. Oh, you can't be deceived by this. It has its own particular, passionate feeling."[33]

The Tempest was a challenging work to produce on such a tight stage. The first scene takes place on the deck of a boat during a ferocious storm. Without a machine to mechanically rock the boat, the actors were asked to sway off-balance as if they were being tossed about: "People fell on each other and shouted out things that were impossible to understand."[34]

That production was to be followed immediately by *The Seagull*. Rehearsals were underway and tickets had been sold when Baryatinsky received a response from Chekhov refusing to allow him to put on the play. Chekhov insisted that the rights to perform *The Seagull* in St. Petersburg and Moscow belonged exclusively to the Moscow Art Theater.[35] Given his skittishness about productions of *The Seagull* and his disdain for Yavorskaya's acting (and improvisations), Chekhov was likely horrified by Baryatinsky's request. Instead, the New Theater moved on to a revival of *The Eaglet*. The opening night attracted a full house. *Theater and Art* attributed this to the public's continuing enthusiasm for pseudo-historical dramas, which in this instance "dragged on until two in the morning." Most successful were the external effects—the sets by the company's talented resident artist Konstantin Eisenberg were painstakingly designed; the costumes were "fresh and attractive." The direction, however, had its shortcomings—pistols failed to fire, the backstage orchestra often missed its cues.[36]

Consistent with its mission to champion new Russian works, in its first season Yavorskaya's theater also presented *Nights of Madness* by Tolstoy's son and namesake Lev L. Tolstoy. The younger Tolstoy was estranged from his father and so aggressively repudiated his teachings that he had earned the nickname "Tiger Tigerovich." The play concerns an ailing, married young journalist who is sent by his doctors to Italy, where he falls in love with his cousin. His wife (played by Yavorskaya) appears and discovers the affair. Distraught and, as one critic wryly put it, "carried away by the example of Anna Karenina," he throws himself in front of a train. The *New Times* concluded that *Nights of Madness* suffered from a multitude of structural flaws and observed that "Miss Yavorskaya has surrounded herself with bad actors."[37] The weakness of the New Theater's troupe was a constant refrain among critics and theatergoers, a problem arising from the fact that many of the city's more talented, established actors were unwilling to submit themselves to Yavorskaya's imperious leadership.

Baryatinsky's social comedy *The Shoals* enjoyed much greater success for its wit and critique of political corruption. It was the first of a trilogy of plays that satirized provincial bigwigs and scoundrels, and was performed forty-seven times before the season ended. The trilogy went on to be widely produced, with performances at Suvorin's and Korsh's theaters, as well as at venues in Paris and London, where one of the plays, *Nablotsky's Career*, was translated into English.

The boldest undertaking of the first season was the production of Ibsen's new play, *When We Dead Awaken*. Anticipating that viewers might find the work incomprehensible, Yavorskaya arranged to have her staff distribute a handout to theatergoers explaining the symbolic meaning of the play. Critics were unreceptive to the allusive, dream state of the play: "The audience doesn't talk about Ibsen's play, but about Ibsen himself, not about the characters, not about the figures of the people he is showing us, but about how all this must be symbolic."[38]

Similarly, Osip Etinger, writing for *Theater and Art*, fumed about having to sit through Yavorskaya's five-hour production of August Strindberg's sardonic comedy *There Are Crimes and Crimes*. He concluded that "the commendable desire of the management of the 'New Theater,' is to familiarize us with plays of so-called 'new art,' but such poorly chosen productions may more likely discredit 'new art' than propagandize in favor of it, particularly when the audience responds to it with mistrust, almost with hostility."[39]

Yavorskaya's commitment to modernist drama, in spite of such criticisms, was serious and prolonged. During the life of the New Theater, she put on three Ibsen plays and four by Strindberg, more than any other St. Petersburg theater. The more liberal intelligentsia was attracted to her as an innovator, as a risk-taker open to Western ideas and influence, as an advocate of political, sexual, and personal emancipation. Yavorskaya started challenging audiences with her modernist repertoire several years before Komissarzhevskaya launched her own Dramatic Theater dedicated to presenting similar fare. Komissarzhevskaya, however, was a more popular, gifted actress, who more single-mindedly pursued an interest in the avant-garde. She hired Meyerhold, then Nikolai Evreinov, both of whom directed productions that baffled viewers and critics alike. Dwindling audiences and hostile reviews were the price that both actor-entrepreneurs paid for staging modernist works.

Yavorskaya had enough of a commercial sense to intersperse these more demanding plays with light comedies and sentimental dramas that were sure to be popular with theatergoers. She ended the season with an adaptation of Sienkiewicz's *Quo Vadis*. Etinger thought Eisenberg's sets worked wonders in creating a historical spectacle (including the burning of Rome) on such a small stage. *Theater and Art* also hinted, based on accounts from people who had seen the same adaptation in Paris, that Yavorskaya had again used stenographers to crib a French production as had been the case with Sardou's *Madame Sans-Gêne*.[40] The play's run came to an abrupt end after a performance in which Boris Nevolin, who was playing an old holy man thrown into a cell with three other Christian converts, says to them: "I saw the coming Christ in a bright cloud. I fell on my knees and asked him: '*Quo vadis*, my Lord?' And he said to me: 'I am going to Rome, which you have left, to save my people.'" He then improvised the line: "Because every government is organized violence." Mikhail Narokov, who played one of the prisoners, recalled that he couldn't believe his ears: "When the scene ended, we rushed up to Nevolin. He replied that he had been at an anarchist gathering and had come straight from there to the performance. What he had said on stage he couldn't remember at all." Nevolin was summarily exiled from the capital.[41]

Yavorskaya was generally more feared than respected among her fellow actors in the troupe, especially among those who had always considered her "not one of us." They found her to be arrogant, insensitive, and undisciplined. Narokov thought Yavorskaya only needed the theater as a framework in which to show off her wardrobe: "In all her roles, she was always the same, with her male-sounding hoarse voice, her naughty eyes, and premeditated stage tricks—only the costumes changed."[42] As a result, professional standards were low. He complained that the backstage crew was generally disorganized, and recalled that when an actor playing the role of a lady's maid in *Nablotsky's Career* took sick, Yavorskaya thought nothing of replacing her with her own dressmaker.

Maria Velizary, a successful provincial actor who grudgingly accepted a low salary at the New Theater when her husband found a prestigious position at the Alexandrinsky Theater, called the place an "insane asylum":

> Rehearsals there didn't start at eleven o'clock, as was done in other theaters, but at two or three o'clock in the afternoon, when the "princess" deigned to arrive . . . The princess arrived at three o'clock and proceeded to her dressing room. A lackey followed her, bringing breakfast on a silver tray. The actors sat and waited. She once invited me to breakfast with her. I blurted out: "How can you eat when hungry actors are sitting and waiting on stage, having waited four hours for rehearsals to begin?" Yavorskaya laughed, "What makes you pay attention to such trivial things? . . . . The princess, having finished breakfast, came out on stage. Rehearsals finished around six or six thirty in the evening. The actors forgot what it was like to eat dinner. The play began in an hour and finished around eleven o'clock, sometimes at one in the morning. In addition, after every premiere we actors always sat for photographs. The photo session also took up a lot of time; hungry and worn out, we stood in our makeup, swearing at the princess's capriciousness. I sometimes demonstratively left for home. Others were afraid, not daring to contradict the owner.[43]

Velizary was equally annoyed by Yavorskaya's onstage behavior. She would use improvisation to extend her most effective scenes: "It would finally reach the height of absurdity when Yavorskaya herself lost the thread of a scene and muddled all of us who were on stage with her."⁴⁴ She used her body not just to strike mannered poses but also to fluster her male colleagues. For the actor Ivan Perestiani, she was "an absolutely unique figure with a clearly expressed sexuality in her stage presence." When Perestiani joined the New Theater, the actor Alexander Mursky warned him to be wary when on stage with her. Mursky told him about an incident in which he was doing a night scene with her:

> She comes out on stage. She was wearing a white, light silk peignoir. She approached me. An embrace, a kiss, and suddenly I notice that this thin, bright silk is being worn on a naked body. She clings to me, presses me, kisses . . . It was horrible. Somehow overcoming myself, I finished the scene. The curtain goes down, and she looks at me and laughs: "I thought it would make is easier for you to play the scene." Easier? I almost lost my senses doing the scene.⁴⁵

In the spring of 1902, after the end of the first season, Yavorskaya took a contingent of her troupe on tour to southern Russia and Western Europe. The goal of the tour was not to make a profit, but to advertise the theater company and attempt to bolster its prestige. Shchepkina-Kupernik went along, occasionally taking on the role of understudy in some of the productions.⁴⁶ The repertoire consisted of five plays: *The Shoals, Nablotsky's Career, The Seagull, The Lady of the Camellias,* and Gorky's first play, *The Philistines.* By the time the tour reached the Theatre Antoine in Paris, Narokov, who had developed a jaundiced view of the constant infighting, Bohemian chaos, and mismanagement on the road, sensed that everyone was exhausted.

At the Antoine, Baryatinsky's two plays went well, but *The Seagull* was a disaster. Unfortunately, Chekhov's ability to control rights to his play did not include foreign productions. Narokov recognized the Paris performance of *The Seagull* as a "conscientious copy" of Stanislavsky's version, but the attempt to borrow the Moscow Art Theater's stylistic subtlety didn't work with French theatergoers: "It was painful to hear coming from the audience the laughter of the French at the Chekhovian pauses, moreover the paucity of the staging crudely wrecked the fabric of Chekhov's Moscow Art Theater production. It was a shameful profanation of a beloved Russian writer."⁴⁷

The performance of Gorky's *The Philistines,* however, turned out to be the highlight of the tour. In December 1901, the New Theater had staged Baryatinsky's adaptation of Gorky's story *Foma Gordeev* over the objections of its author. When Baryatinsky's partner Arabazhin asked Gorky for permission to produce *The Philistines*, the writer, still furious, refused and granted the rights to Stanislavsky's Moscow Art Theater. Stanislavsky premiered the play in St. Petersburg in March in a heavily censored production. Authorities feared that this rambling, comic play about a politically rebellious adopted son raised in the narrow-minded, bourgeois family would provoke unrest. Mounted police patrolled the theater on opening night, but Nemirovich-Danchenko had successfully pleaded with student leaders not to stage demonstrations that would only result in government suppression of his theater company. In Paris, out of Gorky's reach and unconstrained by censorship, Yavorskaya was able to stage the play without cuts. On opening night, the theater was packed with Russian political exiles and émigrés excited to see a performance that would be banned back home. Narokov, who was playing the role of Teterev the choir singer, recalled that when in the second act he intoned "'Damn this household!' the whole theater let out such a stormy rumble that it seemed like the roof would fall in. I was called out three times after this scene in the middle of the act to take a bow, completely perplexed, understanding very well the reason for my success. It was a deeply disturbing political demonstration."[48] Increasingly, Yavorskaya was taking on the role of an "artist protester," a public figure who was aligning herself with the radical forces driving Russia toward a crisis that would result in the 1905 revolution.

On its way back to St. Petersburg, the troupe stopped in Vilnius for a series of engagements. On the last day, Yavorskaya suggested to Shchepkina-Kupernik that they visit Yavorskaya's former governess, Alexandra Pavlova, who was now a senior nurse at the Sisters of Mercy compound deep in the pine forests outside of town. When they arrived, they were told that Sister Pavlova was away on business. The young nurses, recognizing Yavorskaya, insisted that the travelers stay for tea. While sitting on the verandah of the compound's little wooden house, they noticed two people coming up the forest road—a policeman and an old lady carrying something in her arms wrapped in rags.

The police officer told the nurses that they had brought a newborn baby who had been abandoned on the village road. The nurses explained that they did not accept abandoned children. The infant girl would have to be brought to the nursery of the Hospital of the Infant Jesus in Vilnius. The officer and the old lady set off with the infant. On their way back to town Shchepkina-Kupernik noticed that Yavorskaya was unusually silent; but then she suddenly said: "What if fate has determined that I have crossed paths with this girl for a reason? What if I raise her?"⁴⁹

Wary of Yavorskaya's impulsiveness, Shchepkina-Kupernik tried to convince her how impractical the idea was—it was dangerous to take in a strange child knowing nothing about its health; Yavorskaya's chaotic professional life was unsuitable for raising a child. But she could not be dissuaded. Having seen the girl, she couldn't forgive herself if the child ended up suffering "a life worse than death" in an orphanage. They agreed that the best solution would be for Yavorskaya to have the child raised by Sister Pavlova under Yavorskaya's guardianship. They went to the hospital, completed the formalities, and took charge of the infant, whose name was Alexandra "Sasha" Smyslova. Sasha remained under the care of Pavlova until the nurse passed away some years later. At that point Yavorskaya took in her ward, much to her husband's displeasure. He refused to take any steps to legally adopt the child.

The Four Sirens of the Louvre

FIGURE 1. Lidia Yavorskaya

FIGURE 2. Tatiana Shchepkina-Kupernik

FIGURE 3. Varvara Eberle

FIGURE 4. Lidia Mizinova

FIGURE 5. Korsh's theater, designed by the architect Mikhail Chichigov in the Russian Revival style.

FIGURE 6. Fyodor Korsh

FIGURE 7.   Ivan Kramskoy's portrait of Alexei Suvorin (1881)

FIGURE 8.   Suvorin's *New Times* newspaper office

FIGURE 9. Yavorskaya in *The Dream Princess*

FIGURE 10. Sarah Bernhardt in *La Princesse Lointaine*

FIGURE 11. Ilya Repin's sketch of Prince Vladimir Baryatinsky (1909)

FIGURE 12. Shchepkina-Kupernik (*left*) visits with Yavorskaya at her extravagantly decorated two-story "palazzo" at 65 Ligovsky Prospect, St. Petersburg.

FIGURE 13. Maria Krestovskaya

FIGURE 14. Vera Komissarzhevskaya

FIGURE 15. Alexandra Kollontai

FIGURE 16. Margarita Zelenina

FIGURE 17. John Pollock. © National Portrait Gallery, London.

FIGURE 18. Pyotr Kropotkin

FIGURE 19. A London studio portrait of Yavorskaya as Anna Karenina, dressed in a haute couture outfit from the House of Paquin. © National Portrait Gallery, London.

FIGURE 20. Shchepkina-Kupernik as Honored Artist of the Soviet Union, © Sputnik MediaBank via Associated Press.

CHAPTER 10

Marriage

By the spring of 1902, almost ten years had passed since Chekhov, as the "Admiral Avelan," had first surrendered himself to the seductive call of the four "sirens of the Louvre": Lidia Yavorskaya, Tatiana Shchepkina-Kupernik, Lidia Mizinova, and Varvara Eberle. At that time, Shchepkina-Kupernik, not yet twenty years old, rejected the idea that marriage was the only way for a woman to achieve a respectable place in society. She and Yavorskaya had both escaped disastrous teenage marriages in order to pursue artistic careers that they hoped would put them on an equal footing with their male counterparts. But Shchepkina-Kupernik watched with dismay as Yavorskaya used her sexual allure to seduce theater audiences in general and Prince Baryatinsky in particular, entering into a marriage that bestowed on her both a royal status and great wealth. As it turned out, by 1904 all four of the "sirens," now in their early thirties, were married, as well as Chekhov himself.

It was while Olga Knipper was on tour in St. Petersburg in March 1901, resisting the annoying visits from Yavorskaya and being charmed by Krestovskaya, that Chekhov finally wrote to Olga telling her he was ready to get married. Yavorskaya had heard rumors of a marriage but dismissed them as nonsense—how many times in the past had she heard similar rumors that turned out to be only gossip.[1] Chekhov asked

Knipper to come straight to Yalta from St. Petersburg. She stayed for two weeks, then returned to Moscow annoyed by Chekhov's reticence to publicly announce an engagement. He agreed, however, to come to Moscow later in the spring when it was warmer and to marry her there, as long as she kept it a secret. They were married on May 25 with no one from Chekhov's family in attendance. Chekhov did send a telegram to his mother in Yalta. It was left to Knipper to write to Chekhov's sister, also in Yalta, describing the wedding. Knipper's tone was not celebratory. The previous week Chekhov had visited a physician whose diagnosis was chilling—Chekhov's lungs, they were told, were severely damaged by tuberculosis. Immediately following the wedding, on the physician's recommendation, Chekhov and Knipper left by boat for Ufa over seven hundred miles to the east to be treated with koumiss, a drink made from fermented mare's milk that was thought to benefit patients with tuberculosis.

When Chekhov first found himself attracted to Knipper in the fall of 1898, his relationship with Mizinova had already become more distant, both literally and figuratively. Their paths rarely crossed—he was mostly confined to Yalta; she was in Moscow or continuing her voice lessons in Paris. Her letters to him, in which she had previously played along with his bantering tone, now began to sound like the voice of a woman scorned. Writing from Paris in January 1899, after having received a letter from him that she considered full of "nonsense," she replied furiously: "You know very well that I love you more than you deserve and I am much nicer to you than you are to me! . . . I'm not someone you have any interest in! Why have you spent your whole life dumping on me! Enough! This isn't going to get us anywhere, and it's not worth burdening you with all sorts of unnecessary lofty phrases."[2] Over the course of their ten-year relationship, Chekhov enjoyed Mizinova's company, her beauty, intelligence, and high-spirited nature. But she was not the type of woman he could marry—too mercurial, too flighty in her various creative pursuits, and too much of a drinker and smoker to suit his prim tastes.

News of Chekhov's marriage drove Mizinova into depression. Her friend Ekaterina Sanina, the sister of the Moscow Art Theater director Alexander Sanin, wrote to Shchepkina-Kupernik in early June: "I saw Lika yesterday and today. She wanted me to tell you that she's moping, which is why she hasn't written to you. . . . She's indeed sad about something. Her lips smile, but her eyes are mournful, and the tragic corners of her lips are deeply turned down. A poor, wonderful creature.

How life is leaving, slipping away from her. Doesn't she have something to live for?"[3]

Knowing about Chekhov's history with Mizinova, Knipper, as was often the case with her husband's former lovers, was merciless in her criticism. In August 1901 Knipper described to Chekhov Mizinova's unsuccessful audition to enroll in the Moscow Art Theater acting school. Nemirovich-Danchenko had Mizinova read several monologues from roles that Knipper felt she herself had made famous—Elena Andreevna in *Uncle Vanya* and Irina Fyodorovna in *Boris Godunov*. "But everything she read (between you and me) was a blank spot," she told Chekhov, "and I felt sorry for her. Sanin hoped she would open a fashion shop, of course not to her face.... Tell Masha about Lika. I think they'll take her into the theater as an extra, since it's already too late for her to go to school. And anyway, she'll never learn."[4] Mizinova did become an extra at no pay, happy to be on stage, and naively hopeful that it might lead to a speaking role. The theater let her go after one season.

On December 21, 1901, Knipper together with the cast gathered at the Hermitage Restaurant to celebrate the premiere of Nemirovich-Danchenko's *In Dreams* and to await the first reviews in the morning newspapers. Knipper wrote to Maria Chekhova that the mood was lively with much drinking, singing, and dancing but with an underlying anxiousness about how the play would be received: "It was as if we wanted to stifle something." Mizinova, who appeared in a crowd scene in the play, was there as well, drinking "heartily as if rooted to her chair; she smoked and drank. Eventually she wanted to drink to *bruderschaaft* with me, but I declined." What Knipper was telling Chekhova was that she was uncomfortable with Mizinova's invitation to switch from the polite to the intimate form of "you" in addressing each other—something reserved for family members and close friends. Knipper went home at nine in the morning, and soon the entourage from the Hermitage, including Mizinova, arrived, still jovial, still drunk. Mizinova again "hinted at *bruderschaaft* several times, but I evaded her requests. I can't, Mashechka! This can't really offend her, can it? We're really not close and I don't feel any particular sympathy or attraction to her, and without this, any use of the intimate 'you' is strange and incomprehensible."[5] In the end she hoped that Mizinova was too drunk to remember any of this awkward exchange.

Mizinova and Alexander Sanin had moved for a long time in the same social circles. They may have met when they both attended Stanislavsky's celebration of the founding of his Society of Art and Literature in

November 1888, when she was eighteen years old.[6] But they only began to see each other regularly when Mizinova became close friends with his sister Ekaterina. Sanin had once been in love with Maria Chekhova, but she rejected his proposal of marriage.[7] Now, ironically having both been spurned by the Chekhov siblings, they found themselves attracted to each other. On March 6, 1902, Knipper wrote to Chekhov: "I think Sanin is in love with Lika. Maybe I'm mistaken."[8] The next day she was even more confident in her suspicions, although their attraction to each other left her perplexed: "You know, Sanin is going to marry Lika. He's accepting congratulations. It means I have a nose. But I completely don't understand her. I'll ask him about it today."[9] Chekhov wrote back convinced that nothing good would result from this union: "I've known Lika for a long time. She's, above all, a good girl, smart and decent. Her being with Sanin won't be good, she doesn't love him, and most importantly she won't get along with his sister, and it's likely that in a year she'll have a big baby, and in a year and a half she'll start to betray her husband. Well, this is all fated."[10]

Chekhov proved to be profoundly wrong on all counts. They were married without any fanfare sometime in May; no one knows the exact date. Mizinova wrote to her mother: "I'm so happy that at times I can't believe that it's not all a dream."[11] Sanin, in turn, loved her deeply despite her past indiscretions. He wrote to her almost every day when they were apart, and he shared with her every aspect of his successes and failures on stage. And Ekaterina Sanina remained a dear friend who felt abandoned when Sanin and Mizinova moved from Moscow to St. Petersburg in June 1902 after he joined the Alexandrinsky Theater. Sanin accepted the position after having been excluded from the list of shareholders, along with Meyerhold, following the reorganization of the Moscow Art Theater. Nevertheless, Knipper continued to take every opportunity to disparage Mizinova. After a visit from Mizinova and Sanina, Knipper wrote to Chekhov on March 1, 1903: "Lika has grown horribly fat—she is colossal, all dressed up, rustling. I feel so shabby next to her."[12]

Sanin remained with the Alexandrinsky Theater until 1907, when he joined Sergei Diaghilev's company in Europe. In 1908 he staged a very successful production of *Boris Godunov* at the Paris Opera with Fyodor Chaliapin in the lead role. Staying in Paris brought back memories for Mizinova of when she was there in 1898-1899 with Eberle. She wrote to Shchepkina-Kupernik in May 1908: "I delight in Paris—my Paris. Happy-go-lucky, crazy Paris has a particular effect on me. It arouses in me a mass of lyricism. I even become sentimental. I walk along my old places and feel joy when I see an old signboard, when I find everything as before. But there's a lot I don't find, and this becomes painful to me, as if a piece of me is missing."[13]

By 1898 Eberle had greatly surpassed Mizinova as a singer. In 1896 she became a soloist in Savva Mamontov's private opera, performing together with Chaliapin in Rimsky-Korsakov's *The Maid of Pskov*. In fact, it was Mamontov who funded the stay in Paris for Mizinova, Eberle, and also Pyotr Melnikov, a producer-director in Mamontov's company. Eberle married Melnikov soon afterward, but the marriage didn't last. By the time Mizinova returned to Paris in 1908, Eberle was married to Savva Mamontov's son, Sergei, a poet and playwright who was also involved in managing his father's railway empire.

With the founding of the New Theater, Yavorskaya's marriage to Baryatinsky turned into primarily a business arrangement. The prince's financial control over the enterprise made it possible for him to stage his own plays. The press, however, continued to identify the New Theater as Yavorskaya's. She controlled the theater's repertoire, which offered her challenging women's roles that often exceeded her acting abilities. In their private lives, she made no effort to hide her sexual conquests from her husband.[14]

The New Theater launched its fall 1902 season with a production of Tolstoy's *The Power of Darkness*. As preparation, the play's director went to Yasnaya Polyana to receive "instructions from the author," while the set designer accompanied him to sketch ideas for the sets and acquire local costumes.[15] In spite of this effort to obtain Tolstoy's blessing, the production was poorly received.

Modernist drama was represented by several productions. The first was Maurice Maeterlinck's new play *Monna Vanna*, translated by Shchepkina-Kupernik, whom Vladimir Linsky of *Theater and Art* called "Miss Yavorskaya's resident rhymester-translator."[16] Next was *The Dream of Life*, the first play by Fyodor Falkovsky, a young playwright associated with the Russian symbolist movement. The season ended with Ibsen's *The Lady from the Sea* as a benefit for Yavorskaya. Linsky grudgingly admitted that "it's a long time since I have come out of a theater with such a pleasant impression.... This is a surprisingly attractive play. It is both invigorating and inspiring."[17] In the same issue an audience member wrote a letter to the editor complaining that Yavorskaya had turned the production into a costume drama that was inconsistent with the modesty of the play: "Miss Yavorskaya's various dresses flashed across the stage, and poses, endless poses. Everything was almost reduced to the fact that in the first act the beneficiary appeared in a fantastically cut dress with a veil reaching down to the floor, in the second, third, and fourth act she was in lace and gauze dresses."[18]

On top of the bad reviews, the theater had to deal with bad publicity. Aside from the recognized artistry of Eisenberg, the set designer (who was also a sculptor), actors in the troupe often complained about the sloppy work of the stage crews. During a performance of *Mademoiselle Fifi* on December 12, 1902, the actor Alexander Romanovsky, frustrated that the revolver he had to shoot several times on stage kept misfiring, raced backstage and threw the gun at the property master Pyotr Nikolaev, hitting him in the back. Nikolaev collapsed and had to be taken to the hospital. After *Theater and Art* reported in its Rumors and News section that Nikolaev's spine was severely injured and the property master had lost the use of his legs, Romanovsky felt compelled to set the record straight. He wrote a letter to the editor expressing deep regret for what he had done: "Losing my patience more than once at the repeated negligence of the property master, I, running backstage while the play was going on, threw the revolver in the direction of Pyotr Nikolaev." But he didn't hit him in the spine: "The revolver gave Nikolaev a bruise, which swelled up. Fortunately, there was no break of his spine and the injured didn't lose use of his legs, which I was able to confirm by visiting him in Obukhovsky Hospital."[19]

At the same time, several newspapers reported on a civil suit against Baryatinsky being held in the chambers of the justice of the peace. The suit was brought by L. V. Leontiev, an assistant director at the theater. He was seeking to recover two weeks of wages, which he lost because of a fine that was levied against him for "twice allegedly voluntarily leaving a rehearsal." Baryatinsky had filed a countersuit seeking an additional forfeiture of 320 rubles, equivalent to two months' wages. A group of actors from the theater, headed by the director Sergei Ratov, appeared in the court chambers as witnesses who unanimously rejected the fine against Leontiev and "gave the most flattering responses about the plaintiff as an assistant director." The judge ruled in favor of Leontiev and rejected Baryatinsky's countersuit. The affair cast an unflattering light on the theater's management and on Baryatinsky personally. *Theater and Art* reported that "the affair is not without interest as a genre painting, and it draws a picture of the organization of the New Theater, in which Prince V. V. Baryatinsky is a representative of its management."[20]

Separate from public criticism of the management of the New Theater, on December 5 Vyacheslav Plehve, the much-reviled minister of the interior, wrote a secret report to Nicholas II recommending a course of action to stop Yavorskaya's political agitation. The memo was prompted by a reading she gave on November 25 as part of a concert for the benefit of impoverished students. Plehve told the tsar that Yavorskaya's history of inciting students, starting with the disruption of the performance of *The Smugglers*, was a threat to public order. He recommended that the mayor's office no longer allow Yavorskaya to participate in public concerts and that the police summon and inform her of this action and that any future "efforts to influence youths in undesirable directions" would result in the "application of severe administrative measures." The tsar wrote "I approve" in the margin of the report, and one can only assume that Yavorskaya received some sort of warning from the police.[21]

The following season (fall 1903/winter 1904) at the theater saw the same mix of classics, French comedies, European modernist dramas, and the occasional work by Baryatinsky. Toward the end of the season, the critic K. Kolosov (likely a pseudonym), writing about Frank Wedekind's *Erdgeist* for *Theater and Art*, started his review by making an astute observation about the New Theater. Despite the general assumption that the journal's editorial stance was critical of modernist plays, Kolosov noted that the New Theater had one indisputable virtue—a repertoire enlivened with "exotic" new plays: "The undertaking familiarizes our public, used to a clichèd, trite repertoire, with the innovations of Western European literature, which in itself is worthy. But it's very sad that at this theater the worthiness of the play and the worthiness of its performance, for the most part, are in opposition to each other."[22]

Such was the fate, Kolosov concluded, of Wedekind's play. *Erdgeist* (*Earth Spirit*) and Wedekind's subsequent play, *Pandora's Box*, were the basis for the silent film *Pandora's Box* (1929) directed by Georg Pabst and starring Louise Brooks, and for Alan Berg's serialist opera *Lulu* (composed 1929-1935). The seductive, ambivalent role of Lulu was surely what attracted Yavorskaya to the work. But Kolosov felt the New Theater poorly served Wedekind's play. Where artistic restraint was required to "preserve at least a hint of truth and naturalness in a play that lays it on so thick," the production did the opposite. "On the contrary they seized on that which is thrown in your face with vulgarity, piled it on; they made completely black everything that is dark in the play. And all this was depicted in some sort of playfully reckless manner, without restraining pauses." Yavorskaya, instead of conveying the "poetic mysteriousness" of *das ewig Weibliche* (the eternal feminine), merely presented Lulu as a "vulgar creature of the female gender."[23]

Similarly, Linsky, in his review of Gabriele D'Annunzio's decadent tragedy *The Dead City*, wrote: "When I read the tragedy—it amazed me with its greatness and beauty. When I saw it on stage of the New Theater—much in it seemed wild, and much seemed funny. I think this happened because neither the performers nor the director tried or were able to convey the style of the work." In performing the blind Anna, Yavorskaya was following in the footsteps of Bernhardt, who had convinced D'Annunzio to give the play to her rather than her rival Duse. But naturalistic drama (Ibsen, Strindberg, Chekhov) was incompatible with Bernhardt's acting style. Bernhardt's production was a disaster and closed after twelve performances.[24]

The negative reviews by Linsky and others infuriated Popov, the New Theater's leading director. He was growing tired of how Yavorskaya's bad reputation in the press and her grating acting style were dragging down his productions. By the end of the year, he quit, telling Yavorskaya that it was impossible to do serious artistic work in her theater, and that there was no point in arguing with her about it because she wouldn't consider anything but her own "personal fantasies."[25] Further plunging a knife in her back, he joined the rival Dramatic Theater being formed by Komissarzhevskaya.

Although *Theater and Art* dismissed Baryatinsky's new social satire, *The Dance of Life*, as no better than his previous trilogy of plays, it turned out to be hugely popular with audiences, playing around 150 times, an unheard-of run for a private theater.[26] The curtain opened on a tableau of the entire troupe animatedly performing a cakewalk dance. They were rehearsing a charity event to be put on by St. Petersburg's "gilded youth" to benefit peasant victims of a village fire. The rest of the play was a comical attack on the upper class's hypocritical attempt to identify with the Russian peasant. The cakewalk was originated by antebellum slaves in the American South as a parody of the stiff ballroom dancing of their masters. By 1900 it had become fashionable in European salons and cabarets. In the play Princess Livinskaya (Yavorskaya) berates her aristocratic peers: "It's unconscionable. . . . Here's this cakewalk that we're dancing: we're all dressed up to the nines, but think about the fact that starving Negroes created it on their plantations. What if they saw us here, being frivolous with our dancing . . .

It's unconscionable."²⁷ In her husband's plays, Yavorskaya often took on the role of a young lady "with convictions," which helped boost her reputation among students and the liberal intelligentsia as a politically bold actor who identified with progressive causes.

The Dance of Life was so successful that the tsar got word to Baryatinsky that he wanted to see it. It wasn't feasible to have a special performance at the New Theater because the tsar's security couldn't be guaranteed there, so they decided to stage it at the imperial Mariinsky Theater. By statute, an outside private troupe was not allowed to perform at the Mariinsky except as an amateur production for a charitable purpose. Accordingly, Baryatinsky himself was cast in the lead role of Count Kuchurgin and his fiancée, Princess Livinskaya, was played by an amateur actress, a countess from the imperial court. The evening was promoted as a benefit for one of Grand Princess Maria Pavlovna's charitable societies.

On the evening of the performance, the tsar arrived with his retinue. Meanwhile, the actors backstage were becoming frantic—Baryatinsky still hadn't shown up. Several calls were made, and he was found drinking champagne in a private room at a nearby restaurant. Someone raced there to bring him to the theater. He arrived a few minutes later, not very steady on his feet. One actor recalled: "Yavorskaya pounced on him like a hawk." She berated him for thinking a bottle of champagne was more important than this crucial performance, reminding him that the whole court was sitting out front in the theater waiting for the performance to begin. Likely he had been drinking to summon the courage to perform. In any event, he calmly replied to Yavorskaya: "First off, not a bottle but a couple of bottles, and secondly, these cretins can wait." He then commanded, "Give me my cloak," putting it on over his coat. He waved his arm—"Open the curtains"—as the actors took their places for the cakewalk scene. As it turned out, the performance went off without a hitch.²⁸

Shchepkina-Kupernik only infrequently contributed to New Theater productions. Rather than joining Yavorskaya during her summer tours as she had in the past, she was now spending those months at Krestovskaya's estate on the Gulf of Finland. She found the grand dacha and gardens to be magical; they inspired her to write a cycle of verse, "Marioki Fairy Tales." Around this time, Krestovskaya began to suffer from periodic bouts of illness, which would later be diagnosed as cancer. Shchepkina-Kupernik stepped in to help manage the estate.²⁹

In April 1904, Shchepkina-Kupernik invited to dinner four of her closest lady friends—Mizinova, Ekaterina Sanina, and two actors,

Maria Roskanova (who had played Nina in Stanislavsky's production of *The Seagull*) and Liubov Selivanova. The ladies exchanged glances as they sat down at the table, noticing that next to Shchepkina-Kupernik sat a handsome stranger. They assumed this was the beginning of some sort of romance. As the main course was being served, Shchepkina-Kupernik hoisted her champagne glass, intending to make an announcement, but was interrupted by the commotion created by the late arrival of Sanin, who had been held up by rehearsals at the Alexandrinsky Theater. He quickly sat down, looked around, raised an eyebrow, and blurted out: "Listen, listen! Shchepochka [his nickname for Shchepkina-Kupernik] has gotten married!" Sanin had spoiled her plan to surprise her friends by telling them she had just returned from Revel, where she had married the man sitting next to her, Nikolai Polynov, a rising young St. Petersburg lawyer. On the way from the train station early in the morning, they were spotted hugging in their carriage by the Mariinsky Opera tenor Alexander Davydov. Seeing the look of amazement on Davydov's face, Shchepkina-Kupernik explained that they had just gotten married, and later that day Davydov told the news to Sanin.[30]

She knew her lady friends would be shocked. Shchepkina-Kupernik was the last and the least likely of the "sirens of the Louvre" to get married. Her friends were convinced she valued her independence too much to ever submit to a man in marriage. She had met Polynov in 1895 in Sudzha in the south of Russia during the unveiling of a bust in honor of her great-grandfather Mikhail Shchepkin, who was born there. Shchepkina-Kupernik had come with a group of actors from the Maly Theater to take part in the ceremonies; Polynov, still a student and spending his summer in the south, had been assigned to write a report on the event for a local newspaper. Afterward, he sent her a copy of a feuilleton he had written praising her verse, but then their paths diverged. She went to Moscow and he returned to St. Petersburg to get his law degree. They met again nine years later through mutual friends. Within two weeks they were engaged.

Polynov was no longer the timid law student she had met in Sudzha. He was a thirty-year-old sybarite whose marriage to a cousin had recently been annulled. Shchepkina-Kupernik suspected that having learned of her marriage to such a man, "my friends were afraid for me."[31] Krestovskaya felt betrayed. Several months later she had breakfast with Olga Knipper and confessed to her about her love for and disillusionment with Shchepkina-Kupernik. Knipper wrote to Chekhov: "Krestovskaya said with a quiver in her voice that Tanechka is an infinitely malicious creature."[32]

Inevitably there was much speculation about Shchepkina-Kupernik's reason for getting married: Was it an obvious marriage of convenience, especially now that she was over thirty and social norms, even among educated liberals, dictated that it was time for her to become the mistress of a household? The similarities between Polynov and Shchepkina-Kupernik's beloved father—both were charismatic lawyers whom women found irresistible—may explain what initially attracted her to him. In her published memoirs, she looked back on her marriage as "thirty-five years in genuine concord in spite of the predictions of friends," describing his handsomeness as very much like that of Michelangelo's sculpture of *The Thinker* in the Medici Chapel in Florence.[33] But if the knowledge that Polynov would continue to have affairs with other women provided her with the cover to discreetly pursue her own passions, it was not a bargain struck without pain. In her archives is a 150-page album entitled *My Life with My Husband*, in which she describes her struggles with his unfaithfulness:

> [Nikolai] had enormous success with women, putting it tritely, they hung onto him. I took this philosophically, understanding that the majority of women couldn't remain indifferent to such a man. And very often the married and unmarried women who had fallen in love with him cried out their sorrows on my breast. I attained a philosophical attitude toward this as I've always had in my life—through empiricism. And of course, this has not been easy—it cost me confused feelings and internal struggles with myself—from which I've emerged the victor.[34]

In the future she would continue to have her own intimate friendships, most notably with Margarita Zelenina, the daughter of the renowned actress Maria Ermolova (about whom Shchepkina-Kupernik wrote a biography), and with the Bolshevik revolutionary Alexandra Kollontai.

CHAPTER 11

1905 Revolution

In the early morning hours of July 2, 1904, Anton Chekhov died of tuberculosis in his room at the Hotel Sommer in Badenweiler, Germany. His funeral took place in Moscow on July 9—a procession of four thousand people followed his casket to his grave behind the high redbrick walls of Novodevichy Cemetery. Recently married, Shchepkina-Kupernik was traveling abroad with her husband when she got word of Chekhov's death. Yavorskaya was on tour with her troupe in Vilnius. She debated whether to drop everything and go to Moscow, but decided it was impossible—the next night's tickets had already been sold, and she was scheduled to leave for Switzerland immediately after the performance for nasal surgery to treat her strained voice.[1]

The only "siren of the Louvre" to attend Chekhov's funeral was Mizinova. Following the graveside service, she joined the Chekhov family at a small gathering in Maria's apartment. After expressing her condolences, Mizinova remained silent, lost in thought, standing by the window, staring out onto the street below. On the fortieth day after Chekhov's death, when according to Orthodox ritual the soul of the deceased ceases to wander the earth, Yavorskaya was back in Moscow and made an evening visit to Chekhov's grave. Fresh flowers from the church service earlier in the day were mixed among the blackening, wet wreathes left over from the funeral. A single votive candle burned at the base of a temporary cross over the grave.[2] Yavorskaya decided it would be fitting to begin the fall season with a play by Chekhov.

But first she had to talk Baryatinsky into delaying a revival of *The Shoals*, which the censors had just allowed to be performed again. The prince was convinced that the critical and popular success of the play would guarantee a full house on opening night. He also felt the times demanded that the theater should start its season with a play that made it clear they were in sympathy with the public's rapidly escalating discontent with government incompetence and despotism. The year had begun with Japan's humiliating attack on the Russian fleet at Port Arthur, Manchuria, in February. There was little public sentiment for a protracted war with Japan, especially against a background of economic decline and political turmoil. In mid-July, Plehve, the minister of the interior who had approved secretly opening and reading Yavorskaya's correspondence, was assassinated by a member of the Socialist Revolutionary Party. The coming of fall brought a series of strikes, student demonstrations, and other disturbances. The creative class had long felt itself at odds with "official Russia," the heavy-handed bureaucracy that enforced censorship and hired police spies. But now the wider social fabric was starting to tear apart as well. However sympathetic Yavorskaya was to her husband's desire to use his play to poke a finger in the eye of corrupt officialdom, she was even more determined to beat Komissarzhevskaya to the punch by having the New Theater open with *Ivanov* on September 8, a full month before her rival's scheduled production of *Uncle Vanya*.

This was the first time Yavorskaya's company performed a Chekhov play on the Russian stage. The result, according to Linsky in *Theater and Art*, was a wrongheaded production that failed to properly honor the beloved playwright. In his typically caustic fashion, Linsky observed there were two things that always distinguished the launching of the fall season: the sandwiches at the buffet were fresh, and the actors actually knew their parts. But unfortunately, Yavorskaya, who was playing the role of Sasha in *Ivanov*, seemed to be making up about two-thirds of her lines. On the other hand, "the operation performed on Miss Yavorskaya's nose," Linsky noted sarcastically, "in no way damaged her voice. Thank God!"[3] He also pointed out that most newspaper reviewers were restrained in their praise of Yavorskaya's performance, being much more interested in the question of why she had decided to take on the seemingly "colorless and thankless" role of Sasha rather than the tragic

Sarah. Litavrina, Yavorskaya's biographer, thought the answer could be found in her reluctance, given her much publicized recent health issues, to play the role of someone dying of tuberculosis.[4] Linsky, on the other hand, quoted with mordant glee the theory of one reviewer that as the theater's "lead actress," it would be awkward for her, as Sarah, to take a bow after she had just died in the third act. As Sasha, however, she could without constraint come out at the end of the fourth act to receive the audience's adoration.

The end of 1904 saw a surge in illegal political meetings that reflected liberal restlessness with the lack of government reforms. In response, the tsar issued a decree on December 12 loosening some of the oppressive measures that had been instituted under Plehve, including easing restrictions on the press. On that date Kugel and Kholmskaya proclaimed in a front-page announcement that beginning with the current issue, *Theater and Art* was now "being published **without prior censorship**. We consider that it goes without saying how much easier this makes our aim 'to fight against the lie of artistic distortions and the falsehoods of life' that we announced when we started our publication."[5] The tsar's decree at the same time also explicitly banned protest meetings, his assumption being that the promise of reforms now made them unnecessary. But in St. Petersburg, simmering beneath the calm of the Christmas holidays, discontent among the workers at the massive Putilov Ironworks was growing. What had begun with complaints against specific plant managers had turned into a call for a general strike under the leadership of a young prison chaplain, Father Georgy Gapon, who headed a police-sponsored labor society at the plant. Rather than co-opting the workers, Gapon called on them to demand an eight-hour day, wage increases, and free medical care. The appeal was formalized as a petition shared with other factory workers in the city, and a plan to have the workers and their families join in a march on Sunday, January 9, to the Winter Palace to peacefully present the petition to the tsar, who they hoped would be sympathetic to their plight.

The ninth was a cold and gray day. A stiff wind blew lightly falling snow over the deep drifts already covering the streets.[6] Around 11 a.m., the actor Ivan Perestiani, who had joined Yavorskaya's troupe that fall, got into his carriage as usual in front of his apartment on Officer's Street for the short ride to rehearsals at the theater on the Moika embankment. Along the way he noticed a large number of soldiers from the Preobrazhensky Regiment grouped closely together in front of St. Isaac's Cathedral. He was not yet aware that over twenty thousand soldiers had been mobilized throughout the city to support police control of the march. It was only when he got to the theater that he found out from other actors that soldiers were also surrounding the Winter Palace to cut off columns of workers who were heading toward the square to meet with the tsar. The whole idea of workers presenting a petition to the tsar seemed so preposterous to Perestiani that he found it humorous.

Looking out the windows of the theater's foyer, Perestiani saw a small cavalry detachment crossing the Police Bridge on Nevsky Prospect only a short distance away. He went outside onto the embankment and could see a crowd filling the sidewalks on both sides of Nevsky and spilling out into the street. His fellow actor Georgy Baransky, who also worked as a reporter for the *Stock Exchange Gazette*, came up to him, and they agreed to walk together to the bridge, where they parted. Perestiani decided to force his way through the crowd up Nevsky to his favorite tobacco shop. He had just stopped at the shop window when soldiers fired a volley; a bullet flew overhead and shattered the glass in front of him. People scattered in panic. Heading back to the Moika embankment, Perestiani saw another cavalry detachment coming toward him, at its head a young officer "whose face was as pale as a sheet." The throng on the sidewalks began to taunt the soldiers. Perestiani heard them shout:

"Look, they're scared!"
"Scumbags. Get lost. Go to Manchuria!"
"Dammit all. It's easier to beat your own people."
"Because we're unarmed."
"Yeah, I'll show him my mother-fucking fist."

More swearing from the crowd was followed by another volley of fire at the demonstrators. Among those killed was Perestiani's colleague Baransky.[7]

What Perestiani saw at the Police Bridge was repeated in other skirmishes between soldiers and unarmed civilians along Nevsky—at the intersection of Gogol Street, in front of Kazan Cathedral—and elsewhere in the city. Orders to disperse were followed by warning shots, then by firing directly into the crowds.[8] The column of workers being led by Father Gapon had been stopped at the Narva Triumphal Arch far from the center of the city. After a series of volleys from the Irkutsk Rifle Regiment, Father Gapon and the crowd fled. At the end of the day, official figures put the dead and wounded at 429, but journalists later submitted a list to the Ministry of the Interior of 4,600 names of the dead and wounded.⁹ Perestiani was told the police refused to release Baransky's body to his mother. "All the victims of the butchery of January 9th were quickly buried somewhere," he wrote in his memoirs. "They only confirmed the deaths of close ones to their relatives. It was obvious that they feared a mass funeral, threatening new, reciprocal butchery."¹⁰ Equally shocking as the number of deaths was the fact that Russian soldiers had fired on the Russian people. As the historian Sidney Harcave noted: "For the most part, the workers had resisted only vocally—with shouted curses and pleas for an explanation of why the tsar would have his people killed: they had thrown no stones, built no barricades, broken no windows."¹¹

Most Petersburg theaters went dark on Sunday night. Both the Alexandrinsky and Maly Theaters shut down midperformance. Yavorskaya had an announcement posted on the doors of her theater that said: "In view of the disruption of the normal flow of civic life, performances are temporarily stopped." On Monday, troops and police remained deployed throughout the city to prevent any further demonstrations. Stores on Nevsky Prospect were shuttered, the sidewalks were empty.

It wasn't until Thursday that any theaters reopened, but given the horrors of "Bloody Sunday," there was no return to normalcy. The striking Putilov workers were joined by other factory workers. St. Petersburg University went on strike, the students and faculty declaring their solidarity with the striking workers and demanding that the government establish a constituent assembly. Similar demands were made by medical, legal, and agricultural societies, by members of the Academy of Sciences, and by most of the city's newspapers. Theater artists, too, seized the moment, organizing a series of meetings to discuss how best to support the striking workers, improve their working conditions, and unshackle the Russian theater from onerous government control.

In early February 1905, a group of theater writers and actors representing the majority of Petersburg theaters, among them the Alexandrinsky Theater, the New Theater, and Suvorin's Literary-Artistic Society, met to draft a document titled *The Needs of Russian Theater (Notes of Stage Artists)*. Inspired by the attempt of factory workers to organize, it called for the creation of a Union of Stage Artists "as a self-directing corporation." The purpose of the union would be to advocate for the abolition of the special drama censor, the end of arbitrary theater closings by the police, the protection of a theater's civic and property rights, and the protection of actors from expulsions through revocation of their residency permits. Among the document's signatories were Yavorskaya, Baryatinsky, Arabazhin, Komissarzhevskaya, Potapenko, and Kugel.[12] Unfortunately, no mechanism existed to compel the government to take action on these proposals. In a concession to the calls for reform coming from all sectors of society, on February 18 the tsar issued a decree that gave Russians the right to send him petitions "for improving the public well-being," which he would turn over to his Council of Ministers for review.[13] But this act of noblesse oblige, which surrendered none of the regime's absolute powers, could not possibly satisfy a public that was demanding representation through the establishment of some sort of popularly elected constituent assembly.

Over the spring, a core group of activists, among them Komissarzhevskaya, met regularly to continue working through the details of forming a Union of Stage Artists. Yavorskaya was not among them, having left with members of her troupe for their annual tour of southern Russia.

She also missed a hearing in April in the chambers of the justice of the peace having to do with a suit filed against her by a former actor in her company, N. A. Victorov. During the winter 1902–1903 season, Victorov, a beginning actor, was offered an additional temporary position as an assistant director at the rate of three rubles per performance. He remained with the theater for the following summer tour and winter season but was never paid for nine performances in which he served as assistant director. Victorov told the judge that when he would remind Yavorskaya of the money owed to him, she would respond with phrases like: "Don't worry about it, Mr. Victorov, I remember this well and you'll be paid everything. You're sweet. I love you very much. You're so committed to our undertaking and I value this!" His suit was postponed four times, and now that he had joined Komissarzhevskaya's troupe, he no longer felt dependent on Yavorskaya's good graces and decided to sue again. Given the paltry amount involved in the suit, it likely had less to do with money and more to do with Victorov's anger at the high-handed treatment he received.

Yavorskaya's lawyer, I. G. Kharlamov, argued that the suit against her should be voided because she wasn't in fact the official owner of the theater. It was Prince Baryatinsky who signed all agreements. But testimony by two fellow New Theater actors maintained that although Baryatinsky signed the documents, it was Yavorskaya who told him what to sign. The judge ruled in Victorov's favor. It was yet another dispute over arbitrary fines and withheld pay, yet another indication of the financial problems and rancorous atmosphere at the New Theater.[14]

Over the past two years, Yavorskaya had counted on her spring southern tours to generate substantial ticket sales from a reliable group of admirers, especially in her hometown of Kiev. Her 1905 repertoire consisted of a typical mix of popular and challenging plays. She tried to stage Gorky's *The Lower Depths* in Kiev but was turned down by the censor. In Tiflis she played the title role in *Hedda Gabler*. One reviewer attributed Yavorskaya's enthusiastic audiences for the more popular plays to the fact that her performances never changed: "As before Miss Yavorskaya plays her heroines *a la Zaza* [the prostitute music-hall performer], as before she displays herself in see-through lace and gauze housecoats, and assumes seductive poses."[15]

Yavorskaya continued to present herself to the public through seemingly contradictory personas—sometimes as a feminist, sometimes as a political provocateur, sometimes as a celebrity sexpot. The response of the *Odessa News* literally reflected these contradictions. The newspaper's critic observed, "It has always seemed to me that she's not so much an artist of the theater as much as an artist of the rostrum, of the tendentious, of social problems." The paper's publisher countered with an opposite view: "Our negative attitude toward Miss Yavorskaya arises precisely because she serves neither a pure idea of stage art nor of social problems, but serves only herself and her personal goals."[16]

The provincial cities that Yavorskaya's company toured were not free of civic strife. In Tiflis, the city was undergoing a general strike with a large police presence in the streets. Perestiani recalled that in the theater hall in Kutaisi, Georgia, armed soldiers stood in front of the orchestra pit during the performance. He was doing a scene with Yavorskaya in a Baryatinsky play, in which he said to her: "Of course, of course . . . I understand your desire to be free . . . " Suddenly "the Kutaisi audience drowned out these words with a deafening burst of applause, absolutely unexpectedly, and at first it even confused Lidia Borisovna and me."[17]

Back in St. Petersburg, Yavorskaya returned to a capital in turmoil. At the end of May, the Japanese annihilated the Russian fleet at Tsushima Strait. This was followed by an armistice, and eventually by a signed peace treaty in August brokered in Portsmouth, New Hampshire, by Theodore Roosevelt. Around the same time, the tsar made a further concession, finally agreeing to form an elected Duma that would start meeting in January. The end of the war and the apparent movement toward liberalization seemed encouraging to Russian intellectuals.

Knipper, who was staying with friends in the Moscow countryside on the day the tsar's manifesto was issued, wrote to Maria Chekhova that when they got the news "we all shouted hurrah and made everyone else yell, and in the evening we drank champagne."[18] However, the tsar in his decree made it clear that any legislative proposals by the Duma had to be "transmitted through the State Council up to the supreme autocratic authority."[19] He still was not surrendering his absolute powers.

Responding to the rebellious atmosphere in the capital, Yavorskaya decided to open her season on September 15 with a performance of Schiller's *William Tell*, a historical drama set against the backdrop of the Swiss struggle for independence from the Hapsburg Empire. Linsky recognized that in the current political climate the obvious weaknesses of the New Theater ensemble were beside the point. What excited the audience were the sentiments expressed in Schiller's words:

> They applauded Schiller, the great Schiller, whose songs speak over and over again about freedom, and call for a new life, bright and joyful. These songs are full of passion, strong and terrifying, knowing their power, ready at any moment to turn into action. Glittering with anger, then with pain, these songs seized the audience, hearing in them an echo of the contemporary, agitating them, arousing that which hides far, far inside.[20]

William Tell was followed by a second attempt to stage a Chekhov play, this time *The Three Sisters*. Linsky wrote that when audiences watched a Maeterlinck play produced by Yavorskaya, they could conclude that the play struck them as odd because the material was unfamiliar. But with Chekhov it was different: "We ourselves have lived through Chekhovian 'boredom,' have ourselves made sense of his 'twilights.'" Therefore, he concluded, the audience could easily sense when the tone was false, when a performance was a caricature, when Yavorskaya's dress made her look more like Zaza than the provincial Masha.[21]

By October, dissatisfied that the tsar in his August decree had surrendered none of his absolute powers, many sectors of society were ready to take action to demand further concessions. A strike among Moscow railroad workers spread to St. Petersburg and the rest of the country. On October 12 the entire country was enveloped in a general strike, which had expanded beyond the working class to include doctors, students, professors, and teachers. In St. Petersburg all public transportation was shut down. "That night," according to the historian Harcave, "the number of factory workers, railroad-men, teachers, clerks, and students who pushed into and out of the university buildings, listening to speeches and advocating the extension of the strike, was increased to some thirty thousand."[22]

The city's imperial and private theaters were faced with the question of how to respond to the general strike. The next evening, a performance of *The Apostle* went on as usual at the Maly Theater, but at the end of the third act the lead actor, Vsevolod Blumenthal-Tamarin, refused to continue and abruptly walked off the stage; another actor took over for the last act. Most of the private theaters decided to cancel their performances and send representatives to a meeting scheduled for the twentieth at the Panaev Theater to further discuss whether to strike. Yavorskaya and Komissarzhevskaya had already decided before the meeting that their theaters would join the strike. Some theaters had closed simply because they had no electricity. On the seventeenth, the management of the Maly Theater decided to stop striking, but they were nevertheless forced to cancel a performance set for the nineteenth because almost no tickets had been sold. On the fourteenth, Sanin arrived at the Alexandrinsky Theater to find the walls plastered with proclamations demanding they join the strike. The next day's performance was canceled out of fear that it would provoke demonstrations. Ostrovsky's *All Good Things Must Come to an End* went ahead on the eighteenth but was occasionally interrupted by shouts from the audience of "Down with the autocracy!" The actors were barely able to finish. Sanin told the playwright Alexander Yuzhin that he had resumed rehearsing his play on the twentieth, but that the atmosphere was tense: "They're proceeding normally but unevenly, nervously, the mood is crazy, agitated . . . Every bit of news reaching the stage from the street irritates and upsets everyone . . . It's hard to concentrate, it's hard to forget oneself, it's hard to keep the troupe in hand . . . "[23]

That evening three hundred to four hundred people gathered in the foyer of the Panaev Theater. The attendees included members of the public in addition to select delegates from the city's theaters—Yavorskaya represented the New Theater. The meeting was facilitated by Kugel and Baryatinsky's colleague Arabazhin. They announced an agenda: (1) a discussion of the reasons why "all theater people must join up with the rest of society to assist the liberation movement and strengthen the attainment of freedom," (2) "the sorting out of guarantees to be put into a manifesto," and (3) a discussion of "how and why the theater world must express sympathy with and aid in the battle of the liberation movement."[24]

These vaguely stated parameters set the stage for a long and unruly night of speeches that only served to underscore the conflicting political and economic views held by the theater community. When Kugel spoke, he tried to direct the debate toward the development of specific resolutions that echoed the demands of labor unions: the abolition of capital punishment, amnesty for political prisoners, and the immediate convocation of a constituent assembly. But others rose to speak with great passion but little focus. A Social Democratic Party activist painted a picture of the significance of the theater in a future social-democratic republic. Radicalized actors spoke of death threats and exhorted their colleagues to fight against provocateurs and antisemites. A socialist worker castigated the organizers for conducting the meeting in such a "restrained liberal fashion." Another actor told the audience that with the theaters shut down, he hadn't eaten in three days: "How can we strike when there isn't any sort of strike fund, no kind of mutual support!" Blumenthal-Tamarin stood up, declaring through tears, "The cyclone is intensifying. We need to more actively support one another." Komissarzhevskaya spoke in favor of an actors' union. When she had finished and was leaving the podium, she tripped and fell, badly hurting her leg. The meeting ended at 6:30 in the morning "amid horrifying noise and shouts." A cartoon titled "At the actors meeting" in *Theater and Art* depicted a chaotic scene—Kugel standing at the dais ringing a bell, calling for order, while members of the audience in front of him shouted and shook their fists at an unruly crowd literally tumbling from the balcony. The decision whether to strike was put off.[25]

It had become apparent that the situation faced by those who worked in a theater was vastly different from that of those who worked in a factory. The theaters themselves were financially strapped; actors were paid by contract not by piecework; the imperial theaters, as state-supported entities, would never agree to a prolonged strike. In the end the public itself dictated whether a theater was "on strike" by simply refusing to attend.

Perestiani, who was in the audience, felt that his fellow actors were incapable of accomplishing anything but empty posturing and naive political pronouncements. He listened to them making speeches attacking theater directors and their employers, calling them capitalists and demanding they be overthrown. "We applauded," he recalled, "completely aware of the ridiculousness of these performances." They were followed by "orators, people whom no one knew, who had been recommended by Socialist Revolutionaries, Social Democrats, anarchists, and even terrorists. They received ovations, but their speeches, in essence, were confused, not always clear, and mostly pointless."²⁶

Yavorskaya, however, embraced the revolutionary fervor. The religious philosopher Vasily Rozanov recalled a conversation with Yavorskaya and Baryatinsky at the home of the mystical writer Nikolai Minsky during the October unrest. Yavorskaya excitedly described the speech of a radical street orator whom she had just heard. Minsky responded that yes, change was necessary, but it should be gradual. There should be a constitution rather than talk of a socialist republic with complete equality of property. She would have none of it. "But of course, a socialist republic!" she exclaimed. Rozanov could tell that Minsky found this amusing coming from an actress standing before him wearing an expensive silk dress with a four-foot train.²⁷ Working from a sketch of Yavorskaya he had previously drawn, Repin included her in the crowd in his painting *17 October 1905*, commemorating the tsar's signing of the October Manifesto. She is wearing an elegant flaming-red dress holding up a red bouquet matching the revolutionary red banners held aloft by others.

In the manifesto the tsar, responding to the massive unrest, made yet another concession, this time agreeing to the creation of a State Duma, an elected legislative body. He proposed "to establish as an inviolable rule that no law may go into force without the consent of the State Duma and that representatives of the people must be guaranteed the opportunity of effective participation in the supervision of the legality of the actions performed by Our appointed officials."²⁸ The public response was elation tempered with continued defiance. The general strike was called off. By the end of the month Petersburg theaters were all open. At the New Theater, Yavorskaya, with renewed enthusiasm, began scheduling plays with an overt political subtext. The actor Boris Gorin-Goryainov recalled seeing her at a rehearsal, most likely for Arthur Schnitzler's *The Green Cockatoo*, which takes place in a Paris tavern on the eve of the storming of the Bastille. Members of the cast ran around shouting: "To the barricades. To the barricades. Why are you sitting here? What are you waiting for?"²⁹ During the play's performance audiences would sometimes stand and sing "La Marseillaise," the anthem of the French revolution, along with the cast.

Baryatinsky didn't share his wife's radical sentiments and stayed away from the political meetings she organized at the theater. His oppositional politics were liberal and focused primarily on a Tolstoyan disdain for the privileges of high society, a position that was vulnerable to the same charges of hypocrisy that were leveled against the great writer.

When the general strike broke out in Moscow on October 14, Olga Knipper sat alone at home, afraid to leave her darkened ground-floor apartment—Black Hundreds, militant supporters of the tsar, roamed the streets provoking fights. "All life has stopped," she wrote Maria Chekhova. "There's no water, no electricity, no trams, no stores, no milk. At night the city is dark, scary, shadows flash."[30] The Moscow Art Theater had joined the strike and was shut down until October 19. After the tsar's manifesto was announced, Knipper felt emboldened to go out again, joining her theater colleagues in celebrations. "We decided in part to go out onto the streets," she told Chekhova. "We moved along with the crowd along Tverskaya to the Governor-General's with red flags, we sang 'La Marseillaise,' we put up flags everywhere, with shining faces, the sun seemed to look out and light up a triumphant crowd of a thousand."[31] But then someone in the crowd shouted out: "They're shooting." People panicked. "The pounding of hoofs could be heard." Knipper decided to back away from the crowd, fearing she would be crushed in the melee.

On October 24, Knipper appeared in a public dress rehearsal of Gorky's *Children of the Sun*. The play is set during a cholera epidemic in the 1860s, and in the third act an armed mob descends on the home of Professor Protassov, a scientist oblivious to the social turmoil surrounding him. Given the charged political atmosphere, when the actor playing Protassov's wife shoots at the mob and the professor falls to the ground, Vasily Kachalov, in the role of Protassov, recalled:

> The audience, not knowing who had fired at whom and why, took the actors rushing in for members of the Black Hundreds, who were breaking into the theater to kill us and concluded that I was the first victim. There was an unbelievable uproar. Some women had hysterics. Part of the audience launched themselves toward the footlights, evidently ready to defend us. The rest went to the exit doors to cut off the escape. Someone leapt to where his coat was hanging to get a revolver out of its pocket.[32]

Nemirovich-Danchenko had to come on stage to ask the audience to allow the performance to continue, assuring them that the play had a happy ending. The audience didn't settle down until Kachalov got up from the stage to show he was still alive, then lay down again.[33]

Back in St. Petersburg, there was a similar response to Yavorskaya's provocative decision to stage Evgeny Chirikov's play *The Jews*, which premiered in censored form on November 23. It was, at long last, her reply to Suvorin's antisemitic production of *The Smugglers*. *The Jews* has as its final scene the horrifying depiction of a pogrom. Linsky, in reviewing the premiere, was struck by the extraordinary effect the play had on the audience:

> I can't recall a comparable enthusiasm in a performance hall, such solidarity of mood between performers and the audience. People were crying on stage; people were crying in the audience. On stage Jewish women who were being pursued fell dead; in the performance hall women who had become hysterical were taken away. At the beginning of the last act, when the unfortunate Jewish family gathers with their pitiful belongings in expectation of the pogrom, the entire performance hall turned into one continuous moan. A bit later, when from somewhere one hears the threatening shouts of the mob, the mood of the audience reached an apogee; many of the ladies got up from their seats and started to leave the hall almost in a run . . . [34]

By the time the final curtain came down, the audience was stunned. They had called for the author at the end of the third act. When it was announced from the stage that the author wasn't in the theater, someone from the front rows shouted: "He's in prison, for promoting a peasant union." In the smoking room after the play Linsky overheard a Jew talking to a small group of men: "You cry when you see a pogrom on stage, but I experienced it with my own skin."

Several months later Yavorskaya and her husband were summoned before a circuit court accused of allowing a tirade spoken in one of the scenes of the play that had been banned by the censors. They were found guilty and each fined twenty-five rubles.[35] It was yet another example of censorship that turned out to be more of an annoyance than an obstacle.

Rather than reflecting a popular resurgence of the New Theater, *The Jews* marked its last gasp. The political turmoil of the past several months had only exacerbated poor ticket sales. The costs of costumes and sets were out of control. The theater was being poorly managed and kept losing money. The last production, Hauptmann's *And Pippa Dances*, ended on February 12, 1906. As usual, the company then went on the road, but the tour didn't generate enough money to enable Baryatinsky to finance another season in St. Petersburg. In Tiflis the local newspaper reported an incident in which one of Yavorskaya's actors became so infuriated at her for being told once again to be patient when he asked for his salary that he grabbed her umbrella, smashed her on the shoulder, and knocked her hat off.[36] That fall Yavorskaya's theater on the Moika embankment was taken over by Olga Nekrasova-Kolchinskaya, who had been an actor in her company.

Notwithstanding the feeling among actors and critics that the New Theater, with its chaotic management and weak ensemble, hurt Yavorskaya's reputation, by lasting five seasons it ranked among St. Petersburg's longest-lived private theaters. Komissarzhevskaya fared no better as an entrepreneur. She launched her Dramatic Theater in 1904, losing forty-one thousand rubles in the first season, primarily due to weak audience interest in her modernist fare.[37] In 1906, she moved from the Arcade Theater on Nevsky Prospect to the Nemetti Theater on Officer's Street, and committed herself to an even more artistically radical repertoire under Meyerhold's direction, which proved to be even more unpopular with critics and the public. One theatergoer lamented that Komissarzhevskaya had fallen "into the barren quagmire of stylized symbolist theater."[38] She fired Meyerhold, hired the symbolist poet Valery Bryusov to replace him, but continued to lose money. By 1909 she was forced to close the theater. Komissarzhevskaya then decided, as Yavorskaya had after the demise of the New Theater, to improve her finances by forming a touring company.

CHAPTER 12

The Wandering Star

After her marriage to Polynov in 1904 Shchepkina-Kupernik took up permanent residence in St. Petersburg, putting an end to her habit of constantly shuttling back and forth between Moscow and the capital. She nevertheless continued to work for Moscow journals and newspapers, publish her books there, and even wrote a four-act play for Korsh's theater, but all from a distance while, as she described it, "setting up my little corner, coinciding with the Japanese war and the first revolution."[1] The events of 1904–1905 disturbed Shchepkina-Kupernik, and her writing became more overtly political.

Following the outbreak of hostilities with Japan in early 1904, Shchepkina-Kupernik became concerned that her husband, an ensign in the reserves, would be sent to the front in Manchuria. She decided to take some nursing courses so she could join him in the event that he was called up. She wrote to her father in despair about their situation: "How can fate be so cruel and merciless toward me?" Lev Kupernik responded with something he had mentioned more than once regarding her literary activity: "You hardly give space in it to politics and social questions. Just as now, in your personal life, you don't take it into consideration. . . . You blame fate for that which the imperial regime is guilty of and makes all of us have to put up with." Kupernik, ever the implacable foe of autocracy, didn't mince words: "We have to crush this regime, to turn against it in word and deed. People of the word, the pen, the press must constantly shout, raise their voices against the war, some directly, some by beating around the bush, some with articles, some with novels."[2]

As it turned out, Polynov was exempted from serving because of a heart condition. Krestvoskaya's son Vsevolod was not as fortunate. A midshipman in the navy, he was assigned to the cruiser *Svetlana*, which set out in May 1904 on the long journey to the Far East to reinforce the Russian Pacific Fleet. At the battle of Tsushima in May 1905, Japan destroyed the Russian fleet and the *Svetlana* was severely damaged. Pursued by three Japanese ships, it attempted to make its way north to Vladivostok. The destroyer *Murakomo* caught up with it, fired on the *Svetlana*, and sank it with a loss of 169 crewmen. Krestovskaya received word that Vsevolod was among the dead. Already suffering from cancer, she was devastated by the news. But three months later, she learned that her son was actually among the 290 survivors rescued by a Japanese support vessel. She was so overjoyed that when Vsevolod returned home after the war, she built a commemorative church and a small monastic cell on the grounds at Marioki.

Although Shchepkina-Kupernik was spared from being drawn into the war, she did experience the turmoil of Bloody Sunday: "The dark streets, here and there pickets by the fires, armed Cossacks riding about . . . I remember the wave of social indignation seizing all of us as being one of the impetuses toward the later revolution."[3] Taking to heart her father's admonition to respond forcefully to the events of the day, she wrote a poem, "In the Motherland." In it "an exhausted, crippled soldier" returns home from Manchuria, "from the fallen strongholds of Port Arthur" only to find that his wife, son, and mother have been killed in the Bloody Sunday uprising. He also learns that his brother, a mutinous sailor in the Black Sea Fleet "was killed by his own officer / Because he stood up for truth!" The poem ends portentously:

> The soldier said not a word:
> He just raised his eyes to the heavens . . .
> In them was a solemn vow
> And the storm of future revenge.[4]

Suspecting the poem could not be legally published, she allowed it to be circulated by hand in St. Petersburg and was surprised to learn it had become popular among workers and students, who turned it into a song that was frequently performed in factories and mass meetings during the revolutionary ferment toward the end of 1905.

The death of Lev Kupernik in October 1905, on the eve of a general strike that resulted in concessions by the monarchy he so despised, only made Shchepkina-Kupernik more determined to write about the political themes he felt were so important. By 1907 she gathered eight stories into a collection titled *This Was Yesterday*, a book reflecting her impressions of the events of 1904–1905 and dedicated to the memory of her father. The work depicts a merciless state seeking to protect itself at all costs. In one story, a young defense lawyer is at first incredulous that those prosecuting his clients are eager to dine with him, show him how cultured they are, say mildly disapproving things about how the police acted on Bloody Sunday, yet have no qualms about putting those whom he is defending to death. When they start talking about the "humaneness of the guillotine," he is repulsed, concluding they are animals lacking any sense of compassion. In another story, a judge is so conscious-stricken by his decision to order the execution of a man he knows personally, whose children played with his, that he contemplates suicide. To distract himself, he goes off to see a prostitute who sits on his lap, her blouse open, laughing, cheering him up, helping him forget about his victim. In "At the Asylum" a regional official, the patron of a local mental ward for children, attends its Christmas party. He is struck by the beauty of one five-year-old girl, "dark like a gypsy with shining eyes and red lips. Even with a shaved head she looked enchanting." She is a "wayward comet" among the grimaces, dead eyes, and pale faces of the other children. He asks about her and is told that her mother went mad and killed herself after learning of her husband's execution for killing a policeman. The official recalls that he had been the one to sign the death sentence. He takes out a wallet and asks the staff to buy something special for her. The story ends in a moment of bitter irony as the girl, encouraged by the head mistress, goes up to the official to thank him for his generous gift.

The radicalized students and workers depicted in the book are thwarted in their efforts to topple an intractable state and its aristocratic supporters. A revolutionary in exile in Switzerland is tricked into returning to St. Petersburg by a telegram from his mother telling him that his wife is dangerously ill. He enters their apartment and finds his wife to be perfectly healthy. She knows nothing about the telegram. The doorbell rings; a policeman enters. In "Sara Mikhailovna" a Jewish radical finds herself homeless in the city because none of her friends is willing to take the risk of putting up someone whose internal passport says "resident of the Pale of Settlement." After wandering through the city all night, in the early morning she hears church bells. A service is about to begin. She goes into the church, finds a dark corner, puts her head down on a ledge, and goes into a deep sleep, her last thoughts being: "If only they don't throw me out . . . if only they don't find out!"

The most defiant story of the collection is "The First Ball." The widowed wife of a general is bothered that her twenty-year-old daughter Olga is so secretive about her personal life. She often goes off for days to visit her girlfriends and has the odd habit of shooting at bottles in the garden. The mother is pleasantly surprised when Olga, usually uninterested in high society, expresses a desire to go to a ball. She has heard that Prince Gordynsky will be there and says she wants to get a close look at him. The young prince is handsome and has recently become politically influential, having been assigned the task of putting down local strikers. The house bustles with preparations for the ball. Olga's mother is overcome by how radiant her daughter looks in her white gown. Olga is mostly indifferent to the fuss being made. At the ball Olga is asked to dance by several prominent young men. The splendor of the event strikes her as strange, as if she were looking at people from another world. After dancing with a baron, she pauses as Prince Gordynsky passes by. What he sees in her eyes causes him to panic and suddenly turn pale. She pulls out a revolver and shoots him three times. The music stops. Olga stands motionless holding the revolver. Gordynsky lies dead on the floor.[5]

This Was Yesterday was published by the Moscow bookseller A. D. Drutman. Not surprisingly, given the reactionary backlash following the 1905 revolution, the books were confiscated and Shchepkina-Kupernik was accused of slandering the state. She regretted that her father wasn't still alive to mount her defense—she was convinced it was something he would have relished.[6] Her lawyer advised her to refuse to show up for the court hearing. No judgment was made against her personally other than an order to have the books confiscated and destroyed. The publisher managed to save a few copies for her; others have made their way into archives.

Perhaps the best summary of Shchepkina-Kupernik's's thoughts on how her life had evolved over her first thirty-three years can be found in her long, semiautobiographical novella in verse *Marianna Bolkhovskaya*, published serially the same year as *This Was Yesterday*. Bolkhovskaya comes to Moscow to train as an actress, having escaped from Kiev and an overbearing father. She gradually becomes disenchanted with the world of the theater. The fame she desires eludes her, but not the notoriety of being taken for a courtesan-actress. She moves to St. Petersburg, where she begins an affair with Andrei Ardatov, a married lawyer. But over the course of the next several years Ardatov's passion for Bolkhovskaya begins to fade.

One day Bolkhovskaya receives a letter from Ardatov's wife, who writes that she is in despair and, much to Bolkhovskaya's surprise, asks for her help. She reveals that Ardatov is once again in love—the woman is half his age and this time he's demanding a divorce. She begs Bolkhovskaya to use her charm to convince him to come to his senses. Bolkhovskaya arranges to see Ardatov and confront him with the letter he once wrote her: "You wrote to me honestly, bravely. You promised not to abandon your family. And the inevitable has come to pass. . . . I swear to you with my soul, on the day that you desert your family in order to leave forever with someone else—on that very day I will reveal everything to her and, listen to me, I will kill myself."[7]

More years pass. Bolkhovskaya abandons acting to become a hospital nurse. When the Russo-Japanese War breaks out, she volunteers to join a group of church sisters leaving for Manchuria to treat the wounded. At the station waiting for their train to depart, she feels at peace surrounded by "her family given to her by God. . . . Marianna's soul is full of a new feeling that had been foreign to her before: Loving not one person, but everyone; living for others, not for herself." A woman breaks through the crowd and approaches Bolkhovskaya. It is Ardatov's wife. She has come to thank her for saving her family: "You are doing a heroic deed, I know. . . . God grant you more strength. Not for my tranquility . . . What's it to me? My time has passed. But for the children—for their salvation. God bless you, sister!" The novella in verse ends with the train departing into the night. Bolkhovskaya is unable to sleep: "She kept recalling the farewell greeting and heard the sad voice saying to her: 'Sister!'"[8]

Marianna Bolkhovskaya reflected several feminist themes that Shchepkina-Kupernik would return to repeatedly in her work. While Yavorskaya embraced the power that her femininity gave her over men and used it to forge her acting career, Shchepkina-Kupernik in her writing focused on the more pervasive power that society gave to men, as fathers, husbands, or lovers, to victimize, betray, and humiliate their daughters, wives, and mistresses. They are allowed to abandon a relationship with no consequences, making a woman wary of fully surrendering herself emotionally to a man.

Throughout his marriage, Andrei Ardatov maintains an apartment in the city, separate from the house where his wife and children live, so that he can openly pursue a series of love affairs. Lev Kupernik thought nothing of going to a Moscow theater with his mistress when Shchepkina-Kupernik's mother was attending the same performance, or spending evenings and holidays with his mistress rather than with his family. "It ended up that Mama couldn't endure such a life," she wrote in her memoirs, "and taking me—I was then one and a half years old—she left for St. Petersburg so as not to see everything that so tormented her."[9] Similarly, Shchepkina-Kupernik had to endure married and unmarried women coming to her, sobbing on her breast, confessing their love for her husband.

For Shchepkina-Kupernik, the shared oppression that women felt created a sense of solidarity among them. In her letter to Bolkhovskaya, Ardatov's wife admits it appears strange that she is asking her husband's mistress to save her family. But she decides that Marianna in her role as lover had behaved honorably, refusing to destroy or even disturb the life of Ardatov's wife and children. Marianna unequivocally does what she asks and shames Ardatov into abandoning his plans to get a divorce. In the final scene at the train station, the two women are explicitly joined in a bond of sisterhood, a relationship of mutual trust and support that Shchepkina-Kupernik found to be otherwise impossible between a man and a woman.

In 1908 Shchepkina-Kupernik, who previously had limited herself to one-act plays, wrote her first four-act drama, *One of Them*. Recovering at home in St. Petersburg from surgery for appendicitis, she was unable to attend its premiere at Korsh's theater in Moscow in December. Reviews were mixed. Some felt the story of a girl, Marusya, who dreams of becoming a great actor only to become disillusioned, was banal and had been told many times before, even by Shchepkina-Kupernik herself in *Marianna Bolkhovskaya*. She argued that the very familiarity of Marusya's fate was what attracted audiences—many educated Moscow families "recognized in the heroes of the play one or another person they knew." Marusya was "one of a thousand ordinary girls, growing up in intellectual families, who thanks to a complete absence of purpose in life, an undisciplined family in a slushy milieu, despite her talents and opportunities, loses her way and perishes in the wings of a pathetic provincial theater."[10]

While Shchepkina-Kupernik settled into home life in St. Petersburg for the first time (she didn't even make her way to Moscow to see *One of Them* until a year after its premiere), Yavorskaya, having closed down the New Theater, became a "wandering star," spending three years on tour in the provinces. In the first half of 1906 her road company of thirty people performed 114 times in twenty cities from Moscow to Samarkand, grossing on average a modest 761 rubles per performance.[11] Rather than living off their earnings, the prince was likely subsidizing his wife's peregrinations.

After a two-month summer hiatus, staying at the famed Kislovodsk spa, Yavorskaya reassembled her troupe and began her fall tour in Baku. As was the case with St. Petersburg theatergoers, she was not satisfied with offering her provincial audiences an exclusive diet of proven popular fare. A performance of *Zaza*, which earned two thousand rubles, was followed by a production of Knut Hamsun's obscure Nietzchian drama *Sunset Glow* (*Aftenrode*), which in spite of considerable promotion played before an almost empty hall.[12] She then fought with a competing theater over the rights to perform a new play, *Robespierre*. Local authorities, nervous about the play's subject matter, delayed allowing either theater to put it on. But when Yavorskaya was finally able to stage it, the local newspaper sarcastically concluded that the production so vulgarized the French Revolution that after seeing it, it was "possible with certainty to say that all of Russia to a man would rise up against the idea of a constitution and demand the most despotic form of government."[13]

At the start of the new year, the company left Russia for central Europe, performing in Warsaw, Lodz, and Vienna, where Baryatinsky had secured the Burgtheater. Yavorskaya continued to offer audiences a mix of light French comedies—*Zaza, Mademoiselle Fifi*—and more challenging Scandinavian dramas—Strindberg's *Miss Julie* and *Laboremus* by the 1903 Nobel laureate Björnstjerne Björnson. In March 1907 the company returned to the Hermitage Theater in Moscow for twelve performances of Baryatinsky's new play *The Bureau of Happiness*. Small audiences and poor reviews resulted in a loss of three thousand rubles.[14] The price that Yavorskaya was paying for her husband's financial underwriting was the general perception that she put on his plays primarily to assuage his vanity.

On top of this, there were indications that after several years, provincial audiences were beginning to grow tired of Yavorskaya, her company, and her repertoire. Although she toured widely throughout southern Russia, the troupe was primarily based in Tiflis (now Tbilisi). A local reporter, using the pseudonym Pince-Nez, followed her progress in articles for *Theater and Art* as closely as Linsky had in St. Petersburg. In June 1907 he wrote: "Miss Yavorskaya has sung her song in Tiflis. For four spring seasons in a row she has attracted a large Tiflis audience; for the fifth this very same audience, yawning, has turned away from its beloved one. . . . For the past two weeks of the short season, the theater was positively empty."[15]

But broadly speaking, the criticism was unfair—it ignored the fact that Yavorskaya continued to introduce provocative new plays into her repertoire, even if her actors weren't up to the challenge of performing them, and her audiences (and sometimes local authorities) weren't capable of understanding or appreciating them. This certainly was the case with Sholem Asch's play *The God of Vengeance*, which she added to her repertoire when she moved on from Tiflis to Baku.

Asch's play, originally written in Yiddish, is about Yankl, a brothel owner, who is determined to preserve the purity and marriageability of his daughter Rivkele. In the course of the play, he is shocked to discover that Rivkele has fallen in love and run off with Manke, one of his prostitutes. *The God of Vengeance* had its first performance in Russia in April at the Contemporary Theater in St. Petersburg. It was put on by the Society of Dramatic Artists, which included actors from the Alexandrinsky and Komissarzhevskaya companies. However gingerly the actors handled it, critics couldn't help but notice there was something "Sapphic" in the relationship between Rivkele and Manka. Asch himself in a letter to *Theater and Art* protested the mangled translations of his play—from Yiddish to Russian to German back to Russian—expressing particular concern about the scene between the two women in act 2, in which in modern productions the actors kiss and talk of sleeping in the same bed.[16]

It was a bold move on Yavorskaya's part to seize the opportunity to put on the play only a month after its St. Petersburg premiere, and she fearlessly cast herself in the role of the seventeen-year-old Rivkele, a girl half her age. There is no way to determine how "Sapphic" her performance was. Given that the play had been approved by the censors and that Rivkele is described as being "as pure as the Torah itself," it's likely her attraction to Manka the prostitute was depicted as innocent and childlike.

When Yavorskaya returned to Tiflis in September to open her fall/winter season, Pince-Nez, rather than disparaging her repertoire as repetitive and tiresome, now expressed excitement after seeing the list of plays slated for performance: Maeterlinck's *The Blue Bird,* Ibsen's *Rosmersholm,* Strindberg's *The Dance of Death,* and Wedekind's *Spring Awakening.* However, most of these proposed plays were eventually shelved, primarily because of the theater's ongoing conflicts with censors and the local authorities. At the beginning of the season Yavorskaya also decided to split the troupe into two companies capable of simultaneously performing in Tiflis and Stavropol. The financial logic of such a decision was debatable—it was often difficult for her to fill one provincial theater; the expense of supporting two productions at the same time would only further erode any net earnings.[17]

So, while still based in Tiflis, Yavorskaya traveled at the end of October to Stavropol to stage Shchepkina-Kupernik's recent translation of *Cupid and Psyche* by the Polish playwright Jerzy Zulawski. Earlier that month, Shchepkina-Kupernik was startled to read a letter to the publisher in *Theater and Art,* in which Zulawski warned Russian theater managers that he had designated a Mr. Alexander Voznesensky as the only person authorized to translate and stage his play. While recognizing the "formal defenselessness of my authorial rights in Russia," he pleaded with Russian theater managers as "cultured people" to comply with his expressed wishes. Kugel, in an editor's note, was dismissive, reflecting Russia's continuing disregard for copyright conventions: "It is our deep conviction that in the interests of culture, the right of free translation should not be limited. We're a bit communist on this point, and if Russia binds itself to this convention, it will be a great inhibition for Russian literature and Russian theater, and will give rise to a monopoly of literary profiteering."[18]

Shchepkina-Kupernik, for her part, published a response, saying it would be very distressing for her to have to tell theater managers and her publisher that she had usurped the rights to translate the play. In her defense she provided as evidence a letter she had received from Zulawski "in which he asks me to send him my published translation of *Cupid and Psyche* and expresses to me flattering satisfaction regarding my taking on a translation of his work. Thanks to this letter I have a firm basis to consider myself having the right to translate *Cupid and Psyche.*"[19] She felt she was being gracious in notifying Zulawski of her translation. Kugel thought even that was unnecessary. *Cupid and Psyche,* like most other contemporary European plays, was performed throughout Russia in various unauthorized translations without any legal repercussions.

Yavorskaya's productions of controversial recent plays continued to make Tiflis authorities uncomfortable. The police chief told her she could not stage Sunday performances of *The God of Vengeance* or of the modernist Polish tragic-farce *The Morality of Mrs. Dulska* by Gabriela Zapolska. In December she announced plans to put on Victor Protopopov's *Black Crows*, a play about a fanatical sect of religious healers based on John of Kronstadt, an Orthodox archpriest whose claim to be a wonderworker put him in conflict with the church authorities. The play was currently running in St. Petersburg, attracting large audiences.

Most daring of all was her decision to stage *Spring Awakening*, Wedekind's scandalous play about sexual repression in German society. Given that the play dealt with the themes of rape, masturbation, abortion, and homosexuality, one wonders how it ever passed Russian censors in the first place. Needless to say, ticket sales were brisk. Extra seats were crammed into the orchestra section. To tackle the challenge of staging the play's sixteen scenes with only one intermission, the play's director took advantage of the Tiflis Artistic Society's revolving stage, although on the first night "the mechanism started to go haywire after the third scene."[20] An additional challenge confronted the actors, who had to convincingly play the roles of teenagers. Yavorskaya took on the role of Wendla, a fourteen-year-old who is raped and dies during a botched abortion. After two performances the play, which had prompted letters to the local newspaper decrying its immorality, was banned.

As rehearsals proceeded for *Black Crows*, the company remained uncertain whether the authorities would decide to ban it as well. They approved the posters for the play but privately advised Yavorskaya that they were still considering shutting it down. The regional governor attended a rehearsal. He demanded that the actresses must not be dressed to look like Orthodox nuns and the singing must not sound like Orthodox chants. Yavorskaya didn't know until 6 p.m. on the day of the first performance whether they had permission from the governor to proceed. *Black Crows* was performed nine times to overflowing audiences, which helped offset the losses resulting from the banning of *Spring Awakening*. By the end of December, the tsar, siding with the supporters of the now ailing John of Kronstadt, had banned all performances of the play throughout Russia.[21] When Yavorskaya subsequently decided to revive *Jews*, which hadn't been staged in Tiflis for over a year, it too had to undergo administrative review by the censor, who decided it could be performed only if the entire pogrom scene, the play's dramatic climax, was deleted.

Yavorskaya tried in vain to find another play to match the success of *Black Crows*. She staged two English plays, E. W. Hornung's *Raffles* and Oscar Wilde's *The Ideal Husband*, but their British cunning and wit were lost on Russian audiences. Overall, her 1907–1908 winter season turned out to be one of the least successful for the Artist's Society Theater, the Tiflis venue Yavorskaya had rented. Its management began to look for another company to lease the space for the following season. They turned to Margarita Pitoeva-Beletskaya, the twenty-three-year-old scion of an illustrious Georgian theatrical family. Furious, Yavorskaya sent a notarized letter complaining that the theater had been promised to her. She demanded arbitration. But Pitoeva-Beletskaya maintained that no such promise had been made. Yavorskaya and her troupe went on the road, playing in Kharkov, Taraspol, and Baku, where she signed a contract to lease the Tagiev Theater for three years starting in the fall of 1909. In the summer of 1908, she also began discussions with the management of the Georgian Court Theater, which was undergoing the final stages of a major reconstruction project set to be completed in November. Desperate to find a new home for her wandering company, Yavorskaya signed a four-year contract with conditions reported to be "quite draconian." She would pay an annual lease of seventeen thousand rubles plus two thousand rubles a year to cover sets and costumes. She was also responsible for year-round administration and maintenance of the theater, bringing the annual total cost to around fifty thousand rubles. The theater owners would retain the proceeds from the cloak room and buffet. Essential to her ability to recoup her costs was the completion of a new summer amphitheater seating a thousand that was part of the reconstruction project. Pince-Nez was convinced Yavorskaya agreed to such onerous conditions out of sheer stubbornness brought on by spite toward Pitoeva-Beletskaya and the desire "to have a theater in Tiflis no matter what."[22]

For her opening night at the Georgian Court Theater on December 2, Yavorskaya, ever combative, staged Hamsun's *At the Gates of the Kingdom* three days before the premiere of the same play at the Artist's Society Theater (and again on the same day as Pitoeva-Beletskaya's premiere benefit performance). Pince-Nez, dismayed by this unnecessary competition, which would only serve to divide local theatergoers, noted the "not very large audience" at Yavorskaya's opening: "Among this small handful of people one felt a chill just like that in the corridors of the still damp and unheated theater." Yavorskaya chose to start the evening with the same short poetic "conversation" Shchepkina-Kupernik wrote to mark the opening of the New Theater in 1901, a reflection of the significance Yavorskaya attributed to once again having her own theater. Pince-Nez found the piece's advocacy of the "new" hardly relevant to Tiflis, and went on to complain that Yavorskaya may have a new building, but "old habits remain—instead of eight o'clock, the performance began at nine. The intermissions were endless. I left the theater at midnight and two acts of the play still remained."[23] He recognized that Yavorskaya's repertoire was more "literary" than that of Pitoeva-Beletskaya: "But this advantage is completely swallowed up by the weaknesses of the troupe. Plays are put on after one or two rehearsals. The young, inexperienced actors feel absolutely helpless; they pay careful attention to the prompter, stumble, miss their cues.... And to add to all this, drafts continue to blow in the reconstructed theater; the temperature rises to that of a bathhouse, then plunges to almost zero."[24]

After a month of struggling to attract audiences, Yavorskaya finally landed a hit, Protopopov's *Laisa the Hetaira*, the story of a courtesan in ancient Greece. Once again, the formula for success was a combination of the promise of a risqué performance and the threat of censorship. In the title role she wore a "shapely, tightly fitting dress so excessively bare that you're amazed how the outfit stays together." Local officials vacillated whether to allow students to attend, not sure if the play's educational value was offset by Yavorskaya's costumes and her "Dance of the Sacred Flames" in the third act. In the end, they decreed that students could not be admitted. This only convinced adult audiences that the play must be seen. The rest of the repertoire was pushed aside, resulting in twenty-three full houses before it ended its run.

An occasional hit, however, wasn't enough to offset the onerous expense of running the theater. As Lent and the end of the winter season approached, many of the actors complained they were still owed much of their salaries. Those who had received their wages left town; others sued. Baryatinsky felt compelled to gather the entire troupe in the foyer to announce that no one should be concerned, that they would all be paid by the end of the season.

Meanwhile, the owners of the Court Theater faced their own financial crisis. On February 12 there was an extraordinary meeting of the Tiflis nobility to listen to a commission report on the reconstruction costs of the Court Theater. Much to their shock, they found out that rather than the 80,000 rubles that had been allocated in 1906 for the reconstruction work and the building of a new summer theater, expenditures to date had totaled 389,500 rubles. This excluded any work on the summer theater, which they were contractually obligated to build.

The attending noblemen were furious both at the construction commission for allowing the excess expenditures and at the marshal of the nobility for signing the contract with Yavorskaya. Some argued it would be better to annul the agreement than to construct the summer theater. The meeting ended with a decision to select a special committee to find ways to fund the cost overruns. By April the committee had reached an amicable agreement with Yavorskaya to void the entire contract, including the three-year lease, and return the funds she had already deposited with them. Yavorskaya was free of a long-term financial burden, but once again she was without a theater. The deal she had signed to take up residence in the Tagiev Theater in Baku for the winter season had fallen through when on February 21 the theater burned to the ground.

Yavorskaya ended her three years as a provincial "wandering star" and returned to St. Petersburg in the spring of 1909. She had discussions with Suvorin about rejoining his troupe but refused to accept his conditions. Earlier in the year, Kugel had written in his Theater Notes column about the dismay he had felt when Komissarzhevskaya announced she was closing her theater for financial reasons and planned to spend the next two years on tour in the provinces in the hope of generating enough funds to return to the capital to restart her theater. "I don't really believe this," he wrote. "In general, I believe that the journey touring in the provinces is a journey to a country 'from which there is no return.'" He listed examples of a "long martyrology" of actresses who befell such a fate, including "the noisily famous L. B. Yavorskaya."[25] His comments were prescient. In January 1910 Komissarzhevskaya became seriously ill while performing with her company in Tashkent. A little over a week later she died of smallpox. Yavorskaya would return to perform in St. Petersburg six years later, but by then the city would be called Petrograd, and the country would be in the throes of a world war.

CHAPTER 13

English Debut

One day in the summer of 1907, Shchepkina-Kupernik accompanied her husband, Nikolai Polynov, to St. Petersburg's Tauride Palace, where he planned to meet with some legislative deputies on legal business while the State Duma was in session. The body had been reconvened in February, but was now stripped of the ability to make any constitutional demands and existed primarily to rubber-stamp government policies. While sitting in the gallery waiting for the Duma to recess, Polynov pointed out to his wife some of the more prominent politicians and lawyers gathered in the hall. In the midst of this blur of men in uniformly dark suits, Shchepkina-Kupernik caught sight of a female figure:

> She was an unusually graceful young woman in a dark green dress, completely smooth-fitting as if she had been poured into it. Despite the dark color of the dress, she gave off some sort of luminescence.... The woman was surrounded by a golden aura: as if light was emanating from her fair hair, from her bright blue eyes, from her lovely smile. The general impression was as if she were lit from within.[1]

Shchepkina-Kupernik asked Polynov if he knew who she was. He didn't, but guessed that she was probably a journalist, given that she was surrounded by a lively group of Social Democrat politicians. Fascinated, Shchepkina-Kupernik watched how she moved, how she talked. "Was she an actress?" she wondered.

In a remarkable coincidence, the next day Shchepkina-Kupernik called on her friend, the actor Vera Yurieva, only to find the very same woman sitting in Yurieva's study. Yurieva mumbled an incomprehensible introduction. Shchepkina-Kupernik mentioned she had seen her yesterday at the Duma. From their brief conversation, Shchepkina-Kupernik sensed the woman had "a certain masculine way of thinking—precise, clear, slightly stern that contrasted with her completely feminine exterior and manners." Yurieva saw the woman out, and when she returned, Shchepkina-Kupernik blurted out, "Who is this enchanting woman?" Yurieva laughed and replied that the woman had asked about her in almost the same way.

The woman was Alexandra Kollontai, whose closest childhood friend was Yurieva's sister, Zoya Shadorskaya. To the public Kollontai was known as an increasingly prominent and controversial socialist activist who wrote and lectured on workers' rights, advocating in particular for improved conditions for laboring women. They met again at Yurieva's, immediately sensed a shared affection, and started regularly visiting each other in what turned out to be a lifelong friendship. Moscow archives preserve 777 letters from Kollontai to Shchepkina-Kupernik, vastly more than she wrote to any other person.

Both women were the same age and shared a privileged upbringing. Kollontai's father was an aristocratic officer in service to the tsar. Her mother, more unconventionally, was a Finnish divorcee, the daughter of a serf. Both Finnish and Russian were spoken at home. In addition, nannies taught English, French, and German. In 1893 Alexandra married her second cousin, Vladimir Kollontai, who came from a Polish family and was educated as an engineer. A year later they had a son, Mikhail.

Raised in a liberal household, Alexandra read books in the family library by such 1860s radicals as Nikolai Chernyshevsky, Nikolai Dobroliubov, and Dmitri Pisarev. She pressured her parents to give her a proper education outside of the home, something that aristocratic young girls were discouraged from doing in the 1880s. They relented and enrolled her for a time in a private school. When Kollontai showed an aptitude for writing, they arranged for her to be privately tutored by a professor of literature at St. Petersburg University. After her marriage and the birth of her son, she rebelled against being consigned to the role of dutiful mistress of the house, and together with her friend Yurieva began to volunteer at an organization that taught night classes to workers. On one occasion she and Yurieva visited a factory with Vladimir Kollontai, who was overseeing the installation of a ventilator system. Both women were profoundly shocked by the squalid conditions they witnessed. When her husband tried to pacify her by saying he was working to improve the factory, Alexandra became furious: "I don't want to live like this anymore! Go, all of you, from now on we'll go our own separate ways!"[2] Alexandra found herself gradually embracing revolutionary politics. After five years of marriage, she divorced Vladimir, left her son behind, and went to Zurich to study Marxist economics.

Kollontai and Shchepkina-Kupernik were drawn to each other by their shared feminist independence and devotion to career. Kollontai's break with bourgeois respectability, however, was far more radical than Shchepkina-Kupernik's. Looking back on her prerevolutionary years, Kollontai echoed Shchepkina-Kupernik's own thoughts about the lives of her other close women friends:

> How much time and energy we wasted on our endless love tragedies and their complications. But it was also we, the women of the 1890s, who taught ourselves and those who followed us that love is not the most important thing in a woman's life, and that if we must choose between love and work, we should never hesitate: it is work, a woman's own creative work, that gives meaning to her life and makes it worth living.[3]

But the radicalism of Kollontai's "creative work" led her to view the fight for women's rights very differently than Shchepkina-Kupernik did. Shchepkina-Kupernik's feminism focused on upper- and middle-class women's struggle, primarily in the arts, for respect and recognition equal to that of men. She wrote stories sympathetic to those who opposed autocracy but could never be considered anti-capitalist. Kollontai, by contrast, had adopted a proletarian worldview. She was critical of feminist organizations that advocated for suffrage but did little to improve working-class conditions. For her, equality for women remained impossible as long as capitalism remained intact.

Shchepkina-Kupernik recognized this difference and respected Kollontai's boldness:

> As someone used to being in an artistic circle, I was impressed by the seriousness of Kollontai's concerns and her persistent, stubborn work, concealed by a made-up disguise. . . . She went to the theater, was in literary-artistic circles, dressed very elegantly, and to unobservant eyes even appeared to be simply a successful society lady. But all this was a facade for the tsarist police behind which she hid her underground work. Officially she wrote articles for Marxist journals about the women's movement, about land issues, gave lectures on neutral themes. . . . , but unofficially she led circles among workers (primarily in the textile industry), disseminated propaganda, and agitated.[4]

Over the course of the next year, Kollontai was a frequent visitor to Shchepkina-Kupernik's spacious apartment on Kirochnaya Street, regularly mixing with the actors, painters, journalists, and lawyers who gathered there. By September 1908 Kollontai had found out the police had issued a warrant for her arrest. Her 1906 book *Finland and Socialism* had come to the attention of the Ministry of Internal Affairs, and it was accusing her of openly calling for an armed uprising in Russia. She needed a place to hide and accepted Shchepkina-Kupernik's offer to stay at her apartment.

Zoya Shadorskaya thought it prudent for Kollontai to leave the country, but Kollontai was determined to stay in St. Petersburg and find a way, even if it was in disguise, to play a role in shaping the upcoming first All-Russian Women's Congress in December. Concerned that the bourgeois organizers of the event would ignore the issues important to working women, she took to addressing dozens of factory meetings, telling women laborers about the congress. This agitation led the congress organizers to agree to the formation of a Labor Group delegation. When the congress opened in Alexandrovsky Hall, Kollontai attended incognito, having arranged for a textile worker from the Labor Group to read her report on the women's socialist movement. But as this and other issues were presented, a shouting match developed between the women in their elegant gowns on the platform and the laborers in their cheap dresses in the audience. "What do you know of our lives, bowling along in your carriages and splashing us in mud," shouted a member of the Labor Group toward the platform. An organizer replied that their social status was precisely what made them best able to represent the workers' interests. Unable to remain silent, Kollontai joined the raucous debate, provoking hisses and jeers. Two organizers rushed toward her. Kollontai's colleagues spirited her out of the hall.[5]

The next day the police sealed off the hall and began checking documents. Thirteen women from the Labor Group were arrested, and others were subjected to body searches. At Shchepkina-Kupernik's apartment, Kollontai packed her things (including a fake passport) and asked for her son to come by so that she could say goodbye. Shchepkina-Kupernik arranged a small farewell party that evening. She then took Kollontai to the Finland Station to catch the late-night express to Berlin. The train stopped at the Lithuanian border, where Kollontai disembarked and nervously paced the platform waiting to find out if the guards would let her continue her journey. They let her pass, and she crossed into Germany.

Two months later Shchepkina-Kupernik visited Kollontai, who was living in a boardinghouse in Grunewald, a suburb of Berlin. This was the first of several meetings in Western cities during Kollontai's exile. They spent two weeks together, talking, going to museums, enjoying being together—they called each other "soul sisters."[6] For Kollontai, Shchepkina-Kupernik's presence was a welcome holiday, a gift of the spirit, prior to going on a demanding speaking tour of industrial towns in Saxony.[7] She would not return to Russia for eight years. On April 1, 1917, Kollontai arrived at the capital, now called Petrograd. She had been elected as a Bolshevik delegate to the Petrograd Soviet. Two weeks later she joined others in welcoming Lenin at a small station at the Finnish border as his train crossed into Russia. She boarded the train and accompanied Lenin; his wife, Krupskaya; Kamenev; and others for the final leg to the Finland Station, where near midnight they were met by a feverishly excited crowd and a military band playing "La Marseillaise."[8]

During the period when Shchepkina-Kupernik was hiding Kollontai from the police in her apartment, she was also concerned about her other dear friend, Maria Krestovskaya, who was now suffering from late-stage cancer. Krestovskaya's Petersburg apartment was on Kirochnaya Street not far from Shchepkina-Kupernik's. There, to distract herself from her unbearable pain, Krestovskaya continued to organize lavish parties. Shchepkina-Kupernik recalled that during these receptions Krestovskaya's spirits would be temporarily lifted: "Her enormous blue eyes shining, she moved from group to group, invited them to be seated at the dinner table, beautifully decorated with flowers and

Venetian topaz silverware. Her wit shined—and then the next day she would collapse into complete prostration for the next two weeks."[9]

By late 1909 Krestovskaya's husband, Evgeni Kartavtsev, decided to move her from their apartment to the home of Baroness Iskul. The baroness had already taken on responsibility for Krestovskaya's care. When she had previously learned that Krestovskaya had gone abroad for an operation accompanied only by her doctor and a servant (Kartavtsev's work kept him from going), Iskul bought a train ticket, visited her, and spent two weeks by her bedside, easing her loneliness as she recovered. Now the baroness offered the whole lower floor of her house so Krestovskaya wouldn't be alone while Kartavtsev attended to his business affairs.

Shchepkina-Kupernik looked on in dread as she watched the torment of Krestovskaya's last days. One incident stood out in particular. The baroness had organized a "grand evening affair," the performance of an excerpt from Dmitri Merezhkovsky's banned play, *Paul the First*. Krestovskaya, already bedridden, convinced her doctor to let her attend the event. Shchepkina-Kupernik and a few friends got her ready to go upstairs, feeling "as if we were dressing up a corpse":

> The light white dress hung on her as if she were a skeleton. She tossed on a white lace shawl to hide her emaciation. She touched up her cheeks with rouge—her eyes blazed with an unnatural blue brilliance. She desperately wanted to deceive herself for a moment, to go out for a moment into a live world, among live people . . . My husband took her hand, not so much to lead her as to carry her into the hall: she weighed almost nothing. They seated her on a couch. Her acquaintances pretended not to be surprised by her appearance. Those who didn't know her looked with terror at this apparition of a woman who was ruining the celebratory atmosphere. Many didn't know that she lived here and were dumbfounded how a dying person was able to be brought into the party.[10]

Krestovskaya caught sight of Fyodor Chaliapin, a striking "bogatyr-like" figure among the elegantly dressed guests in the room. She insisted on being introduced to him, and when he came over to her, she asked him to sing something to her. Hiding his irritation at the request, he smiled and said, "Please allow me this time to simply be a guest at the party." When she continued to implore him, he added, "Allow me to send you a ticket to my concert."

At this, she cried out plaintively: "But you have to understand. I may not live to see your concert!"

Indignant, he replied so sharply that Shchepkina-Kupernik's husband rushed in to lead Chaliapin away, who was overheard saying to Polynov, "If I sang for everyone who was dying, I would have lost my voice a long time ago!"

Krestovskaya became hysterical. The baroness and Shchepkina-Kupernik stepped in to escort the sobbing woman out of the room. Shchepkina-Kupernik felt that Chaliapin would have acted differently if he realized the significance of his snub. She could see the episode terribly upset her friend: "The unhappy woman had reached out to people, to life—and life refused her last request. She endured this with difficulty, and she was left with a sense of unnecessary cruelty."[11]

Krestovskaya died at her beloved estate, Marioki, on July 7, 1910. At the time, Shchepkina-Kupernik was visiting Kollontai in Frankfurt. She had recently found out that Polynov was once again having an affair, this time with one of her cousins. She demanded that he drop this dalliance and join her in Germany. He agreed, but Shchepkina-Kupernik also told him that from now on she considered their marriage to be a formality. She would be a "sister and a mother" to him, not a wife.[12]

Marriage for Yavorskaya and Baryatinsky, as well, had by now become a formal arrangement. By the summer of 1909 the couple had to make a decision about how best to continue that arrangement. Three years of performing in the provinces had been tumultuous and, in the end, financially unsustainable. Returning to St. Petersburg was problematic. Many of the city's theater critics had long been hostile toward Yavorskaya and, more troubling, she knew she was under police surveillance. In addition, the era of the leading lady was coming to an end. The model now was the ensemble, exemplified by Stanislavsky's Moscow Art Theater. It made sense to go abroad.

Given Yavorskaya's theatrical training, past tours, and Francophilia, one would have expected her to look to Paris. But during a brief stay there, she was unable to find anything that suitably encompassed her ambitions. After her trip to Paris, she settled into the Hotel de France in St. Petersburg. She was desperate to talk to Shchepkina-Kupernik privately about a decision she had just made about her future—she would go to England to establish herself on the London stage. Yavorskaya went to Shchepkina-Kupernik's Petersburg apartment. Only Polynov was there, and Yavorskaya was shocked to learn from him that he had no idea where his wife was. She guessed that Shchepkina-Kupernik must be at Marioki, caring for Krestovskaya, who would die a year later. As it turned out, Yavorskaya and Baryatinsky had plans to visit Repin at his dacha in Kuokkala (now Repino) on the Gulf of Finland not far from Marioki. But the two women were unable to connect until they both returned to St. Petersburg several days later. Yavorskaya spent a night at Shchepkina-Kupernik's apartment a few days before departing for Western Europe. She and Shchepkina-Kupernik looked through a collection of press clippings that she planned to show English producers as bona fides of her theatrical reputation in Russia. Shchepkina-Kupernik could not have been pleased by Yavorskaya's decision to leave, something she herself would never contemplate doing. In a final note to her, Yavorskaya lamented that the two couples weren't able to arrange a farewell celebration: "After all, when will we ever see each other again?"[13]

We don't know whether Yavorskaya's decision to move to London was calculated or impulsive, but it couldn't have been more fortuitous. Britain, at the time, was going through a period of "Russomania,"[14] a newfound fascination with Russian culture. Aylmer and Louise Maude and Constance Garnett had translated novels by Tolstoy and Turgenev. The Proms at Queen's Hall had premiered works by Tchaikovsky, Rachmaninov, Glazunov, and other Russian composers. Productions of Russian plays, however, were mostly limited to private Sunday performances by the Incorporated Stage Society of London. The society premiered Gorky's *The Lower Depths* in 1903, Tolstoy's *The Power of Darkness* in 1904, Gogol's *The Inspector General* in 1906, and Turgenev's *The Bread of Others* in 1909. Its members came to expect a level of "philosophical gravitas" in Russian plays that distinguished them from contemporary British theater's emphasis on amusement.[15]

Soon after arriving in London in July 1909, Yavorskaya gave an interview to the *Daily Mirror* in which she said the purpose of her visit was "to study the British stage, and, if possible, open for a short season with a Russian play at one of the London theaters."[16] The reporter noted her striking beauty: "She is a tall, handsome woman, with fine, large, expressive eyes." Yavorskaya made sure to mention both her husband's links to the Russian royal family and his liberal opposition to the autocracy. She talked about how his newspaper, the *Northern Courier*, had been suppressed by the censor for championing the poor, and that one of his most successful plays, *The Silkworms*, was a denunciation of Russian aristocracy. Yavorskaya also emphasized how impressed she was by London and the British people, how after checking into her hotel the previous night, she had gone for a walk in Westminster, "saw your Houses of Parliament in the moonlight, with the light all shining in the river. It was a fairyland—a beautiful enchanted town.... You English people are wonderful—everybody seems so calm and takes things so easily. There is no hurry or rush."

The Baryatinskys stayed in London for more than two months, attending the theater (she went to see *King Lear* three times at the Haymarket), making important social and artistic contacts, and basking in the flattering attention of the popular press. Of particular help was Gabriel Veselitsky, a former diplomat who had been serving as the London correspondent of Suvorin's *New Times* for the past twenty years. He may have had something to do with the fact that by the time Yavorskaya returned to St. Petersburg at the end of September, she had an agreement with Sir Herbert Beerbohm Tree to return in November with her own troupe to put on a series of matinee performances in Russian at His Majesty's Theatre. In October, the *Illustrated London News*, *The Tatler*, and *The Sketch* featured spreads announcing Yavorskaya's upcoming debut on November 30 in *The Lady of the Camellias*. In *The Tatler* Yavorskaya was shown in profile in a provocative publicity photograph (from the 1902 production of *The Dream of Life*)—she's wearing a narrow-waisted, tight-fitting dress with a low-cut pleated flounce emphasizing her amble bosom. Much was made of her being "the daughter of a Russian general" and the wife of a playwright-prince.[17]

Yavorskaya returned to London with a small company of actors to begin preparations for her London debut. Four days before the premiere she gave another interview to the *Daily Mirror* in which she again sang the praises of being in England: "The life here is so artistic, so logical, so clear." She expressed confidence that audiences would appreciate her performances notwithstanding the language barrier: "From what I have seen of the English people, I am led to hope that they will fully appreciate these plays, all of which are well-known. They are simple, realistic, and emotional. It is not important that the words should be understood. I rely absolutely on my own artistic acting."[18]

Yavorskaya and her company gave five afternoon performances over the course of two weeks. The repertoire consisted of *The Lady of the Camellias* (performed in Russian once in its entirety, once abbreviated to the last three acts), act 5 of Ostrovsky's *Vasilisa Melentieva*, Ibsen's *Hedda Gabler*, and Strindberg's *The Stronger* (part of which Yavorskaya performed in pantomime). She wrote Shchepkina-Kupernik about the joy she felt following her debut performance: "I'm madly happy.

Strange as it may seem, the audience listened attentively and appeared to understand me. . . . How sad it is that you're not with us."[19]

The exoticness of seeing performances by a Russian princess who was also a professional actor attracted considerable press and public attention. In the audience were curious theatergoers, Russian expatriates, and London actors (including Sir Herbert Tree). The translator Constance Garnett attended the December 7 performance of *Hedda Gabler* as part of "quite a gay week" of going to the theater with her sister-in-law Olive.[20] *The (London) Times* declared that Yavorskaya's decision to open with *The Lady of the Camellias* "was a bold choice," inviting comparisons with Bernhardt and Duse: "In London the majority of every audience understands French pretty well; a good sprinkling have enough Italian to know what Duse is saying. Russian is comprehensible to very few indeed . . . . a strange tongue to those ignorant of it, with passages of liquid beauty queerly mixed up with crowding sibilants and gutturals." Nevertheless, the *Times* critic concluded that Yavorskaya overcame this barrier and revealed herself to be "a great actress. . . . Mme. Yavorskaya's Marguerite should be seen by all who love good acting; and in the face of such acting as hers, all difficulties of language simply do not exist."[21] Veselitsky was so pleased with the press response that he sent a dispatch to the *New Times* reporting Yavorskaya's "exceptional success in London" and providing excerpts of flattering reviews by six London newspapers. "It remains for us to be only sincerely happy for our Russian actress," Veselitsky declared.[22]

The British literary journal *The Athenaeum*, looking back on the fortnight of Yavorskaya's performances, was more circumspect in its response and pointed out weaknesses in her acting style that were well known to Russian critics: "A woman of graceful carriage and fine presence, an actress of unusual emotional sensibility, she was at her best in depicting the sorrows of Dumas's sentimental courtesan. In her capacity for abandoning herself to the luxury of grief she has no equal on the English stage." But the critic found that this approach ("Hysteria seems to be the note of her art") simply didn't work in her portrayal of Hedda Gabler: "Her Hedda is resourceful and dangerous; but she acts the melodramatic scenes with too melodramatic a fervor, and is always on the lookout for effects. . . . Hers is, indeed, an interesting, but not very plausible reading of the character."[23]

Celebrating her success, the Russian Embassy hosted a breakfast in Yavorskaya's honor. But more significantly, on December 5 she was invited to attend a luncheon for Henry James at the chambers of Sir

Frederick Pollock, a gathering that would shape the course of her future life. Pollock was an eminent jurist, an Oxford don who played an influential role in shaping English legal education. His son John, like his father, was educated as a lawyer, but was more interested in pursuing a career in journalism and the theater. Also at the luncheon was Ezra Pound, who found the meeting between the flamboyant Yavorskaya and the reserved James sufficiently memorable to describe it almost forty years later in his *Cantos*: "her holding dear H. J. (Mr. Henry James) literally by the button-hole . . . in those so consecrated surroundings (a garden in the Temple, no less) and saying, *for once*, the right thing namely: 'Cher maitre' to his checqued waistcoat, the Princess Baryatinsky, as the fish-tails said to Odysseus."[24] Echoing Chekhov's analogy, Pound likened Yavorskaya to a siren (a "fish-tail") who button-holes James in a garden of the Temple law courts and flatters him by calling him "Dear Master" just as Odysseus had been seduced by the sirens' song. She invited James to see *Hedda Gabler* on December 7. He didn't much like her performance, but nevertheless found her charming. Yavorskaya accepted his invitation to visit him at Rye. She was accompanied by Baryatinsky and John Pollock, who photographed the couple with James in front of Lamb House.

Prior to the abbreviated performance of *Vasilisa Melentieva*, Baryatinsky, who as one reporter commented "speaks better English than any Englishman," came out on stage, sat at a small table, and gave an animated fifteen-minute introduction to the play and its author. His talk was nuanced, slyly humorous, "commanding and winning over the audience as completely as his wife."[25]

After the curtain came down on the final performance of *Vasilisa Melentieva* on December 10, 1909, Yavorskaya returned to the stage to recite Shchepkina-Kupernik's poem "Lais' Farewell," accompanied by music from Camille Saint-Saëns' *Samson and Delilah*. Shchepkina-Kupernik was inspired to write the poem by Protopopov's recent popular play *Lais the Hetaira*, in which Yavorskaya had appeared with great success in Tiflis at the beginning of the year. The poem was derived from several classical Greek epigrams in which Lais, the famous courtesan, now old, bequeaths her mirror to Aphrodite. Where once the mirror reflected her allure, it now only reveals "How the rosy cheeks have withered, / How the gaze of love no longer burns, / How beauty no longer has the power to enchant . . . "[26] By the end of her first London engagement Yavorskaya, however, felt reassured that she still had the power to enchant, and had found a way to point her career in a new direction in a new country. She returned to St. Petersburg before Christmas, declaring that she was "enraptured by the English."[27] The response of the returning actors in her troupe was a bit more muted. They told *Theater and Art* that they were "elated by the gentlemanliness of the English . . . but complained a lot about the conditions of life in London and the climate." The actors joked that the English press was so courteous that theater critics wrote reviews before plays were even performed. On the financial side, it was reported that proceeds from the tour "were moderate."[28]

In early March 1910 the Baryatinskys were again in Western Europe, traveling to Florence following the death of the prince's brother Alexander. His affair with the singer Lina Cavalieri had poisoned his life, and neither his marriage to Princess Yekaterina Yurievskaya, whose mother was the morganatic wife of Alexander II, nor the birth of his two sons could prevent him from squandering his wealth and drinking himself to death at the age of forty. The Baryatinskys stayed for two months at the Villa Papiniano in Fiesole, consoling the princess, who in her grief had taken to her bed, and trying to help her sort out the complexities of her inheritance. In spite of these grim affairs, Yavorskaya was delighted to be able to spend early spring in such luxurious surroundings that were so reminiscent of the joy she felt traveling through Italy with Shchepkina-Kupernik in 1894. "The landscape here is shrouded in the distance by a blue fog," she wrote to Shchepkina-Kupernik, "like in an ancient fresco. . . . How I wish you were here, and saw this villa, drowning in roses and wisteria. . . . There's nothing I would like more than to once again inhale this beauty together with you."[29] Pyotr Kropotkin, the doyen of Russian anarchists in exile, whom Yavorskaya had met soon after arriving in London, was staying in Rappolo and came to visit. She marveled at his youthful energy at age sixty-eight: "For days on end we devour paintings, frescos, and statues together with him."

Princess Yurievskaya's financial situation turned out to be maddeningly complex. Yavorskaya came up with the idea of having Baryatinsky suggest to the princess that she contact Polynov, Tatiana's husband and a highly respected lawyer, to ask him to come to Italy to help sort things out. She made the proposal in expectation that Shchepkina-Kupernik would accompany her husband. She was deeply offended when he arrived at the Florence train station alone. Polynov solemnly promised Yavorskaya that he and his wife would come to London in the summer. That was not to be. In spite of countless invitations over the next several years, Shchepkina-Kupernik would never visit Yavorskaya in England.

At the Villa Papiniano, Polynov managed to charm Yavorskaya and, more importantly, Princess Yurievskaya. "Such an amazing ability to please and such a lightning-fast ability to immediately master the circumstances," Yavorskaya wrote to Shchepkina-Kupernik. "Now the secret of your great love for him has been revealed to me," she added, glossing over the pain caused by Polynov's many marital indiscretions.[30]

From Italy the Baryatinskys went on to Paris, where Yavorskaya performed in several small-scale musical matinees and recitals, but no theatrical engagements. She was back in London in July, continuing to cultivate her social contacts and the attention of the press. The *Daily Mirror* quoted her in an article on the preservation of courtly manners. "In Russia," Yavorskaya explained, "it is quite the rule for a young man to propose on his knees, also to kiss the hand of ladies of his acquaintance. Such customs are a pretty reminder of days of chivalry, and I am pleased to hear Englishmen are reviving them."[31]

By this time Yavorskaya had drawn John Pollock into her professional and personal circle, so much so that he accompanied the Baryatinskys to Paris in the fall for rehearsals of *Le Meilleur Moyen*, a three-act comedy, "an undemanding little thing about adultery," at the small Théâtre Michel on Rue des Mathurins. The theater fancied itself as modernist, a bit "over the top," and somewhat naughty, evoking "the atmosphere of the boudoir, but always with humor and even some self-irony."[32] Mata Hari was a member of its ensemble; in 1923 it was the scene of a famous brawl between Dadaists and Surrealists involving Pablo Picasso and André Breton.

During one rehearsal Pollock witnessed an awkward exchange in which the play's two authors started arguing about whether Yavorskaya deserved to be given a leading role. When the author who opposed the idea started making disparaging comments about her, Baryatinsky, who was sitting next to Pollock in the stalls, yelled out that he was a *goujat* (Black Guard). The playwright became furious, was ready to challenge Baryatinsky to a duel, but thought better of it and left the theater. The prince admitted to Pollock that when it came to his wife, "You either adore her or you can't bear her."[33] Yavorskaya considered the play's three-week run in Paris a success, even if the earnings were only five thousand francs. The money did, however, allow her to buy several haute couture dresses from the House of Paquin.[34]

In his memoirs, published in 1950, Pollock, with typical British reserve, refrained from expressing any romantic feelings toward Yavorskaya but did describe how mismatched the Baryatinskys were as a couple. She "was ever driven on by a demon of energy that barely gave her time to sleep or to eat. She had absolutely no sense of time, and invariably tried to crowd into twenty-four hours the normal activity of a week." In the prince, however, he witnessed "a typically Russian slothful disposition."

> I never saw a man more averse to exertion. Apart from endless talk with friends over slowly consumed light beer and innumerable cigarettes, his chief pleasure was in long walks so slow that it was difficult to keep pace with him.... Only great mutual devotion could have kept such a couple together, buttressed by the defensive armor of the prince's lethargy.... In the end the bond broke, to the Princess's long, inconsolable grief.[35]

In public, for the most part, they played their roles without displaying much mutual affection.

Yavorskaya recognized that collaborating with Pollock, with his connections, could lead to more significant theater engagements, which to date had been on a modest scale. On December 3 the *Illustrated London News* devoted its Art, Music and the Drama page to a write-up on the *Causeries du Jeudi* (Thursday Chats) being held at the three-hundred-seat Little Theatre on John Adam Street. The article featured photographs of Yavorskaya, Pollock, and Baryatinsky, who were organizing the next causerie, set for December 8. The event turned out to be something between a salon gathering (the *Daily Mirror* reported that "the social and artistic world were present in full force")[36] and a theatrical performance—Yavorskaya appeared as a temptress in Pollock's one-act medieval drama *Rosamond* and as a comic princess in one act of Baryatinsky's satirical *Nablotsky's Career*. During the pause between the two plays, the prince gave a talk on Tolstoy, who had just died.

Significantly Yavorskaya, for the first time, performed both roles in English. She had been receiving coaching from the actor Kate Rorke.[37] Yavorskaya was already fluent in French and German, but she had a hard time mastering a proper British-sounding accent. This would pose less of a problem in roles as a continental European character where her foreign-sounding English seemed appropriate, sometimes fooling audiences into believing that she was putting on the accent intentionally. The review in the *Daily Telegraph* made no mention of her debut in English, commenting that she was "received by a crowded house with remarkable favor.... Madame Yavorskaya is without doubt a very distinguished actress, accomplished in technique, subtle in suggestion, full of resource, and inspired through and through with a nervous energy which, at times, rises to tragic height."[38] For the next five years, Yavorskaya would devote herself to acting exclusively on the London stage. Perhaps more due to English reserve and good manners than any remarkable displays of artistry on her part, Yavorskaya felt more generally accepted in London than she had ever felt in Moscow and St. Petersburg.

CHAPTER 14

"I Don't Need a 'Happy Life,' I Need the Stage"

By 1911 Shchepkina-Kupernik had been involved in theatrical productions, either in collaboration with Yavorskaya or with others, for almost twenty years. Over the course of those years, most of her work for the stage consisted of translations of classical and contemporary Western European plays in support of Yavorskaya. Only recently had she started writing her own full-length plays. She readily admitted that the first one, *One of Them* (1908), came across as four one-act plays strung together. Her next play, *The Happy Woman*, was better structured and premiered (like *One of Them*) at Korsh's theater, on September 9, 1911. She still had a large following among theatergoers in Moscow, and Korsh knew she would attract an audience from the intelligentsia that normally stayed away from his theater. No longer attached to Yavorskaya's theatrical career, Shchepkina-Kupernik's flourished.

She felt *The Happy Woman* "was and wasn't a success." Initially the actor Alexander Yuzhin, who headed the troupe at the Maly Theater (her favorite Moscow venue), expressed interest in performing the play, but the theater's administration refused, citing the play's "leftist leanings." Witnessing through her friendship with Kollontai how high society sometimes intersected with the world of radical youth, Shchepkina-Kupernik wrote a play about how, as she described it, "a refined, charming 'happy woman,' overlooked the fact that her young student son had become a revolutionary, and only comes to her senses when he is sent off to Siberia.... From a happy woman, she is turned into an unhappy mother."[1] In the final act, against the wishes of her husband and friends, she makes the arduous journey to Siberia, only to find her son on his deathbed.

When *The Happy Woman* was submitted to the censors for approval, it was banned. However, one of the censors, Baron Nikolai Drizen, stood up for the play and suggested to Shchepkina-Kupernik that it could be performed if she rewrote the last act to eliminate the scenes in Siberia. She reworked it: the fourth act ends with Lidia Stozharova, the mother, making preparations to go to Siberia. While she's offstage packing, two of her friends open a telegram stating that her son has died. Lidia returns to find one of the friends crying uncontrollably. When Lidia asks what's happened, the other friend says, "Lidia, I must . . . I must tell you . . . " and the curtain drops.

Shchepkina-Kupernik went to Moscow to attend the dress rehearsal. She wasn't happy with the play's director, Nikolai Krasov, whom she found to be "very colorless and uncultured." She felt he didn't have "the least understanding of the lifestyle, habits, and manners of Petersburg 'high society' (the world of *Anna Karenina*)." Getting these touches right in the play was very important to her because they made palpable the contrast between the sanctimonious sense of privilege enjoyed by the aristocracy and the hints we get of a seething discontent among the lower classes. It disturbed her that Krasov had staged a society salon in a living room with small tables and carafes of rowanberry vodka and snacks reminiscent of a Moscow tavern, "which to him was the height of extravagance."[2] Fortunately, Krasov didn't protest and let Shchepkina-Kupernik make last-minute changes to the props to create a more accurate mise-en-scène.

Another concern in advance of the premiere was the play's lead actress, Elsa Krechetova. She was, as Yavorskaya had been, an attractive ingenue plucked by Korsh from the provinces. He had decided to begin the fall season with a production of Ostrovsky's *The Storm*, on the occasion of the twenty-fifth anniversary of the playwright's death, featuring Krechetova in her debut in the lead role of Katerina. Her performance was savaged by critics, who found her interpretation of the tormented, unhappily married Katerina to be excessive in its self-laceration. Korsh was crushed by the response, and Krechetova considered quitting the company. But he decided to give her another chance and cast Krechetova as Stozharova in *The Happy Woman*.

Fortunately, this time the critics' response to Krechetova was more favorable, if not glowing. She had played her role "convincingly and with a great sense of measure," most noticeably in the last scene, "at a moment where you expect a cry, hysterics," instead she "suddenly without a sound goes down on her knees with the sorrowful prayer of a mother on her pinched, pale face."[3] Emmanuil Beskin, the regular contributor to the Letter from Moscow column in *Theater and Art*, was less charitable: "I won't say it was good. No. But it wasn't as bad as in *The Storm*. Miss Krechetova—one can say this now—doesn't have the temperament. She is cold, like a carafe of water. She doesn't experience drama. And in place of nervous agitation, she simply offers empty spots."[4] Shchepkina-Kupernik's recollection of the reaction to Krechetova's performance was more positive, saying that in her role "all her gifts were on display, and she was very much in her element."[5] Krechetova looked on the role as her savior and often performed it when she went on tour with Korsh's company.

Beskin was not only uncharitable toward Krechetova, he was highly critical of Shchepkina-Kupernik's attempt to inject politics into her play. He damns her with faint praise as primarily a "talented 'woman,' . . . . a poet of intimate experiences," whose theatrical pinnacle would always be *The Dream Princess*. But with *The Happy Woman*, she "wants to toss aside the silk peignoir and put a toga on her shoulders." He found the political point she was trying to make "hackneyed; . . . she is pounding on a door that has long ago been opened." To him, the play "smells slightly like the year 1905."

On this score, history would prove Beskin wrong. If the door had already been open, the censors would not have banned the first version of act 4, just as they had previously attacked her collection of stories, *This Was Yesterday*, for slandering the state. In addition, the play as performed makes it clear in hindsight that the upper classes were ignoring the seething peasant and workers' protests at their peril. At a soiree, the well-connected Baron Shvert, who is in love with Stozharova but refuses to intercede on her son's behalf when he is arrested, pompously recalls speaking with an American president, who told him: "In our country we, the grown-ups and old people, do the politics and the young people are busy with their own personal lives, but in your country, it's the other way around and that's very dangerous." But Shvert dismisses the president's concern: "Young people in Russia have to grow out of their attraction to politics—it's like getting the measles, the earlier the better."

Shchepkina-Kupernik felt she eventually achieved a "moral victory" over those who had dismissed *The Happy Woman* as politically naive when she was awarded the Griboyedov Prize for the best play of 1911 by the Society of Drama Writers and Composers. Suvorin told her he wanted to put on the play in St. Petersburg, but his leading actress, Valentina Mironova, who had succeeded Yavorskaya in his troupe, refused because she found it offensive that she was being asked to play the role of a mother with a grown son. The idea was dropped. *The Happy Woman* went on to be widely performed throughout Russia and, although not Shchepkina-Kupernik's best play, it was included in a 2009 Russian anthology of women's drama of the Silver Age.[6]

The success of *The Happy Woman* encouraged Shchepkina-Kupernik to start working on another play, revising the plot she had used in her short story "Backstage," published in 1893 at the very beginning of her writing career. Theater life was a subject that she had repeatedly turned to in her prose, poetry (*Marianna Bolkhovskaya*), and plays (*One of Them*). What interested her most, not surprisingly given her close collaboration with Yavorskaya, was the attraction that acting had for women of her era: celebrity, power over men, financial independence, and not least of all, artistic expression. But Shchepkina-Kupernik understood that pitfalls and disappointments accompanied these opportunities: the general assumption that an actress was sexually promiscuous; the recognition that fame, when not completely elusive, was often fleeting; the constant professional jealousies and bitter rivalries; and the realization that the pursuit of art most often meant sacrificing personal happiness. These were the themes that dominated her stories of theater life.

As described previously, in Shchepkina-Kupernik's story "Backstage" Bronislava Lesnovskaya, a provincial actress, decides to take revenge on her lover, Rudnev, for abandoning her to become engaged to a seventeen-year-old girl, Natasha. Using her charisma and expressions of sexual desire to flatter the impressionable Natasha, Lesnovskaya seduces the young girl, convincing her that she has what it takes to become an actress. The story ends with Natasha deciding to call off her marriage to Rudnev to join Lesnovskaya's troupe as it leaves town. Lesnovskaya, through her successful act of revenge, humiliates Rudnev, telling him, in effect, "You should never play with the affections of a good actor."

Her play, *The Girl with Violets*, has the same basic story line (the actress even has the same last name), but this time (Marina) Lesnovskaya is a Moscow leading lady with the star power of Yavorskaya. Shchepkina-Kupernik draws on her experience and observations working alongside Yavorskaya, at both Korsh's and Suvorin's theaters, to create a more complex portrait of the theater world, and she gives her heroine a more conflicted attitude toward a life on stage. "The plot was simple," she recalled, "but the pictures of life backstage, the actors, and lawyers were painted rather life-like, and much was taken from nature."[7]

Marina has been in a relationship with Boris Neradov, a successful lawyer in his late thirties, but now suspects he is in love with someone else (Shchepkina-Kupernik knew a thing or two about handsome lawyers with a wandering eye). She confronts him, and Neradov confesses that he has fallen in love with the nineteen-year-old Nelly Chemezova, a rich orphan chafing under the watchful eye of a domineering aunt. When Lesnovskaya's fellow actors explain to Ivan Porokhovshchikov, the owner of the theater company, that she's been behaving strangely because of the stress of her personal life, he goes on a tirade reminiscent of Korsh's and Suvorin's well-known diatribes about the agonies of running a theater company:

> If an actress's nerves aren't shot—she's not worth a penny! In the theater, everyone's nerves should be shot, so it is with this theater, with the actors, the box office, down to the last stage hand. Haven't you noticed how fat I am. God made me this way, and you think my nerves aren't shot? Every night I hallucinate that Velinsky [an actor] has run off, that expropriators have made off with the till, that the other actors are begging for advances . . . I wake up in a cold sweat. If Marina crashes, just haul me away to the sanitarium for the exhausted and spiritually worn-out.[8]

In act 2 there is a dressing room scene reminiscent of the seduction in "Backstage." An assistant brings Lesnovskaya a bouquet of violets sent by Neradov's new lover, Nelly. Seizing the opportunity, Marina asks that Nelly be brought to her and that they be left alone. Nelly, who dreams of becoming an actress, is flattered by Marina's attentiveness. But this time, unlike the sensuous embrace described in "Backstage," Marina simply asks Nelly, "Do you want to kiss me?" The stage directions call for "a quick, robust kiss." At the end of the scene, Marina cryptically announces that she has now found a way to quiet the agitation in her soul.

Marina lets Nelly know that she has used her influence to convince Porokhovshchikov to audition her. But here the plot takes a significant turn not found in "Backstage"—Marina tells Nelly not to go on stage:

"I fear that all your illusions will be crushed." Nelly is dumbfounded. Why is Marina saying this after all the encouragement she has given? Because, she responds, "you don't know what it takes to attain true artistry. We approach it through shattered happiness, through shattered love. . . . Why would you want to experience this?"

Nelly rejects Marina's advice: "I don't need a 'happy life,' I need the stage. The stage! The stage represents the ideal of freedom for a modern woman. An all-conquering, widely recognized freedom. It lets you use all of your powers to assert 'I AM' . . . An actress is a free person!" Marina tells Nelly she doesn't know what she's talking about:

> You want to know what being an actress is? It means that every man will look at you like a woman who's available; that if you fall in love, the man you love will only see it as a temporary romance and will never, never believe in your sincerity; that if you feel attached to someone, they will pour out a tub of filth onto you, that your every good impulse or generous act will be considered a false pose, bravado, an advertisement; and for the rest of your life until the grave, all sorts of legends, like snakes, will crawl after you, and for the rest of your life you will feel yourself tangled up in a mesh of disbelief, suspicion, and foul intents—that's what awaits you!

The Lesnovskaya of "Backstage" had no qualms about using an innocent girl to take revenge on the man who spurned her. Twenty years later, *The Girl with Violets* reflected the evolution of Shchepkina-Kupernik's thinking about relations between women. It was as if her sexual attraction to women in her twenties had matured into a sense of feminist solidarity in her forties. She now believed it wrong to exploit another woman as part of confronting male dominance.

Marina's attempt to save Nelly fails. "You're just trying to scare me," she says, "after having opened the doors for me." Nelly is accepted into the company. Contrary to the advice she gave Nelly, Marina herself can't turn her back on the theater. She tells Neradov, after rejecting his plea to reconcile, that the life of an actor has placed an awful burden on her that she now willingly accepts:

> You have rightly noticed that I'm performing like I never have before, that across the footlights I'm giving people both my love and my despair. . . . And it's you who did all this! . . . Love is temporary. Art is forever. I will no longer betray it. You have destroyed my happiness, and I forgive you for this. But if you had destroyed

what is genuinely me, if you had destroyed the artist in me, this I would never have forgiven.

The Girl with Violets leads its audience to conclude that Marina, in deciding to continue her career, has made a Faustian bargain. Her celebrity has been achieved at the price of personal happiness, her only consolation being that it is a price worth paying in the pursuit of art. The play reflects Shchepkina-Kupernik's doubts about whether, as the young Nelly puts it, "the stage represents the ideal of freedom for a modern woman." For most women, achieving success on stage is an illusion. With its sprightly comedy and complex view of theater life, *The Girl with Violets* is the one Shchepkina-Kupernik play worthy of a modern-day revival. It was the play that she recalled most fondly, the one that "had the most success of anything I have written for the stage."[9]

Two premieres of *The Girl with Violets* opened just weeks apart in January 1913. In Moscow, the play was Korsh's first of the year, with Krechetova in the lead role. In St. Petersburg, Shchepkina-Kupernik convinced the Alexandrinsky Theater to take on the play in a production led by the actor-director Mikhail Darsky. The veteran actress Vera Michurina-Samoilova was cast as Lesnovskaya. Either Darsky or Michurina, or both, insisted that the play's title be changed because it gave audiences the false impression that Michurina, who was forty-six years old, would be playing a "girl." Shchepkina-Kupernik didn't object to having to sacrifice her ironic allusion to *The Lady of the Camellias*, and retitled it *Backstage*, like the original story.

Korsh's production was a success, given the public's interest in the repeated pairing of Krechetova and Shchepkina-Kupernik, but the critical response was muted. The *Moscow Gazette* thought the play lacked fresh ideas, but succeeded in enlivening things with its scenes of contemporary business and artistic life, and its use of a "strong flavoring" of onstage and backstage music.[10] At the Alexandrinsky, Shchepkina-Kupernik felt that Maria Vedrinskaya as Nelly "was sufficiently poetic" but lacked the "simplicity and sincerity" that she saw as important attributes of her character. Nevertheless, she was enraptured by the reception the play received at its premiere on January 23. Always one to be impressed by the hubbub of opening-night curtain calls, Shchepkina-Kupernik recalled that after the final curtain, the stage was so filled with flowers that she and the lead actors could hardly make their way through them to take their bows. When she was called out again alone, she noticed her husband, "his fine figure in a tailcoat," standing in one of the nearest loges with the rest of the audience, applauding, "sharing in my joyous pride and looking happier than I was."[11] One wonders what he thought of his wife's characterization of Neradov, the philandering lawyer who destroyed Marina's happiness.

The continued popularity of *The Girl with Violets* was a source of great pride for Shchepkina-Kupermik. Years after its debut, while trapped in Yalta during the civil war, she was visited by actors from a provincial troupe who invited her to attend their performance of the play. The weather was horribly cold, and the audience in the poorly heated hall remained dressed in their overcoats and galoshes. Nevertheless, she found the performance to be lively and the two lead actresses to be charming. Returning home frozen and standing at the stove heating a kettle for tea, she thought back to the premiere at the Alexandrinsky, how that moment now seemed like a dream, as war and an icy, northeast wind blew across the city.[12]

CHAPTER 15

"A Princess in Real Life, but in the Theater a Queen"

By 1911 Yavorskaya and her husband had settled into a flat at Bedford Court Mansions in Bloomsbury, in London's West End, that would remain her primary residence for the next several years. By the summer of 1913 Sasha, her ward, had come to live there as well, following the death of Alexandra Pavlova, the Sister of Mercy who had cared for the child since 1902. Baryatinsky, meanwhile, was increasingly absent, preferring to spend long periods of time back in St. Petersburg. While he was away, Yavorskaya couldn't rely on his financial support. She resorted to writing to Shchepkina-Kupernik to ask for a loan to cover Sasha's schooling and the cost for the child's stay at a sanitarium for treatment of eczema.[1] Responsibility for Sasha's future welfare weighed on Yavorskaya. She put the girl's education in the hands of Fanny Stepniak, a longtime resident of London who was the widow of the émigré Ukrainian nihilist Sergei Stepniak and a mutual friend of the Kropotkins. She also had Shchepkina-Kupernik write a brief account of how Sasha came to be adopted, something that Yavorskaya wanted to share with Sasha when she was older and had questions about her birth.[2]

Professionally Yavorskaya now had the confidence and the connections to organize her own productions, often with assistance from Pollock. She acted exclusively in English, with mixed reactions from critics and audiences. Sometimes her exotic charisma on stage lent charm to her heavy accent; sometimes the accent made her acting feel labored. She herself admitted to Shchepkina-Kupernik that acting in English was hard, telling her that "a dramatic role in a foreign language is the fruit of extraordinary effort in order not to appear strange or humorous."[3] Yet in spite of these difficulties, 1911 turned out to be her most successful year yet on stage in England.

Yavorskaya's winter season began with Ibsen's *A Doll's House* at the seven-hundred-seat New Royalty Theatre. It was a bold choice given the difficulty of mastering the role of Nora. As the critic for the *London Daily News* astutely pointed out, Nora is like Shakespeare's Juliet: "an actress young enough to look the part could not play it." In his opinion, Yavorskaya's interpretation "was not altogether successful. Her insouciance and naïveté of the early Nora were very deliberate and unconvincing." However, "in the last act, when Nora is awake, the Russian actress was quite excellent and held the audience with her quiet power."[4] But, as was often the case with Yavorskaya, the critical response in no way dampened the public's enthusiasm. The February premiere at the New Royalty was followed by engagements at the Royal Court and Kingsway Theatres.

In large part, the production's popularity can be attributed to Yavorskaya's conscious desire to connect Nora's rebellion ("Before all else I am a human being just as you are," she tells her husband) with the increasingly clamorous English suffragist movement. The connection was not lost on *The Times* reviewer, who offered the advice that "in these days of Hyde Park demonstrations, the woman's case has to be presented without bias, if sympathy is to be presented without bias." Unfortunately, he came to the conclusion that "brilliant as it is, the play made the impression of a Limehouse speech," alluding to Lloyd George's famous speech in 1909 to a crowd of four thousand in support of a graduated income tax to fund social welfare measures.[5] A newly committed activist herself, Yavorskaya had recently joined the Actresses' Franchise League, which had been formed in 1908 to convince theater professionals to extend the vote to women.

Her success in *A Doll's House* led to an invitation to speak at a dinner reception in her honor given by the New Vagabond Club at the grand Hotel Cecil on the Thames embankment. As described by a reporter for the *Kent & Sussex Courier*, she used the occasion to expound on the high moral and intellectual seriousness of theater in Russia in contrast with the greater emphasis on amusement and entertainment on the

English stage: "In Russia, as the Princess assures us, drama is looked upon as much more of an educational force than it is in England, and exercises a greater influence in the forming of intellectual opinion. For this reason, the Princess prefers what we call the problem play or the play with an intellectual motif. For this reason, the Princess made her English debut in that much discussed problem play, *A Doll's House*." The reporter referred to an interview Yavorskaya had previously given in which she insisted the Russian people would never tolerate a theater that existed only to make money. "I think it a crime," she said, "to give up such a great power as the theater to mere amusement. The great need in England is for intellectual theater."[6]

Two weeks after the closing of *A Doll's House* at the Kingsway, Yavorskaya premiered *Hedda Gabler* with Pollock as its producer. Once again, she attracted large audiences, and once again theater critics pointed out how difficult it was to judge her acting skills when performing in English. "Personality this clever Russian actress undoubtedly has," wrote the *London Daily News*, "but unfortunately she has so rudimentary a knowledge of the English language that she can only deliver herself in slow, halting, detached words which, spoken in the only way in which a learner can speak them, hardly admit of light and shade."[7] She compensated by employing "a feverishness of gesture," "pantomime," and "much physical activity." Her boldness in even attempting to interpret Ibsen in English made Yavorskaya impervious to such criticism, and contributed to her rise as a female theatrical impresario and a celebrity.

Not surprisingly, public sentiment and critical responses were less at odds with each other in her next production, Henri Becque's *La Parisienne*, a light, risqué comedy translated by Pollock. She played Clothilde du Mesnil, a strong-willed woman eminently capable of manipulating both her husband and a lover, all the while dressed in the latest Parisian fashions. Theatergoers were titillated by a full-page, three-photo spread in *The Sketch* depicting Clothilde and her paramour half-reclining on a loveseat engaged in "Three Stages of a Kiss."[8] This time the *London Daily News* concluded that "for almost the first time in London, she found a part which suited her in every respect and to which she could, even with the imperfections of her diction, do justice."[9]

After the successful run of *La Parisienne*, Yavorskaya decided to travel to Russia accompanied by Pollock. While in St. Petersburg, they stayed with Shchepkina-Kupernik at her apartment rather than with Baryatinsky. It was yet another sign of Yavorskaya's estrangement from her husband and of an increasingly close personal relationship between her and Pollock, since his coming to Russia with her didn't involve any theater business.

During her stay, Yavorskaya likely regaled Shchepkina-Kupernik with stories of her growing fame in London. It was, in fact, remarkable how swiftly she had managed to become part of London's cultural and artistic elite. She had already told Shchepkina-Kupernik about witnessing the endless sparring between H. G. Wells and G. B. Shaw: "I see Wells often . . . . and Bernard Shaw. These are two brilliant men. When they are together, you can't get a word in edgewise."[10]

Back in London in the fall of 1911, Yavorskaya's socializing in bohemian circles embroiled her in a highly publicized divorce proceeding in which the conductor Thomas Beecham was named the co-respondent. The pretrial phase of the suit dragged on for two years before making its way into court. The plaintiff's allegations focused on a series of events that transpired in the summer of 1909, when the Baryatinskys had only just come to England. Yavorskaya had become friends with Maud Foster, an American-born painter who was married to George Foster, a dilettante who "organized arts balls, turned biggish houses into flats, lived on the rents, and painted portraits."[11] Mrs. Foster's friends included Beecham, whom she offered to help with her connections in the musical world. Their behavior became overly familiar (he too was unhappily married), but whether it was adulterous is an unanswered question. In any event, George Foster found several amorous notes from Beecham to his wife, hired a private detective, and asked his lawyers to sue for divorce.

Central to George Foster's suit was an incident in which Beecham loaned his cottage at Boreham Wood to the Baryatinskys, with Maud as their guest, so that, it was alleged, under the pretext of visiting the Baryatinskys, the conductor could have an assignation with Maud. At the trial Maude was harshly cross-examined by her husband's lawyer about what transpired: "Did you appreciate that he [Beecham] was going to spend the night there?" "It is suggested that you had your arm around his neck when he was at the piano." "Is it true that on any occasion you came down to dinner in your nightdress with your dressing gown over it?" "It is suggested the day the Prince and Princess left, he spent the night with Miss Heyman [a pianist friend accused of being a go-between] and yourself and the two servants." Maud denied each of these accusations.[12] When called to testify, Yavorskaya maintained that she saw nothing improper in the relations between Foster and Beecham. The proceedings took up eight days in court spread over two weeks. Press coverage was extensive. The *Daily Mirror* published a photo of "Maud Christian Foster taking veal and red wine with her friends Katherine Ruth Heyman and Princess Baryatinsky in the Law Courts restaurant."[13] In the end, George Foster's petition for divorce was granted.

During the trial, Yavorskaya was appearing in *The Great Young Man*, Pollock's translation of *Nablotsky's Career*, at the Kingsway Theatre. When the verdict was announced, a reporter visited her backstage after a performance to get her reaction. She was livid:

> The Divorce Court is a place of horrible indignities. There is, I am sure, nothing like it anywhere else in the whole civilized world. France would not have it, and Russia—backward Russia—would scorn it. It is an outrage on public taste, a blot on your boasted freedom. Where else would private letters be read out for the public to laugh at, and all the sacred domestic relations be detailed to provide a cheap sneer? Justice should be clothed with dignity. In the Divorce Court it grovels in the mud and the mire to provide a nasty entertainment for nasty-minded people. . . . I sat in Court, and as I heard the attempts made to put the worst possible construction on the most innocent of things, I could have torn the skin off my face. It dazed me. I thought I must be living three hundred years back, in the days when they burned witches.[14]

Implicit in Yavorskaya's reaction was her conviction that the court and the public misinterpreted the nature of the relationship between Foster and Beecham—they were fellow artists and collaborators, not lovers. "You kill the sacred comradeship which ought to exist between man and woman," she told the reporter. "You stop men and women from working together. It is cruel. What can you know of these things, you ignorant people? What can a jury know who cannot understand? When we get votes for women and we have women on juries . . . " The reporter interrupted her: "You will find them harder than the men." "That's impossible," she replied. "And certainly, they cannot be more stupid." Adding to her sense of outrage, and that of her fellow suffragists, about the whole spectacle was the fact that in English law at the time only a husband, not a wife, could sue for adultery, based on the long-standing premise that marriage was an unequal relationship in which the wife was the property of the husband.

The Great Young Man enjoyed a monthlong run, interspersed with matinees of *A Doll's House*. Reviews, however, were lukewarm, with several critics commenting that the satire on Russian officialdom was largely lost on English audiences. The *London Daily News* couldn't resist pointing out that Yavorskaya's irritating English pronunciation "no longer had the charm of the unexpected."[15]

As often was the case when Yavorskaya scheduled productions, she chose to follow this light fare with a drama designed to challenge and provoke her audiences—London's first full-fledged staging of Gorky's *The Lower Depths* (there had been a single performance by the Stage Society in 1903). The play was produced by Pollock and translated by the dramatist Laurence Irving, whom Yavorskaya had previously met in St. Petersburg, where he had become an avid theatergoer while spending three years preparing to join the Foreign Office. In 1910 Irving adapted *Crime and Punishment* for the stage with performances in London and Manchester.

Yavorskaya directed *The Lower Depths*, performed a small role as Nastya, and, according to Pollock, was responsible for "the whole design of the production down to the smallest details,"[16] which she based on Stanislavsky's 1902 Moscow Art Theater staging.[17] Pollock declared that the play—"four acts of sordidness and misery,"[18] as the *Daily Mirror* described it—"marked an epoch in London stage production. Nothing like it had ever been seen." Critics, even while finding the play at times to be too raucous and melodramatic, recognized its artistic and polemical significance. "The play is remarkable," wrote the *London Daily News*, "and its revival justifies Lidia Yavorskaya's management."[19] In fact, starting with Chekhov's *The Bear*, followed by *The Lower Depths* and subsequent productions, she was establishing herself as an early pioneer in presenting Russian plays and adaptations on the London stage, only surpassed when the director and stage designer Fyodor Komissarzhevsky (Vera's half-brother) came to London in 1919 and gained fame for his groundbreaking and extraordinarily well-received productions of Chekhov's plays.

Gorky, who in 1911 was living in self-imposed exile in Capri, was best known by the British as the Russian writer most vocally critical of his country's monarchy. The popular and critical success of *The Lower Depths* prompted Yavorskaya and her husband to join Shaw, John Galsworthy, and other British literary notables in sending a congratulatory telegram to Gorky. He responded with a letter to *The Times* saying he was flattered by the attention: "I am happy to have succeeded in arousing the interest of English people in a Russian play, in Russian life: and I hope that this interest is more than passing—that it will not die, but that it will live and help in the wider growth of good feeling."[20] Yavorskaya wrote to Shchepkina-Kupernik that Gorky's warm words about the production had greatly encouraged her.[21] Baryatinsky sent Gorky press clippings about the play, initiating a correspondence in which the two men argued back and forth for the next two years about Russian history and current events.[22]

During the run of the play, Baryatinsky also presided over a lecture on Gorky delivered to a large audience at the Kingsway by George Calderon. After graduating from Oxford, Calderon had spent two years teaching in Russia, then returned to England, taking up a position as an assistant librarian at the British Museum and pursuing an interest in Slavonic folklore. He was the first English translator of Chekhov's *The Seagull*, which premiered in Glasgow in 1909. After meeting Yavorskaya, Calderon invited her to act in an upcoming London performance being planned by the Adelphi Play Society. Unable to judge the quality and accuracy of Calderon's translation, she went to Brighton to have it vetted by Kropotkin, whose English was flawless, having lived in England for the past twenty-five years. They had become very close—he attended her plays and talked to her about returning to Russia to work toward a future revolution. Kropotkin pointed out a few errors in the translation to be corrected, and Yavorskaya agreed to do the play. Not surprisingly, Yavorskaya at age forty-one, rather than taking on the role of Madame Arkadina, whom Chekhov had modeled after her, insisted on playing the teenage ingenue Nina Zarechnaya, as she had done, more plausibly, sixteen years earlier for Suvorin's production. Calderon devilishly noted in his revised translation of Chekhov's play that this is exactly what the *cabotine* Arkadina would have demanded.[23]

Calderon had previously remarked that the English method of acting was "ill-suited" for a Chekhov play: "A sportsmanlike code has been established to give everyone a fair chance.... As each actor opens his mouth to speak, the rest fall petrified into an uncanny stillness." Such was the fate of the Adelphi production of *The Seagull*. John Palmer in the *Saturday Review* wrote that neither Gertrude Kingston as Arkadina nor Yavorskaya as Nina "seemed to realize that her individual part was important only in correlation with the rest.... They succeeded in completely upsetting the balance and rhythm of the play."[24] British audiences would not come to appreciate Chekhov's innovative approach to drama until Komissarzhevsky's productions in the mid-1920s.

As happened in provincial Russia, Yavorskaya could generally count on more flattering attention when she toured the English countryside.

After premiering a well-received performance in Zola's gritty *Thérèse Requin* in London, she took the play (in rotation with *La Parisienne*) in May 1912 to the fashionable spa towns of Tunbridge Wells and Cheltenham. Local reporters, most likely after being fed old newspaper clippings by Yavorskaya, went along with the fanciful image she had created for herself as an aristocratic Russian princess deigning to appear before the public on stage. "Her passion for the theater," wrote the *Cheltenham Looker-On*, "made her prefer the struggles of her difficult profession to a calm and brilliant social life."[25] Similarly, the reporter for the Tunbridge Wells newspaper, having trotted out a quote from 1907 by the French tragedian Jean Mounet-Sully, who declared that Yavorskaya "is a princess in real life, but in the theater a queen," went on to point out that "she is devoting a large part of her life to the stage, and her society life has become a secondary matter in the achievement of those dramatic laurels which are shared with her distinguished husband, who is himself a playwright of proved skill,"[26] not to mention also the one responsible for her aristocratic title.

Yavorskaya thoroughly enjoyed spinning fables for the press. The theater director Emmanuil Krasnyansky in his memoirs recalled an anecdote (told to him secondhand) in which her chambermaid was straightening out her Bedford Court apartment when she found a photograph of a decorated general. Yavorskaya had no idea who he was and told the chambermaid to toss it in her suitcase. That day a newspaper reporter came to interview her. She proceeded to tell the reporter that perhaps one of the reasons she was drawn to performing in London was that "English blood flowed in her veins." She pulled out the photo from her suitcase and explained that this was a portrait of her grandfather, a Russian general who was the descendant of an Englishman.[27] This was a complete fiction.

That summer Yavorskaya again made a short visit to Russia, this time to visit her dying mother. She rented a dacha on Kamenny Ostrov in St. Petersburg and begged Shchepkina-Kupernik to come visit her. But the reunion was a disappointment. Yavorskaya found Shchepkina-Kupernik to be distracted and indifferent. She thought it ironic that her friend was now urging her to return to St. Petersburg, recalling all the times when Shchepkina-Kupernik had complained about the city's damp, cold climate and said she could never live in such a place. At its core, their disagreement about the importance of living and working in Russia was a reflection of their different origins. Yavorskaya was born into a family of Russified Huguenots. She was barely twenty when she went to France for the first time to study acting. Never having thought of herself as deeply Slavic, leaving Russia was not something wrenching for her. Shchepkina-Kupernik, on the other hand, came from an illustrious Russian theater family. As a successful translator of European plays into Russian, she couldn't picture herself maintaining a professional life in the West. As a poet, she couldn't imagine leaving the enchanted land of Russian versification.

Back in London, Yavorskaya wrote Shchepkina-Kupernik a "farewell letter," not for the first time and, as it turned out, not for the last time either. Feeling abandoned by her closest friend, she melodramatically jumbled some lines from *Uncle Vanya* and *The Three Sisters*: "All is gone and you have gone . . . It's painful, so very painful . . . Yes, the brigade has left. One has to live. We will live . . . "[28] In reality, Yavorskaya was flourishing and wishing that Shchepkina-Kupernik could see her success in London with her own eyes, as Alexandra Kollontai had when she attended one of Yavorskaya's performances at the Kingsway and dined with her afterward at the Waldorf Hotel.[29]

By December, Yavorskaya had already renewed her correspondence with Shchepkina-Kupernik, sharing with her the excitement and challenges of preparing to put on Tolstoy's *The Living Corpse*. Tolstoy considered the play unfinished, and it was never performed before his death in 1910. The play premiered in the fall of 1911 in a Moscow Art Theater production codirected by Stanislavsky and Nemirovich-Danchenko. For the London production, the play was retitled *The Man Who Was Dead* in a translation by Pollock and Zinaida Vengerova, a literary critic and noted proponent of symbolism, who had become Yavorskaya's friend. Yavorskaya admitted to Shchepkina-Kupernik that she didn't have "a direct interest" in staging the play but sensed there was considerable public curiosity about it. The production was a complex endeavor for a single afternoon performance with a cast of more than thirty plus a chorus of gypsy singers. During rehearsals, Yavorskaya found herself "trying to teach Russian ways to English actors," while also acting as an interpreter for Alexander Andreev from the Theater Royal in Belgrade, whom she had brought in to produce the play.

Shchepkina-Kupernik's response was to again insist that this was work she should be doing in Russia—Baryatinsky was in St. Petersburg at the time and Yavorskaya should be where her husband was. She disagreed—returning to Russia, rather than opening opportunities, would stifle her. "What for?" she replied. "To again earn some money playing with Russian ham actors? I've experienced everything on the

Russian stage . . . both great success and failure . . . I've lived through the groveling of Russian art before revolutions, then pornography, etc. . . . If I leave London, stop speaking English, I will live again in Russian surroundings and say goodbye to all my plans for the future, for going to America . . . ."[30] It's not surprising that Yavorskaya had dreams of touring the United States, given that Bernhardt had achieved great success there.

In March of 1913, through the efforts of the theatrical manager Eric Wollheim, Yavorskaya was signed to perform in *Lolotte*, a risqué one-act French comedy adapted by Pollock, at the London Coliseum, the city's most famous variety theater. According to Pollock, it was a "riotous success." He marveled at the ability of "an unknown foreign actress to sweep audiences of two or three thousand Britons off their feet."[31] Yavorskaya wrote excitedly to Shchepkina-Kupernik that the "public is coming to see me in throngs," and wished her friend could see "the electric lights on the theater marquee spelling out 'Lidia Yavorskaya *Lolotte*.'"[32]

But then, she suffered a setback. While opening a package in her apartment, she fell against a sharp corner in the entryway, painfully bruising her chest. At first, she thought she could tough it out and went ahead with a scheduled out-of-town engagement. But the tight corset and bodice she had to wear on stage caused such excruciating pain that after returning to London, she went to see a doctor, who told her she had to stop performing until he was able to make a diagnosis. Her left breast became swollen, turned blue, then darkened. When palpated, the swelling felt like a tumor. Yavorskaya wrote to her husband in St. Petersburg that she feared she might need an operation. Shchepkina-Kupernik's predictable reaction was to demand that she get treated by Russian doctors, whom she considered the best in Europe. "I'm afraid you're a bit mistaken," Yavorskaya wrote back. "Here I'm encountering an attentiveness and serious study of my illness the likes of which I have never encountered in Russia . . . One doctor has already refused payment three times because he hasn't yet been able to make a diagnosis."[33] By May, her doctors were able to conclude that she did not have cancer. After a two-month hiatus, she was now able to take advantage of the success of *Lolotte* at the Coliseum and go on the road with it to music halls throughout England and Scotland. "I've just returned from Manchester," she told Shchepkina-Kupernik, "where I did 14 performances of *Lolotte* at the Music Hall . . . And this in terrible 'chronic' heat! In a huge hall! And right after being ill! And to boot, in the very cities and with the same repertoire where Sarah Bernhardt and Réjane had performed! The hall is magnificent. Now I will perform again in London . . . to an audience of 3,500."[34]

At the end of the spring season, rather than returning to Russia for the summer as she had in previous years, Yavorskaya vacationed on the Dorset coast in the south of England. She was joined by Baryatinsky, and the two of them were featured in a full-page photo spread in *The Tatler* "resting and reveling in the simple life" as "Princess Baryatinsky prepares for a strenuous autumn."[35] The publicity photos of the couple splashing about in their bathing costumes and, as captured in a photo in the *Daily Mirror*, sleeping together "in the open each night lying on the bare ground protected only by warm sleeping bags"[36] belie the real state of their marriage. Baryatinsky's inability to provide financial support during his long absences drove Yavorskaya to intensify her efforts to work with Pollock to ensure herself a successful career on the London stage. While Baryatinsky was in Russia, she relied on Shchepkina-Kupernik to keep her informed about how he was doing, concerned that the prince was too susceptible to the dissipation of his St. Petersburg friends. It came as no surprise when Shchepkina-Kupernik told her of an incident in which her husband, Polynov, and Baryatinsky got drunk at a celebration and started a fight that resulted in the police showing up and the scandal being reported in the newspapers. "It's shameful," she wrote, "that both Valya and Nikolai Borisovich now have to waste their energy on smoothing over the matter."[37]

The Tatler feature also announced that Yavorskaya had booked the Ambassadors Theatre from September on to produce, for the first time in English, Tolstoy's *Anna Karenina*: "At present she is studying the part in a secluded spot on the south coast, where, as she says, she 'wants to take the English summer in her arms.'" Yavorskaya and Pollock, together with several other investors, had formed a company, the International Theatre Ltd., to produce a series of plays at the Ambassadors through the end of the year. Her season at the Ambassadors began with a series of light French plays sure to please a broad audience, followed by the premiere of *Anna Karenina* on December 1. It was to be Yavorskaya's greatest success on the British stage. Pollock was commissioned to do the dramatization. "I may say without vanity," he recalled, "that my effort bore fruit, for *Anna Karenina* ran for nearly a year at the Ambassadors and Scala Theatres, followed by a triumphant tour, and was only prevented from resumption in London by the course of the First World War."[38]

Chapter 16

Anna Karenina

Toward the end of 1913, Margarita Zelenina, the daughter of the famed Maly Theater actor Maria Ermolova, renewed a childhood friendship with Shchepkina-Kupernik that would become increasingly intimate over the course of the next forty years. Shchepkina-Kupernik met Zelenina in the early 1880s when she first visited Moscow as a little girl, most likely through her aunt, Alexandra Shchepkina-Chernevskaya. Ermolova was at the height of her fame, and Shchepkina-Kupernik noticed that she had little time for her daughter, "a charming, pensive child with the tragic eyes of her mother."[1] From an early age, Zelenina had been turned over to a nanny who tormented the timid child for years.

Ermolova's neglect of her daughter came to an abrupt end when Zelenina was around eight years old. The actor's marriage to the lawyer Nikolai Shubinsky was an unhappy one, and she was considering leaving him for another man. But Shubinsky, although he cared little for his daughter, threatened to insist on his legal right to keep the child if Ermolova left him. This, together with the shocking discovery that Zelenina had been all but tortured by her nanny, made Ermolova change her mind, sacrifice her happiness, and begin to be properly attentive to her daughter. "My mother," Zelenina wrote in her unpublished diary, "took on everything that touched my life, my sicknesses. My feelings for her grew, and I felt that my mother had started to understand me."[2]

Both Zelenina and Shchepkina-Kupernik were now in their thirties. Zelenina had just separated from her husband, a prison doctor, and fled from Moscow to St. Petersburg with their young son. Shchepkina-Kupernik took her in: "I loved her when she was a pensive, tender child, and later as a young girl, poetic and deep.... My husband loved Margarita like a sister. I fell in love with Margarita's son as if he were my own—and we constituted a unique family, though not related by blood, but much deeper than many genuine families."[3] Later Ermolova thanked Shchepkina-Kupernik for providing a place of refuge for her daughter: "I am so grateful that you have shown such affection for Margarita. You have warmed and given light to her soul.... Suddenly she has found in your household a glimmer of light. She herself says that 'it's as if I have fallen into a pure spring!' ... You and your husband are real people in the midst of this complete maelstrom that we're living in."[4] The maelstrom that Ermolova referred to was the outbreak of World War I.

Around the same time that Zelenina and her son sought refuge in Shchepkina-Kupernik's St. Petersburg apartment, Yavorskaya began rehearsals for *Anna Karenina* in London. She took advantage of every opportunity to publicize the upcoming premiere. On November 14, 1913, she invited a reporter from the *Pall Mall Gazette* to visit her in her home. She showed him an autographed photograph of Tolstoy that he had given her in December 1899 at a meeting in which she confided to Tolstoy that she wasn't sure she wanted to continue acting in Suvorin's company. "He comforted me," Yavorskaya said, and reminded her that "there was nothing so beautiful as the art of the theater."[5]

A week later another reporter at the *Daily News & Leader* was invited to attend a rehearsal, and during a break Yavorskaya sat down with him for an extensive interview. "She is a vivid and interesting talker," the correspondent wrote, "and in conversation her expressive hands play almost as great a part as her curiously arresting contralto voice." After briefly discussing the production, Yavorskaya went on to expound on one of her favorite themes—British misunderstanding of Russians—and to present herself as an expert on all things having to do with Russian culture and politics:

> We are full of joy and the gladness of living, and pleasure is our great goal. Outward circumstances make us miserable naturally, but in our own natures there is nothing but gaiety and

gladness.... There is no city in the world where there is such night life as there is in St. Petersburg. Life only begins there at midnight, callers commence to come at one o'clock, and supper is usually at four in the morning. The fashionable restaurants are open till five o'clock in the morning, and sometimes even after that, parties go out to gypsy restaurants on the outskirts of town. It is all one ceaseless hunt for pleasure.[6]

She insisted that when it came to women's rights and the rise of liberalism, Russia was already surpassing England: "We in Russia have already achieved what the English suffragists are striving for here.... Nowadays women are entering all the professions, and are on terms of absolute equality with men. In Russia the man who does not regard women as his equal is looked upon as a hooligan." Of course, actual conditions in Russia, Yavorskaya's own experiences, and the very play she was rehearsing contradicted such rosy pronouncements. After all, Anna is ostracized by society for her infidelity, while Vronsky is unaffected. Pollock himself pointed out to the reporter that Anna Karenina symbolized "the struggle of the soul of Russia against oppression." Similarly, Yavorskaya chose to interpret the recent acquittal of Menahem Beilis, who had been prosecuted by the Russian government for the ritual murder of a thirteen-year-old boy, as evidence of the rise of Russian liberalism: "There is a great wave of regeneration sweeping over Russia at present," she told the reporter, "a great Liberal movement against oppression of which the judgment given at the Kiev blood-ritual trial, the verdict of a jury of the people, is a triumphant and splendid expression."[7] In reality, the jury, displaying no liberal sentiments, had concluded that a Jewish ritual murder had taken place, but that Beilis, who had a strong alibi, could not have been the perpetrator. Most London theatergoers didn't have a very sophisticated understanding of Russia. Indeed, part of the attraction of a play like *Anna Karenina* was that it took place in an unfamiliar, exotic setting. Yavorskaya and Pollock understood that the production's haute couture costumes, ornate settings, and domestic melodrama were the things that would most appeal to audiences.

The opening-night reviews were uniformly tepid. *The Times* set a tone echoed by other critics, concluding that Pollock had "written an emotional and a rather lachrymose play, but it is not the *Anna Karenina* that we know. How should it be, when Levin only appears for a moment in Act One and again for a moment in Act Two, and is never seen in his country home?"[8] Striking him as more melodramatic than tragic, one critic thought the play was "worth seeing as a study of feminine weakness and sexual attraction."[9] Several reviewers commented that the play felt like a Muscovite *East Lynne*, a fabulously successful but critically maligned dramatization of a Victorian novel by Mrs. Henry Wood. Others said the three-hour play dragged, Yavorskaya's acting lacked subtlety, and her English was still too labored. One critic so disliked the play that he took up the first half of his review complaining that the new seats in the stalls had such exceptionally powerful springs that to sit down you had to firmly push down the cushion and quickly slide onto it to avoid being ejected. As for the production itself, he noted, "Though I had read *Anna Karenina* some time before, I would never have imagined that this play had anything to do with it, were it not for the names on the program."[10]

But much like *East Lynne*, *Anna Karenina* proved to be impervious to criticism. Yavorskaya wrote to Shchepkina-Kupernik: "We started with a half-empty theater and are finishing with overflow crowds."[11] Audiences turned out to care less about fidelity to Tolstoy's novel than the pageantry and spectacle offered on stage. One theatergoer wrote a letter to the editor of the *Pall Mall Gazette* wondering if there were some Russians in London who could comment on whether the atmosphere of the play was truly Russian. Three Russians and an Irishman, who had lived for twenty years in Russia, enthusiastically affirmed that it was. "It was all so deliciously Russian," replied the Irishman, "fur coats and snow boots, ice, large, high, warm rooms, real Russian log balcony, and the fine old custom of kissing ladies' hands." Yavorskaya's friend Gabriel Veselitsky sprang to the play's defense, expressing pleasure at "seeing actors dressed in the uniforms of our smartest regiments of the Guards behaving with the exact manner of those exclusive bodies." In preparing the costumes, Yavorskaya had consulted with retired émigré Russian officers to ensure that the uniforms of the guards were accurate. The reporter for the *Russian Word* affirmed that "there has, to my knowledge, never been in London a play in which the social, emotional, and pictorial sides of upper-class Russian society were shown with such fidelity."[12]

Yavorskaya had indeed put considerable energy into creating what one critic called "the illusion of Moscow 50 yards from Charing Cross."[13] The first act featured a ball at Prince Shcherbatsky's with a mazurka arranged by Leonid Zhukov of the Imperial Russian Ballet. The music score for the production included works by Tchaikovsky, Glinka, and Rimsky-Korsakov. An Orthodox priest was consulted to make sure the church bells sounded authentic. One area where Yavorskaya allowed herself creative license was in the anachronistic costuming of Anna and the other aristocratic ladies in modern gowns from the House of Paquin, which attracted the attention of the fashion writers in several newspapers, one of whom noted that Yavorskaya was "one of the most expensively dressed women on the English stage."[14]

With packed houses came a punishing schedule. Yavorskaya wrote back to Russia: "One day after another, and the work never lessens, as if a great mountain stands in front of me. . . . But as a result, *Anna Karenina* is a great success."[15] On April 5, the cast celebrated its 150th performance and the move from the Ambassadors Theatre, London's smallest, to the Scala Theatre, the city's largest. *Anna Karenina* ended its run by late May followed by a revival of *The Lady of the Camellias* in June and July, featuring a modernist set design.

As a celebrity, Yavorskaya attracted press attention not only for her performances but also as a fashion trendsetter. It was reported that she had enlarged her Bedford Court Mansions apartment to more adequately house her wardrobe, consisting of dresses "created on Futurist lines by Madame Paquin," and "wraps which must have run well into four figures."[16] The entire front page of the May 6, 1914, edition of *The Daily Mirror* was taken up with two photos of Yavorskaya arriving at Victoria Station wearing an unusual skirt. "In an instant," the caption read, "the buttons, which are fastened down the front were undone, the skirt cast aside, and the Princess was standing before the camera clad in breeches." Two weeks later the Reverend Richard Free, the vicar of St. Clements Fulham, wrote a letter to the *Standard* decrying the "wave of indelicacy" overspreading the country. His "condemnation of the shocking styles forced upon women by Parisian creators" was so widely reported that it even led to an article in *The New York Times*. The manager at Paquin's insisted "the dress of today is both artistic and beautiful." Yavorskaya eagerly jumped into the fray: "Must women be supposed to have only faces and hands? . . . What is more beautiful than the human body? Did not God make our bodies as well as our souls? Down with hypocrisy!"[17]

That summer Yavorskaya vacationed for six weeks on the Dorset coast. Pollock, who accompanied her, noted that she, "like most Russians, enjoyed doing things in a crowd." Her holiday entourage included the Cambridge mathematician Andrew Forsyth and his wife, Marion Pollock; Dr. Nodel, a Russian dentist with a practice in the East End; and Elizaveta Blagoveschenskaya ("Miss Blago"), the exiled editor of a

Tiflis newspaper who had become one of Yavorskaya's closest friends. Baryatinsky wasn't among the group, having already made plans to leave London for St. Petersburg, as it turned out, never to return. "Life in England began to bore him," Pollock recalled with derision. "He yearned for Romanov's, the oyster shop in the Nevsky Prospect, whither he could stroll, there over a dozen of them and a bottle of champagne to write another witty scene in a new comedy."[18]

War clouds dampened the vacationers' summer idyll. On July 30, 1914, Russia declared war on Germany, followed by Britain's declaration a few days later. "One morning we were all standing on a cliff and looking out to sea," wrote Pollock, "when before our eyes the British fleet that had been at Portland for dispersal after maneuvers steamed back up-Channel. So we knew, Russians and British, that war with Germany was upon us."[19] When Baryatinsky sailed for Russia via Norway in September, Yavorskaya became very worried for his safety. She wrote both Burenin and Shchepkina-Kupernik that she feared his ship would hit a mine or be sunk by a German battleship.[20]

In spite of the disruptions to domestic life caused by the outbreak of war, Yavorskaya was able to proceed as planned with her provincial tour of roughly eighty performances of *Anna Karenina*, which began in Cardiff on September 7 and ended in Brighton on December 12. Baryatinsky had previously signed an agreement with Pollock to help underwrite the tour but left for Russia without providing the funds. Once again, provincial newspapers proved to be more generous in their praise of Yavorskaya than their London counterparts. In Liverpool, the local critic found the play to be melodramatic, "but there was always the emotional genius of Lidia Yavorskaya to compensate us. She is a wonderful actress..."[21] It now became a common practice for Yavorskaya to make a short speech after her performance reminding the audience that Britain and Russia were allies in a common struggle; in Liverpool some of the week's proceeds were set aside for the two countries' Red Cross funds. She attended a luncheon given by the Liverpool Vegetarian Society at the invitation of the Anglo-Irish writer James Cousins and his wife, Margaret, arriving an hour and a half late, the result of an impromptu visit to the Russian steamer *Kursk* with two thousand Russian refugees onboard. "The glow of genius and the inspiration she gave us made the delay worthwhile," Cousins concluded, quickly finding himself charmed by her eccentric behavior.[22] Yavorskaya had been introduced to vegetarianism by Repin's wife, Natalia Nordman, although Shchepkina-Kupernik found Yavorskaya's commitment to it suspect, given that she insisted that cold ham was a vegetarian dish.[23]

A week later Yavorskaya sent Cousins a telegram inviting him to spend the weekend with her in Sheffield, where *Anna Karenina* was now playing at the Lyceum Theatre. He met her backstage after a performance and was startled when she suggested that they set off "from the theatre through streets of diminishing respectability" to have a drawn-out supper at "a most unappetizing house." Cousins learned that this kind of louche late-night outing was typical of Yavorskaya while she was on tour, "she being a Tolstoyan and aristocrat to whom mean streets were a treat." The next morning the tireless Yavorskaya was at Cousins's door in a waiting taxi to take him to visit the socialist poet Edward Carpenter, whom he already knew. "When we walked into Edward's garden," Cousins recalled, "we were met by George Merrill, his trusted man [they lived openly as a couple], in short sleeves and knickers. The Princess . . . . called: 'Hello George! You're not the only person who wears knickers,' and whisked off her skirt and flung it like a flying witch's cloak over a hedge,"[24] revealing the breeches that she had recently modeled for the press at Victoria Station.

After *Anna Karenina* ended its provincial tour in Brighton in December, Yavorskaya, now deeply affected by the plight of the bedraggled refugees she had seen on the *Kursk*, was devoting most of her time to the cause of supporting Russians who had been displaced by the war. Together with Kropotkin's wife, Sophia, she established the Great Britain to Poland Fund to send food and clothing to those who had been driven east by the German advance in Poland, which at the time was part of Russia. The following month Yavorskaya combined her fundraising appeals with performances of *For Russia*, a one-act historical drama written by Pollock. In it she played Nadezhda Durova, a real-life figure who, disguised as a soldier, fought as a Hussar during the Napoleonic Wars and was decorated for gallantry by Alexander I. Pollock himself appeared as "a dashing young Cossack captain."[25] He knew that taking on a role dressed as a man in an officer's uniform would appeal to Yavorskaya, reminding her of her success in Rostand's play *The Eaglet*. *For Russia*, with its martial, patriotic theme, enjoyed a successful run at the Coliseum and Scala in London before moving on to Bristol, Glasgow, and Manchester. In St. Petersburg, *Theater and Art* took note of the play's success, publishing a photograph of Yavorskaya in her Hussar uniform.[26]

Although Yavorskaya's husband had left her and England for Russia, the press in its patriotic fervor continued to make, perhaps with her encouragement, patently false statements about her background and relationship with the prince. The *Daily Mirror* wrote: "She comes from a high Russian military family herself. . . . All Mme. Yavorskaya's theatrical affairs are in the hands of her husband Prince Baryatinsky, who was a great friend of Tolstoy's. The Prince's father . . . . was an aide-de-camp and intimate friend of the Emperor Alexander III."[27]

Throughout the first year of the war, Yavorskaya tried to maintain a correspondence with Shchepkina-Kupernik, whose infrequent responses distressed her: "Why have you completely forgotten about me? Write me immediately about what's happening in Russia. Are you getting mail from abroad?"[28] She sent Shchepkina-Kupernik New Year's greetings on the eve of 1915, expressing the hope that the war would soon come to an end and normal life would resume.

Yavorskaya painted for Shchepkina-Kupernik a picture of wartime London in winter: "All of London is enveloped in perpetual gloom. Particularly Trafalgar Square, around the British Museum and near the Admiralty—you can't see a thing. . . . London theaters are completely empty in the evenings. . . . Enemy planes and the bombing of Scarborough have changed life in the provinces. In coastal cities almost all lights are turned off after four o'clock and no one goes out on the streets."[29] The authorities were beginning to remove paintings from the British Museum and the National Gallery.

Yavorskaya also complained to Shchepkina-Kupernik about her financial situation. In the four months since Baryatinsky left England, he had only managed to send her sixteen pounds as a Christmas present. Concerned that Shchepkina-Kupernik would report her desperation to the prince and further aggravate things, she added: "For God's sake, let this all remain between us. Don't think I'm judging someone."[30] Yavorskaya couldn't bring herself to speak of it openly, but she feared that Baryatinsky was ready to end the marriage. Without his support, how would she be able to pay for Sasha's medical bills and education? The child was now fully recovered from her eczema after a long stay in a sanitarium. Yavorskaya enrolled her in a prestigious boarding school, Downs Junior in Brighton. She arranged for Sasha to stay with Kropotkin, who lived near the school, on Sundays, pleased that the child would be "under the influence of this remarkable person!"[31]

After Yavorskaya sent her three letters in January in quick succession, pleading for a reply, Shchepkina-Kupernik finally responded in mid-February. Her explanation for her silence confirmed Yavorskaya's worst fear: Baryatinsky was openly talking about getting a divorce and "all this time I wasn't able to write you because I myself had to get used to this somehow." Now she advised Yavorskaya to face the facts: "Your marriage has taken on a form that has long been devoid of any passionate attraction."[32] It could only be saved if she lived together with her husband, and that would mean sacrificing her career. She told Yavorskaya to think about her future, about her financial security, which with the closing of the London theaters had become even more tenuous. Shchepkina-Kupernik at first was upset when she found out Baryatinsky was thinking of retaining her husband to pursue the matter, but then came to the conclusion that Polynov would do a better job of considering Yavorskaya's interests than some outside lawyer who would be completely indifferent to her plight. In any event, it was impossible for Baryatinsky to pursue a contested divorce without Yavorskaya's presence in Russia. Her financial situation improved after successful runs in January and February of *For Russia*, and twice daily, sold-out performances of *Lolotte* in Glasgow and Manchester, for which she was paid a percentage of ticket sales.

By the spring of 1915 both Yavorskaya and Pollock had fully committed themselves to the war effort. They assembled a delegation to travel to Russia and on to Poland with the goal of distributing relief from the Great Britain to Poland Fund for refugees. The fund was now out of necessity affiliated with the Russian Red Cross, since it was impossible for civilians to travel to and work in the war zone. Pollock became an International Red Cross commissioner outfitted with the uniform and sword of a Russian ensign.[33]

The delegation set out for Petrograd in March, traveling by sea to Norway and then overland to Finland and into Russia to avoid areas of conflict. Arriving in a torrential downpour, they were met, according to Pollock, by a "deputation of distinguished professors, men of letters, and economists [who] had been waiting over two hours at the dismal Finland station."[34]

Over the past five years the Russian press had reported sporadically on Yavorskaya's career in England. The May 17 issue of *Theater and Art* for the first time put a portrait of Yavorskaya on its cover, a photograph of her wearing an elegant gown and holding a parasol on the occasion of her "arrival in Russia with an English deputation."[35] A week later the magazine announced that "L. B. Yavorskaya has decided to base herself in Petrograd for the upcoming fall season and look for an appropriate venue."[36]

CHAPTER 17

Divorce and Revolution

Soon after arriving in Petrograd, Yavorskaya and Pollock set off for Poland with the fund delegation to establish feeding stations in Warsaw and Przemysl, farther south on the Ukrainian border close to the German front lines. But by early summer 1915, the continued German advance drove Yavorskaya and her fellow relief workers back to Petrograd, where they started feeding the thousands of retreating refugees streaming into the city's Warsaw train station. Pollock stayed behind, visiting Lvov, then returned to Warsaw. Just before the city's capture by the Germans in August, he managed to board a train to Kiev.

That summer Yavorskaya signed an agreement to lease the Luna Park Theater and busied herself with forming a troupe and deciding on a repertoire. Unlike the darkened stages of London, Petrograd's theaters managed to maintain a sense of normalcy, announcing their regular fall season seemingly unaffected by the war except for the occasional disruption caused by actors leaving to enlist. Overall, after an initial surge of patriotism, the response of Petrograd artists to the war was muted, ambivalent. For some, the war amplified a long-standing dread of an impending apocalypse. Others remained completely detached, choosing to further explore the inner worlds of symbolism, abstraction, and sensuality that were the hallmarks of the Silver Age. Neither the imperial nor the private theaters presented productions intended to spur patriotic fervor or benefit the war effort. Yavorskaya didn't feel free to use her celebrity status to go on stage to ask audiences to donate to her war refugee efforts, as she had in London, because as a member of a British benevolent organization, she would be seen as an agent of a foreign, albeit friendly, government.

In July, Yavorskaya indulged in a brief flirtation with film acting. She agreed to appear in the "cinema-play" *The Lonely Soul* (now lost) with a scenario by Natalia Bakhareva, the granddaughter of the writer Nikolai Leskov. Her one and only experience with this medium was a negative one. "Several days ago, I encountered for the first time this 'new' art form called cinema," she told a correspondent for the *Theatrical News*. "My participation in the film was by chance. It turned out that I had a few free hours one day, and I gave them to the movies." She understood that her film acting should be lifelike, not theatrical, but was frustrated that the director seemed uninterested in her performance and only cared about how far she was positioned from the camera and where the light was coming from. She ended her interview with the question: "Are movies really art?"[1]

By late August, Yavorskaya had finished putting together her troupe and began rehearsals for her September 18 premiere of Sheridan's *School for Scandal*, to be followed by Shaw's *Fanny's First Play*. Over the course of the season, which lasted until March, her productions fell into three categories: English comedies and satires, provocative new Russian works, and her reliably popular "Sarah Bernhardt plays" (*Madame Sans-Gêne* and *The Lady of the Camellias*, among others). Of the season's plays, Kugel thought two were deserving of lengthy reviews, and one became the object of Rasputin's wrath.

Kugel appreciated Yavorskaya's desire to introduce an English repertoire to Russia but doubted it would take root. He noted that neither Wilde nor Shaw had much success in Russia because the humor of their plays depended on a kind of wit that remained untranslatable: "We can only reproduce the external form, not the internal meaning." In addition, Yavorskaya was constrained by having to work with a fixed group of actors: "In Russia we don't have the ability to adjust the cast to the play," something he felt was essential to finding the right actors to successfully convey the highly stylized tone of light comedy.[2] Nevertheless, Kugel found much to praise in *Fanny's First Play*, which enjoyed brisk ticket sales. He found it "more entertaining and wittier . . . . sharper and more piquant" than Meyerhold's production of *Pygmalion*, which was running at the Alexandrinsky Theater at the same time.[3] For years Kugel had been critical of Meyerhold's directorial control over his actors, some of whom felt it turned them into puppets.

Yavorskaya's next play, *The Law of the Savage* by Mikhail Artsybashev, caused an even bigger stir among Petrograd theatergoers. Artsybashev first gained notoriety as the author of *Sanin*, a frankly sensual novel advocating a woman's right to engage in premarital sex. The book was banned as pornographic. Like *Sanin*, *The Law of the Savage* exposed the hypocrisy of upper-class Russian attitudes toward women. In the play, Boris Veryesov, a serial philanderer, seduces Larissa, his best friend's wife, and Ninochka, his wife's sister, without suffering any consequences. In the last act, Duganovich, a cavalry officer who is in love with Boris's wife, challenges him to a duel. Boris admits that dueling is absurd, a vestige of the law of the jungle. He confesses to having lived a life of lies and deceit: "I am what nature has created and what society has raised! . . . I cannot be anything else and don't want to be! . . . I'm a child of my age: I believe in nothing and want only one thing in life—variety and pleasure! . . . I was raised to have contempt toward a woman, and to look upon her above all as an instrument of pleasure! . . . Perhaps that's reprehensible, or maybe she deserves no better!"[4] Boris refuses to peacefully resolve the dispute, shooting and killing Duganovich even before his opponent has a chance to raise his pistol, an act of murder.

Shocking in its depiction of amorality, the play ran for two months to full houses. Kugel had admired Artsybashev's previous play, *Jealousy*, recognizing in it the "genuine temperament of a dramaturg." But he felt disappointed by *The Law of the Savage*: "It's hack-writing, and bad hack-writing to boot. . . . The structure of the play was striking in its incoherence, lack of proportion." Kugel found the theme compelling— the supposed right of a husband to betray his wife as much as he wants while rejecting an even "minimal" right of the wife to betray her husband. But how did such a gifted writer produce such a clumsy play? The reason, he concluded, was that the story began as a film scenario called *The Husband*. Artsybashev had taken cinematic action and stuffed it with words, creating a sort of "literary stew." Like Yavorskaya, Kugel rejected film as art, except as "the art of making money. . . . Film with the fast rhythm of its photographic logic sneaks into the very heart of our art and literally sucks out our blood and brains." On top of this he thought the production suffered from Yavorskaya's long-standing inability to convey psychological complexity on stage.[5]

The popularity of *The Law of the Savage*, however, encouraged Yavorskaya to end the year with another work that focused on the war of the sexes. She decided to stage *Maybe Tomorrow*, a new play by Anatoly Kamensky, already quite well known as a writer of Freudian erotic stories. On December 7, Baron Nikolai Drizen, the official drama censor, attended the play's dress rehearsal and had no objection to it being performed. But the next day, Stefan Beletsky, the deputy minister of the interior, demanded to see a copy of the play after being contacted by a furious Rasputin. Apparently, Kamensky had based a scene in the play and one of its characters, a seductive peasant spiritual healer with a "magnetic gaze," on a party he had attended for Rasputin. At dinner Rasputin was visibly attracted to the writer Teffi, who was seated next to him, and tried to lure her to his apartment, an encounter that she later described in detail.[6] At 6 p.m. on December 8, a police officer appeared at the Luna Park Theater. He announced that the play had been banned and demanded the removal of all posters.[7] Two hours later the theater was packed, with the audience waiting for the curtain to go up. Yavorskaya told someone from her administrative staff to go out on stage to inform everyone that the premiere had been canceled by the Ministry of the Interior and that they would be receiving refunds.[8] Coincidentally, while Yavorskaya was forced to contend with the abrupt cancellation of her production, less than two miles away Shchepkina-Kupernik was enjoying the revival of her play *Backstage* at the Alexandrinsky Theater. Working with the imperial theater, Shchepkina-Kupernik surrounded herself with friends and colleagues who were traveling a path that was closely parallel to but separate from Yavorskaya's.

Kamensky, after lengthy discussions with the censors, made cuts and revisions to his script. The play's premiere was rescheduled for December 20. The peasant monk was now a philandering Swede. The theme of *Maybe Tomorrow*, however, remained unchanged—the right of women to free themselves from a sexual repression hypocritically demanded by a patriarchal society. In the first act we are introduced to two "new women," Yulia and Lara, at a feminist club. Yulia is a secretary to a prominent railroad baron, Tikhmenov. She knows he is attracted to her, but something is holding her back from reciprocating. Her friend Lara comes from a more "earthy" peasant background. She looks at love more simply and isn't opposed to having multiple affairs. Two writers, Boretsky and Gagarin, arrive at the club, soon followed by Tikhmenov. Yulia sees Tikhmenov in private; he declares his love, passionately kisses her, and she falls into a faint. The next act takes place at an evening gathering at Tikhmenov's—the scene inspired by the dinner that had been organized for Rasputin. Yulia meets the Swede Johan Johansson and is won over by his gaze and ingratiating talk. Unnoticed by the others, she leaves the party with him. In a final scene at a restaurant where Yulia, Lara, and their friends are getting drunk, Tikhmenov confronts Yulia, telling her how offended he is by her actions. But she rejects him, responding that he doesn't understand her. She leaves the restaurant with the writer Boretsky.[9]

The play's radical take on female emancipation was not greeted sympathetically. The *Theater and Art* critic found Yulia's habit of going off with different men "deeply and thoroughly pornographic. . . . It has something in it that is disturbing and suggestive." He was confused by Yavorskaya's performance: "An abstraction and an extraction, so to speak, of an agitated and disturbed female essence."[10] After a brief run in Petrograd, the play was banned everywhere else in Russia, apparently at the insistence of Rasputin.[11]

Pollock returned from the front to Petrograd in late 1915, experiencing for the first time the full brunt of a Russian winter. Outside the temperature was minus twenty-two degrees Fahrenheit: "The air in my room, despite a stove kept baking hot, has never managed to be warmer than 60°. . . . Winter, the master magician, spreads a pall of beauty over fur and fustian, palace and hovel alike; but his smile is relentless and his touch upon the head or the heart of man spells death."[12] With both Pollock and Yavorskaya still active in relief work, we can safely assume they saw each other often that winter. In April 1916, Pollock filed a civil suit in the Petrograd Circuit Court against Baryatinsky claiming that the prince, as part of a prior business agreement, had failed to pay him the equivalent of eighteen thousand rubles to support Yavorskaya's tour of *Anna Karenina* throughout Britain. As security, Baryatinsky presented the court with twenty thousand rubles to be held while the matter was being adjudicated.[13]

Yavorskaya was distressed that Baryatinsky had been refusing to see her since her return to Russia. She hoped she could convince him to maintain the marriage and continue to provide financial support, which she needed to supplement her professional earnings. It was an unreasonable hope. She should not have been shocked to learn that now that she was in Russia, the prince had taken steps to divorce her against her will. On May 8, 1916, Baryatinsky approached Nicholas II with a request "to possibly speed up the dissolution of his marriage." The tsar forwarded the prince's petition to the Holy Synod, which had absolute control over marriages and divorces. Two weeks later the Synod instructed the Petrograd Ecclesiastical Consistory to "fulfill His Excellency's resolution" and resolve the matter expeditiously.[14]

Because marriage was considered a sacrament by the Orthodox Church, the Synod was particularly reluctant to grant contested divorces. In filing his suit with the consistory, Baryatinsky declared that while they were living in London, his wife had entered into an adulterous relationship with Pollock, now serving as the secretary of the British-Polish charitable fund. Yavorskaya denied this charge and filed a countersuit against the prince, claiming that he had in fact been cheating on her and now needed a divorce in order to remarry. She found out that Baryatinsky had been seeing Olga Berestovskaya, an Alexandrinsky Theater actor (her stage name was Panchina). On August 23, the consistory declared that both spouses were guilty of infidelity and therefore refused to grant the divorce, much to the annoyance of Baryatinsky, who felt he had pulled all the right strings.

The prince filed an appeal. In the meantime, Nikolai Raev, the newly installed chief procurator of the Synod, had decided to take the case back from the consistory without informing Yavorskaya. Rasputin had recommended Raev for the position after Empress Alexandra summarily removed his predecessor. Pollock saw the evil hand of Rasputin guiding Raev's actions in support of Baryatinsky. Yavorskaya suspected bribery.

On September 22 Yavorskaya went to the consistory office to request some documents, only to find out that two weeks previously everything had been given back to the Synod. The next day she went to the Synod to review the documents. The clerk told her the decision of the consistory had just that day been overturned, that the marriage had been dissolved with a declaration of her guilt, and that Raev had specifically instructed him not to turn over any documents to her. Five days later Baryatinsky married Panchina.

When Raev finally agreed to meet with Yavorskaya, he encouraged her to drop the whole matter. She told him he had violated court procedures. He replied: "You're right, that's true, but these illegalities don't constitute a threat against state security, and therefore I don't see the need to deal with them." When she accused him of accepting bribes from Baryatinsky, he shrugged it off: "Apparently, you're right here too, but I don't understand what's wrong if a civil servant of the Synod receives a hundred or, let's say, a thousand rubles, since their salaries are so miserly, and everyday life gets insanely more expensive."[15] Raev's brazen responses reflected his certainty that he enjoyed the protection of Rasputin and the royal court. Yavorskaya was furious. Not only was she now cut off from Baryatinsky's financial support, but she had been treated dismissively, and the resolution of the case reeked of corruption. On October 23, she requested that the Synod undertake a review of the matter but received no reply. Nevertheless, she had no intention of giving up.

A week later, the Petrograd Circuit Court ruled in favor of Pollock, affirming that Baryatinsky owed him eighteen thousand rubles to cover his British tour expenses.[16] The prince surrendered the sum held by the court, extricating himself from what he surely felt were the long-standing, onerous burdens of his relationship with Yavorskaya. In 1897, in the first year of their marriage, Baryatinsky wrote an article for the *New Times* on the nature of marital love. He recognized that for most couples the intensity of passion eventually dissipates: "The period of such cooling is a critical and decisive moment: if at such a time the beloveds feel an emptiness in their internal *I* towards each other—then all is done, disillusionment arises."[17] Passion, even friendship had faded away long ago. Now, finally, the last vestige of their remaining professional collaboration was settled for eighteen thousand rubles.

The fall 1915 season at Luna Park Theater was the last time Yavorskaya was in charge of her own theater company. She didn't undertake a similar effort in 1916, understandable given her preoccupation with contesting the legality of her divorce. Shchepkina-Kupernik, however, continued to have success as a playwright and was busy that fall with a new play, *Flavia Tessini*. She attended the rehearsals and made some final suggestions to the cast before its premiere at the Alexandrinsky Theater on November 7.

Once again, as was the case with *Backstage*, Shchepkina-Kupernik reworked one of her short stories into a play. Like *Backstage*, *Flavia Tessini* was a play about the lives of performing artists. Zhenya Brailovskaya, the daughter of a family of Kievan Jews, takes on the stage name of Flavia Tessini and goes on to a dazzling career as celebrated singer in France and Italy. She marries a gifted violinist, Grisha Tesman, her sometime accompanist, whose career suddenly ends when he injures his hand in a carriage accident.

In the short story, Zhenya maintains a busy concert schedule as Tesman comes down with tuberculosis and his health deteriorates. Delirious on his deathbed, Tesman calls for Zhenya. She is at his bedside, but looking at her, he says, "No, I need Zhenya. You're Flavia Tessini. You look like her, but where is Zhenya?" He is seeking comfort from his wife, not from the celebrated singer. In the play the ending is thematically and dramatically different. After Tesman suffers his accident, Zhenya abandons her career to care for him. "The behavior of Flavia Tessini toward poor Grisha to whom she is totally devoted," wrote Kugel in his review, "is depicted delicately and believably, without any melodramatic maliciousness," by Ekaterina Roshchina-Insarova.[18] But, as Kugel describes it, "there's the implication that this sacrifice diminishes her, makes her capricious and feel oppressed." He sees something tragic in Zhenya turning from an artist into a "shrewish non-entity" as she cares for her dying husband. But Kugel felt that Shchepkina-Kupernik missed an opportunity to delve more deeply into the implications of this choice. While the twenty-nine-year-old Shchepkina-Kupernik in her short story asked us to judge Zhenya's choice of a celebrated career over an act of loving self-sacrifice, the forty-two-year-old Shchepkina-Kupernik in her play shifted the emphasis to the emotional toll that such a sacrifice has on an artist. It's as if in the two versions, she was saying that married women artists, unlike married men, are faced with two unsatisfactory options: either accept being criticized for choosing a career over family life, or make yourself miserable by abandoning art to fulfill family responsibilities.

On February 21, 1917, less than two months after Rasputin's gruesome murder, Yavorskaya, still seething from the injustice of the divorce decree, submitted a petition to Nicholas II, accusing Chief Procurator Raev of exceeding his authority. She requested a review of the Holy Synod's decision. Revolutionary events, however, conspired to push her entreaty aside. Two days later, mass demonstrations and riots broke out in Petrograd over shortages of bread and coal. The city garrison, mobilized to put down the mutineers, joined them instead. By March 2, Nicholas II abdicated, appointing Prince Georgy Lvov prime minister, who together with prominent Duma leaders and politicians formed a provisional government. For the next eight months, the provisional government sought to establish a constitutional democracy while struggling to control the growing power and authority of the rival socialist Petrograd Soviet of Workers' and Soldiers' Deputies.

Both Yavorskaya and Pollock embraced the February 1917 revolution. Consistent with their pro-British sentiments, they supported the provisional government's decision to continue to prosecute the war against Germany. On March 24, Pollock expressed his hope in the direction that the events unfolding before his eyes were taking: "All that an

Englishman and a lover of their country can do is wish them God-speed in a task that cannot but be troubled."[19] Shchepkina-Kupernik chose to avoid the tumult in Petrograd, settling in for the summer at Marioki with her husband and Zelenina.[20]

Still an officer of the British-Polish Fund, Yavorskaya was now also chosen to head the newly formed Union of Russian Dramatic Actresses. At a general meeting in April, made up of around forty stage performers from Petrograd and provincial theaters, the union established as its first goal the dissemination of the concept of equal rights for women in Russia, which included petitioning the provincial government to establish voting rights for women. It also decided to create in the near future an "Actresses' House," modeled after the English "Women's House," where women arriving in Petrograd would have a place to stay and resources to help them pursue work in the city.[21]

Yavorskaya continued to act sporadically. She had a brief engagement at the ornate People's House theater, performing in *The Lady of the Camellias*, Andreev's *The Days of Our Life*, and, most interestingly, Octave Mirbeau's *Les Mauvais Bergers* (*The Bad Shepherds*), a play first performed by Sarah Bernhardt and subsequently banned in imperial Russia because it dealt with a brutally suppressed workers strike. Also in April, she participated in an evening of poetry at Tenishev Hall. At the reading, she recited a translation of Walt Whitman's "Beat! Beat! Drums!" Other performers included Teffi, Sergei Yesenin, Fyodor Sologub, and Anna Akhmatova.

Hoping that the provisional government would be more favorably disposed toward her, Yavorskaya renewed her quixotic efforts to have her divorce reviewed and overturned. The Ministry of Justice of the provisional government had set up an Extraordinary Investigatory Commission charged with looking into illegal actions taken by tsarist authorities. She requested that the commission investigate the former Chief Procurator Raev, once again accusing him of violating court procedures and accepting bribes. The commission opened an investigation in early June.[22]

That summer Yavorskaya traveled to the Hermitage Theater in Moscow to appear in three of her well-worn "Sarah Bernhardt plays": *Zaza, Madame Sans-Gêne*, and *Mademoiselle Fifi*. "The public for old time's sake attended the engagement," wrote one critic. "But the actress didn't achieve her former success. Something exhausted, fading appeared in her performance, lacking any brightness, liveliness."[23] For the next six months she stayed away from the stage, working on something fresh—a

Russian translation of J. M. Barrie's *The Admirable Crichton*. On October 10, the same day that Trotsky and the Petrograd Soviet voted to support an armed uprising against the provisional government, Yavorskaya submitted further evidence to the Extraordinary Investigatory Commission, which was building a substantial case against Raev. On October 25, the Bolshevik Red Guards seized government buildings, and the next day they stormed the Winter Palace. In the ensuing turmoil the commission was shut down. Raev fled to the Caucasus without having to suffer the consequences of his actions.

"The revolution of March 1917," wrote Pollock in 1919, "began as a patriotic movement directed against the corrupt intrigues of the Court by men who wanted Russia and her allies to win the war." The Bolsheviks who carried out the October revolution were different: they "were for the most part not Russians at all, but Jews who had suffered persecution at the hands of the Russian government. . . . The Bolsheviks were aided by countless German agents and spies, and they succeeded so well in their work that within eight months the Russian army had ceased to exist, and they themselves, the paid agents of Russia's enemy, had seized the machinery of government."[24] With Red Cross activities stopped by the Bolsheviks, Pollock now devoted himself full-time to writing about events in Russia and sending dispatches to the British press, an undertaking that opened him up to accusations of being a foreign spy.

Remarkably, on the evening of October 25, Shchepkina-Kupernik's *Flavia Tessini* was performed in repertory at the Alexandrinsky Theater as scheduled. In Moscow, both the Bolshoi and Maly Theaters were shelled, but on November 7, the *Theater Review* reported: "Petrograd theaters are undamaged, and the majority of them didn't interrupt their activities over the course of recent days. Performances went on even on the most deadly days. Actors made their way to theaters while under fire, and, leaving the theater, they didn't know if they were going to make it home safely. Nonetheless, artistic life in the capital didn't shut down."[25]

The night the Winter Palace was stormed, Fyodor Chaliapin performed *Don Carlo*s at the People's House. Leaving the theater, the audience was subjected to a barrage of deafening cannon fire coming from Palace Square. "It was indeed an unusual combination of emotions aroused by peaceful art and the sense of a terrifying and militant civil war," wrote the *Theater Review*. "Theaters steadfastly fulfilled their obligation, and art didn't die during those bloody days of death and destruction. Does this not mean that art is in truth eternal, that its spirit is indomitable?"[26]

Yavorskaya's translation of *The Admirable Crichton* (its Russian title was *A Journey Around Equality*) opened at the Crooked Mirror on December 28, 1917. The Crooked Mirror was unique among Petrograd venues. Founded in 1908 by Kugel and Kholmskaya, herself a comic actor, it started as a midnight cabaret devoted to parodies of all the current theater trends: naturalism, symbolism, futurism, and "Meyerholditis."[27] In 1910, they hired Evreinov, a dramatist drawn to the avant-garde, as artistic director and moved to the 750-seat Catherine Theater so that they could present full-length works. For years in his influential articles in *Theater and Art*, Kugel had been critical of the dominance of the auteur director in modernist theater, particularly Stanislavsky and Meyerhold. His involvement with the Crooked Mirror and Evreinov's experiments with monodrama and medieval performance styles created a forum to demonstrate Kugel's belief that the actor, not the director, should be the one to have the dominant voice on stage.

As a satire on rigid British class structure, *The Admirable Crichton*, with an expansive Yavorskaya in the role of Lady Mary, fit in very well with the comic fare that Crooked Mirror's audiences had come to expect. "Barrie's idea is witty, and biting, and true," wrote one critic, "but the play itself unfolds as a clichéd English comedy—funny and not deep. But it's all very lively to watch, and unfolds in front of the viewer like an engaging fable."[28] Adding to the production's fancifulness, the "eccentric and curious costumes" worn by the characters on the deserted island, where class roles are reversed, looked like patchwork rags from an art nouveau ballet.

The Crooked Mirror attracted sophisticated theatergoers who understood the modernist trends being parodied and satirized. But on the heels of the Bolshevik revolution, political condemnation of such forms of "bourgeois art" was gradually increasing, fed by a grievance-filled proletariat eager to smash the privileges of a wealthy, educated class that had oppressed them. In February 1918 Yavorskaya again returned to Moscow for a brief engagement at the Nikolsky Theater. The writer Ivan Bunin, a friend of Shchepkina-Kupernik, noted in his diary: "Over on Strastnaya Street, people are advertising that Yavorskaya will give a benefit performance. An old woman, fat, rosy-red, mean-spirited, and coarse, cries out: 'Just take a look at that! They're smearing paste all over the place! And who's going to clean up that mess? And the bourgeois will be going to theaters. They shouldn't be allowed to go. After all, we don't go.'"[29]

In the March 25 issue of *Theater and Art*, Kugel expressed his despair over what was happening to theaters after the revolution: "How sad it is! How dead has the life of the theater become! It has lost all its charm, all its excitement, and has been turned into a toy." He recalled recently attending a meeting at which Anatoly Lunacharsky, the head of the People's Commissariat for Education, said that theaters are now empty because they don't have a "socialist repertoire." Kugel's response to Lunacharsky's observation dripped with sarcasm and vitriol: "Take your socialist eyes and see; bend your socialist ears and listen; take in the air with the socialist nostrils of your socialist nose and smell what is happening in your beloved socialist fatherland, and in particular, in the socialist theater of your socialist fatherland."[30] Seven months later *Theater and Art* was shut down.

As Yavorskaya later recalled, by the summer of 1918 almost all theaters "had already been taken over by the local councils, their owners and managers being summarily turned out, and the wardrobes and all other property requisitioned."[31] Hoping to escape the hostility facing her in Petrograd, she thought things might be better if she performed in the provinces, specifically in Saratov, a city on the Volga River in southwestern Russia. She had memories of Saratov as a place with a traditionally strong theater with a repertoire very similar to that of her New Theater. But her time in Saratov turned out to be a miserable failure. The city was in Red hands. The Bolshevik sympathizers running the theater made it clear to her that she was "not one of them," that her time had passed.[32] Soviet theater no longer needed a Yavorskaya.

Yavorskaya returned to Petrograd determined to find a way to get papers that would allow her to go abroad. She had thought of trying to get across the Czech border or escape via Vladivostok, which was not yet under Bolshevik control. But she hesitated—she had been warned that the very act of submitting an application for exit papers would arouse suspicion and the possibility of being arrested.[33] As an English citizen, Pollock's situation was even more dire. In August he had managed to be on a train en route to Moscow on the night when the Red Guards rounded up and arrested English and French citizens. Told by a colleague not to return to his Petrograd apartment, Pollock changed his name, obtained false papers, and went into hiding. He knew it would be impossible to leave the country through legal, diplomatic channels; he had to find a way "to make my exit without permission."[34]

Kugel recalled that sometime in the fall of 1918, he saw Yavorskaya for the last time. He dined with her and Pollock, whom he called her "new husband" (they were not married). Kugel found her to be uncharacteristically "very subdued in appearance and behavior."[35] She was suffering from what Pollock would later call "the seeds of illness, aggravated by her indomitable efforts against the Bolsheviks."[36] At dinner Yavorskaya told Kugel that only by returning to London would she be able to continue to live and work.

CHAPTER 18

"Out of the Bolsheviks' Clutches"

In December 1918 Yavorskaya was invited to appear in Shaw's *How He Lied to Her Husband* at the theater hall on the second floor of the Eliseev building on Nevsky Prospect. The theater was run by a Bolshevik council under the patronage of the wife of Grigory Zinoviev, the chairman of the Petrograd Soviet.[1] Pollock was hired by the theater for two months as a producer. One evening a man, whom Yavorskaya described as an "influential Bolshevist" she had known before the revolution, visited her in her dressing room. He complimented her on her performance and asked if there was anything he could do for her. "Get me a passport for abroad," she replied without hesitation. "You shall have it tomorrow, he promised."[2]

The next day her Bolshevik friend accompanied Yavorskaya to the Commissariat of Foreign Affairs. They issued her a passport to leave through the Belo-Ostrov train station on the Finnish border and granted her permission to take almost fifteen hundred pounds of baggage. She told the authorities she was going on tour in America, fearing that saying she was going to "arch-enemy" England would arouse suspicion. When she arrived at the Finnish border, the Russian guards turned her back. Her papers were no longer valid because the person who had signed them had been dismissed. She returned to Petrograd and obtained "fresh papers with a different signature" from the commissariat. This time the border guards accepted the papers as valid but refused to allow her to leave with the forty-four trunks she had brought with her. She returned again to the commissariat. This time an official called the border guards and insisted that she had permission to take the trunks with her. For Yavorskaya there was nothing comic about this bureaucratic run-around. While it was going on, she decided to stay with a friend rather than return to her apartment, having been warned that the Extraordinary Commission for Combating Counter-Revolution was about to receive a denunciation against her "for harboring agents in a British plot."[3]

In early February, Yavorskaya gathered her luggage for the third time and took the short train ride to the Belo-Ostrov station. The guards did a thorough search, confiscating some items, including a silver sugar bowl and tray that had been used in the production of *The Admirable Crichton*. They discovered a pistol with cartridges hidden in a satin cushion, but she somehow managed to convince them it was a prop. Finally, after several hours, the guards completed their search and porters wheeled all the trunks over the bridge crossing the River Sestra, which marked the boundary between Russia and Finland. On the other side, Yavorskaya boarded a train to Helsingfors (Helsinki) and freedom. "It was only afterwards," she wrote, "that I learned how narrow had been my escape. . . . The very next day the denunciation of which I had warning materialized, and agents of the Gorokhovaya [the Cheka] were sent to arrest me at my flat in Petrograd."[4]

One day later Pollock too managed to flee across the Finnish border, but his escape was clandestine and dangerous. Living in hiding, he knew there were individuals in Petrograd who, for a considerable fee, were smuggling people across the Finnish border, providing guides, horses, and maps of a safe route. The man Pollock found, whom he called Ivan Petrovich in his memoir, "was young and energetic, and was reputed to have piloted many persons from barbarism to civilization."[5] On the appointed night, Pollock took a train to a village on the Russian side of the border. But when he met up with Ivan Petrovich in the village safe house, Pollock was told that leaving that night was impossible—the party that had left the previous day had been stopped. Ivan Petrovich failed to mention that "the whole party had been nabbed on the border itself, with fatal consequences."[6]

Ivan Petrovich returned to Petrograd. No longer with a place to stay in the city, Pollock spent the night in the village. The next day he took the train back to the Finland station, got on a tram, and went to Petrovich's apartment: "The door opened in answer to my ring; I stepped in; 'Hands up!' and two revolvers were at my head."[7] Instead of Petrovich, Pollock was greeted by two agents of the Cheka. Under questioning, he claimed ignorance of any smuggling operation, insisting that he knew Petrovich through his work at the Eliseev theater. Pollock was then taken to No. 2 Gorokhovaya Street. While sitting unguarded on a bench waiting to be interrogated, Pollock managed to slip out the door, go through a kitchen, down some backstairs, and out onto an interior courtyard: "In my military coat and high fur hat and the Cossack-like beard I had grown in the course of the last two months, they doubtlessly took me for one going about the ordinary business of the place."[8] Pollock knew he still would have to present a pass to get out of the building: "I approached the gateway. 'Pass?' called out one of the guards. Without stopping I answered in an absolute manner: 'From room No. 36.' The phrase acted like magic; no one attempted to stop me, and without further query I passed under the arch and into the street."[9]

For the next week, Pollock went into hiding again, taken in by various friends, changing locations four times. One of his friends suggested that he go see "Madame R., the daughter of a well-known general," who had already helped several people get across the border. She arranged for him to be taken in one of three sledges across the ice of the Gulf of Finland: "In any other circumstances my position would have seemed one of extreme discomfort, for I had half to lie, half to recline on the bottom of the sledge with my back to the horse, so that every jolt of the vehicle over the rough ice sent a jar from the top of my spine to the bottom; but my spiritual content was such that I hardly noticed physical annoyances."[10] Eight hours later the Finns delivered Pollock to the town of Terioki. "Fifteen minutes more, and we were knocking up a young farmer and his wife, who gave us unlimited coffee—with milk!—and bread, and butter, such luxuries as are not to be found in all Petrograd."[11]

Both Yavorskaya and Pollock remained in Finland for three months. He was hired as a special correspondent for *The Times*, reporting on events in Russia. Yavorskaya, returning to England on May 18, settled into her London apartment never to leave the country again. Four days after her arrival, she gave an interview to the *Daily Mirror* in which she described in detail the privations suffered by the Russian people at the hands of the Bolsheviks. She told the reporter: "In January and December last each person existed on one herring a day, with a small portion of oats. Bread was practically unprocurable." She hoped that Western forces would intervene: "If they do not, the Germans will, and they are already doing their best to exterminate the intellectual people of Russia and to reconstruct the country in a manner to suit themselves."[12] Pollock too returned to England in mid-May, but after submitting his memoir *The Bolshevik Adventure* to his publisher, he went back to Finland, staying until the end of the year.

It turns out that Terioki, where Pollock had finally reached safety after fleeing Russia, was also the closest Finnish village to Marioki, the estate of the late Maria Krestovskaya, which Shchepkina-Kupernik continued to visit regularly after Krestovskaya's death. In the period between the February and October 1917 revolutions, Shchepkina-Kupernik escaped the tumult in Petrograd by settling in at Marioki for the summer with her husband, Zelenina, and Zelenina's son.[13] In March 1919, the foursome, joined by Zelenina's father, Nikolai Shubinsky, and constituting a family of sorts, made their way south, first to Kiev, then on to Odessa. They were joining an exodus of upper-class, educated Russians fleeing the revolution and hoping to find a way out of the country. By the time they reached Odessa, the city was occupied by the Red Army after being abandoned by the French expeditionary force that had first arrived in November 1918. Those hoping to escape now feared what the future would bring. "The only thing we live for is to gather in secret and to exchange news with each other," wrote Ivan Bunin in his diary. "For us the main source for such counterintelligence is on Khersonskaya Street, at the home of Shchepkina-Kupernik."[14] Her attitude toward the revolution was not as virulent as Bunin's. She told Bunin about her friendship with Kollontai, now a member of the Communist Party's central committee. "I know her very well," she told Bunin. "She once resembled an angel." Bunin confided to his diary: "The judicial system and psychiatric medicine have long classed this (angelic-looking) type as belonging to inbred criminals and prostitutes."[15]

By August 1919 the White Army was rapidly advancing on Odessa, poised to take it back. Zelenina recalled: "We went to bed at night, couldn't sleep, kept dreaming of steps, a knock on the gate in the alley, somebody's deafening wail. Odessa was already seized with confusion."[16] She saw office workers burning papers, changing their clothes. Bunin came by, happy and excited, saying, "Come watch how the Bolsheviks are running out of the Cheka." When the White forces arrived, Zelenina "cried, feeling myself freed, and there was joy in my soul. Tania and I embraced in our room and on our knees thanked fate.... [We] went to bed, turned off the light. Across from the house someone was wonderfully playing a Beethoven sonata, and it was apparent that someone's soul was celebrating being set free in sound."[17]

The opportune moment had come to leave Russia. On January 26, 1920, Bunin and his wife boarded the last French ship to leave Odessa sailing for Constantinople. Zelenina, her father, and her son left as well, perhaps on the same ship as Bunin. But when Zelenina's father died in Constantinople in 1921, she decided to return to Russia.[18] Shchepkina-Kupernik and her husband, however, did not leave. Having previously accused Yavorskaya of turning her back on Russia, Shchepkina-Kupernik couldn't bring herself to do it. Lunacharsky convinced her to return to Petrograd, where for the next three years she endured the deprivations of the early Soviet period.[19] She avoided any sort of political visibility, relying on the protection afforded by her close friendship with Kollontai, who was grateful for the times when Shchepkina-Kupernik let her hide in her Petrograd apartment before the revolution.

In England, Yavorskaya once again took advantage of her celebrity status to campaign against Bolshevism, promoting an antisocialist viewpoint that put her in the company of reactionaries with whom she would never have associated in prerevolutionary Russia.

On March 6, 1920, Lidia Yavorskaya and John Pollock were married before the civil registrar of St. Giles parish in London. Newspapers reported it was a quiet ceremony, "the Princess having recently suffered a sad bereavement in her family owing to the atrocities committed by the Bolsheviks."[20] It is unknown how she came to know Count Arthur Cherep-Spridovich, who gave away the bride at the ceremony. Cherep-Spiridovich was a rabid antisemite who soon afterward moved to the US, where he formed a branch of the Anglo-Latino-Slav League, which promoted a "world union of white people against the dominance of the colored peoples."[21] Such unfortunate associations could possibly have been the result of Yavorskaya's and Pollock's participation in meetings and debates held by the British Empire Union, which had evolved from an anti-German organization during the war to an antisocialist movement concerned about possible Bolshevist sympathies in the Labour Party.

It was becoming obvious to Pollock that Yavorskaya's health was deteriorating. Although she performed in a one-act play, *In the Darkness of the Night*, written by Pollock, at the London Coliseum on July 5, 1920, she devoted most of her diminishing energy to supporting refugees fleeing Russia. In March of 1921, she organized, as a fundraiser, two one-act plays at the Ambassadors Theatre, after which she became seriously ill. It would be the last time she performed on stage. In May, the *Westminster Gazette* reported that Yavorskaya was "now making a rapid recovery and has been moved to Brighton for her convalescence."[22] In reality, she was dying of cancer.

Pollock settled his wife into a friend's house on Carlisle Road in Hove, just outside Brighton. Weakening rapidly following an unsuccessful operation, Yavorskaya died on September 3, 1921, at the house on Carlisle Road with Pollock at her side. Death came from a combination of "cancer of the womb" and asthma, the lifelong ailment that had caused the often-noted hoarseness in her voice. She was fifty years old. Four years after Yavorskaya's death, Pollock remarried. Although we don't know who cared for Sasha while Yavorskaya was in Russia between 1915 and 1919, the ward was living with her at Hove at the time of Yavorskaya's death. The young woman, now nineteen years old, plagued by poor health and most likely forced to find a way to support herself, lived only a few more years. At the time of her death of typhoid fever in 1927, she was working as a house servant.

Yavorskaya's death was widely reported in the British press. *The Stage* described her as "a Russian actress seen a good deal on the London stage, on which she can scarcely be said to have realized her ambitions as 'the Russian Sarah Bernhardt.'"[23] Many obituaries described her "harrowing" escape from Petrograd and dramatically attributed her death "to privations suffered in Russia." One reporter called her a figure of romance whose death "removes one of those amazing personalities sometimes encountered in a novel by Turgenev, but rarely in real life."[24]

As a prerevolutionary actor who escaped while her country was in the midst of a bloody civil war, Yavorskaya's death received less attention in Russia than in England. However, when the news reached Russia, the theater critic Nikolai Efros wrote an extensive obituary in the journal *Theater Culture*. It was a perceptive, unsparingly frank, and complex portrait of the actor. From the very beginning of her career, Efros noted, Yavorskaya was a new type of Russian actor at odds with what actors and audiences found acceptable: "Hers was a stormy and combative nature with an enormous will to action . . . . a will for self-affirmation and praise." Similar to Bernhardt, she "choked on the thought of obscurity." But for Russians, Efros maintained, the ideal was Ermolova, whose artistic persona was shy, humble, restrained. Yavorskaya's "theatrical egocentrism" prevented her from developing a reputation as a serious artist, but, Efros added, her "importunate" nature did manage to turn her into a celebrity: "There were seasons when none of our stage artists were talked about more, and even with fervor—never mind with praise or disapproval—than Yavorskaya."[25]

Returning to Petrograd in 1921, Shchepkina-Kupernik and her husband discovered that they had no way to make a living. Her prerevolutionary works had become unfashionable and unpublishable. For a while, they "lived on handouts and by selling their possessions."[26] Conditions gradually improved after Lenin instituted his New Economic Policy, which permitted limited privatization of the economy. Kollontai arranged for Shchepkina-Kupernik to receive a pension for "revolutionary services."[27] Polynov resumed his career as a defense attorney. She was allowed to publish her memoirs, and she became well known as a translator of Shakespeare's plays, for which she was officially recognized as an Honored Soviet Artist.

The Polynovs were even able to travel to France, although they kept their visits with émigrés to a minimum, fearing that it might get them into trouble. Even though Shchepkina-Kupernik had become good friends with Bunin, having suffered with him through the Bolshevik occupation of Odessa in 1919, she didn't risk going to see him in Paris: "I feared that he . . . . wouldn't let me in—only because I dared remain in Soviet Russia."[28] They did however visit Lika Mizinova, who was in poor health. She died in Paris in February 1939.

During this period Shchepkina-Kupernik started splitting her time between living with Zelenina in Moscow and staying with Polynov in their Leningrad apartment, a reflection of the strains in their marriage. She admitted to a friend: "All my life I pursued my husband, but he pursued other women."[29] She described having to leave Moscow for Leningrad as being like "leaving a comfortable warm room, wearing just a dress, for the freezing cold."[30] When Polynov died in April 1939, she moved into Zelenina's apartment. They lived together for the rest of Shchepkina-Kupernik's life. Zelenina's son took over Polynov's apartment and died there during the siege of Leningrad. In her last years, Shchepkina-Kupernik became a deputy of the Supreme Soviet, and in 1948 she published another volume of her memoirs. She died in July 1952, having outlived Yavorskaya by more than thirty years.

In recent decades there has been a modest revival of interest in Shchepkina-Kupernik due in large part to Donald Rayfield's previously mentioned monograph, "The Forgotten Poetess" (2001), followed by his involvement in the publication of a Russian volume of her selected verse (2008). The poet Yevgeny Yevtushenko, echoing continuing ambivalence about Shchepkina-Kupernik's reputation in post-Soviet Russia, thanked Rayfield for his essay, but felt he exaggerated her poetic gifts. Yevtushenko did, however, praise her translations, particularly *Cyrano de Bergerac*. He noted in his monumental *Ten Centuries of Russian Verse*: "Shchepkina-Kupernik lived two long lifetimes—one decadent, the other Soviet;" he admired neither. Yevtushenko wrote a caustic poem about "Tatiana Topsy-Turvy" (a nickname her Hotel Louvre friends gave her), in which the nineteenth-century decadent is a "provincial young lady playing the role of a *hetaera*," a Greek courtesan, and the twentieth-century Soviet citizen pays a price for being decorated "an honored artist" by the Communist Party:

> Who's clean, who's not clean?
> She was in a class by herself.
> In Moscow, a Chekist drank with her.
> In Crimea, she dined with Wrangel.
> In her new life
> Tatiana Topsy-Turvy
> In topsy-turvy Moscow
> Got used to the words "Tsk" [Central Committee of the
>   Communist Party]
> And "Obkom." [Regional Committee of the Communist Party]
> But here's one
> Unknowable secret that remains:
> How did Kollontai kiss you
> In a way consistent with Party dictates?[31]

Tatiana Shchepkina-Kupernik is buried in a place of honor in the artists' corner of Novodevichy Cemetery in Moscow. Her gravestone simply says "Writer." Immediately adjacent, across a narrow path, is the grave of the painter Isaac Levitan, whom she had impulsively insisted accompany her to Melikhovo in 1895 to see Chekhov, thereby ending an estrangement between the two men that had lasted almost three years.

Far away, separated by a revolution and almost two thousand miles, lies the grave of Lidia Yavorskaya in the quiet village churchyard of St. Nicolas in Old Shoreham on the coast of Sussex, England. Today its recently restored white Portland stone gleams in the sun, making it easy to make out the inscription that John Pollock ordered incised onto its face: "The youngest of the four great actresses of her generation: Noble heart, lofty mind, burning soul, she devoted her life & gifts to the worship of beauty and to the cause of freedom."

It's a mystery whom Pollock had in mind as the other three great actresses of her time. We have come to know, however, that Yavorskaya's life was far more controversial and complex than what is reflected in these words. But for those who pass by her grave, Pollock fittingly memorialized those attributes of Yavorskaya that so fascinated her contemporaries, both in Russia and in England: her passion for performance, her desire to inspire, and her commitment to a just society. In the end, it was the critic Nikolai Efros who best expressed the essence of Lidia Yavorskaya—she wanted a "glory that was beyond her capacity.... and she received less praise than she deserved."[32]

Notes

Introduction

1. Murray Frame, *School for Citizens: Theatre and Civil Society in Imperial Russia* (New Haven, CT: Yale University Press, 2006), 107.
2. Donald Rayfield, "The Forgotten Poetess: Tatiana L'vovna Shchepkina-Kupernik," *The Slavonic and East European Review* 79, no. 4 (October 2001): 601–637.
3. Catherine A. Schuler, *Women in Russian Theatre: The Actress in the Silver Age* (London: Routledge, 1996).
4. Schuler, *Women in Russian Theatre*, 139.

Prologue

1. A. Ia. Glama-Meshcherskaia, *Vospominaniia* (Moscow-Leningrad: Iskusstvo, 1937), 70.
2. Glama-Meshcherskaia, *Vospominaniia*, 128.
3. Glama-Meshcherskaia, 128.
4. Glama-Meshcherskaia, 133.
5. Paul du Quenoy, *Stage Fright: Politics and the Performing Arts in Late Imperial Russia* (University Park: Pennsylvania State University Press, 2009), 25.
6. Schuler, *Women in Russian Theatre*, 125.
7. Glama-Meshcherskaia, *Vospominaniia*, 209.
8. Anton Chekhov, *Polnoe sobranie sochinenii i pisem v tridtsati tomakh* [Complete Works and Letters in Thirty Volumes], ed. N. F. Belchikov et al. (Moscow: Nauka, 1975), *Letters* 1:61 (hereafter cited either as *Works*, volumes one through eighteen, or *Letters*, volumes one through twelve, with volume and page number indicated).
9. Chekhov, *Works*, 16:48.
10. Chekhov, 16:150–151.
11. Chekhov, 16:151.
12. Chekhov, 16:151.
13. Chekhov, 16:152.
14. D. M. Iazykov, *Kratkii ocherk dvadtsatipiatiletnei deiatel'nosti Teatra F. A. Korsha* (Moscow: A. A. Levinson, 1907), 27.
15. Chekhov, *Works,* 16:172–173.
16. Chekhov, *Letters,* 1:260.
17. Chekhov, 1:61.
18. Chekhov, 1:259.

19. Chekhov, *Works*, 11:208
20. Chekhov, 11:212, 214.
21. Chekhov, *Letters*, 2:128.
22. Chekhov, 2:142.
23. Chekhov, 2:142.
24. Glama-Meshcherskaia, *Vospominaniia*, 258.
25. Chekhov, *Letters*, 2:150.
26. Vladimir Giliarovskii, *Sochineniia v dvukh tomakh* (Kaluga: Zolotaia alleia, 1994), 1:441.
27. Chekhov, *Letters*, 2:150–152.
28. Chekhov, 2:153–154.
29. A. P. Kuzicheva, *A. P. Chekhov v russkoi teatral'noi kritike* (Moscow: Chekhovskii poligraficheskii kombinat, 1999), 47.
30. Kuzicheva, *Chekhov*, 52.
31. Chekhov, *Letters*, 2:433.
32. E. M. Sakharova, ed., *Vokrug Chekhova* (Moscow: Pravda, 1990), 253.
33. Louise McReynolds, *The News under Russia's Old Regime: The Development of a Mass-Circulation Press* (Princeton, NJ: Princeton University Press, 1991), 74, quoted in Frame, *School for Citizens*, 114.
34. Chekhov, *Letters*, 2:158.
35. Chekhov, 2:159.
36. Chekhov, 3:8.
37. Frame, *School for Citizens*, 109–110.
38. Chekhov, *Letters*, 3:14.
39. Chekhov, *Works*, 11:426.
40. Chekhov, 11:427.
41. du Quenoy, *Stage Fright*, 44.
42. Chekhov, *Letters*, 3:50.
43. Chekhov, 3:50.
44. Chekhov, 3:60.
45. Glama-Meshcherskaia, *Vospominaniia*, 245.
46. Chekhov, *Letters*, 3:94.
47. Chekhov, 3:162.
48. Chekhov, 3:250.

1. "Ma Petite Sappho"

1. Glama-Meshcherskaia, *Vospominaniia*, 286.
2. Tat'iana Shchepkina-Kupernik, *Vospominaniia* (Moscow: Zakharov, 2005), 252.
3. Chekhov, *Works*, 16:81.
4. "Teatr g. Korsha," *Artist*, no. 30 (October 1893): 137.
5. "Teatr g. Korsha," 137. See also "Teatr g. Korsha," *Artist*, no. 31 (November 1893):169; "Teatr i Muzika," *Moskovskie vedomosti*, September 26, 1893.
6. Iurii Beliaev, *Stat'i o teatre* (St. Petersburg: Hyperion, 2003), 67.
7. Beliaev, *Stat'i o teatre*, 67.

8. Aleksei Suvorin, *Dnevnik Alekseia Sergeevicha Suvorina* (Moscow: Nezavisimaia Gazeta, 1999), 217.

9. O. M. Skibina, "... i moia bezumnaia liubov' k vam, sviatoi, nepostizhimyi, divnyi!" (Pis'ma L. B. Iavorskaia A. P. Chekhovu), in *Chekhoviana: Polet "Chaiki"* (Moscow: Nauka, 2001), 81n3.

10. Beliaev, *Stat'i o teatre*, 67.

11. Marina Litavrina, *Iavorskaia, bezzakonnaia kometa* (Moscow: MIK, 2008), 23.

12. Litavrina, *Iavorskaia*, 26–27.

13. Chekhov, *Works*, 16:17.

14. Robert Gottlieb, *Sarah: The Life of Sarah Bernhardt* (New Haven, CT: Yale University Press, 2010), 192.

15. N. Tamarin, "Novosti dnia," *Revel'skie izvestiia*, May 25, 1893.

16. Shchepkina-Kupernik, *Vospominaniia*, 100.

17. Tat'iana Shchepkina-Kupernik, *Teatr v moei zhizni: memuary moskovskoi fify* (Moscow: AST, 2015), 82.

18. "Teatr g. Korsha," *Artist*, no. 24 (November 1892): 166.

19. Schepkina-Kupernik, *Vospominaniia*, 250.

20. Ivan Ivanov, "Teatr g. Korsha—Zametki i vpechatleniia," *Artist*, no. 2 (October 1889): 107.

21. F. A. Korsh, *Kratkii ocherk desiatiletnei deiatel'nosti russkogo dramaticheskogo teatra Korsha v Moskve* (Moscow: Kushnerev, 1892), 50.

22. Shchepkina-Kupernik, *Teatr v moei zhizni*, 89.

23. "'Letniaia kartinka' v 1 d. T. Kupernik," *Artist*, no. 24 (November 1892): 155.

24. Shchepkina-Kupernik, *Teatr v moei zhizni*, 88.

25. Shchepkina-Kupernik, 88.

26. T. Shchepkina-Kupernik, "Kulisy (Raskaz)," *Artist*, no. 27 (February 1893): 91.

27. T. Shchepkina-Kupernik, "Kulisy (Raskaz)," *Artist*, no. 27 (February 1893): 95.

28. Shchepkina-Kupernik, *Vospominaniia*, 82.

29. Shchepkina-Kupernik, 99.

30. Shchepkina-Kupernik, *Teatr v moei zhizni*, 338.

31. Shchepkina-Kupernik, 304.

32. Yu. A. Koroleva, *Soprikosnovenie sudeb: A. P. Chekhov i I. I. Levitan* (Moscow: Gelios, 2011), 240.

33. Shchepkina-Kupernik, *Vospominaniia*, 194.

34. Shchepkina-Kupernik, 190.

35. Shchepkina-Kupernik, 191.

36. Shchepkina-Kupernik, 191–192.

37. Shchepkina-Kupernik, 191–192.

38. Shchepkina-Kupernik, 193.

39. Donald Rayfield, "Tongues Wagged," *London Review of Books* 19, no. 4 (February 1997), accessed January 23, 2024, https://www.lrb.co.uk/the-paper/v19/n04/donald-rayfield/tongues-wagged.

40. Laura Engelstein, *The Keys to Happiness: Sex and the Search for Modernity in Fin-de-Siecle Russia* (Ithaca, NY: Cornell University Press, 1992), 83.
41. Engelstein, *Keys to Happiness*, 156.
42. Yavorskaya's letters and telegrams to Shchepkina-Kupernik, 1893, Moscow State Archive for Literature and Art (RGALI), 571-1-1204, l. 43 (hereafter cited as RGALI, 571-1-1204).
43. RGALI, 571-1-1204, l. 47.
44. RGALI, 571-1-1204, l. 30.

2. "I Spent Two Weeks in Some Sort of a Daze"

1. Anton Chekhov, *Perepiska A. P. Chekhova v trekh tomakh*, vol. 2 (Moscow: Nasledie, 1996), 311.
2. Chekhov, *Perepiska*, 2:313.
3. Chekhov, *Letters*, 5:235.
4. L. D. Gromova, *Letopis' zhizni i tvorchestva A. P. Chekhova*, vol. 3 (Moscow: Nasledie, 2004), 434.
5. Chekhov, *Perepiska*, 2:387.
6. Chekhov, 2:313.
7. Chekhov, 2:314.
8. Chekhov, 2:388.
9. Chekhov, *Letters*, 5:243.
10. Chekhov, 5:248.
11. Shchepkina-Kupernik, *Vospominaniia*, 202.
12. Shchepkina-Kupernik, 200.
13. Shchepkina-Kupernik, 201.
14. Kuzicheva, *A. P. Chekhov v russkoi teatral'noi kritike*, 346.
15. Donald Rayfield, *Anton Chekhov: A Life* (New York: Henry Holt, 1997), 302.
16. Skibina, *Chekhoviana*, 77.
17. Shchepkina-Kupernik, *Vospominaniia*, 210.
18. Ivan Shcheglov, "Iz dnevnika I.L. Shcheglova," *Literaturnoe nasledstvo* 68 (1960): 484.
19. Skibina, *Chekhoviana*, 79.
20. Chekhov, *Perepiska*, 2:315.
21. Chekhov, 2:317.
22. RGALI, 571-1-1204 l. 13-14.
23. RGALI, 571-1-1204, l. 72.
24. RGALI, 571-1-1204, l. 43-46.
25. T. Shchepkina-Kupernik, "Credo," *Artist*, no. 33 (January 1894):115.
26. "Teatr g. Korsha," *Artist*, no. 34 (February 1894): 244-246.
27. Sakharova, *Vokrug Chekhova*, 270.
28. Sakharova, 270-271.
29. Sakharova, 269.
30. Chekhov, *Letters*, 5:263.
31. Skibina, *Chekhoviana*, 78.

32. Skibina, 78.
33. Beliaev, *Stat'i o teatre*, 70.
34. For an overview of Kovalevskaya's life and works, see Sofya Kovalevskaya, *A Russian Childhood*, translated, edited, and introduced by Beatrice Stillman (New York: Springer-Verlag, 1978), 1–47; see also Don H. Kennedy, *Little Sparrow: A Portrait of Sophia Kovalevsky* (Athens: Ohio University Press, 1983) and Ann Hibner Koblitz, *A Convergence of Lives, Sofia Kovalevskaia: Scientist, Writer, Revolutionary* (Boston: Birkhauser, 1983).
35. Kovalevskaya, *A Russian Childhood*, 27.
36. S. V. Kovalevskaia, *Vospominaniia, Povesti* (Moscow: Nauka, 1974), 437.
37. Beliaev, *Stat'i o teatre*, 70.
38. Shchepkina-Kupernik, *Vospominaniia*, 253.
39. Chekhov, *Letters*, 5:270.
40. T. L. Shchepkina-Kupernik, "O pervom predstavlenii dramy S. Kovalevskoi i A. Sh. Leffler Bor'ba za schast'e," in *Pamiati S. V. Kovalevskoi* (Moscow: Akademiia Nauk, 1951), 143.
41. "Sovremennoe obozrenie, Moskva, Teatr g. Korsha 'Bor'ba za schast'e.'" *Artist*, no. 36 (April 1894):246.
42. Shchepkina-Kupernik, *Vospominaniia*, 211.
43. Shchepkina-Kupernik, "Sapho, listki iz dnevnika," in *Mezhdu prochim*, edited by F. A. Kumanin (Moscow: Artist, 1894), 17–49.
44. Kuzicheva, *A. P. Chekhov v russkoi teatral'noi kritike*, 342.

3. "In Paris Things Don't Happen So Quickly"

1. Rayfield, *Anton Chekhov*, 316.
2. Skibina, *Chekhoviana*, 80.
3. Skibina, 79.
4. Skibina, 79.
5. Leonid Munshtein, "Moskva dalekaia . . . Klochki vospominanii (v sokrashenii)," in *Pervoprestol'naia dalekaia i blizkaia: Moskva i moskvichi v poezii russkoi emigratsii* (Moscow: Russkii mir, 2005), last modified April 17, 2022, http://az.lib.ru/m/munshtejn_l_g/text_1931_moskva_dalekaya.shtml.
6. Shchepkina-Kupernik, *Vospominaniia*, 209.
7. Yavorskaya's letters and telegrams to Shchepkina-Kupernik, 1894, Moscow State Archive for Literature and Art (RGALI), 571-1-1205, l. 5-6 (hereafter cited as RGALI, 571-1-1205).
8. RGALI, 571-1-1205, l. 7,13.
9. RGALI, 571-1-1205, l. 15.
10. RGALI, 571-1-1205, l. 14.
11. RGALI, 571-1-1205, l. 28-29.
12. RGALI, 571-1-1205, l. 32-35.
13. Shchepkina-Kupernik, *Vospominaniia*, 256-257.
14. Shchepkina-Kupernik, 259.
15. Shchepkina-Kupernik, 260-261.
16. Shchepkina-Kupernik, 268.

17. Shchepkina-Kupernik, 267.
18. Shchepkina-Kupernik, 271.
19. Shchepkina-Kupernik, 261.
20. Potapenko's letter to Maria Chekhova, May 31, 1894, Manuscript Division of the Russian State Library, 331-95-2.
21. Kuzicheva, *A. P. Chekhov v russkoi teatral'noi kritike*, 348.
22. Rayfield, "The Forgotten Poetess," 608.
23. RGALI, 571-1-1204, l. 48-50.
24. Shchepkina-Kupernik, *Vospominaniia*, 272.

4. "Don't Forget the One Who Loves Only You"

1. See Chekhov's letter to Suvorin. Chekhov, *Letters*, 6:54.
2. "Teatr g. Korsha," *Artist*, no. 43 (November 1894): 184.
3. Lev Tolstoi, *Polnoe sobranie sochinenii*, vol. 27 (Moscow: Izdatel'stvo khudozhestvennoi literatury, 1936), 662.
4. Chekhov, *Perepiska*, 2:323.
5. Chekhov, 2:324.
6. V. A. Nelidov, *Teatral'naia Moskva: sorok let moskovskikh teatrov* (Moscow: Materik, 2002), 46.
7. "Teatr i Muzika," *Moskovskie vedomosti*, December 13, 1894.
8. "Teatr i Muzika."
9. S. N. Durylin, *V svoem uglu* (Moscow: Moskovskii rabochii, 1991), 185-186.
10. Litavrina, *Iavorskaia*, 36.
11. See Munshtein, "Moskva dalekaia," Chapter Four: *Madame Sans-Gêne*, I-VII.
12. "Teatr i Muzika," *Moskovskie vedomosti*, October 15, 1894.
13. Chekhov, *Perepiska*, 2:390.
14. Skibina, *Chekhoviana*, 81.
15. Shchepkina-Kupernik, *Teatr v moei zhizni*, 341.
16. Chekhov, *Perepiska*, 2:390-391.
17. RGALI, 571-1-1204, l. 11.
18. Tatiana Shchepkina-Kupernik, *Schast'e*, 2nd ed. (Moscow: D.P. Efimov, 1903), 252.
19. RGALI, 571-1-1204, l. 12.
20. Shchepkina-Kupernik, *Teatr v moei zhizni*, 345.
21. Koroleva, *Soprikosnovenie sudeb*, 242.
22. Chekhov, *Letters*, 5:349.
23. "Teatr g. Korsha," *Artist*, no. 45 (January 1895): 210.
24. Chekhov, *Perepiska*, 2:391.
25. Tat'iana Shchepkina-Kupernik, *Stranichki zhizni* (Moscow: M. Merkusheva, 1898), 17.
26. Shchepkina-Kupernik, *Teatr v moei zhizni*, 360.
27. Skibina, *Chekhoviana*, 81-82.
28. Rayfield, *Anton Chekhov*, 338.

29. Skibina, *Chekhoviana*, 82.
30. Chekhov, *Letters*, 6:11.
31. "Teatr i Muzika," *Moskovskie vedomosti*, February 5, 1895.
32. Chekhov, *Letters*, 6:17.
33. Chekhov, *Perepiska*, 2:392.
34. Chekhov, 2:392.
35. Chekhov, 2:393.
36. Chekhov, *Letters*, 6:17.
37. Chekhov, 6:107.
38. "Teatr i Muzika," *Moskovskie vedomosti*, March 2, 1895.
39. Skibina, *Chekhoviana*, 83–84.
40. Chekhov, *Letters*, 6:18.

5. *The Dream Princess*

1. Skibina, *Chekhoviana*, 84–85.
2. Shchepkina-Kupernik, *Vospominaniia*, 275.
3. Aleksandr Kugel', "Iz moikh vospominanii (L. B. Yavorskaya)," *Zhizn' iskusstva*, no. 33 (1924): 8.
4. Chekhov, *Letters*, 6:44.
5. Skibina, *Chekhoviana*, 85.
6. E. I. Strel'tsova, *Chastnyi teatr v Rosii: ot istokov do nachala xx veka* (Moscow: GITIS, 2009), 371.
7. "Teatr i Muzika," *Novoe vremia*, April 7, 1895.
8. Aleksei Suvorin, "Teatr i Muzika," *Novoe vremia*, April 8, 1895.
9. "Teatr i Muzika," *Sankt-Peterburgskie vedomosti*, April 8, 1895.
10. Chekhov, *Letters*, 6:55.
11. "Teatr i Muzika," *Novoe vremia*, April 11, 1895.
12. Shchepkina-Kupernik, *Vospominaniia*, 274.
13. Shchepkina-Kupernik, 274.
14. Chekhov, *Letters*, 6:59.
15. "Teatr i Muzika," *Novoe vremia*, April 20, 1895.
16. Strel'tsova, *Chastnyi teatr v Rosii*, 400.
17. Chekhov, *Letters*, 5:344.
18. Chekhov, *Works*, 9:111–112.
19. Shchepkina-Kupernik, *Vospominaniia*, 277.
20. Chekhov, *Works*, 9:117.
21. Chekhov, *Perepiska*, 2:331.
22. Chekhov, *Works*, 9:126.
23. Chekhov, *Works*, 9:130–131.
24. A. P. Chekhov, *Aleksandr i Anton Chekhov: Vospominaniia, perepiska* (Moscow: Zakharov, 2012), 338.
25. Shchepkina-Kupernik, *Vospominaniia*, 278.
26. Litavrina, *Iavorskaia*, 58.
27. "Teatr i Muzika," *Novoe vremia*, September 10, 1895.
28. "Teatr i Muzika," *Sankt-Peterburgskie vedomosti*, September 19, 1895.

29. "Teatr i Miuzika," *Sankt-Peterburgskie vedomosti*, September 20, 1895.
30. "Teatr i Muzika," *Novoe vremia*, September 19, 1895.
31. Litavrina, *Iavorskaia*, 59.
32. Glama-Meshcherskaia, *Vospominaniia*, 294.
33. Shchepkina-Kupernik, *Vospominaniia*, 211–212.
34. Shchepkina-Kupernik, 280.
35. Chekhov, *Letters*, 6:112–113.
36. Shchepkina-Kupernik, *Vospominaniia*, 283.
37. Shchepkina-Kupernik, 283.
38. "Teatr i Muzika," *Novoe vremia*, January 6, 1896.
39. Litavrina, *Iavorskaia*, 64.
40. Litavrina, 65.
41. Shchepkina-Kupernik, *Vospominaniia*, 284.
42. Shchepkina-Kupernik, 284.
43. Litavrina, *Iavorskaia*, 67.
44. "Teatr i Muzika," *Sankt-Petersburgskie vedomosti*, January 5, 1896; January 6, 1896.
45. Quoted in D. S. Yarovenko, "Perevod p'esy *La Princesse Lointaine* (*Printsessa Greza*) T. L. Shchepkina-Kupernik: russkoe prochtenie," *Vestnik Leningradskogo gosudarstvennogo universiteta* 1, no. 2 (2013): 246.
46. "Teatr i Muzika," *Novoe vremia*, January 6, 1896.
47. "Zapisi o Chekhove v dnevnikakh S. I. Smirnovoi-Sazonovoi," *Literaturnoe nasledstvo* 87 (1977): 307.
48. Maksim Gorkii, *Nesobrannye literaturno-kriticheskie stat'i* (Moscow: Khudozhestvennaia literatura, 1941), 246–248.

6. Princess Baryatinskaya

1. "Zapisi o Chekhove v dnevnikakh S. I. Smirnovoi-Sazonovoi," *Literaturnoe nasledstvo* 87 (1977): 307–308.
2. "Teatr i Muzika," *Novoe vremia*, January 13, 1896; January 16, 1896.
3. "Teatr i Muzika," *Sankt-Peterburgskie vedomosti*, January 13, 1896.
4. Suvorin, *Dnevnik*, 204.
5. Litavrina, *Iavorskaia*, 69.
6. Suvorin, *Dnevnik*, 214.
7. Suvorin, 219.
8. L. Ia. Gurevich, ed., *O Stanislavskom: sbornik vospominanii* (Moscow: Vserossiiskoe teatral'noe obshchestvo, 1948), 72.
9. Gurevich, *O Stanislavskom*, 73.
10. Gurevich, 73–74.
11. A. R. Kugel, quoted in Liudmila Chernichenko, *Kniaz' V. V. Bariatinskii: Pisatel' v rossii i v emigratsii* (Moscow: Rossiiskaia politicheskaia entsiklopediia, 2006), 68.
12. Litavrina, *Iavorskaia*, 71.
13. Suvorin, *Dnevnik*, 250.

14. Suvorin, 247.
15. For a description of the Baryatinsky family's attempt to annul the marriage, see Princess Anatole Marie Bariatinsky, *My Russian Life* (London: Hutchinson, 1923), 78–80.
16. Suvorin, *Dnevnik*, 240.
17. Suvorin, 241–242.
18. Rayfield, "The Forgotten Poetess," 611.
19. Suvorin, *Dnevnik*, 249–250.
20. Tat'iana L. Shchepkina-Kupernik, *Teatr v moei zhizni* (Moscow-Leningrad: Iskusstvo, 1948), 140–141.
21. Chernichenko, *Kniaz' V. V. Bariatinskii*, 72.
22. Chernichenko, 72.
23. Suvorin, *Dnevnik*, 253–255.
24. "Teatr i Muzika," *Novoe vremia*, October 22, 1896.
25. Suvorin, *Dnevnik*, 259.
26. Rayfield, *Anton Chekhov: A Life*, 394.
27. Chekhov, *Letters*, 6:85.
28. "Zapisi o Chekhove v dnevnikakh S. I. Smirnovoi-Sazonovoi," *Literaturnoe nasledstvo* 87 (1977): 309.
29. Rayfield, *Anton Chekhov: A Life*, 394.
30. "Zapisi o Chekhove v dnevnikakh S. I. Smirnovoi-Sazonovoi," *Literaturnoe nasledstvo* 87 (1977): 309.
31. "Teatr i Muzika," *Sank-Peterburgskie vedomosti*, October 19, 1896.
32. Aleksei Suvorin, "Teatr i Muzika," *Novoe vremia*, October 19, 1896.
33. Kuzicheva, *A. P. Chekhov v russkoi teatral'noi kritike*, 114.
34. Suvorin, *Dnevnik*, 263.
35. Suvorin, 263, 265.
36. Tat'iana L. Shchepkina-Kupernik, *Schast'e* (Moscow: D. P. Efimov, 1903), 24–25.
37. Tat'iana L. Shchepkina-Kupernik, "Lozanna," in *Pis'ma iz daleka* (Moscow: D. P. Efimov, 1903), 22.
38. Shchepkina-Kupernik, 40.
39. Shchepkina-Kupernik, 42–43.
40. Shchepkina-Kupernik, 45–46.
41. Shchepkina-Kupernik, 46.
42. Shchepkina-Kupernik, 47–48.
43. Shchepkina-Kupernik, 17.
44. Shchepkina-Kupernik, 17.

7. Reconciliation

1. Litavrina, *Iavorskaia*, 82.
2. "Teatr i Muzika," *Sankt-Peterburgskie vedomosti*, February 7, 1897.
3. "Teatr i Muzika," *Sankt-Peterburgskie vedomosti*, February 14, 1897.
4. "Teatr i Muzika," *Novoe vremia*, February 14, 1897.
5. Suvorin, *Dnevnik*, 279.

6. Suvorin, 288.
7. Chekhov, *Works*, 16:85–86.
8. "Teatr i Muzika," *Novoe vremia*, February 27, 1897.
9. "Teatr i Muzika, *Novoe vremia*, April 24, 1897.
10. "Teatr i Muzika," *Sankt-Peterburgskie vedomosti*, April 25 1897.
11. Quoted in Schuler, *Women in Russian Theatre*, 155.
12. Schuler, *Women in Russian Theatre*, 155.
13. "Teatr i Muzika," *Novoe vremia*, May 13, 1897.
14. Suvorin, *Dnevnik*, 299.
15. Shchepkina-Kupernik, *Pis'ma iz daleka*, 112.
16. Suvorin, *Dnevnik*, 300–301.
17. The title of Litavrina's biography refers to Yavorskaya as a "wayward comet" ("bezzakonnaia kometa").
18. Suvorin, *Dnevnik*, 308–309.
19. "Teatr i Muzika," *Novoe vremia*, November 15, 1897.
20. "Teatr i Muzika," *Sankt-Peterburgskie vedomosti*, November 28, 1897.
21. Chekhov, *Aleksandr i Anton Chekhov*, 760.
22. Shchepkina-Kupernik, *Vospominaniia*, 284.
23. Shchepkina-Kupernik, 286–287.
24. "Teatr i Muzika," *Novoe vremia*, February 8, 1898.
25. "Teatr i Muzika," *Novoe vremia*, February 12, 1898.
26. Shchepkina-Kupernik, *Vospominaniia*, 288.
27. "Teatr i Muzika," *Novoe vremia*, February 12, 1898.
28. Shchepkina-Kupernik, *Vospominaniia*, 288–290.
29. Suvorin, *Dnevnik*, 321.
30. Jean Benedetti, *Stanislavski* (London: Routledge, 1988), 60.
31. Shchepkina-Kupernik, *Vospominaniia*, 309.
32. Benedetti, *Stanislavski*, 74.
33. Benedetti, 82.
34. Chekhov, *Perepiska*, 2:394.
35. Chekhov, 2:395–396.
36. Chekhov, 2:398.
37. Benedetti, *Stanislavski*, 83.
38. Chekhov, *Perepiska*, 2:400.
39. Chekhov, 2:401.

8. *Sons of Israel*

1. Chernichenko, *Kniaz' V. V. Bariatinskii*, 189–190.
2. Chernichenko, 77.
3. Chernichenko, 87–88.
4. Chernichenko, 87–88.
5. Shchepkina-Kupernik, *Vospominaniia*, 443.
6. Shchepkina-Kupernik, 453.
7. Shchepkina-Kupernik, 454.
8. Alexei Suvorin, "Malenkie pis'ma," *Novoe vremia*, December 10, 1897.

9. Chernichenko, *Kniaz' V. V. Bariatinskii*, 131.
10. Shchepkina-Kupernik, *Vospominaniia*, 290.
11. Shchepkina-Kupernik, 295.
12. Chernichenko, *Kniaz' V. V. Bariatinskii*, 131.
13. Chernichenko, *Kniaz' V. V. Bariatinskii*, 160.
14. Chekhov, *Letters*, 9:10.
15. Suvorin, *Dnevnik*, 376.
16. Suvorin, 377.
17. See Lina Cavalieri, *Le mie verità* (Rome: Paolo D'Arvanni, 1936).
18. See Paul Fryer and Olga Usova, *Lina Cavalieri: The Life of Opera's Greatest Beauty, 1877–1944* (London: McFarland & Company, 2004) 18–29.
19. Litavrina, *Iavorskaia*, 87.
20. Suvorin, *Dnevnik*, 385.
21. Suvorin, 386–387.
22. Litavrina, *Iavorskaia*, 87.
23. Chernichenko, *Kniaz' V. V. Bariatinskii*, 173.
24. Suvorin, *Dnevnik*, 393.
25. Laurence Senelick, "Anti-Semitism and Tsarist Theatre: The Smugglers Riots," *Theatre Survey* 44, no. 1 (May 2003): 73.
26. V. Krylov and S. Litvin, *Syny Izrailia* (St. Petersburg: Tipografiia A. S. Suvorina, 1899), 11–12.
27. Krylov and Litvin, 45.
28. Krylov and Litvin, 48.
29. Senelick, "Anti-Semitism and Tsarist Theatre," 77.
30. Senelick, 78.
31. Senelick, 86.
32. Senelick, 78.
33. "Teatr i Muzika," *Novoe vremia*, November 16, 1900.
34. Litavrina, *Iavorskaia*, 92–93.
35. Senelick, "Anti-Semitism and Tsarist Theatre," 77.
36. Chernichenko, *Kniaz' V. V. Bariatinskii*, 183.
37. "Teatr i Muzika," *Novoe vremia*, November 22, 1900.
38. Chernichenko, *Kniaz' V. V. Bariatinskii*, 183–184.
39. Senelick, "Anti-Semitism and Tsarist Theatre," 79.
40. Senelick, 80.
41. Eyewitness accounts of the premiere have been widely published. Several authors have relied on the memoirs of B. A. Gorin-Goriainov, a student attendee who later became an actor in Yavorskaya's company. B. A. Gorin-Goriainov, *Aktery (iz vospominanii)* (Leningrad-Moscow: Iskusstvo, 1947) 79–93. My summary is based on descriptions provided by Senelick, Chernichenko, Litavrina, and Suvorin.
42. Litavrina, *Iavorskaia*, 94.
43. Senelick, "Anti-Semitism and Tsarist Theatre," 84.
44. Litavrina, *Iavorskaia*, 96–97.
45. Litavrina, 189–190.
46. Suvorin, *Dnevnik*, 401.

47. "Pis'mo v redaktsiiu," *Novoe vremia*, November 25, 1900.
48. "Pis'mo v redaktsiiu."
49. Suvorin, *Dnevnik*, 402–403.
50. Suvorin, 403.
51. Suvorin, 404–405.
52. Suvorin, 406.
53. Suvorin, 407.
54. Suvorin, 407.
55. Chernichenko, *Kniaz' V. V. Bariatinskii*, 189.
56. Litavrina, *Iavorskaia*, 102.
57. Litavrina, 191.
58. Suvorin, *Dnevnik*, 408.
59. Shchepkina-Kupernik, *Vospominaniia*, 298.
60. Shchepkina-Kupernik, 299.
61. Yavorskaya's letters and telegrams to Shchepkina-Kupernik, 1901–1910, Moscow State Archive for Literature and Art (RGALI), 571-1-1206, l. 15–16 (hereafter cited as RGALI, 571-1-1206).
62. Rayfield, "The Forgotten Poetess," 614.
63. Suvorin, *Dnevnik*, 412.
64. RGALI, 571-1-1206, l. 9.
65. RGALI, 571-1-1206, l. 11. The word "insisting" is underscored in the original letter.
66. RGALI, 571-1-1206, l. 12–13.

9. The New Theater

1. Maria Vsevolodovna Krestovskaya (1862–1910) is not to be confused with the actress Maria Alexandrovna Krestovskaya (1870–1940).
2. Shchepkina-Kupernik, *Vospominaniia*, 455.
3. Shchepkina-Kupernik, 458.
4. Shchepkina-Kupernik, 456.
5. Rayfield, "The Forgotten Poetess," 614.
6. Shchepkina-Kupernik, *Pis'ma iz daleka*, 287.
7. Shchepkina-Kupernik, 289.
8. Shchepkina-Kupernik, 291.
9. Shchepkina-Kupernik, 292.
10. Shchepkina-Kupernik, 293.
11. Shchepkina-Kupernik, 295–296.
12. Rayfield, "The Forgotten Poetess," 614.
13. A. P. Chekhov, *Perepiska s zhenoi* (Moscow: Zakharov, 2003), 173. For the unexpurgated version, see Rayfield, "The Forgotten Poetess," 613.
14. O. L. Knipper and M. P. Chekhova, *Perepiska 1899–1927*, vol. 1 (Moscow: Novoe literaturnoe obozrenie, 2016), 56.
15. Litavrina, *Iavorskaia*, 123.
16. Chekhov, *Perepiska s zhenoi*, 161.
17. "Khronika teatra i iskusstva," *Teatr i iskusstvo*, no. 9 (February 25, 1901): 188.

18. Chekhov, *Perepiska s zhenoi*, 164.
19. Chekhov, 164. For the unexpurgated version, see Rayfield, *Anton Chekhov: A Life*, 528.
20. Chekhov, 167.
21. Chekhov, 171-172.
22. Gottlieb, *Sarah*, 139.
23. Shchepkina-Kupernik, *Vospominaniia*, 300.
24. RGALI, 571-1-1205, l. 6.
25. Litavrina, *Iavorskaia*, 136.
26. Litavrina, 130.
27. Suvorin, *Dnevnik*, 420.
28. "Teatr i Muzika," *Novoe vremia*, September 17, 1901.
29. T. L. Shchepkina-Kupernik, *"Novyi teatr" razgovor v 1 diestvii v litsakh* (St. Petersburg: Narodnaia pol'za, 1901), 4.
30. Shchepkina-Kupernik, *"Novyi teatr,"* 8.
31. Shchepkina-Kupernik, 13-14.
32. Shchepkina-Kupernik, 15.
33. Shchepkina-Kupernik, 15.
34. "Teatr i Muzika," *Novoe vremia*, September 17, 1901.
35. "Teatr i Muzika," *Novoe vremia*, September 22, 1901.
36. "Khronika teatra i iskusstva," *Teatr i iskusstvo*, no. 30 (September 30, 1901): 710.
37. "Teatr i Muzika," *Novoe vremia*, October 10, 1901.
38. "Teatr i Muzika," *Novoe vremia*, November 4, 1901.
39. "Khronika teatra i iskusstva," *Teatr i iskusstvo*, no. 51 (December 16, 1901): 950.
40. "Khronika teatr i iskusstva," *Teatr i iskusstvo*, no. 8 (February 17, 1902): 171.
41. M. S. Narokov, *Biografiia moego pokoleniia* (Moscow: Vserossiiskoe teatral'noe obshchestvo, 1956), 123.
42. Narokov, *Biografiia moego pokoleniia*, 121.
43. Litavrina, *Iavorskaia*, 140.
44. Schuler, *Women in Russian Theatre*, 227-228.
45. I. N. Perestiani, *75 let zhizni v iskusstve* (Moscow: Iskusstvo, 1962), 187.
46. Rayfield, "The Forgotten Poetess," 613.
47. Narokov, *Biografiia moego pokoleniia*, 123-124.
48. Narokov, 123-124.
49. Yavorskaya's letters to Shchepkina-Kupernik, July 2, 1913-February 15, 1915, Moscow State Archive for Literature and Art (RGALI), 571-1-1210, l. 14-15. (hereafter cited as RGALI, 571-1-1210).

10. Marriage

1. Litavrina, *Iavorskaia*, 121.
2. Chekhov, *Perepiska*, 2:340.
3. N. Kinkul'kina, *Aleksandr Sanin: Zhizn i tvorchestvo* (Moscow: Iskusstvo, 2001), 114.

4. Chekhov, *Perepiska s zhenoi*, 208–209.
5. Knipper and Chekhova, *Perepiska 1899–1927*, 1:79–80.
6. Kinkul'kina, *Aleksandr Sanin*, 44.
7. Kinkul'kina, 124.
8. Chekhov, *Perepiska s zhenoi*, 415.
9. Chekhov, 416.
10. Chekhov, 424.
11. Kinkul'kina, *Aleksandr Sanin*, 125.
12. Chekhov, *Perepiska s zhenoi*, 631.
13. Kinkul'kina, *Aleksandr Sanin*, 202.
14. Chernichenko, *Kniaz' V. V. Bariatinskii*, 205.
15. "Khronika teatra i iskusstva," *Teatr i iskusstvo*, no. 39 (September 22, 1902): 699–700.
16. Vladimir Linskii, "Khronika teatra i iskusstva," *Teatr i iskusstvo*, no. 40 (September 29, 1902): 718–720.
17. Vladimir Linskii, "Khronika teatra i iskusstva," *Teatr i iskusstvo*, no. 5 (January 25, 1903): 114.
18. "Khronika teatra i iskusstva," *Teatr i iskusstvo*, no. 5 (January 25, 1903): 115.
19. "Ot kontory," *Teatr i iskusstvo*, no. 52 (December 22, 1902): 1002.
20. "Khronika teatra i iskusstva," *Teatr i iskusstvo*, no. 52 (December 22, 1902): 1006.
21. Litavrina, *Iavorskaia*, 190–191.
22. K. Kolosov, "Khronika teatra i iskusstva," *Teatr i iskusstvo*, no. 52 (December 21, 1903): 1011.
23. Kolosov, "Khronika teatra i iskusstva," 1011.
24. Gottlieb, *Sarah*, 146.
25. Litavrina, *Iavorskaia*, 162.
26. Litavrina, 145.
27. Chernichenko, *Kniaz' V. V. Bariatinskii*, 259.
28. Litavrina, *Iavorskaia*, 144–145.
29. Rayfield, "The Forgotten Poetess," 614.
30. Shchepkina-Kupernik, *Teatr v moei zhizni*, 374–375.
31. Shchepkina-Kupernik, *Teatr v moei zhizni*, 374.
32. Rayfield, "The Forgotten Poetess," 615.
33. Shchepkina-Kupernik, *Teatr v moei zhizni*, 373, 376.
34. Rayfield, "The Forgotten Poetess," 616.

11. 1905 Revolution

1. Litavrina, *Iavorskaia*, 164. A cartoon in an August issue of *Theater and Art* shows Yavorskaya with a bandage over her nose with the caption "Miss Yavorskaya after her operation." *Teatr i iskusstvo*, no. 34 (August 22, 1904): 624.
2. Litavrina, *Iavorskaia*, 165.
3. Vladimir Linskii, "Khronika teatra i iskusstva," *Teatr i iskusstvo*, no. 37 (September 12, 1904): 667.

4. Litavrina, *Iavorskaia*, 165.
5. Aleksandr Kugel', "Ot redaktsii," *Teatr i iskusstvo*, no. 50 (December 12, 1904): 881.
6. Sidney Harcave, *The Russian Revolution of 1905* (London: Collier Books, 1970), 88.
7. Perestiani, *75 let zhizni v iskusstve*, 192-193. See also "Khronika teatra i iskusstva," *Teatr i iskusstvo*, no. 3 (January 16, 1905): 42.
8. Harcave, *Russian Revolution*, 92.
9. Harcave, 93.
10. Perestiani, *75 let zhizni v iskusstve*, 193.
11. Harcave, *Russian Revolution*, 94.
12. "Nuzhdy russkogo teatra (Zapiska tsenicheskikh deiatelei)," *Teatr i iskusstvo*, no. 7 (February 13, 1905): 98-99.
13. Harcave, *Russian Revolution*, 129.
14. "Khronika teatra i iskusstva," *Teatr i iskusstvo*, no. 15 (April 10, 1905): 234.
15. "Provintsial'naia letopis'," *Teatr i iskusstvo*, no. 22 (May 29, 1905): 357.
16. "K sezonu v provintsii," *Teatr i iskusstvo*, no. 23 (June 5, 1905): 363.
17. Perestiani, *75 let zhizni v iskusstve*, 196.
18. Knipper and Chekhova, *Perepiska 1899-1927*, 1:169.
19. Harcave, *Russian Revolution,* 162.
20. Vladimir Linskii, "Khronika teatra i iskusstsva," *Teatr i iskusstvo*, no. 38 (September 18, 1905): 602.
21. Vladimir Linskii, "Khronika teatra i iskusstva," *Teatr i iskusstvo*, no. 39 (September 25, 1905): 619.
22. Harcave, *Russian Revolution*, 183.
23. Kinkul'kina, *Aleksandr Sanin*, 170.
24. "Eti dnii . . . ," *Teatr i iskusstvo*, nos. 42-43 (October 23, 1905): 670.
25. "Eti dnii . . . ." The cartoon appeared in nos. 45-46 (November 13, 1905): 718.
26. Perestiani, *75 let zhizni v iskusstve* 194.
27. V. V. Rozanov, *Mysli o literature* (Moscow: Sovremennik, 1989), 584-585.
28. Harcave, *Russian Revolution*, 196.
29. Chernichenko, *Kniaz' V. V. Bariatinskii*, 302.
30. Knipper and Chekhova, *Perepiska 1899-1927*, 1:183-184.
31. Knipper and Chekhova, 1:183-184.
32. Benedetti, *Stanislavski*, 150.
33. Benedetti, 150.
34. Vladimir Linskii, "Khronika teatra i iskusstva," *Teatr i iskusstvo*, no. 48 (November 27, 1905): 740.
35. "Khronika teatra i iskusstva," *Teatr i iskusstvo*, no. 11 (March 12, 1906): 162.
36. Litavrina, *Iavorskaia*, 174.
37. Du Quenoy, *Stage Fright*, 30.
38. Du Quenoy, 229.

12. The Wandering Star

1. Shchepkina-Kupernik, *Vospominaniia*, 379.
2. Shchepkina-Kupernik, 50.
3. Shchepkina-Kupernik, 379–380.
4. T. L. Shchepkina-Kupernik, *Izbrannye stikhotvoreniia i poemy* (Moscow: O-G-I, 2008), 177–178.
5. T. L. Shchepkina-Kupernik, *Eto bylo vchera* . . . (Moscow: Drutman, 1907).
6. Shchepkina-Kupernik, *Vospominaniia*, 51.
7. Shchepkina-Kupernik, *Izbrannye stikhotvoreniia i poemy*, 314.
8. Shchepkina-Kupernik, 323.
9. Shchepkina-Kupernik, *Vospominaniia*, 8.
10. Shchepkina-Kupernik, 383–384.
11. "Khronika teatra i iskusstva," *Teatr i iskusstvo*, no. 34 (August 20, 1906): 510.
12. "K sezonu v provintsii," *Teatr i iskusstvo*, no. 43 (October 22, 1906): 656.
13. "K sezonu v provintsii," *Teatr i iskusstvo*, no. 46 (November 12, 1906): 705.
14. "Khronika," *Teatr i iskusstvo*, no. 16 (April 22, 1907): 261.
15. "Provintsial'naia letopis'," *Teatr i iskusstvo*, no. 22 (June 3, 1907): 369.
16. *The God of Vengeance* had a notorious premiere on Broadway in 1923 that resulted in the cast being arrested and jailed for obscenity. The scandal forms the basis of Paula Vogel's 2015 play *Indecent*, which had its Broadway premiere in 2017.
17. "Provintsial'naia letopis'," *Teatr i iskusstvo*, no. 41 (October 14, 1907): 675.
18. Aleksandr Kugel', *Teatr i iskusstvo*, no. 40 (October 7, 1907): 643.
19. Tat'iana Shchepkina-Kupernik, "Pis'ma k redaktsiiu," *Teatr i iskusstvo*, no. 41 (October 14, 1907): 672.
20. "Provintsial'naia letopis'," *Teatr i iskusstvo*, no. 50 (December 16, 1907): 850.
21. "Provintsial'naia letopis'," *Teatr i iskusstvo*, no. 1 (January 6, 1908): 20.
22. "Provintsial'naia letopis'," *Teatr i iskusstvo*, no. 28 (July 13, 1908): 492.
23. "Provintsial'naia letopis'," *Teatr i iskusstvo*, no. 1 (January 4, 1909): 22.
24. "Provintsial'naia letopis'," *Teatr i iskusstvo*, no. 4 (January 25, 1909): 83.
25. Aleksandr Kugel', "Teatral'nye zametki," *Teatr i iskusstvo*, no. 7 (February 15, 1909): 135.

13. English Debut

1. Shchepkina-Kupernik's unpublished memoirs of Kollontai, archives of the St. Petersburg Theater Library, quoted in "Byloe: Tat'iana L'vovna Shchepkina-Kupernik—Nezhnaia zhenshchina," *Strakhi* (September 2008), https://coollib.com/b/271023-zhurnal-russkaya-zhizn-strahi-sentyabr-2008/read.
2. Cathy Porter, *Alexandra Kollontai: A Biography* (Chicago: Haymarket Books, 2014), 54.

3. Porter, *Alexandra Kollontai*, 44.
4. Unpublished memoirs quoted in *Strakhi* (September 2008).
5. Porter, *Alexandra Kollontai*, 139.
6. Rayfield, "The Forgotten Poetess," 618.
7. Emilii Mindlin, *Ne dom, no mir. Povest' ob Aleksandre Kollontai* (Moscow: Politizat, 1969), 124.
8. Porter, *Alexandra Kollontai*, 242.
9. Shchepkina-Kupernik, *Vospominaniia*, 458.
10. Shchepkina-Kupernik, 459.
11. Shchepkina-Kupernik, 460.
12. Rayfield, "The Forgotten Poetess," 618.
13. RGALI, 571-1-1206, l. 31.
14. See Rebecca Beasley, *Russomania: Russian Culture and the Creation of British Modernism, 1881–1922* (Oxford: Oxford University Press, 2020).
15. Stuart Young, "'Formless,' 'Pretentious,' 'Hideous and Revolting': Non-Chekhov Russian and Soviet Drama on the British Stage," in *Russia in Britain, 1880–1940: From Melodrama to Modernism*, ed. Rebecca Beasley and Philip Ross Bullock (Oxford: Oxford University Press, 2013), 89–90.
16. "Princess Actress in London," *Daily Mirror*, July 12, 1909.
17. See "The Only Princess on the Stage," *Illustrated London News*, no. 3678 (October 16, 1909): 12; "The Only Princess Who Is a Professional Actress," *The Sketch*, no. 872 (October 13, 1909): 11.; "A Russian Princess-Play-Actress, *The Tatler*, no. 433 (October 13, 1909): 49.
18. "Princess-Actress. Russian Artist Who Is to Produce Plays in Russian in London," *Daily Mirror*, November 27, 1909.
19. RGALI, 571-1-1206, l. 35-36.
20. Richard Garnett, *Constance Garnett: A Heroic Life* (London: Sinclair-Stenson, 1991), 226.
21. "The Afternoon Theatre. 'La Dame Aux Camélias,'" *The Times* (London), December 1, 1909.
22. "Khronika," *Novoe vremia*, no. 48 (November 29, 1909): 851.
23. "Drama. This Week," *Athenaeum*, no. 4285 (December 11, 1909): 741-742.
24. Ezra Pound, *Cantos: LXXIX* (New York: New Directions, 1965), 488.
25. "Khronika—Prodolzhenie," *Teatr i iskusstvo*, no. 51 (December 20, 1909): 941.
26. Shchepkina-Kupernik, *Izbrannye stikhotvoreniia i poemy*, 107.
27. "Teatr i Muzika," *Novoe vremia*, December 24, 1909.
28. "Khronika—Prodolzhenie," *Teatr i iskusstvo*, no. 51 (December 20, 1909): 942.
29. RGALI, 571-1-1206, l. 48.
30. RGALI, 571-1-1206, l. 53.
31. "Men Must Kneel When Proposing," *Daily Mirror*, July 14, 1910.
32. Litavrina, *Iavorskaia*, 213.
33. John Pollock, *Time's Chariot* (London: John Murray, 1950), 208-209.
34. RGALI, 571-1-1206, l. 65.

35. Pollock, *Time's Chariot*, 208.
36. "This Morning's Gossip," *Daily Mirror*, December 9, 1910.
37. Pollock, *Time's Chariot*, 209.
38. "Little Theatre," *Daily Telegraph*, December 9, 1910.

14. "I Don't Need a 'Happy Life,' I Need the Stage"

1. Shchepkina-Kupernik, *Vospominaniia*, 384.
2. Shchepkina-Kupernik, 385.
3. "Teatr F. A. Korsh," *Studio*, no. 1 (1911): 25.
4. Em. Beskin, "Moskovskie pis'ma," *Teatr i iskusstvo*, no. 38 (September 18, 1911): 700–701.
5. Shchepkina-Kupernik, *Vospominaniia*, 385.
6. All excerpts from *The Happy Woman* are translations from the text in M. Mikhailova, ed., *Zhenskaia dramaturgiia Serebrianogo veka* (St. Petersburg: Hyperion, 2009).
7. Shchepkina-Kupernik, *Vospominaniia*, 388.
8. All excerpts from the play are translations from the text in T. L. Shchepkina-Kupernik, *Baryshnia s fialkami (Kulisy)* (Moscow: Izdatel'stvo S. Possokhina, 1913).
9. Shchepkina-Kupernik, *Vospominaniia*, 388.
10. "Teatr Korsha," *Moskovskie vedomosti*, January 13, 1913.
11. Shchepkina-Kupernik, *Vospominaniia*, 388.
12. Shchepkina-Kupernik, 388–389.

15. "A Princess in Real Life, but in the Theater a Queen"

1. Litavrina, *Iavorskaia*, 268.
2. RGALI, 571-1-1210, l. 117.
3. Litavrina, *Iavorskaia*, 244.
4. "'The Doll's House.' A Russian Actress Plays in English," *London Daily News*, February 15, 1911.
5. "Kingsway Theatre. 'A Doll's House,'" *The Times* (London), April 24, 1911.
6. "Princess Bariatinsky at the Opera House," *Kent & Sussex Courier*, May 24, 1912.
7. "Madame Yavorska at Kingsway Theatre," *London Daily News*, May 29, 1911.
8. "Three Stages of a Kiss (Stage): 'The Parisienne,'" *The Sketch*, no. 962 (5 July 1911): 455.
9. "'La Parisienne.' Madame Yavorska in a Clever Comedy," *London Daily News*, June 27, 1911.
10. Litvarina, *Iavorskaia*, 233.
11. Charles Reid, *Thomas Beecham: An Independent Biography* (London: Victor Gollancz, 1961), 79.
12. "Artist's Divorce Suit," *Daily Telegraph & Courier* (London), October 25, 1911.

13. Reid, *Thomas Beecham*, 112.
14. "The Divorce Court: Should Cases Be Heard in Public?," *Dundee Evening Telegraph*, November 2, 1911.
15. "'The Great Young Man,'" *London Daily News*, November 1, 1911.
16. Pollock, *Time's Chariot*, 209.
17. Litavrina, *Iavorskaia*, 277.
18. "Princess Bariatinsky in 'The Lower Depths,'" *Daily Mirror*, December 4, 1911.
19. "'The Lower Depths.' Maxim Gorki's Play at the Kingsway," *London Daily News*, December 4, 1911.
20. "Maxim Gorki's Creed," *The Times* (London), January 31, 1912.
21. Litavrina, *Iavorskaia*, 278.
22. Chernichenko, *Kniaz' V. V. Bariatinskii*, 360-364.
23. See Patrick Miles's blog, "Kitty Absolved, Lydia Looks In," last modified September 8, 2016, https://www.patrickmileswriter.co.uk/calderonia/?p=7083. Miles is the author of *George Calderon: Edwardian Genius* (Cambridge: Sam & Sam Publishers, 2018).
24. Beasley, *Russomania*, 12-13.
25. "Dramatic Doings. 'Thérèse Raquin,'" *Cheltenham Looker-On*, June 1, 1912.
26. "Visit of Princess Bariatinsky to the Opera House: The Russian Sarah Bernhardt as 'Thérèse Raquin," *Kent and Sussex Courier*, May 17, 1912; and "Princess Bariatinsky at the Opera House," *Kent and Sussex Courier*, May 24, 1912.
27. Litavrina, *Iavorskaia*, 252.
28. Litavrina, 258.
29. Litavrina, 256.
30. Litavrina, 253-255.
31. Pollock, *Time's Chariot*, 210.
32. Litavrina, *Iavorskaia*, 256.
33. Litavrina, 260.
34. Litavrina, 261.
35. "'Resting' and Revelling in the Simple Life: Princess Bariatinsky Prepares for a Strenuous Autumn," *The Tatler*, no. 633 (August 13, 1913): 204.
36. "Prince and Princess Sleep in the Open on Dorset Cliffs," *Daily Mirror*, September 1, 1913.
37. Litavrina, *Iavorskaia*, 269.
38. Pollock, *Time's Chariot*, 210-211.

16. *Anna Karenina*

1. Shchepkina-Kupernik, *Vospominaniia*, 128.
2. Nikolai Liubimov, *Neuviadaemyi tsvet: kniga vospominanii* (Moscow: Iazyki russkoi kultury, 2000), 1:286.
3. Shchepkina-Kupernik, *Vospominaniia*, 474.
4. Rayfield, "The Forgotten Poetess," 619.
5. "Tolstoy and Mme. Yavorska," *Pall Mall Gazette*, November 15, 1913.

6. "The Land of Joyous Hearts," *Daily News & Leader*, November 25, 1913.
7. "The Land of Joyous Hearts."
8. "'Anna Karenina.' A Tolstoy Play at the Ambassadors," *The Times* (London), December 2, 1913.
9. "Anna Karenina," *The Era* (London), December 3, 1913.
10. "'Anna Karenina' at the Ambassadors," *Illustrated Sporting & Dramatic News*, no. 2100 (December 6, 1913): 616.
11. Litavrina, *Iavorskaia*, 271.
12. See "Letters to the Editor: 'Anna Karenina,'" *Pall Mall Gazette*, December 4, 1913; December 5, 1913; December 6, 1913.
13. Litavrina, *Iavorskaia*, 272.
14. "Wealth of Ideas at the West End Theatres," *Manchester Courier*, February 6, 1914.
15. Litavrina, *Iavorskaia*, 270.
16. "A Princess's Wardrobe. Extensive Dress Repertoire Owned by Mme. Yavorska," *Manchester Courier*, November 27, 1913.
17. "Priest Denounces Indelicate Modes. 'Hypocrisy,' Says Actress," *New York Times*, May 31, 1914.
18. Pollock, *Time's Chariot*, 212.
19. Pollock, 211.
20. Litavrina, *Iavorskaia*, 285–286.
21. "Shakespeare Theatre," *Liverpool Echo*, September 22, 1914.
22. James H. Cousins and Margaret Gretta, *We Two Together* (Madras, India: Ganesh & Co, 1950), 23.
23. Shchepkina-Kupernik, *Vospominaniia*, 449.
24. Cousins and Gretta, *We Two Together*, 234.
25. "Theatres and Music," *The London Evening Standard*, January 18, 1915.
26. "Zametki," *Teatr i iskusstvo*, no. 10 (March 8, 1915): 177.
27. "This Morning's Gossip. Allies All," *Daily Mirror*, January 7, 1915.
28. Litavrina, *Iavorskaia*, 287.
29. RGALI, 571-1-1210, l. 37-42.
30. RGALI, 571-1-1210, l. 39.
31. RGALI, 571-1-1210, l. 39.
32. Shchepkina-Kupernik's Letters to Yavorskaya, 1915, Moscow State Archives for Literature and Art (RGALI), 571-1-401, l. 1.
33. Pollock, *Time's Chariot*, 221.
34. John Pollock, *War and Revolution in Russia: Sketches and Studies* (London: Constable, 1918), 18.
35. "L. B. Iavorskaia (k priezdu v Rossiiu s angliiskoi deputatsiei)," *Teatr i iskusstvo*, no. 20 (May 17, 1915): cover.
36. "Khronika," *Teatr i iskusstvo*, no. 21 (May 24, 1915): 361.

17. Divorce and Revolution

1. Litavrina, *Iavorskaia*, 313–314.
2. Aleksandr Kugel', "Zametki," *Teatr i iskusstvo*, no. 39 (September 27, 1915): 735–736.

3. Aleksandr Kugel', "Zametki," *Teatr i iskusstvo*, no. 40 (October 4, 1915): 737.

4. Mikhail Artsybashev, "Zakon dikaria," *Sobranie sochinenii*, vol. 8 (Moskovskoe knigoizdatel'stvo, 1916): act 5, scene 1.

5. Aleksandr Kugel', "Zametki," *Teatr i iskusstvo*, no. 43 (October 25, 1915): 793-796.

6. Douglas Smith, *Rasputin: Faith, Power, and the Twilight of the Romanovs* (New York: Farrar, Straus and Giroux, 2016), 393-397. Teffi's description of the evening can be found in Teffi, "Rasputin," in *Subtly Worded and Other Stories* (London: Pushkin Press, 2014), 91-136.

7. "Khronika," *Teatr i iskusstvo*, no. 50 (December 13, 1915): 944.

8. "Khronika," *Rampa i zhizn'*, no. 50 (December 13, 1915): 9.

9. See "'Zavtra,'" *Obozrenie teatrov*, no. 2972-2973 (December 25-26, 1915): 35.

10. "Khronika," *Teatr i iskusstvo*, no. 52 (December 27, 1915): 1002-1003.

11. Smith, *Rasputin*, 397.

12. John Pollock, *War and Revolution*, 118-119.

13. "Khronika," *Teatr i iskusstvo*, no. 14 (April 3, 1916): 279.

14. A detailed summary of the archival records on the Baryatinsky divorce proceedings and their aftermath can be found in Arsenii Vladimirovich Sokolov, "Delo ober-prokurora sinoda N. P. Raeva v 1917 godu," *Izvestia rossiiskogo gosudarstvennogo pedagogicheskogo universiteta im. A. I. Gertsena*, no. 151 (2012): 26-33.

15. Sokolov, "Delo ober-prokurora sinoda N. P. Raev b 1917 godu," 30.

16. "Khronika," *Teatr i iskusstvo*, no. 44 (October 20, 1916): 891.

17. Chernichenko, *Kniaz' V. V. Bariatinskii*, 204.

18. Aleksandr Kugel', "Zametki," *Teatr i iskusstvo*, no. 46 (November 13, 1916): 931-933.

19. Pollock, *War and Revolution*, 178.

20. Rayfield, "The Forgotten Poetess," 619.

21. "Khronika," *Teatr i iskusstvo*, nos. 13-14 (April 2, 1917): 240.

22. Sokolov, "Delo ober-prokurora sinoda N. P. Raev v 1917 godu," 30.

23. "Iz Moskvy," *Teatr i iskusstvo*, no. 30 (July 23, 1917): 510.

24. John Pollock, *The Bolshevik Adventure* (London: Constable, 1919), 26-27.

25. "Posle pereryva," *Obozrenie teatrov*, no. 3590 (November 14, 1917): 7.

26. "Posle pereryva," *Obozrenie teatrov*, no. 3590 (November 14, 1917): 7.

27. See Laurence Senelick, *The Crooked Mirror: Plays from a Modernist Russian Cabaret* (Evanston, IL: Northwestern University Press, 2023).

28. A. Tumanskii, "Krivoe zerkalo," *Teatr i iskusstvo*, no. 1 (January 7, 1918): 7.

29. Ivan Bunin, *Cursed Days: A Diary of Revolution*, trans. Thomas Gaiton Marullo (Chicago: Ivan R. Dee, 1998), 36.

30. Aleksandr Kugel', "Zametki," *Teatr i iskusstvo*, nos. 10-11 (March 25-April 7, 1918): 119-120.

31. Lidia Yavorskaya, "Out of the Bolsheviks' Clutches," *Chambers's Journal* 10, no. 503 (July 17, 1920): 514.

32. Litavrina, *Iavorskaia*, 355-368.

33. Yavorskaya, "Out of the Bolsheviks' Clutches," 514.
34. Pollock, *Time's Chariot*, 233; Pollock, *The Bolshevik Adventure*, 240.
35. Rebecca B. Gauss, "Lydia Borisovna Yavorskaya: Her Life, Her Work, Her Times" (master's thesis, University of Colorado, 1992), 63.
36. Pollock, *Time's Chariot*, 212.

18. "Out of the Bolsheviks' Clutches"

1. Yavorskaya, "Out of the Bolsheviks' Clutches," 515.
2. Yavorskaya, 513.
3. Yavorskaya, 542.
4. Yavorskaya, 544.
5. Pollock, *The Bolshevik Adventure*, 241.
6. Pollock, 242.
7. Pollock, 244.
8. Pollock, 258.
9. Pollock, 259.
10. Pollock, 273.
11. Pollock, 275.
12. "Princess Armed with Gun," *Daily Mirror*, May 22, 1919.
13. Rayfield, "The Forgotten Princess," 619.
14. Bunin, *Cursed Days*, 122.
15. Bunin, 122.
16. Liubimov, *Neuviadaemyi tsvet: kniga vospominanii*, 1:292.
17. Liubimov, 1:294.
18. E. Bapabanovich, "Sovremenniki vspominaiut," *Voprosy literatury*, no. 1 (1980): 138–145.
19. Rayfield, "The Forgotten Poetess," 619.
20. "Princess Weds Well-Known Playwright," *Dundee Evening Telegraph*, March 8, 1920.
21. "For World-Union of White Races," *Brooklyn (NY) Daily Eagle*, June 19, 1921.
22. "Russian Actress's Convalescence," *Westminster Gazette*, May 7, 1921.
23. "Mme. Lydia Yavorska," *The Stage*, September 8, 1921.
24. "A Figure of Romance," *Daily Record and Mail*, September 6, 1921.
25. Nikolai Efros, "Lidiia Iavorskaia," *Kul'tura teatra*, nos. 7–8 (1921): 63–65.
26. Rayfield, "The Forgotten Poetess," 619.
27. Rayfield, 621.
28. Liubimov, *Neuviadaemyi tsvet: kniga vospominanii*, 1:356.
29. Liubimov, 1:345.
30. Rayfield, "The Forgotten Poetess," 622.
31. Yevtushenko's comments and poem "Tatiana Topsy-Turvy" were published in *Noviye Izvestiia*, February 29, 2008, and can be found online at https://www.peoples.ru/art/literature/poetry/national/tatiana_schepkina-kupernik and https://vk.com/wall77068267_16643?ysclid=ll2lugs35i561683886.
32. Efros, "Lidiia Iavorskaia," 64.

Bibliography

Primary Sources

Archives

MOSCOW STATE ARCHIVE FOR LITERATURE AND ART (RGALI)

571-1-401	Shchepkina-Kupernik's letters to Yavorskaya, 1915
571-1-1204	Yavorskaya's letters and telegrams to Shchepkina-Kupernik, 1893
571-1-1205	Yavorskaya's letters and telegrams to Shchepkina-Kupernik, 1894
571-1-1206	Yavorskaya's letters and telegrams to Shchepkina-Kupernik, 1901–1910
571-1-1207	Yavorskaya's letters to Shchepkina-Kupenik, March 23, 1911–May 1912
571-1-1208	Yavorskaya's letters to Shchepkina-Kupernik, July–September 1912
571-1-1209	Yavroskaya's letters to Shchepkina-Kupernik, October 1912–June 25, 1913
571-1-1210	Yavorskaya's letters to Shchepkina-Kupernik, July 2, 1913–February 15, 1915

MANUSCRIPT DIVISION OF THE RUSSIAN STATE LIBRARY (RGB)

331-95-2	Potapenko's letter to Maria Chekhova, May 31, 1894

Published Plays, Poems, Stories, Correspondence, and Memoirs

Artsybashev, Mikhail. *Sobranie sochinenii*. 8 vols. Moscow: Moskovskoe knigoizdatel'stvo, 1912–1916.

Bariatinsky, Princess Anatole Marie. *My Russian Life*. London: Hutchinson, 1923.

Bunin, Ivan. *Cursed Days: A Diary of Revolution*. Translated by Thomas Gaiton Marullo. Chicago: Ivan R. Dee, 1908.

Cousins, James H., and Margaret Gretta. *We Two Together*. Madras, India: Ganesh, 1950.

Chekhov, A. P. *Aleksandr i Anton Chekhov: Vospominaniia, perepiska*. Moscow: Zakharov, 2012.

——. *Perepiska A. P. Chekhova v trekh tomakh*. 3 vols. Moscow: Nasledia, 1996.

——. *Perepiska s zhenoi*. Moscow: Zaharov, 2003.

———. *Polnoe sobranie sochinenii i pisem v tridtsati tomakh*. Edited by N. F. Belchikov et al. 30 vols. Moscow: Nauka, 1974–1988.
Giliarovskii, Vladimir. *Sochineniia v dvukh tomakh*. 2 vols. Kaluga: Zolotaia alleia, 1944.
Glama-Meshcherskaia, A. Ia. *Vospominaniia*. Moscow-Leningrad: Iskusstvo, 1937.
Gorin-Goriainov, B. A. *Aktery (iz vospominanii)*. Leningrad-Moscow: Iskusstvo, 1947.
Gor'kii, Maksim. *Nesobrannye literaturno-kriticheskie stat'i*. Moscow: Khudozhestvennaia literatura, 1941.
Gurevich, L. Ia., ed. *O Stanislavskom: sbornik vospominanii*. Moscow: Vserossiskoe teatral'noe obshchestvo, 1948.
Knipper, O. L., and M. P. Chekhova. *Perepiska*. 2 vols. Moscow: Novoe literaturnoe obozrenie, 2016.
Kovalevskaya, Sofya. *A Russian Childhood*. Translated by Beatrice Stillman. New York: Springer-Verlag, 1978.
Kovalevskaia, S. V. *Vospominaniia, Povesti*. Moscow: Nauka, 1974.
Krylov, V., and S. Litvin. *Syny Izrailia*. St. Petersburg: Tipografia A. S. Suvornia, 1899.
Liubimov, Nikolai. *Neuviadaemyi tsvet: kniga vospominanii*. 2 vols. Moscow: Iazyki russkoi kultury, 2000.
Munshtein, Leonid. "Moskva dalekaia . . . Klochki vospominanii (v sokrashenii)." In *Pervoprestol'naia dalekaia i blizkaia: Moskva i moskvichi v poezii russkoi emigratsii*. Moscow: Russkii mir, 2005. Last modified April 17, 2022. http://az.lib.ru/m/munshtejn_l_g/text_1931_moskva_dalekaya.shtml.
Narokov, M. S. *Biografia moego pokoleniia*. Moscow: Vserossiiskoe teatral'noe obshchestvo, 1956.
Perestiani, I. N. *75 let zhizni v iskusstve*. Moscow: Iskusstvo, 1962.
Pollock, John. *The Bolshevik Adventure*. London: Constable, 1919.
———. *Time's Chariot*. London: John Murray, 1950.
———. *War and Revolution in Russia: Sketches and Studies*. London: Constable, 1918.
Pound, Ezra. *Cantos: LXXIX*. New York: New Directions, 1965.
Sakharova, E. M., ed. *Vokrug Chekhova*. Moscow: Pravda, 1990.
Shchepkina-Kupernik, Tatiana L. *Baryshnia s fialkami (Kulisy)*. Moscow: Izdatel'stvo S. Possokhina, 1913.
———. *Eto bylo vchera . . .* Moscow: Drutman, 1907.
———. *Izbrannye stikhotrvoreniia i poemy*. Moscow: O-G-I, 2008.
———. *"Novyi teatr" razgovor v 1 diestvii v litsakh*. St. Petersburg: Narodnaia pol'za, 1901.
———. "Odna iz nikh." In *Zhenskaia drama Serebrianogo veka*. St. Petersburg: Hyperion, 2009. Last modified January 25, 1918. http://az.lib.ru/s/shepkinakupernik_t_l/text_0180.shtml?ysclid=lrqmhc7aeq533429293.
———. "O pervom predstavlenii dramy S. Kovalevskoi i A. Sh Leffler Borba za schast'e." In *Pamiati S. V. Kovalevskoi*, 133–143. Moscow: Akademiia Nauk, 1951.
———. *Pis'ma iz daleka*. Moscow: D. P. Efimov, 1903.
———. "Sapho, listki iz dnevnika." In *Mezhdu prochim*, edited by F. A. Kumanin, 17–49. Moscow: Artist, 1894.

———. *Schast'e*. 2nd ed. Moscow: D. P. Efimov, 1903.
———. *Stranichki zhizni*. Moscow: M. Merkusheva, 1898.
———. *Teatr v moei zhizni*. Moscow-Leningrad: Iskusstvo, 1948.
———. *Teatr v moei zhizni: Memuary moskovskoi fify*. Moscow: AST, 2015.
———. *Vospominaniia*. Moscow: Zakharov, 2005.
Skibina, O. M. ". . . i moia bezumnaia liubov' k vam, sviatoi, nepostizhimyi, divnyi! (Pis'ma L. B. Iavorskaia A. P. Chekhovu)." In *Chekhoviana: Polet "Chaiki,"* 74-87. Moscow: Nauka, 2001.
Suvorin, Aleksei. *Dnevnik Alekseia Sergeevicha Suvorina*. Moscow: Nezavisimaia Gazeta, 1999.
Teffi, N. A. "Rasputin." In *Subtly Worded and Other Stories*, 91-136. London: Pushkin Press, 2014.
Tolstoi, L. N. *Polnoe sobranie sochinenii*. 90 vols. Moscow: Izdatel'stvo khudozhestvennoi literatury, 1928-1958.

Newspapers and Periodicals

RUSSIA

Artist [Artist]
Kul'tura teatra [Theater Culture]
Literaturnoe nasledstvo [Literary Inheritance]
Moskovskie vedomosti [Moscow Gazette]
Noviye izvestiia [New News]
Novoe vremia [New Times]
Obozrenie teatrov [Theater Review]
Rampa i zhizn' [Footlights and Life]
Revel'skie izvestiia [Revel News]
Sankt-Peterburgskie vedomosti [St. Petersburg Gazette]
Severnyi kur'er [Northern Courier]
Studio [Studio]
Teatr i iskusstvo [Theater and Art]
Voprosy literatury [Literary Questions]
Zhizn' iskusstva [Life of Art]

GREAT BRITAIN

Athenaeum
Cheltenham Looker-On
Daily News & Leader
Daily Mirror
Daily Record and Mail
Daily Telegraph & Courier
Dundee Evening Telegraph
The Era
The Evening Standard
Kent & Sussex Courier
Illustrated London News
Illustrated Sporting & Dramatic News

Liverpool Echo
London Daily News
London Review of Books
Manchester Courier
Pall Mall Gazette
The Sketch
The Stage
The Tatler
The Times
Westminster Gazette

UNITED STATES

Brooklyn Daily Eagle
The New York Times

Secondary Sources

Beasley, Rebecca. *Russomania: Russian Culture and the Creation of British Modernism, 1881–1922*. New York: Oxford University Press, 2020.

Beliaev, Iurii. *Stat'i o teatre*. St. Petersburg: Hyperion, 2003.

Benedetti, Jean. *Stanislavski*. London: Routledge, 1988.

Chernichenko, Liudmila. *Kniaz' V. V. Bariatinskii: Pisatel' v rossii i v emigratsii*. Moscow: Rossiskaia politicheskaia entseklopedia, 2006.

Du Quenoy, Paul. *Stage Fright: Politics and the Performing Arts in Late Imperial Russia*. University Park: The Pennsylvania State University Press, 2009.

Durylin, S. N. *V svoem uglu*. Moscow: Moskovskii rabochii, 1991.

Engelstein, Laura. *The Keys to Happiness: Sex and the Search for Modernity in Fin-de-Siecle Russia*. Ithaca, NY: Cornell University Press, 1992.

Frame, Murray. *School for Citizens: Theatre and Civil Society in Imperial Russia*. New Haven, CT: Yale University Press, 2006.

Fryer, Paul, and Olga Usova. *Lina Cavalieri: The Life of Opera's Greatest Beauty, 1877–1944*. London: McFarland, 2004.

Garnett, Richard. *Constance Garnett: A Heroic Life*. London: Sinclair-Stenson, 1991.

Gauss, Rebecca B. "Lydia Borisovna Yavorskaya: Her Life, Her Work, Her Times." Master's thesis, University of Colorado, 1992.

Gottlieb, Robert. *Sarah: The Life of Sarah Bernhardt*. New Haven, CT: Yale University Press, 2010.

Gromova, L. D. *Letopis' zhizni i tvorchestva A. P. Chekhova*. 3 vols. Moscow: Nasledie, 2000–2004.

Kennedy, Don H. *Little Sparrow: A Portrait of Sophia Kovalevsky*. Athens: Ohio University Press, 1983.

Kinkul'kina, N. *Aleksandr Sanin: Zhizn' i tvorchestvo*. Moscow: Iskusstvo, 2001.

Koblitz, Ann Hibner. *A Convergence of Lives: Sofia Kovolevskaia; Scientist, Writer, Revolutionary*. Boston: Birkhauser, 1983.

Koroleva, Ya. A. *Soprikosnovenie sudeb: A. P. Chekhov i I. I. Levitan*. Moscow: Gelios, 2011.
Korsh, F. A. *Kratkii ocherk desiatiletnei deiatel'nosti russkogo dramaticheskogo teatra Korsha v Moskve*. Moscow: Kushnerev, 1892.
Kuzicheva, A. P. *Chekhov v russkoi teatral'noi kritike*. Moscow: Chekhovskii poligraficheskii kombinat, 1999.
Harcave, Sidney. *The Russian Revolution of 1905*. London: Collier Books, 1970.
Iazykov, D. M. *Kratkii ocherk dvadtsatipiatiletnei deiatel'nosti Teatra F. A. Korsha*. Moscow: A. A. Levinson, 1907.
Litavrina, Marina. *Iavorskaia, bezzakonnaia kometa*. Moscow: MIK, 2008.
McReynolds, Louise. *The News under Russia's Old Regime: The Development of a Mass-Circulation Press*. Princeton, NJ: Princeton University Press, 1991.
Miles, Patrick. "Kitty Absolved, Lydia Looks In." Last modified September 8, 2016. https://www.patrickmileswriter.co.uk/calderonia/?p=7083.
Mindlin, Emilii. *Ne dom, no mir. Povest' ob Aleksandre Kollontai*. Moscow: Politizat, 1969.
Nelidov, V. A. *Teatral'naia Moskva: sorok let moskovskikh teatrov*. Moscow: Materik, 2002.
Porter, Cathy. *Alexandra Kollontai: A Biography*. Chicago: Haymarket Books, 2014.
Rayfield, Donald. *Anton Chekhov: A Life*. New York: Henry Holt, 1997.
———. "The Forgotten Poetess: Tatiana L'vovna Shchepkina-Kupernik." *Slavonic and East European Review* 79, no. 4 (October 2001): 601–637.
Reid, Charles. *Thomas Beecham: An Independent Biography*. London: Victor Gollancz, 1961.
Rozanov, V. V. *Mysli o literature*. Moscow: Sovremennik, 1989.
Schuler, Catherine A. *Women in Russian Theatre: The Actress in the Silver Age*. London: Routledge, 1996.
Senelick, Laurence. "Anti-Semitism and Tsarist Theatre: The Smugglers Riots." *Theatre Survey*. 44, no. 1 (May 2003): 68–101.
Smith, Douglas. *Rasputin: Faith, Power, and the Twilight of the Romanovs*. New York: Farrar, Strauss and Giroux, 2016.
Sokolov, A. V. "Delo ober-prokurora sinoda N. P. Raeva v 1917 godu." *Izvestia rossiiskogo gosudarstvennogo pedagogicheskogo universiteta im A. I. Gertsena*, no. 151 (2012): 26–33.
Strel'tsova, E. I. *Chastnyi teatr v Rosii: ot istokov do nachala xx veka*. Moscow: GITIS, 2009.
Yarovenko, D. S. "Perevod p'esy *La Princesse Lointaine* (*Printsessa Greza*) T. L. Shchepkina-Kupernik: russkoe prochtenie." *Vestnik Leningradskogo gosudarstvennogo unversiteta* 1, no. 2 (2013): 243–251.
Young, Stuart. "'Formless,' 'Pretentious,' 'Hideous and Revolting:' Non-Chekhov Russian and Soviet Drama on the British Stage." In *Russia in Britain, 1880–1940: From Melodrama to Modernism*, edited by Rebecca Beasley and Philip Ross Bullock, 87–111. New York: Oxford University Press, 2013.

Index

Adelphi Play Society, 244
Admirable Crichton, The (Barrie), 267–268, 272
Alexander II, 6, 136, 226
Alexander III, 1, 6, 68
Alexandrinsky Theater, 1, 4, 16, 18, 23–24, 80, 97, 104–107, 116, 138, 180, 196, 236, 261, 264, 267
Alexandrov-Krylov, Victor, 15
Alexeev, L., 23, 43, 53–54, 99
All Good Things Must Come to an End (Ostrovsky), 196
Ambassadors Theatre, 248, 253, 276
And Pippa Dances (Hauptmann), 200
Anna Karenina (Tolstoy), 248, 250–255, 262
Anthill, The (Sazonova), 95–97, 106
antisemitism, 134, 138, 140–142, 145, 147, 275
Aphrodite's Necklace (Burenin), 114, 118
Apostle, The, 196
Arabazhin, Konstantin, 134, 140, 143, 145, 164, 193, 196
"Ariadne" (Chekhov), 76, 83–85
Artist's Society Theater, 212
Asch, Sholem, 209
"At the Asylum" (Shchepkina-Kupernik), 204
"At the Cemetery" (Shchepkina-Kupernik), 130
At the Gates of the Kingdom (Hamsun), 212–213
"At the Station" (Shchepkina-Kupernik), 47

"Backstage" (Shchepkina-Kupernik), 29–30, 233–235
Backstage (Shchepkina-Kupernik), 236, 261
Bakhareva, Natalia, 259
Bakhrushin, Alexei, 9

Baransky, Georgy, 191–192
Barrett, Wilson, 113
Barrie, J. M., 267–268
Baryatinsky, Alexander, 136, 226
Baryatinsky, Anatoly, 99–100
Baryatinsky, Vladimir
  The Bureau of Happiness and, 208
  charity events and, 119–120
  as columnist, 92, 96–97
  Cyrano de Bergerac and, 123
  death of grandmother of, 118–119
  departure of from London, 254
  divorce and, 256–257, 262–264
  financial difficulties of, 108–109
  Gorky and, 244
  Jewish population and, 135
  Ligovsky Prospect residence and, 132
  in London, 222–223, 225, 238
  marriage and, 99–104, 221
  New Theater and, 157–158, 160, 163–164, 181–185, 189, 193
  Northern Courier and, 134, 136
  Pollock's suit against, 262, 264
  press and, 136–137
  publicity photos of, 248
  Pushkin commemoration and, 131
  revolution and, 198–199
  sketch of, 171fig
  Sons of Israel and, 140–143, 145–147
  suicide attempt of, 150
  in Tiflis, 213
  translations by, 114
  Yavorskaya and, 177, 227–228
Bear, The (Chekhov), 16–19, 21, 25, 243
"Beauties, The" (Chekhov), 51
Becque, Henri, 240
Beecham, Thomas, 241–242
Beilis, Menahem, 251
Belle Hélène, La (Offenbach), 11
Belot, Aldolphe, 55

309

310 INDEX

"Beneath the Mask" (Mikheev), 51
Benois, Albert, 93
Berestovskaya, Olga (Panchina), 263
Berg, Alan, 183
Bernhardt, Sarah, 21, 25, 45, 57, 59–60,
  73, 79, 85, 114, 117, 125, 156,
  170fig, 184, 247–248, 266
Beskin, Emanuil, 232
Björnson, Björnstjerne, 208
Black Crows (Protopopov), 211–212
Bloody Sunday, 190–192, 203–204
Blue Bird, The (Maeterlinck), 210
Blumenthal, Oscar, 66
Blumenthal-Tamarin, Vsevolod, 196–197
Bolshevik Adventure, The (Pollock), 274
Bolshoi Theater, 25, 41, 94
Boris Godunov (Pushkin), 131, 179–180
Bread of Others, The (Turgenev), 222
Brenko, Anna, 5–7
Bryusov, Valery, 201
Bukharin, Mikhail, 121
Bunin, Ivan, 268–269, 274–275, 277
Bureau of Happiness, The (Baryatinsky), 208
Burenin, Viktor, 78–79, 83, 97, 101–103,
  114, 118–120, 146, 254
Burlak, Vasily, 5, 7–8, 82
By the Way, 51–52

Calderon, George, 244
Carpenter, Edward, 255
Causeries du Jeudi, 228
Cavalieri, Lina, 136, 226
censors/censorship, 17, 93, 105, 145–146,
  164, 190, 200, 211–212, 231, 261
Chaliapin, Fyodor, 180–181, 220–221, 267
Chekhov, Alexander, 120–121
Chekhov, Anton
  Bernhardt and, 25
  in Crimea, 53
  death of, 188–189
  The Dream Princess and, 90, 92–93
  Knipper and, 155–156, 177–180
  Korsh and, 8–10, 12–13
  Kugel and, 157
  on Lent, 115–116
  Levitan and, 278
  Literary-Artistic Circle and, 83
  M. Chekhov and, 45–47
  Markevich and, 21
  Mizinova and, 32, 37–40, 42–43,
    64–65
  New Theater and, 159–160
  Northern Courier and, 135–136

Ozerova and, 82
play writing and, 1, 11–12, 14–15,
  18–19
royalties for, 121
The Seagull and, 88, 104–108, 126–130,
  163
Shchepkina-Kupernik and, 3, 61,
  68–75, 127–130
Suvorin and, 142
views on women, 85
Yavorskaya and, 3, 42–43, 47, 50–51,
  55, 68, 72–79, 95
See also individual works
Chekhov, Mikhail, 46
Chekhova, Maria, 32, 38, 41–43, 61, 70,
  106, 127–128, 155, 179, 199
Cherep-Spridovich, Arthur, 275
Chernevsky, Sergei, 26, 28
Chestnuts out of the Fire (*Les Marrons du feu*;
  de Musset), 97
Chichigov, Mikhail, 9–10, 168fig
Children of the Sun (Gorky), 199
Chirikov, Evgeny, 199–200
Chitau, Maria, 105
Christmas Party, The (Nemirovich-
  Danchenko), 43
Comédie-Française, 24–25, 59, 79, 132
Contemporary Theater, 209
Court Theater, 212–214
Cousins, James and Margaret, 254–255
Covetous Knight, The (Pushkin), 97
"Credo" (Shchepkina-Kupernik), 44–45
Crime and Punishment (Dostoevsky), 243
Crooked Mirror, 268
Cupid and Psyche (Zulawski), 210–211
Cyrano de Bergerac (Rostand), 121–125,
  135, 278

Dalsky, Mamont, 97
Dame aux Camélias, 118
Dance of Death, The (Strindberg), 210
Dance of Life, The (Baryatinsky), 184–185
D'Annunzio, Gabriele, 184
Darsky, Mikhail, 236
Davydov, Alexander, 186
Davydov, Vladimir, 11–12, 14–15, 23–24,
  64, 79
Days of Our Life, The (Andreev), 266
de Musset, Alfred, 97
Dead City, The (D'Annunzio), 184
Derzhavin, Gavriil, 120
Diaghilev, Sergei, 180
Diana Fornari (Burenin), 97

INDEX 311

Dobrovolsky, Nikolai, 151
Doll's House, A (Ibsen), 27, 86–87, 239–240, 242
Domasheva, Maria, 120–121, 140
Don Carlos (Verdi), 267
Donna Più Bella del Mondo, La (*The Most Beautiful Woman in the World*), 136
Dostoevsky, Fyodor, 48
Dramatic Theater, 161, 184, 201
Dream of Life, The (Falkovsky), 181, 223
Dream Princess, The, 88–94, 97–98, 103–104, 108, 117, 136, 170fig
Drizen, Nikolai, 231, 261
Duma, formation of, 194–195
Dumas, Alexandre, 61–62, 117
Durnovo, Ivan, 146
Durova, Nadezhda, 255
Duse, Eleonora, 45, 79, 125, 184, 224

Eaglet, The (*L'Aiglon*; Rostand), 156–157, 160, 255
Eberle, Varvara, 38–39, 41, 51–53, 57, 59, 167fig, 181
Efros, Nikolai, 276–277, 279
Eisenberg, Konstantin, 160–161, 182
Eliot, George, 48–49
Enemy of the People (Ibsen), 27
Erdgeist (*Earth Spirit*; Wedekind), 183
Ermolova, Maria, 125, 187, 249–250, 276
Eternity in a Moment (Shchepkina-Kupernik), 53, 129
Etinger, Osip, 161
Eugene Onegin (Pushkin), 131
Eugene Onegin (Tchaikovsky), 30, 41
Evreinov, Nikolai, 161, 268

Falkovsky, Fyodor, 181
Fanny's First Play (Shaw), 259
Far-Away Princess, The (Rostand), 85
Faust (Goethe), 118
Faust (Gounod), 59
Faydeau, Georges, 56
Finland and Socialism (Kollontai), 218
"First Ball, The" (Shchepkina-Kupernik), 205
Flavia Tessini, 264–265, 267
Fleurs de Russie (Shchepkina-Kupernik), 57
Flirt, The, 79
Folies Bergère, 136
Foma Gordeev (Gorky), 163–164
For Russia (Pollock), 255, 257

"Forgotten Poetess, The" (Rayfield), 277
Foster, George and Maud, 241–242
Fragments of Moscow Life, 1, 8
From Crime to Crime, 27
"From the Diary of a Superfluous Woman" (Shchepkina-Kupernik), 152–154
Fruits of Enlightenment, The (Tolstoy), 64
Fyodorov, Mikhail, 79–80

Gapon, Georgy, 190–191
Garnett, Constance, 222, 224
Ge, Grigori, 103
Georgian Court Theater, 212
Giacosa, Giuseppe, 73
Gilyarovsky, Vladimir, 13, 38
Girl with Violets, The (Shchepkina-Kupernik), 233–237
Glama-Meshcherskaya, Alexandra, 4–8, 10, 13–14, 17–18, 20, 87
Gnedich, Pyotr, 90–91
God of Vengeance, The (Asch), 209, 211
Gogol, Nikolai, 7, 222
Goltsev, Victor, 26, 42, 46, 90
Goreva, Elizaveta, 18–19
Gorin-Goryainov, Boris, 198
Gorky, Maxim, 27, 93, 134–135, 163–164, 199, 222, 243–244
Gôt, Edmund, 24
Gounod, Charles, 59
Gradovsky, Grigory, 118
Gradov-Sokolov, Leonid, 13
"Grasshopper, The" (Chekhov), 32, 72
Great Young Man, The (Baryatinsky), 242–243
Green Cockatoo, The (Schnitzler), 198
Griselda (Silvestre and Morand), 114

Halm, Friedrich, 125
Hamlet (Shakespeare), 97, 118
Hamsun, Knut, 27, 208, 212
Hannele (Hauptmann), 80–83, 118–119
Happiness (Shchepkina-Kupernik), 60, 68–70, 109
Happy Day: Scenes from Life in a Provincial Backwater (Ostrovsky and Solovyov), 105
Happy Woman, The (Shchepkina-Kupernik), 230–233
Harcave, Sidney, 192, 195–196
Harvieu, Paul, 87
Hauptmann, Gerhart, 80–82, 119, 200
Haze of Life, The (Markevich), 21

INDEX

Heart Responded, The, 26–27
Hedda Gabler (Ibsen), 194, 223–225, 240
Heureuse comme le reine (As Happy as a Queen), 22
Homeland (Sudermann), 87
Hornung, E. W., 212
How He Lied to Her Husband (Shaw), 271
Husband, The, 260

Ibsen, Henrik, 27, 86, 160, 181, 210, 223, 239–240
Ideal Husband, The (Wilde), 212
Imperial Theater Committee, 105
In a Vice (Les Tenailles; Harvieu), 87–88
In Dreams (Nemirovich-Danchenko), 179
"In Memory of Pushkin" (Shchepkina-Kupernik), 131
In the Darkness of the Night (Pollock), 275
"In the Motherland" (Shchepkina-Kupernik), 203–204
In the Name of Love (Gradovsky), 118
Incorporated Stage Society of London, 222
Inspector General, The (Gogol), 7, 9, 222
International Theatre Ltd., 248
Iskul von Hildebrandt, Varvara, 133–134, 143, 220–221
Ivanov (Chekhov), 1, 12–16, 18–19, 127, 138, 189–190
Ivanov, Pyotr, 108–109
Izeÿl (Silvestre and Morand), 114–115, 117–118
Izmail (Bukharin), 121

James, Henry, 224–225
Jealousy (Artsybashev), 260
Jews, The (Chirikov), 199–200, 211–212
Julius Caesar (Shakespeare), 118
Justice, La, 117

Kachalov, Vasily, 199
Kamensky, Anatoly, 261
Karpov, Evtikhy, 88, 95, 106, 139–140, 143
Kartavtsev, Evgeny, 152, 220
Kholeva, Nikolai, 120–121, 140
Kholmskaya, Zinaida, 86, 95, 155, 157, 190, 268
Khotyaintseva, Alexandra, 128
Kicheev, Pyotr, 14–15
Kingsway Theatre, 242
Kiselevsky, Ivan, 9, 14
Kiselyova, Maria, 10–11
Knipper, Olga, 128, 130, 154–156, 177–180, 186, 195, 199
Kollontai, Alexandra, 51, 173fig, 187, 215–219, 230, 246, 274–275, 277

Kolomnin, Alexei, 100, 102–104, 142–145
Kolomnin, Mikhail, 216
Kolomnin, Vladimir, 216–217
Kolosov, K., 183
Komissarzhevskaya, Vera
  death of, 214
  Dramatic Theater and, 184, 201
  The Fruits of Enlightenment and, 64
  general strike and, 196–197
  The Needs of Russian Theater and, 193
  photograph of, 172fig
  Savina and, 140
  The Seagull and, 105–106
  Yavorskaya and, 2, 116–117, 161, 189
Komissarzhevsky, Fyodor, 243–244
Korsh, Fyodor
  The Bear and, 17
  Brenko and, 6–7
  Chekhov and, 12–13, 18–19
  criticism of, 1, 27
  Cyrano de Bergerac and, 124–125
  French opera productions and, 75
  Glama-Meshcherskaya and, 17–18, 20
  Ivanov and, 12–13, 15–16
  Krechetova and, 231
  Madame Sans-Gêne and, 65–67
  Maly Theater and, 79
  photograph of, 168fig
  The Seagull and, 88
  Shchepkina-Kupernik and, 3, 26–29, 230, 236
  The Struggle for Happiness and, 48
  theater of, 168fig
  theaters of, 7–11
  Vasantasena and, 67–68
  Vasilieva and, 20–21
  Yavorskaya and, 3, 43, 53, 56–57, 60–61, 63
Kovalevskaya, Sophia, 48–50
Krasnyansky, Emmanuil, 245
Krasov, Nikolai, 90–91, 231
Krechetova, Elsa, 231–232, 236
Krestovskaya, Maria, 23, 150–152, 154–155, 172fig, 185–187, 219–222, 274
"Kreutzer Sonata" (Tolstoy), 83
Kropotkin, Pyotr, 174fig, 226, 244, 256
Krylov, Victor, 138, 140
Kugel, Alexander, 78, 157, 190, 193, 196–197, 210, 214, 259–260, 265, 268–270
Kumanin, Fyodor, 38, 47, 51
Kupernik, Lev Abramovich, 26, 155, 202–204, 207

INDEX 313

Laboremus (Björnson), 208
Lady from the Sea, The (Ibsen), 181–182
Lady of Challand, The (Giacosa), 73
Lady of the Camellias, The (Dumas), 21, 25, 43–45, 61–62, 82, 138, 163, 223–224, 236, 253, 259, 266
"Lais' Farewell" (Shchepkina-Kupernik), 225
Lais the Hetaira (Protopopov), 213, 225
"Lausanne" (Shchepkina-Kupernik), 110–111, 117
Lausanne University, 109–112
Law of the Savage, The (Artsybashev), 260–261
Leffler, Anna-Carlotta, 49
Lenin, Vladimir, 219, 277
Lensky, Alexander, 19, 125
Leontiev, L. V., 182
Lermontov, Mikhail, 136
Levitan, Isaac, 31–32, 59, 72, 76, 278
Levkeeva, Elizaveta, 105, 107
Light but No Heat (Ostrovsky and Solovyov), 21
Linsky, Vladimir, 181, 184, 189, 195, 200
Literary Fund, 152
Literary-Artistic Circle, 80–83, 103–104, 140–141, 146
Litvin, Savely, 138
Litvinne, Felia, 58, 60
Living Corpse, The (Tolstoy), 246
Lolotte, 247, 257
London Coliseum, 247, 255, 275
"Loneliness" (Shchepkina-Kupernik), 70–71
Lonely Soul, The, 259
Love and Intrigue (Schiller), 116
Lower Depths, The (Gorky), 194, 222, 243–244
Lulu (Berg), 183
Luna Park Theater, 258, 261, 264
Lunacharsky, Anatoly, 269, 275
Lyceum Theatre, 255

Madame Sans-Gêne (Sardou), 60–61, 65–67, 73, 78–81, 92, 161, 259, 266
Mademoiselle Fifi, 182, 208, 266
Mademoiselle Giraud, Ma Femme (Belot), 55
Maeterlinck, Maurice, 181, 210
Maid of Orleans, The (Schiller), 87
Maid of Pskov, The (Rimsky-Korsakov), 181
Malkiel, Samuel, 5–6, 12
Maly Theater, 1, 3, 19, 28, 78, 85–86, 97, 117, 125, 157–158, 196, 230
Mamontov, Savva, 8, 93–94, 181
Mamontov, Sergei, 181

Man Who Was Dead, The (Tolstoy), 246
Maria Fyodorovna, Dowager Empress, 99
Maria Pavlovna, Grand Princess, 185
Marianna Bolkhovskaya (Shchepkina-Kupernik), 205–207, 233
Mariinsky Theater, 185
"Marioki Fairy Tales" (Shchepkina-Kupernik), 185
Markevich, Boleslav, 21
Marriage of Belugin, The (Ostrovsky and Solovyov), 64
Mary Stuart (Schiller), 24, 79
Masquerade (Lermontov), 136
Mauvais Bergers, Les (*The Bad Shepherds*; Mirbeau), 266
Maybe Tomorrow (Kamensky), 261–262
Medvedeva, Nadezhda, 26–27
Meilleur Moyen, Le, 227
Men above the Law (Pisemsky), 50
Merezhkovsky, Dmitri, 90–91, 220
Metropol Hotel, 93–94
Meyerhold, Vsevolod, 130, 161, 180, 201, 259–260, 268
Michurina-Samoilova, Vera, 236
Mikhailov, Mikhail, 146
Mikhailovsky Theater, 24
Mikheev, Vasily, 33, 51
Minsky, Nikolai, 198
Mirbeau, Octave, 266
Mironova, Valentina, 233
Miss Julie (Strindberg), 208
Mizinova, Lidia
  "Ariadne" and, 84
  Chekhov and, 37–40, 42–43, 51, 53, 64–65, 72, 178–181
  Chekhova and, 32
  Chekhov's death and, 188
  death of, 277
  Eberle and, 41
  in Paris, 58–59
  photograph of, 52, 167fig
  The Seagull and, 88, 104, 106
  Shchepkina-Kupernik and, 61, 185
  Yavorskaya and, 57, 61
Monna Vanna (Maeterlinck), 181
Month in the Country, A (Turgenev), 87
Morality of Mrs. Dulska, The (Zapolska), 211
Morand, Eugene, 114
Mordovtsev, Daniil, 143
Moscow Art Theater, 119, 126–127, 154, 156, 159, 163–164, 179–180, 199, 221, 243, 246
Moscow Faraway (Munshtein), 56

314 INDEX

Moscow Society of Art and Literature, 64
Motley Tales (Chekhov), 68
Mounet-Sully, Jean, 132, 245
Mounet-Sully, Paul, 132
Munshtein, Leonid, 30–31, 55–56, 67
Murakomo, 203
Mursky, Alexander, 163
My Life with My Husband (Shchepkina-Kupernik), 187

Nablotsky's Career (Baryatinsky), 160, 162–163, 228, 242
Nana (Zola), 151
Narokov, Mikhail, 161–164
Needs of Russian Theater, The, 192–193
Nekrasov, Nikolai, 95
Nekrasova-Kolchinskaya, Olga, 201
Nemetti Theater, 156
Nemirovich-Danchenko, Vladimir, 25, 43, 126–127, 130, 154, 164, 179, 199, 246
Nevolin, Boris, 161–162
New Royalty Theatre, 239
New Theater, 3, 125, 157–165, 181–185, 193–194, 200–201, 213
New Times
  The Anthill and, 95
  Baryatinsky and, 134, 264
  Al. Chekhov and, 120
  Cyrano de Bergerac and, 123
  The Dream Princess and, 91
  Hannele and, 81
  Knipper and, 155
  Korsh and, 77–79
  Literary-Artistic Circle and, 104
  London correspondent for, 223
  New Theater and, 158
  office of, 169fig
  Ozerova and, 82
  The Seagull and, 108
  Shchepkina-Kupernik and, 110, 128, 130–131
  Sons of Israel and, 140–141, 145, 147
  Suvorin and, 15
  Yavorskaya and, 86–87, 115, 119, 224
New Vagabond Club, 239–240
New World, A, 113–115, 118
Nicholas II, 3, 98–100, 183, 185, 190, 193–195, 198, 262–263, 265
Nights of Madness (Lev L. Tolstoy), 160
Nikolaev, Pyotr, 182
Nikolsky Theater, 268
Nobodies of This World, The (series; Shchepkina-Kupernik), 128
Nordman, Natalia, 133, 254–255

Northern Courier, 134–136, 140–142, 147–149, 153–154, 222
Nouvelle Revue, 58

Offenbach, Jacques, 11
One of Them (Shchepkina-Kupernik), 207–208, 230, 233
Orest, 123–124
Ostrovsky, Alexander, 21, 25, 64, 86, 105, 196, 223, 231
Othello (Verdi), 59
Ozerova, Lyudmilla, 82–83, 116–117

Panaev Theater, 80, 93, 104, 108, 158, 196
Pandora's Box (Wedekind), 183–184
Paris Opera, 180
Parisienne, La (Becque), 240, 245
Paskhalova, Anna, 103
Paul the First (Merezhkovsky), 220
Pavlova, Alexandra, 164–165, 238
People's House, 266–267
Perestiani, Ivan, 163, 190–192, 194, 197–198
Petrovich, Ivan, 272–273
Philistines, The (Gorky), 163–164
Pince-Nez, 209–210, 212–213
Pisarev, Modest, 7–8, 106
Pisemsky, Alexei, 50
Pitoeva-Beletskaya, Margarita, 212–213
Platon Andreevich (Al. Chekhov), 120–121
Plehve, Vyacheslav, 183, 189–190
Pobedonostsev, Konstantin, 100
Pollock, John
  Anna Karenina and, 251
  Baryatinsky and, 262, 264
  flight from Russia of, 269–270
  marriage and, 275
  photograph of, 174fig
  revolution and, 265–267, 271–274
  For Russia and, 255
  translations/adaptations by, 242, 246–247
  war effort and relief work of, 257–258, 262
  Yavorskaya and, 225, 227–228, 238, 240–241, 243, 248, 253–254, 263
  Yavorskaya's grave and, 278–279
Polynov, Nikolai, 186–187, 202–203, 215–216, 221–222, 226–227, 248, 257, 277
Potapenko, Ignaty, 38, 43, 45, 53, 58, 61, 64–65, 104–106, 108, 193
Pound, Ezra, 225

INDEX   315

Power of Darkness, The (Tolstoy), 181, 222
Princesse Lointaine, La (Rostand), 85, 87–88, 170fig
Proposal, The (Chekhov), 18–19
Protopopov, Victor, 211, 213, 225
Pushkin, Alexander, 97, 131
Pushkin Theater, 5–7
Pygmalion (Shaw), 259–260

Quo Vadis (Sienkiewicz), 161–162

Raev, Nikolai, 263–267
Raffles (Hornung), 212
Rasputin, 261–264
Rayfield, Donald, 2, 35, 104, 277–278
Red Cross, 254, 257
Réjane, Gabrille, 59–60, 66, 80, 248
Repin, Ilya, 133, 171fig, 198, 222
Richelieu, 9
Rimsky-Korsakov, Nikolai, 181
Robespierre, 208
Rodionov, Lev, 122–123
Romanovsky, Alexander, 182
Romantics, The (Rostand), 59, 68, 70, 78, 82
Rosamond (Pollock), 228
Roshchina-Insarova, Ekaterina, 265
Roskanova, Maria, 130, 186
Rosmersholm (Ibsen), 210
Rossi, Ernesto, 82
Rostand, Edmond, 59–60, 68, 70, 82, 85, 117, 121, 125, 132, 156
Royal Court Theatre, 239
Rozanov, Vasily, 198
Russian Dramatic Theater, 7
Russian Theatrical Society, 147
Russo-Japanese War, 202–203
Rybchinskaya, Natalia, 17–18

Sablin, Mikhail, 38, 46, 53, 58, 90
Sakhalin Island (Chekhov), 42
Saltykov-Shchedrin, Mikhail, 95
Sand, George, 85
Sanin, Alexander, 178–180, 186, 196
Sanina, Ekaterina, 178, 180, 185
"Sappho" (Shchepkina-Kupernik), 51–52
"Sara Mikhailovna" (Shchepkina-Kupernik), 204–205
Sardou, Victorien, 60–61, 65–67, 81, 117, 161
Savina, Maria, 105, 116, 140
Sazonova, Sophia, 87, 92, 95–96, 106–107

Scala Theatre, 248, 253, 255
Schiller, Friedrich, 24, 79, 87, 116, 195
Schnitzler, Arthur, 198
School for Scandal (Sheridan), 259
Schuler, Catherine, 2
Seagull, The (Chekhov), 88, 93, 104–108, 117, 126–130, 159, 244
Sergeenko, Pavel, 38
Sergei Mikhailovich, Grand Duke, 99
17 October 1905 (Repin), 198
Shadorskaya, Zoya, 216, 218
Shakespeare, William, 97, 158
Shaw, George Bernard, 25, 241, 243, 259, 271
Shcheglov, Ivan, 18–19, 42
Shchepkin, Mikhail, 26
Shchepkina, Olga Petrovna, 26
Shchepkina-Chernevskaya, Alexandra, 26, 249
Shchepkina-Kupernik, Tatiana
  "Avelan's squadron" and, 40
  "Backstage" and, 29–30
  Baryatinsky and, 99
  Bloody Sunday and, 203–204
  Chekhov and, 38–40, 42, 52–53, 68–75, 127–130
  Chekhov's death and, 188
  Cyrano de Bergerac and, 121–125
  The Dream Princess and, 88–93
  The Eaglet and, 156–157
  Gorky and, 135
  grave of, 278
  Happiness and, 68–70
  Knipper and, 155
  Kollontai and, 215–219
  Korsh and, 26–29
  Krestovskaya and, 150–152, 219–221
  at Lausanne University, 109–112
  Ligovsky Prospect residence and, 132–133
  M. Chekhov and, 46
  marriage and, 177, 186–187, 202, 221
  Mizinova and, 178–181
  Monna Vanna and, 181
  Moscow Art Theater and, 126–127
  New Theater and, 158–159, 185, 213
  Ozerova and, 82
  photographs of, 52, 167fig, 171fig, 176fig
  press and, 83
  Pushkin commemoration and, 131
  renewed interest in, 277–278
  Repin and, 133
  revolution and, 266, 274–275

INDEX

Shchepkina-Kupernik (*continued*)
  "Sappho" and, 51–52
  The Seagull and, 88, 129–130
  Shilovsky and, 30–31
  Smyslova and, 238
  Stanislavsky and, 98
  The Struggle for Happiness and, 48
  Summer Picture and, 28–29
  Suvorin and, 85, 87
  writings of, 203–208, 225, 230–237, 264–265
  Yavorskaya and, 2–3, 32–36, 41, 44–45, 47, 50–51, 53–59, 61–62, 73–74, 77–78, 88, 100–102, 112–113, 117, 149–150, 153–154, 163–165, 221–224, 226, 240–241, 245–248, 252, 254, 256–257
  Zelenina and, 249–250
  Zulawski and, 210
Sheridan, Richard, 259
Shilovsky, Konstantin, 26–27, 30–31, 34
Shoals, The (Baryatinsky), 160, 163, 189
Shubinsky, Nikolai, 249, 274–275
Sienkiewicz, Henryk, 161
Sign of the Cross, The (Barret), 113
Silkworms, The (Baryatinsky), 222
Silvestre, Armand, 114–115
Sipyagin, Dmitri, 148
Slums of St. Petersburg, The (Krestovsky), 151
Smugglers, The, 140–141, 145, 148, 183, 200
  See also Sons of Israel (Litvin and Krylov)
Smyslova, Alexandra (Sasha), 165, 238, 256, 276
Society of Art and Literature, 97, 119, 126
Society of Christian Assistance, 5
Society of Drama Writers and Composers, 124, 233
Society of Dramatic Artists, 209
Solovtsov, Nikolai, 18–20, 105
Solovyov, Nikolai, 21, 64
Sons of Israel (Litvin and Krylov), 138–149, 154
Spring Awakening (Wedekind), 210–211
Stanislavskaya, Lilina, 130
Stanislavsky, Konstantin, 64, 97–98, 119, 126–127, 129, 154, 156–157, 164, 246, 268
State Duma, 198, 215
Stenbock-Fermor, Nadezhda, 109, 118
Stepniak, Fanny, 238

Stockmarket Fever (Suvorin), 134
Stone Guest, The (Pushkin), 131
Storm, The (Ostrovsky), 86, 231
Strindberg, August, 27, 49, 161, 208, 210, 223
Stronger, The (Strindberg), 223
Struggle for Happiness, The (Kovalevskaya and Leffler), 48–51, 82
Struve, Peter, 134
Sudermann, Hermann, 87
Summer Picture (Shchepkina-Kupernik), 28–29
Sunken Bell, The (Hauptmann), 119
Sunset Glow (Aftenrode; Hamsun), 208
Suvorin, Alexei
  The Anthill and, 95–97
  antisemitism and, 134
  Baryatinsky and, 108–109
  Chekhov and, 15–16, 40, 64, 76–80
  Al. Chekhov and, 120–121
  The Dream Princess and, 88–89, 91, 97, 108
  fire at Maly Theater and, 157–158
  on Lent, 115–116
  Literary-Artistic Circle and, 80–81, 83
  Maly Theater and, 117
  New Times and, 223
  A New World and, 114
  Northern Courier and, 135–136, 149
  Ozerova and, 82
  portrait of, 169fig
  The Seagull and, 105, 107–108, 130
  Shchepkina-Kupernik and, 74–75, 85, 87, 100–101, 233
  Sons of Israel and, 139–140, 142–148
  Yavorskaya and, 3, 73–75, 77, 79–80, 88, 101–104, 113–115, 117–118, 125, 138, 214
Suvorov, Alexander, 121
Svetlana, 203
Svetlov, Nikolai, 13
Svetlovidov, Vasily, 11–12
"Swan Song" (Chekhov), 11–12, 15

Tagiev Theater, 212, 214
Tatiana Repina (Suvorin), 119, 134
"Tatiana Topsy-Turvy" (Yevtushenko), 278
Tchaikovsky, Pyotr Ilyich, 30, 41
Teffi, Nadezhda, 261
Telyakovsky, Vladimir, 138
Tempest, The (Shakespeare), 158–159
Ten Centuries of Russian Verse (Yevtushenko), 278

Theater and Art
  actors' union and, 197
  Asch and, 209
  Baryatinsky and, 182
  censors/censorship and, 190
  The Dance of Life and, 184
  The Eaglet and, 160
  Erdgeist and, 183
  Krechetova and, 232
  Kugel and, 268
  on *Maybe Tomorrow*, 262
  prominence of, 157
  revolution and, 269
  Shchepkina-Kupernik and, 181
  Yavorskaya and, 161, 189, 226, 255, 257
Theatre Antoine, 163
Théâtre de la Porte Saint-Martin, 121
Théâtre de la Renaissance, 25, 57, 85, 114
Théâtre du Vaudeville, 60
Théâtre Michel, 227
There Are Crimes and Crimes (Strindberg), 161
Thérèse Requin (Zola), 245
This Was Yesterday (Shchepkina-Kupernik), 204–205, 232
Three Sisters, The (Chekhov), 155, 195, 246
Tiflis Artistic Society, 211
Tikhomirov, Dmitri, 45–46
Tinsky, Yakov, 124, 139–143
Tolstoy, Alexei, 126
Tolstoy, Lev, 64, 83, 137, 181, 222, 228, 246, 248, 250
Tolstoy, Lev L., 160
Tree, Herbert Beerbohm, 223–224
Tsar Fyodor Ivanovich (A. Tolstoy), 126
Tsar Vasily Ivanovich Shuisky, 8
Turchaninova, Evdokia, 125–126
Turgenev, Ivan, 25, 87, 222

Ukhtomsky, Esper, 137
Un fil à la patte (*Tied by the Leg*) (Faydeau), 56
Uncle Vanya (Chekhov), 155, 179, 189, 246
Union of Russian Dramatic Actresses, 266
Union of Stage Artists, 192–193

Vasantasena, 67–68
Vasilieva, Nadezhda, 20–21, 25
Vasilisa Melentieva (Ostrovsky), 223, 225
Velizary, Maria, 162–163
Vengerova, Zinaida, 246
Veselitsky, Gabriel, 223–224, 252

Victorov, N. A., 193
Vladimir Alexandrovich, Grand Prince, 90
Volgina, Sophia, 9
Volodin, V. V., 92
Vrubel, Mikhail, 93–94

Weary Soul, The, 104
Wedekind, Frank, 183, 210–211
Wells, H. G., 241
When We Dead Awaken (Ibsen), 160
Wild Winds (*Wildfeuer*), 125–126
Wilde, Oscar, 212
William Tell (Schiller), 195
Women in Russian Theatre (Schuler), 2
Wood, Mrs. Henry, 252
World War I, 254–259

Yavorskaya, Lidia
  Anna Karenina and, 248, 250–255, 262
  The Anthill and, 95–97
  background of, 22–24
  Baryatinsky and, 99–104
  benefit performances for, 47–51, 73, 88, 104, 114, 121, 123–124, 181
  "Bloody Sunday" and, 192
  charity events and, 119–120
  Chekhov and, 38–39, 42–43, 47, 53, 68, 72–79
  M. Chekhov and, 46
  Chekhov's death and, 188–189
  critical response to, 22, 80, 82, 86–87, 92, 194, 224, 238–240, 245, 252, 254
  Cyrano de Bergerac and, 121–124
  death of, 276–277
  decision to go to England and, 221–222
  divorce and, 262–267
  The Dream Princess and, 88–89, 91–92, 97, 108
  Dumas and, 61–62
  The Eaglet and, 156–157
  expulsion of, 150
  fame of, 40–41
  fashion and, 253
  film acting and, 259
  grave of, 278–279
  Happiness and, 69–70
  in Italy, 226
  The Jews and, 200
  Knipper and, 155–156
  Korsh and, 20–21, 25–26, 60–61, 63
  legacy of, 2–3
  Ligovsky Prospect residence and, 132

Yavorskaya (*continued*)
   Literary-Artistic Circle and, 83
   in London, 222-229, 238-248, 250-251, 273, 275-276
   Madame Sans-Gêne and, 65-67
   at Maly Theater, 78
   marriage and, 177, 221
   The Needs of Russian Theater and, 193
   New Theater and, 157-163, 181-185, 189-190, 193, 195, 200-201
   Northern Courier and, 148-149
   in Paris, 24-25, 117-118, 125, 132
   in Petrograd, 258-262
   photographs of, 52, 167fig, 170fig-171fig, 175fig
   Pollock and, 227-228
   popularity of, 119-120
   press and, 137-138
   Pushkin commemoration and, 131
   Repin and, 133
   revolution and, 196, 198, 269-274
   in *The Romantics*, 70
   The Seagull and, 88, 104-105
   Shchepkina-Kupernik and, 32-36, 44-45, 47, 50-51, 53-59, 61-62, 73-74, 77-78, 88, 100-102, 112-113, 117, 149-150, 153-154, 226, 240-241, 245-248, 256-257
   Sons of Israel and, 140-148, 154
   Stanislavsky and, 97-98
   The Struggle for Happiness and, 48-49
   Suvorin and, 113-115, 136, 214
   in Tiflis, 210-212
   on tour, 117, 208-210, 212-213
   Vasantasena and, 67-68
   ward of, 164-165, 238
Yevtushenko, Yevgeny, 278
Yurevskaya, Ekaterina, 136
Yuriev, Yury, 131-132
Yurieva, Vera, 216-217
Yurievskaya, Yekaterina, 226-227
Yuzhin, Alexander, 196, 230

Zapolska, Gabriela, 211
Zaza, 208, 266
Zelenina, Margarita, 173fig, 187, 249-250, 266, 274-275, 277
Zola, Émile, 151
Zulawski, Jerzy, 210

www.ingramcontent.com/pod-product-compliance
Lightning Source LLC
Chambersburg PA
CBHW031722230426
43669CB00007B/214